spotlight

second edition

on Paragraph and Essay Skills

CAROLE ANNE MAY
CAMOSUN COLLEGE

spotlight

second edition

on Paragraph and Essay Skills

PEARSON

Prentice Hall

Toronto

Library and Archives Canada Cataloguing in Publication

May, Carole Anne, 1948–
    Spotlight on paragraph and essay skills / Carole Anne May.—2nd ed.

Includes index.
ISBN 978-0-13-206805-5

1. English language—Paragraphs.   2. Essay—Authorship.   I. Title.

PE1439.M39 2009   808'.042   C2008-900025-0

ISBN-13: 978-0-13-206805-5
ISBN-10: 0-13-206805-2

Vice President, Editorial Director: Gary Bennett
Acquisitions Editor: Christopher Helsby
Marketing Manager: Sally Aspinall
Supervising Developmental Editor: Suzanne Schaan
Developmental Editor: Rose Grotsky
Production Editor: Richard di Santo
Copy Editor: Camille Isaacs
Proofreaders: Nancy Carroll, Susan McNish
Production Coordinator: Avinash Chandra
Composition: Integra
Art Director: Julia Hall
Cover and Interior Design: Anthony Leung
Cover Image: Getty Images/Adam Taylor

1 2 3 4 5   12 11 10 09 08

Printed and bound in the United States of America.

*This book is dedicated to the memory of my kind
and loving parents—Annie and Harry.*

brief contents

detailed contents

preface

Welcome to the new edition of *Spotlight on Paragraph and Essay Skills*. Through its philosophy and structure, this book will help encourage students at the college preparatory or first-year level to become capable, confident writers, eager to handle higher-level challenges in their writing. It teaches paragraph structure, organization, and rhetorical patterns, first through the reading and analyzing of samples, and then by developing composition through analysis and practice of five rhetorical patterns. It also offers an introduction to essay and research paper writing and provides extensive information and practice in English grammar and mechanics.

This latest edition has many improvements based on the suggestions of both reviewers and students. It has been completely revised in a number of ways that capitalize on the strengths of the first edition while incorporating the following key changes:

- improved format

- redesigned exercises

- altered chapter sequencing

- expansion of the essay chapter (Chapter 9)

- a new research chapter, including sample research essays (Chapter 10)

- more paragraph samples

- new readings (Chapters 18 and 19)

- the addition of writing topics for paragraphs and essays to accompany the readings chapters (Chapters 18 and 19)

- a specific chapter for ESL common skill concerns, tips, and exercises (Chapter 17)

Format

The trimmed explanations of key concepts, often streamlined into a clearer bulleted format, will assist students enormously. We reviewed the content of each chapter, paying particular attention to its layout to increase student interest, comprehension, and skill development.

Redesigned Exercises

We have carefully reviewed all exercises and improved the content while keeping objectives focused. We paid particular attention to Chapters 11–16, the main grammar chapters. Students will find the grammar exercises redesigned to **suit their skill levels**.

Each grammar chapter contains a variety of exercises at *three different levels of difficulty*: 1—introductory; 2—intermediate; and 3—advanced. Students may choose level 1 if they feel they need to do a lot of work on the topic, level 2 if they have some knowledge of the topic and simply need to refresh ideas, and level 3 if they feel they have mastered the ideas and want to challenge their knowledge. As with the first edition, we placed some of the answers directly in the Answer Key at the back of the text, but placed others—especially Review Test answers—in the *Instructor's Manual*.

It is important to stress the value of the way in which the grammar chapters (11–17) have been structured, all beginning with **Self-Tests** and culminating in **Review Tests** and **Check Outs**. The design of these chapters is based on valuable research in adult education from renowned practitioner/researchers.[1] Adult learners learn best when they have input and control of their learning. Most adults prefer to develop a starting point in their learning by sorting out what they know from what they don't know. Self-Tests at the start of key grammar and mechanics chapters provide that opportunity. Having exercises designed by levels of difficulty offers students clear choices after the self-tests have helped them determine what they need to know. The explanations are also part of the philosophical framework from adult education that respects learners' needs for clarity and focus, particularly at the college preparatory or first-year level of entry. The Review Test is a distinct point of reference in terms of what students have learned from the chapter and what they need to review from it. Some instructors like to use the Review Tests as class tests while others prefer to have students work through them on an individual basis. The *Instructor's Manual* provides extra exercises for those students who may require them after they have completed the Review Test for each chapter. The Check Outs round out each chapter and offer students a chance to conceptualize some of the material from the chapter. Rather than merely providing a summary of key concepts, the Check Outs offer a "thinking person's rest stop"—a place to consider how ideas not only consolidate, but branch out to other ideas.

Chapter Sequencing

Based on reviewers' suggestions, this edition contains a new chapter sequence. This sequence is important in the grammar/mechanics section of the text, but it is also critical to the writing development chapters.

- "Punctuation and Capitalization" (Chapter 14) now follows "Modifiers" (Chapter 13).

- "Patterns of Sentences" has been moved to Chapter 15.

- "The Beginning Research Paper" has been added as a new chapter (10).

- The material specific to ESL now has its own chapter (17).

Expansion of the Essay Chapter

Reviewer and student suggestions have sparked the further development of this chapter. Since college preparatory and first-year students often require more explanation for new concepts, the chapter provides more detail about beginning essays. Chapter 19, "Longer Readings," also contains essay topics for 500-word papers to develop students' writing by offering a choice of topics based on each reading.

---

[1]Brookfield, Stephen D. (1991). *Understanding and facilitating adult learning: A comprehensive analysis of principles and effective practices.* San Francisco, Jossey-Bass.

Merriam, Sharan B., Caffarella, Rosemary S., and Baumgartner, Lisa M. (2006). *Learning in adulthood: A comprehensive guide* (3rd ed). San Francisco, Jossey-Bass.

Knowles, Malcolm S. (1998). *The adult learner: The definitive classic in adult education and human resource development* (5th ed). Houston, TX: Gulf Publishing.

A New Research Chapter

The addition of a new chapter on writing a beginning research paper enhances this new edition tremendously. Chapter 10 introduces students to what a standard academic research paper is, discusses two main styles of documentation—MLA and APA—explains the problems of plagiarism, and offers a step-by-step approach for students to plan and write their first research papers. Chapter 10 provides three sample research papers: one in MLA style and two in APA style. The exercises will help students think, discuss, organize, and write.

More Paragraph Samples

This second edition of *Spotlight on Paragraphs and Essays* provides some new paragraph samples for students to read in the writing development chapters and **ten** new readings in Chapter 18, "Paragraph Readings." It also includes **suggested paragraph topics for paragraph compositions** after each paragraph reading in Chapter 18; the topics are arranged to provide student writers with practice in using the rhetorical modes discussed in the paragraph development chapters (4–8).

New Readings

Based on reviewers' suggestions, Chapter 18, "Paragraph Readings," contains **ten** new readings, and Chapter 19, "Longer Readings," offers **four** new longer readings. All **new topics** for paragraph and essay writing have been added to both Chapter 18 and 19.

A Specific Chapter for ESL Common Skill Concerns, Tips, and Exercises

On the advice of most reviewers, the ESL tips, information, and exercises have been moved to a separate chapter for ease of access. Now ESL instructors and their students can examine Chapter 17 in depth to help meet English language challenges. An Answer Key is available at the back of the text and in the *Instructor's Manual*.

FACULTY SUPPLEMENTS

Spotlight on Paragraph and Essay Skills, Second Edition, is accompanied by an *Instructor's Manual* that is an invaluable resource to instructors using the text. Included in the *Instructor's Manual* are answers to the Review Tests, a set of suggested activities for each chapter, and additional tests with answers. Instructors can download the manual from Pearson Education Canada's online catalogue at **vig.pearsoned.ca**; they should contact their sales representative to obtain a password.

ACKNOWLEDGEMENTS

I am especially grateful to Pearson Education Canada for their continued support and encouragement. My thanks go to Marianne Minnaker, Matthew Christian, Richard di Santo, Carmen Batsford, the reviewers, my students and colleagues for their wonderful assistance in the first edition. For the second edition, I wish to acknowledge the clear direction and warm support of Christopher Helsby, Suzanne Schaan, and Richard di Santo once again from Pearson Education. They have been invaluable at all times. Thanks also to Camille Isaacs and Nancy Carroll for their editing and proofreading talents. My gratitude also includes the reviewers, for their insightful, useful comments and suggestions, including:

Jane Barley, Thompson Rivers University

Rose Caruso, Seneca College

Debbie Hlady, Camosun College

Chandra Hodgson, Humber College

Bonnie Holtby, Northern Alberta Institute of Technology

Moira Langley, Kwantlen University College

Helene Littmann, British Columbia Institute of Technology

John Patterson, Vancouver Community College

Jill Singleton-Jackson, University of Windsor

Al Valleau, Kwantlen University College

As always, thank you to my family, students, and colleagues who have helped lighten the work by generously offering their advice and humour when most needed.

chapter 1

Preparing and Planning to Write

Chapter Objectives

After completing this chapter, you will be able to

- recognize what a paragraph composition is
- recognize and apply a number of prewriting and organizing strategies
- use brainstorming to generate ideas
- use freewriting to generate ideas
- create outlines for paragraph compositions

INTRODUCTION

Most of the time you write because you need to explain or remember something. You might jot a note or two in a week, write a list of things to remember, or send a short letter or email to someone, but unless you are taking a course, you probably do not write compositions. Most adults do not expect to write much every day unless they are journalists, writers, or professionals who do a lot of writing as part of their work. However, you may be surprised by how much and how often you have to communicate in writing, both in your future courses and in the workplace.

Like most people, you may feel wary of writing for a number of reasons. You may not have written anything in "formal" English for a long time and may feel unsure about the rules of formal grammar. You may be uncertain how to start writing a college- or university-level paper.

This section will help you build confidence in your writing. You will begin with smaller compositions called **paragraph compositions**. This work will help prepare you for longer pieces of writing called **essays**.

As you learn to write for academic courses, you will be introduced to rules and conventions. Conventions are accepted practices in academic writing. The chapters that follow provide exercises to prepare you for that formal writing. The written work you will do in college and university courses is called **academic writing** with its own rules, different from those of other types of writing. Usually, the writing you see in newspapers and magazines, for instance, is not academic writing. As an academic writer, however, you will learn about the standards of writing expected of you.

Most of the time, academic writing is judged and graded. You, your instructors, professors, other students, friends, and even family may all play a part in evaluating your written assignments. You will learn to become a more effective writer through all of these experiences.

Applying Standard Writing Conventions

As an academic student writer, you should know about guidelines of practice called **conventions**. Grammar, spelling, punctuation, formatting, structure of arguments, presentation, and organization are all parts of academic writing conventions.

Although some may argue that judgments about writing are a matter of taste, others maintain that university and college writing is evaluated on the basis of accepted standards. They claim that conventions exist in academic writing for certain reasons. Writing conventions help writers express complicated thoughts clearly and assist readers in grasping what the writer is expressing.

When you write for academic purposes, you want to persuade your reader that your point of view is worth considering. Therefore, your writing should be forceful. You want interesting and informative writing. You want to express your viewpoints, but do not want to sound like a dull textbook or a self-appointed expert. Above all, you want your writing to be clear.

Remember: instructors are looking for good writing, including the application of standard writing conventions in your papers. They will look at how your writing develops over a semester, and how your writing makes meaning clear. *Spotlight on Paragraph and Essay Skills* begins with an overview of what a paragraph composition is, along with some ideas for preparing to write.

WHAT IS A PARAGRAPH COMPOSITION?

A paragraph composition is usually a short piece of writing on one general topic. It begins with a **topic sentence**, a sentence that contains the **main idea** of the paragraph. Next, it contains separate **points** about the topic. After each point, elaborate by providing examples, reasons, facts, or other **ideas that support** the point. End the paragraph composition in a sentence that closes the discussion.

To write a good paragraph composition, you need to plan carefully. You need to include convincing ideas and a logical construction. Writing paragraph compositions will prepare you to write essays and term papers. Using paragraph compositions as an entry point to academic writing, you will have the opportunity to practise without having to write long papers. You will also gain experience in editing, revising, and presenting papers.

Pre-Test: What Is a Paragraph?

On a separate piece of paper, write down what you think makes a good paragraph. What parts must a paragraph have? Be prepared to share your answers with the class.

Exercise 1   *Reading Examples of Paragraph Compositions*

Read the three examples of paragraph compositions below. Then answer the following five questions on a separate piece of paper.

What is the topic sentence in each paragraph?

What are the points each writer is making?

What is the support for each point?

What is the closing sentence in each paragraph composition?

Did you notice any differences between the paragraphs?

PARAGRAPH 1 Buying a new mattress may be one of the most stressful situations for couples. First of all, partners have to agree on what type of mattress they are going to purchase. They must agree on the price, size, quality, and construction. Getting agreement on all four points may not be easy. As a matter of fact, couples may enter the store with the intention of purchase, but may not be in agreement about what exactly they want to purchase. Next, once in the store, partners must assess what the salesperson tells them and then must negotiate with each other. This business is a tricky one because as they negotiate, partners often feel they must not reveal too many personal secrets to the salesperson. They might even be guarding the price they are willing to pay to try to negotiate a better price. Perhaps the most difficult, even embarrassing, part is revealing sleep preferences to a perfect stranger. Usually the salesperson will ask questions such as, "Which side of the bed do you prefer to sleep on? Are you a restless sleeper?" He or she may then invite couples to "try out the bed." So couples may find themselves lying stiffly side-by-side while a salesperson smiles down on them. Since most couples only buy two or three mattresses in their lifetime together, they should discuss not just what they will purchase, but also how they plan to make their purchase once they are in the store: a little more planning could turn stress into an adventure.

PARAGRAPH 2 The columbine, a wildflower native to Western Canada, is easy to identify. Hikers may recognize any of the five species of columbine by a particular feature common to all varieties. Each species has a hornlike spur that protrudes from the back of each petal of the flower. Flourishing from Ontario to British Columbia, this wildflower is distinctly coloured. It may possess blue, lavender, red, yellow, or white blossoms. Finally, nature lovers may be able to distinguish the columbine by its leaves. They are divided into three distinct leaflets. The columbine provides quiet, beautiful elegance in unexpected places in the wild, and walkers can discover the flower by looking for these details.

PARAGRAPH 3 The Canadian Wildlife Service (CWS) is a unique department in the Government of Canada. First it began as a unit responsible for monitoring migratory birds in Canada and protecting them. Both Canada and the United States signed The Migratory Birds Convention in 1916, regulating the hunting of game birds and protecting other non-game birds. Later the government expanded CWS's mandate to manage all wildlife found in Canada's national parks. This responsibility included looking after game and fur animals through planning and scientific study. Over the years under the direction of the CWS, 40 national wildlife areas and 80 nesting sites for birds have been placed under preservation. The CWS's work in these areas became world renowned. Today, the

CWS is part of Environment Canada, yet its distinguished history has become largely invisible to the average Canadian.

Exercise 2   Group Activity: What Makes a Good Paragraph?

Form a group of three to five people. Discuss the answers to four of the following questions. One member of the group should write the group's response in the spaces provided. Be prepared to share your answers with the rest of the class.

1. What is a paragraph?

    _____

    _____

2. Look over Exercise 1. What makes the three paragraphs effective?

    a. _____

    b. _____

    c. _____

3. How can paragraphs differ?

    a. _____

    b. _____

    c. _____

4. In what ways must paragraphs be the same?

    a. _____

    b. _____

    c. _____

PREPARING TO WRITE

What Is Prewriting?

Prewriting is what you do as a writer to prepare for the writing task. There are many ways to prepare; you may find some work more effectively than others. Some writing experts call these *strategies* for prewriting. Others prefer to view prewriting as a *series of stages*. In any case, remember that preparing for writing is as important as the actual writing itself.

Think of prewriting as a crucial part of *composing*. When you are composing, you are setting down ideas on the page. You are trying to discover what you know or think about something. You are attempting to discover your ideas. When you compose, try to let ideas flow without stopping or censoring them. Set out ideas as they occur to you. Correcting errors in spelling, grammar, punctuation, or usage is not important at this stage. In fact, if you stop to correct something, you will interfere with the stream of ideas that come to mind. Think of this little rule when you start prewriting for a project: Write now; fix later!

For the purposes of this book, think of prewriting and organizing in the following ways:

- brainstorming and freewriting

- clustering ideas

- arranging ideas into a logical order (different ways of outlining: formal outlines, informal outlines, mapping, spokes and wheels, box charts)

Brainstorming

Brainstorming is the activity of writing down all the ideas that pop into your mind when you think about a particular topic. It is a technique for generating or creating ideas. There are no right or wrong answers; instead, you will have a rush of ideas that you want to put down on the page. Let the ideas flow.

Brainstorming has three purposes:

1. It lets you know what you know about a topic. If after a few minutes you find you have written down very little in your brainstorming session, you may decide that you need to change your topic.

2. It helps unblock ideas; it gets the creative juices flowing.

3. It is an excellent method of overcoming the dreaded writer's block—a stoppage of writing thoughts.

Exercise 3   *Individual Brainstorming Activity*

Find a quiet space that allows you to work without interruption. Use a clean sheet of paper for this exercise.

1. Look over the "Topics for Brainstorming" below.

2. Quickly choose one topic.

3. Scribble down as many ideas, words, or phrases that come to mind regarding the topic. Continue brainstorming for several minutes.

4. Stop writing when you feel you have exhausted what you have to say about the topic.

5. Look over your scribbles. Did you have quite a lot to say? Can you organize your ideas in some way?

Topics for Brainstorming

tea	cars
watching television	fashion
backpacking	vacations
insomnia	soap operas
snow sports	smoking
studying	relaxation
restaurants	keeping fit
MP3 players	playing baseball

Exercise 4   Group Brainstorming Activity

Part A

Your instructor will divide the class into five or six groups. Together your group will brainstorm for ideas. You may use the board in the classroom, large sheets of paper, or note sheets. One person should take notes. Another person should keep group members focussed on their task by asking questions and making sure the note-taker has enough time to take down each note. Write down everything the group suggests, no matter how silly.

The instructor will tell the groups when to begin. Everyone will brainstorm, using the same topic: *bargains*.

Part B

The instructor will tell the groups when to stop. If your group used sheets of paper or note sheets, you will post them in the classroom. Be sure to give your group a name and write it at the top of your page or at the top of the board so that your group's work can be distinguished from another's. Next, the instructor will ask everyone to read each set of notes. Then all of the groups will meet as a class to discuss how the brainstorming session went, what was effective, and what was not. You will also discuss how the sets of notes differ.

Part C

Each group should take another group's notes to organize them so that ideas are clustered. Each group should use large sheets of paper or the board to do the organizing. The organizing group should write its name and the original group's name on the organized set of notes. Post the new organized notes. Then groups should review the new notes. Groups should discuss how they organized the notes and why. Groups can debate why some notes may have been left out and others included.

Freewriting

Freewriting means writing on a topic for a set time without stopping. It is a way to

- gather ideas

- focus on what you might think of a topic

- write without stopping to check spelling, grammar, or punctuation.

When you freewrite, you are "free-falling with words." Try writing without lifting your pen or pencil from the page. Write and write, even if you happen to be repeating the same words; do not stop the flow of writing.

Usually, freewriting works best if you limit your time as it is difficult to freewrite for long. You can freewrite at any time, in virtually any place, as long as you have a pen or pencil and notepaper or a computer.

Limit distractions when you freewrite, if you can. You must intensely concentrate on the activity as you do it. You cannot have someone talking to you or interrupting your flow of ideas. Try to choose a private place in which to freewrite.

To freewrite follow these steps:

1. Take five to ten minutes for the activity. Your instructor may have given you a topic already. If you do not have one, you can always look through a magazine or newspaper for some topics.

2. Write five or six of these topics on a clean sheet of paper.

3. Take another clean sheet of paper, a pen or pencil, and a timer.

4. Start the timer and set it for five minutes.

5. Choose one of your topics and write, without stopping, for the full five minutes.

6. Do not let the pen or pencil come away from the page.

7. When the timer sounds, look over what you have written.

Are you surprised that you had so much to say? Can you organize your ideas to write a paragraph composition?

Exercise 5   *Freewriting in Class*

Your instructor will provide you with a topic and give you a set time to freewrite. Your instructor will then ask you to look over your writing to see if you can organize it into a paragraph form. You may wish to add ideas during the class discussion. Pay attention to what others in the class say. You may learn that many different points of view emerge from one topic.

Clustering Ideas

Another method to get ideas flowing is **clustering**. Clustering is a way of *mapping out ideas* by using associations or connections.

To begin, write a single word (usually a thing or idea) in the centre of a clean sheet of paper. Put a circle around it. Now think of an idea that associates with your central idea and write it down. Connect it with a line to your central idea and put a smaller circle around it. As another idea occurs to you, add it, but make sure that the idea connects with one of the other ideas on your page. Put all new ideas in circles.

Look over your page. Do you see one cluster that you might be able to develop? Do you see associations between any of the clusters? Do any clusters interest you more than others?

Exercise 6   Clustering

Choose one of the topics below. Place it in the centre of your page. Add and circle related ideas, connecting associated ideas. Use circles and lines: circles signify the ideas; lines represent the connections. Your instructor may want to see your work.

Topics for Clustering

movies
hobbies
friendship
accidents

lunches
work
families
trends

Organizing Ideas: Mapping

Indoor plants require a good deal of care.

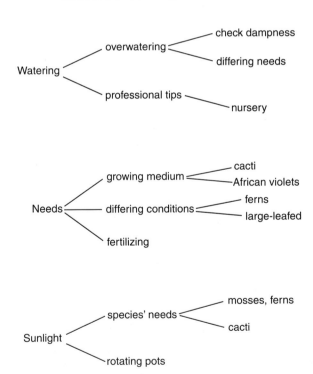

Organizing Ideas: Spokes and Wheels

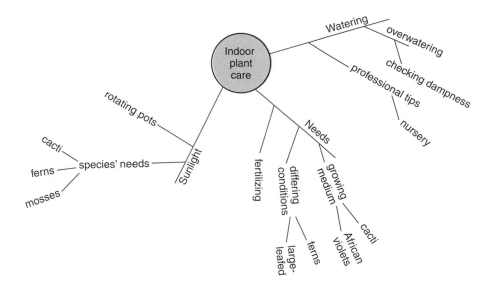

Organizing Ideas: Box Charts

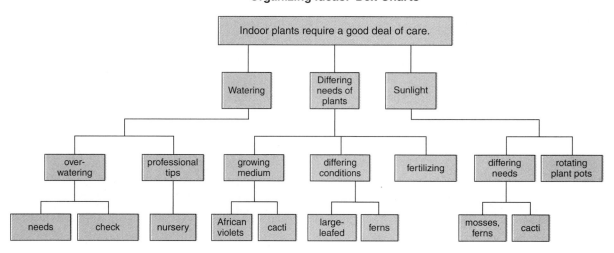

Organizing Ideas: Outlining

After you have decided what you want to say, use **outlining** to arrange your ideas. An outline is an organized way of fitting ideas together.

An outline is like a blueprint for writing. Making an outline is very important because it makes clear to writers what they are going to say and how they are going to say it. An outline arranges the topic sentence (main idea) and the supporting details, often using

Outline in Point Form for a Paragraph Composition

I. Topic sentence: Indoor plants require a good deal of care.

Major point A. Watering

Support

1. overwatering

a. check dampness; insert finger into soil

b. different watering needs

2. find out from nursery

Major point B. Differing needs of plants

Support

1. growing medium

a. cacti

b. African violets

Support

2. different conditions

a. ferns

b. large-leafed

Support

3. fertilizing

Major point C. Sunlight

Support

1. different species' needs

a. mosses, ferns

b. compared to cacti

Support

2. rotating plant pots

Wrap-up sentence: Plant owners must pay particular attention to the watering, specific needs, and sunlight requirements of their houseplants, if they want them to be beautiful and healthy.

Paragraph Coming from the Outline

Indoor plants require a good deal of care. The first concern is the watering needs of different plants. Many plant owners make the mistake of overwatering their plants. It is always important to check the dampness of the soil by pressing a finger down into the soil about 5 centimetres. All houseplants do not require the same amount of watering. A nursery can advise customers how much water is enough for each variety of plant. Another factor to remember is that, like people, plants have varying needs. For example, the growing medium for a cactus contains almost no soil at all: instead, it is a grit, sand, and light peat moss combination. An African violet, on the other hand, prefers a rather rich, light humus to grow in. Ferns prefer a moist, rather dark situation, whereas broad-leafed plants generally grow well in airy, bright positions. Each species of plant will also have differing needs when it comes time to fertilize. Some, like cacti, require very little fertilizer while broad-leafed plants must be given fertilizer on a regular basis. Finally, indoor plants differ in the amount of sunlight they require. Some plants, like mosses and ferns, do not like direct sunlight. Many other plants thrive in direct sun. If plant owners pay particular attention to these basic needs of their household plants, they will find their plants will respond by thriving and continuing to provide pleasure for several years.

point form. Point form means you will write notes rather than full sentences for the points and supporting details. Some instructors prefer that outlines be written in sentence form. Check with your instructor to see which she or he prefers. The next few pages will provide you with some extra practice in outlining or arranging your ideas for a paragraph composition. You have already seen some ideas organized by mapping, spoke and wheel, and box charts. Now, you will see an outline for a paragraph composition developed into a complete paragraph.

Exercise 7   Creating Outlines from Paragraphs

Below are some paragraph compositions. After each one, you will see the form for an outline. Write in the topic sentence. In note form, write in the major points and the support (explanation or supporting details for the points). Also write in the wrap-up or concluding sentence. Check your answers in the Answer Key.

PARAGRAPH 1 Cell phone use should be banned from the public domain. First of all, most cell phone users who make calls in unrestricted places do not respect the privacy of others around them. They make the mistaken assumption that they can talk as loudly or aggressively as suits their mood. In fact, many are downright obnoxious as they yell over the noise of the mall to get their words across. Another reason for the suggested ban is that cell phone users are often discourteous. Many cell phone users employ profane language or say offensive things in their conversations. Some claim that to do so is their right because they are making a private call, which they are paying for, and even exclaim that if someone else is listening in on their conversation, then the other person is at fault for eavesdropping. Finally, cell phone use is actually an incursion into once quiet and relaxing public places. It's not unusual to hear walkers or joggers shouting over their headsets as they make their way along trails through public parks. Park benches are now often occupied by people who are talking on their cell phones as they work on their laptops. Cell phone use should be prohibited from public spaces because it is removing the rights of people to enjoy open places in relative peace in favour of the individual who co-opts the space for his or her own private purpose.

Topic sentence: _____

Major point 1: _____

Support: _____

Support: _____

Support: _____

Major point 2: _____

Support: _____

Support: _____

Major point 3: _____

Support: _____

Support: _____

Support: _____

Wrap-up sentence: _____

PARAGRAPH 2 Consumers can "food-shop" wisely. The first idea for shoppers is planning. It is important to prepare a weekly menu and then base the shopping trip on what is needed for the menu. Many stores feature "specials" that are sold in bulk and are cheaper. Having a grocery list in hand stops consumers from "impulse buying" along the aisles. The next objective is for consumers to avoid convenience foods. Premixed and convenience foods are costly and non-nutritional. Most of these items are high in fat, salt, and food additives. Almost all convenience foods leave people feeling hungry because they do not satisfy the appetite. Finally, shoppers should think about what food item packs the most nutritional "bang for the buck." Whole-grain foods like whole wheat, unprocessed rice, beans, lentils, and other grains, for example, are rich in complex carbohydrates and are inexpensive to purchase. Also, many cheaper cuts of meat can be prepared to make delicious, wholesome meals if consumers are ready to spend extra time on preparation. Finally, shoppers should pay attention to the freshness of the produce they buy. Overripe produce, for instance, should not be purchased as it will soon spoil. With some planning and attention, consumers can do some careful shopping in the grocery store, while saving money and avoiding unnecessary buying trips.

Topic sentence: _____

Major point 1: _____

Support: _____

Support: _____

Support: _____

Major point 2: _____

Support: _____

Support: _____

Major point 3: _____

Support: _____

Support: _____

Support: _____

Wrap-up sentence: _____

Exercise 8   *Group Activity: Adding Major Points and Support*

Form groups of five to seven people. For three of the following topic sentences, think of three major points and supporting details. One person in the group should write down the group's responses. Another should be prepared to report on the group's answers. Your instructor will advise you how much time you will have to work in your group.

Topic sentence 1:   Moving house can be very stressful.

Topic sentence 2:   Sharks are highly adapted predators.

Topic sentence 3:   A hobby can make someone money.

Topic sentence 4:   Finding good student accommodation is difficult.

Topic sentence 5:   The latest movie I saw was terrible.

Topic sentence 6:   What is "comfort food"?

Topic sentence 7:   Travelling by bus has its advantages.

CHECKOUT

1. A paragraph composition usually has these parts:

   • topic sentence

   • major points

   • support (examples and explanation that provide details for each major point)

   • wrap-up sentence

2. Prewriting helps prepare you for writing. You can use

   • brainstorming

   • freewriting

   • clustering

   • outlining

chapter 2

Analyzing Paragraph Development

Chapter Objectives

After completing this chapter, you will be able to

- recognize modes of paragraph development
- apply five basic rhetorical modes of organization
- identify the rhetorical mode through reading paragraphs

INTRODUCTION

Writers organize their ideas clearly to help a reader understand what they have to say. Academic writing, in particular, requires a clear arrangement of ideas. Most often, composition experts advise using **rhetorical modes**, methods of organizing paragraphs and essays. Not everyone agrees on just how many rhetorical modes are possible. *Spotlight on Paragraph and Essay Skills* will introduce you to five basic methods of development, that is, five rhetorical modes.

In this chapter you will first be introduced to each rhetorical mode. Then you will read a paragraph composition that uses the particular mode, and work on some related exercises. Later on, in other chapters, you will write paragraph compositions based on each rhetorical mode. After working through all of these chapters, you will begin to recognize and use the five rhetorical patterns.

As you develop writing skills, you will learn to appreciate that sometimes one mode is more effective in a particular context than another. As you read, you will begin to recognize rhetorical modes used by writers. Thinking about ways of developing ideas in writing can help you conceptualize abstract thoughts. Paying attention to how someone else writes will also help you to become a better writer. Rhetorical modes will provide a framework for your writing, so that you do not feel as if you have nothing to "hang on to" as you write. Remember: the more practice you get using a method, the more effective and inventive you can become when you apply it.

FIVE BASIC MODES OF PARAGRAPH DEVELOPMENT

Mode One: Time-Order, or Process, Development

Time-order mode, sometimes called **chronological order**, clearly sets out ideas as steps or stages, and by doing so, you take readers either through a process of how to do something, the order of events, or the explanation and analysis of a process. For example, accounts from history or stories from your own life often use time-order. Recipes, for instance, use time-order to describe to the reader what to do first, second, and so on. Instruction manuals use time-order to describe a process. You can use time-order when you write about anything from your life, such as raising children, fixing a car, playing a game, or planning a wedding. If you wish to inform readers about how something works, you can also use this mode. For example, you might want to explain how the tax system in local or municipal government works, how the anti-locking mechanisms on a car's braking system operate, or how an insect uses natural chemicals to battle its enemies.

The steps used in time-order must be arranged in a specific order. Details are arranged in the order they occur, that is, chronological order. A step-by-step sequence is vital. Your reader will become confused if you present steps or stages in an incorrect order of presentation. After all, readers imagine your explanation as they read. Therefore, you must pay close attention to logical connections and progression of steps, stages, or events.

Example: Time-Order Mode

A famous Canadian actor, Kate Reid, had a memorable career in theatre and film. She was born in London, England, and first went on the stage during the 1950s. She then moved to Canada. Kate Reid's acting career really began in 1959, when she played in Canada's famous Stratford Shakespeare Festival. Soon her skills as an actor became recognized by critics, theatre directors, and the public. By 1958 her reputation was growing, and in 1962 she was featured in the main role in *Who's Afraid of Virginia Woolf?* on Broadway. By 1974 she received a great honour—she was made an Officer of the Order of Canada because of her contribution to the performing arts in Canada. She went on to earn major parts in movies, including *The Andromeda Strain* (1971), *Equus* (1977), *Atlantic City* (1980), *Sweet Hearts Dance* (1988), *Bye Bye Blues* (1990), and *Deceived* (1991), her last film. She continued to promote the arts and Canadian actors throughout her lifetime. She died of cancer in 1993. Because of her distinguished career, Kate Reid will always be remembered for her rich performances as one of Canada's great character actors.

Notice that the above paragraph uses a sequence of dates to reveal information. The **topic sentence** is the **first sentence** of the paragraph.

You will learn more about time-order development in Chapter 4.

Mode Two: Comparison and Contrast Development

Writers can write about how things are the same or different. A **comparison** piece discusses how things are similar. **Contrast** explains how things are different. Often, writers will use details to present likenesses (comparison) and differences (contrast) in order to establish elaborate ideas. Each approach provides a particular focus. Writers may employ both comparison and contrast as a single mode in one paragraph, while others may use only comparison or only contrast.

You may choose to use comparison and contrast together in a single piece of writing, or you may decide to develop your ideas by using either one. For example, you can discuss all the similarities first and then move through the differences. Or you may choose to discuss one thing first, and then compare and contrast it to something else. For instance, if you want to discuss how coaching hockey was different when you were a child, you might begin with a discussion of coaching today in the first part of the composition, and following that, you might discuss what coaching was like some years ago. In so doing, you could highlight differences for your reader as you draw the discussion to a close.

Example: Comparison and Contrast

Journalism, as the saying goes, is "history in a hurry"; photography, by contrast, is "history in an instant." Journalists try to capture a scene, a moment, or an event through carefully chosen words so that the public can get a feel for it quickly. Photography, however, registers an image more indelibly in the public's heart and imagination than the printed word. Moreover, words take time to read and understand. If someone does not understand the language, he or she might not benefit from the journalist's story. A picture, in contrast, needs no words. A viewer can take in the image whether he or she speaks the journalist's language or not. In addition, in an "instant" world, what is faster, and perhaps easier, seems to be preferred. Since so much in advertising and the media compete for the public's attention, to stop and read may lose out to the rapid glance. Pictures and images are simply faster and more convenient. Despite these subtle differences, both print journalism and photography are closely linked to bring the public what contemporary news reporting has become today.

The writer is showing the differences between journalism and photography related to the news and has chosen contrast in details to get this idea across to readers. The writer provides three distinctions between the two things and talks about what makes the distinction interesting, using a point-by-point organization of ideas.

You will learn more about comparison and contrast development in Chapter 5.

Mode Three: Classification and Division Development

Classification is a method that uses a clustering analysis as a framework. In classification, you group or cluster ideas, concepts, or items into categories. Let's suppose, for instance, that you wanted to discuss salmon. One way of organizing information is to arrange the varieties into groups or categories—pink, chum, and coho. You might then discuss the characteristics of each group. Classification is a valuable tool for thinking, organizing, and writing.

Your classification clusters can be of your design, but you must have reasons for clustering the groups as you do. Make sure that in the body of your paragraph you can distinguish the categories for your reader.

Division is somewhat different. You do not think in terms of clusters or groups; instead when you use division, you consider a subject, topic, or idea by breaking it into component parts. Usually you state the parts or divisions in your topic sentence, and you follow this by examining each part in turn, by providing supporting details. For example, you might discuss the parts of a computer, a stereo, a debate, a real estate contract, or whatever seems to suit a discussion of parts. This mode is often used in scientific writing. You may notice in your biology textbook, for instance, a discussion of the parts of an ecosystem, a bird's wing, or the respiratory system of a mammal. These explanations all divide a larger topic into constituent parts.

Classification and division are generally placed together in textbooks as one rhetorical method because the two have a common ground: in different ways, they separate items or ideas into groups (categories) or parts. You, however, will use each separately. Including both in a short piece of writing is difficult since talking about groups of things and talking about component parts can be complex.

Example: Classification

Three kinds of bus riders—the shy, the curious, and the aggressive—seem to be in every city. The shy bus passenger tends to try to make himself invisible. He will often wait at the end of the line to get on board and then will move to the back of the bus. Once there, he will often look out the window or read a book to avoid eye contact. The second type, the curious bus rider, seems to want to look around. She will climb on the bus, take the first available seat, and then have a good look around at her comrades in ridership. She might smile and say hello to the passenger next to her as she begins taking in the sights, sounds, and smells around her. Perhaps the most noticeable is the aggressive rider. He will make his way to the head of the line, tread on other passengers' toes, elbow his way to the best seat, and generally strike out like a person with a mission. He will make eye contact with almost all the passengers he meets on board, but does not give a friendly greeting. Often he will stare around in a grimace with his belongings spilling into the aisle or onto the seat next to him. He seems to be saying, "Stay away from me!" Bus riders may come in many sorts or types, but these three are unmistakeable.

This author uses classification; the topic sentence shows what the method of development will be. The writer classifies bus riders into three types and then discusses what each type is like. In the same fashion, you can classify or divide your topic in any manner that seems reasonable to you. You might name three or four types of things or ideas as in classification, or you might discuss four or five parts that make up something, employing a division method of arrangement of ideas.

You will learn more about classification and division development in Chapter 6.

Mode Four: Cause and Effect Development

Cause and effect is a rhetorical mode that describes a close relationship between two ideas or events. You must link how something causes something else and clearly establish the effects. Science writers, for instance, might use this method to explain the significance of an experiment that supports their research results. Suppose that they investigated how fertilizers of different types affect plant growth—corn, for example. Their findings, written in an article, would then present evidence of the outcomes of their experiment. They may describe the conditions under which a particular fertilizer would or would not produce the best crop. In other words, they would describe results.

Social scientists also examine the relationships between things and use the cause and effect method of development in their writing. They might, for instance, be studying the effects of television watching, stress, drug abuse, partnerships, and so on. They may also choose to examine the causes of something rather than the effects. Cultural anthropologists, for example, might be interested in why people use certain products, like computers. They might want to consider what reasons humans have for using convenience foods, buses, services, and so forth.

The cause and effect method of development is complicated because you cannot rely on your personal impressions and experience alone to guide you when you write. It is more abstract than a process, or a comparison and contrast method. In using cause and effect, you must reason your way through. Your reasons must be convincing, and the relationship between ideas must be clear. If you develop a piece of writing using this mode, you establish verifiable or reasonable connections between causes and effects. Sometimes, you may have to rely on the results of documented research to "back up" your assertions in order to provide first-hand evidence for your points. This method of development is perhaps the most difficult to use because a clear cause (reason) must be convincingly related to effects (results).

Example: Cause and Effect

Caffeine has come under suspicion as contributing to one disorder or another. It stimulates the body in a number of ways. First, it speeds up the nervous system. It also increases heartbeat and the basal metabolic rate. In addition, it promotes secretion of stomach acid and steps up production of urine. Furthermore, in some cases, drinking too much caffeine may cause lumps to form in the breast. Many doctors advise women against drinking beverages high in caffeine for this very reason. Finally, excessive intake of caffeine can cause physical dependence. Some individuals have experienced "withdrawal" symptoms if foods like coffee, tea, cola drinks, or chocolate have been taken out of their diets. These people experience withdrawal symptoms such as tiredness, headaches, and muscle pain. Caffeine, therefore, must be considered as a powerful drug, having definite and damaging effects.

In this paragraph the cause is stated in the first sentence, the topic sentence—that caffeine produces certain negative effects in the body. The details that follow are the effects of caffeine in the body. Notice that examples and an explanation are included in the discussion of the effects.

You will learn more about cause and effect development in Chapter 7.

Mode Five: Definition Development

The **definition** mode is more complex than the others. Writers must define or tell what something is. You must carefully construct how the ideas relate together to form a definition. Its development should answer these questions: "What is *x*?" and "What are the characteristics of *x*?" To begin, you can situate your idea in a general class of things, so it can be understood as a concept. Next, you must explain the distinguishing features of the thing or idea you wish to define and then examine its characteristics.

Suppose you choose definition as the rhetorical mode to write about friendship. You must first decide what friendship is by thinking about what things it might resemble—about what general class of things it belongs to. Perhaps you decide to place it in the class of things called "human relationships." Next, you must determine how friendship can be distinguished from something else in that class—love, for instance. Then, you must explain the distinguishing features of friendship. In other words, ultimately, you must bring out the special features of the idea in order to define it.

In another example you might examine what a good hockey player is. You spend time thinking over the context in which a player functions. That context might be described by "street hockey," for instance. From this specific context, determine the distinguishing player qualities you want to include in your definition. In the case of a good street hockey player, you could set out the qualities or characteristics you believe to be defining ones; accordingly, you would establish that the qualities you have described are relevant to your choice of context. In other words, you would connect the characteristics with the context in order to form your definition.

You will see definition paragraphs in a variety of sources. A journalist, for example, could be writing about what it means to be a French-Canadian living abroad today. Another writer may be working to define what it means to be a good writer for a rural community newspaper, or perhaps a philosopher may want to explain what is entailed by the definition of "good citizen." Doctors describe the healthy person, psychologists label human behaviours, and other experts work to explain what it means to be something.

Example: Definition

What is a memory? A psychologist considers memory by thinking about how people act and how the brain processes experience. Ralph W. Gerard suggests that memory is "the modification of behaviour by experience." A cognitive psychologist tries to link experience and the mind, examining the relationship between recognition and recall in the study of human memory. A musician, however, may consider memory in a different way: what the hand, eye, ear, and voice can do together is memory. An athlete may talk about memory in terms of a moment frozen like a photograph, the play forever there to be studied or glimpsed. To a writer, memory may be many things. Perhaps like Proust, a writer hopes to make the past into a series of tangible objects through the remembering, using involuntary memory rather than deliberate recollection. Memory can thus be perceived differently depending on the point of view.

In the above paragraph, the writer uses four different perspectives to create the definition of memory. Of course, memory is viewed as a complicated, problematic issue. To get at a complex idea, you may sometimes want to explore the ways other writers or theorists have defined it.

You will learn more about definition development in Chapter 8.

Exercise 1   Group Activity: Reading for Modes

Form a group of three to five people. Read each of the paragraph compositions below. Together decide what mode of development the author has used to organize each paragraph: time-order, comparison or contrast, cause and effect, division or classification, or definition. Discuss why you believe the method is successful. Suggest other modes of development the writer could have used. Write down your answers and be prepared to share them.

PARAGRAPH 1 My happy childhood has influenced me as an adult. When I was little, I was taught to share. Sometimes that was hard to do because there were six children in my family. Even though it was difficult, we learned to cooperate. Today I remember that sharing, and I think I am a more generous person because of it. In addition, although we were poor, we respected ourselves and each other. We never went hungry, and we were always cleanly dressed. As an adult, I think that experience taught me that money has nothing to do with self-respect. Finally, the good parenting I had really helps me today because I have children of my own. Even though my parents were busy people, they took time to talk to us kids and took us everywhere with them. They taught us a number of skills and values; they gave us discipline. Learning all of that as a child helps me now as I struggle to raise my own family. Remembering positive things about my childhood, I realize how these experiences helped shape me as an adult and parent.

PARAGRAPH 2 Inexpensive, delicious homemade soup is easy to prepare. First, you should buy some plump, meaty short ribs, cheap cuts of chicken, or (if you are a vegetarian) extra vegetables. Then assemble your ingredients: garlic, onion, celery stalks and leaves, green cabbage, carrots, one large can of tomatoes, lentils or buckwheat, peas, one bay leaf, one beef/chicken bouillon cube, parsley, salt, and pepper. Now follow these cooking steps: Cut the short ribs or chicken into four-inch pieces, removing the extra fat. Heat a large soup kettle and add a dash of cooking oil. Add chopped onions, celery stalks and leaves, and minced garlic. Sear these vegetables, stirring rapidly to prevent any burning. After two to three minutes, add the short ribs or chicken to the vegetables in the kettle. Sear the meat on all sides. Add six to eight cups of water or enough to cover the meat. Add one bay leaf and a few peppercorns. Cover the kettle and turn the element to medium to low heat. As the stock is simmering, skim off the excess fat with a large, slotted metal spoon. After two to three hours, add two cups of chopped cabbage, one cup of carrots, the can of tomatoes, one-half cup of washed lentils or buckwheat, a bouillon cube, one-third cup of parsley, and additional celery leaves. Mix the soup thoroughly. Let the soup simmer for about 45 minutes. Then remove the short ribs or chicken and strip off the meat from the bones. Return the meat to the soup. Finally, add peas, salt, and pepper. Taste the soup and adjust the seasoning. This hearty soup is ready to serve. It is especially nutritious with thick slices of heavy rye or brown bread. A nourishing meal for four to six people, this soup is inexpensive, delicious, and easy to freeze.

PARAGRAPH 3 Is female handwriting different from that of males in Western society? Some handwriting experts claim that it is easy to spot female handwriting because it is "tidier" than that of males. Although both genders can have a tendency to "open" handwriting, most females tend to tolerate fewer handwriting botch-ups and will clean them up for the reader. Secondly, some experts say a reader can recognize male handwriting because it is even and uses a smaller form. Some samples studied showed that the small, even writing seemed to be created by males three out of five times. Finally, most female handwriting tends to be somewhat fancier than that of males. Special loops and curlicues, along with particular care applied to punctuation marks and the formation of capital letters, seem to be the hallmarks of the female hand. Of course, many disagree and claim this is an oversimplified view; however, when you read handwriting, see if you can judge whether the writing was done by a male or female. You might be able to distinguish the writer's gender.

PARAGRAPH 4 What is "realism" in fiction? Writers became interested in "writing from the real" because they found romantic literature boring and unhelpful. Romantic literature referred to writing that depicted people, places, and situations in the ideal. Heroes were noble and greater than the average person could ever hope to be. Characters struggled with issues that were great universal themes. Their anguish was larger than life, and they were more beautiful and strong—beyond ordinary. Eventually, writers began to try to get at some kind of truth in the world by using realistic material from it. They tried to incorporate accuracy and detail in their writing, including providing precise background information. Details became almost like a photograph. In addition, realist writers became concerned with social and psychological issues so that characters suffered and saw some of life's ugliness, disorder, and disharmony. Readers may gain a sense of authenticity when they read realist fiction, something the writers hoped to achieve—a closer glimpse at the "truth" in experience.

PARAGRAPH 5 Three components make up a first-rate community theatre. The first necessary element is a cooperative group of people who are enthusiastic and energetic. Most people who work in community theatre are volunteers, willing and able to give up their time. Since few people are paid, it becomes important for all contributing members to feel valued and respected. Next, community theatres require a home base. In other words, to flourish in a community, a theatre needs a designated space or building. The local government can then provide tax reduction support, special grants, and so on to the group. Also, the physical space itself can become important to the community. Advertising becomes easier. Word-of-mouth, community newspapers, and passersby all become good sources of information about the theatre's shows. The final ingredient is skill. Good community theatres can attract knowledgeable people who are willing to contribute voluntarily. Citizens may know about directing, writing, marketing, carpentry, and technical theatre knowledge, such as lighting, sound, and set design. In addition, good community theatres help give young people a start in theatre, a career often difficult to break into. These aspects make community theatre the special thing that it is.

PARAGRAPH 6 The company offers its customers three types of billing. "Direct Account" billing allows customers to not have to be reminded of payment. The company debits customers' accounts directly. The second form of billing is "E-Billing." This billing is all done electronically. The company emails customers when their account is due, giving the amounts and payment due dates. Customers then respond by sending their credit card numbers directly to the web site of the company. The third type of billing is called "Prepayment Plan." This plan allows customers to pay in advance. The company gives a 5% discount to those customers who choose the third billing plan. All of the plans are flexible and can be changed in favour of one of the others; however, the company requires 30 days' written notice of customers' intentions to change their type of plan.

PARAGRAPH 7 Learning to play a musical instrument is like taking a vacation. First of all, if a person has not played the instrument before, the experience is like going to a new place. There are many new things to discover about the place and about the person who travels or is learning to play. Secondly, just as a vacation takes someone's mind off his or her troubles, so does learning to play an instrument such as the piano. Each person knows how refreshing it is to be able to forget stresses and problems and concentrate deeply on how his or her fingers are moving on the keyboard; reading the music and trying to keep time really is like a "time-out," similar to the feeling of a short, enjoyable trip. Most important is the satisfaction a person feels at doing and succeeding at something new. Vacations can offer a sensation of well-being because something new may have been tried—a new place visited, a new challenge accepted. The music student can also feel a similar satisfaction in achieving a new and difficult set of skills. In these three ways, learning to play a musical instrument can be as refreshing as a little holiday.

Exercise 2   *Identifying Rhetorical Modes in Paragraphs*

Read and examine the following paragraphs. Decide if the mode is time-order, comparison or contrast, cause and effect, division or classification, or definition. Write the mode after the paragraph. Check your answers in the Answer Key.

PARAGRAPH 1 What is the "underground economy"? Some experts define it as business transactions between people trying to escape paying taxes or to escape government control. Skilled workers can take advantage of "under-the-counter deals." Transactions usually take place in cash with no paper trail or means of tracing the work or payment. The underground economy includes all illegal activities, too. Prostitution, drug trafficking, tax evasion, smuggling, and stealing are some examples. Interestingly enough, any average citizen can participate without knowing it. Canadians who do not report income become part of the underground economy. Some experts believe that the underground economy is part of the growing disrespect for the law, while others say it is simply a response to tough economic times.

Mode: _____

PARAGRAPH 2 The northwest coast Aboriginal peoples' artistic tradition and community differed significantly between the genders. In the past, villages and patrons supported a special group of male artists who were exempt from the everyday chores of the tribe. Some members of this artistic group made items for individuals or families within the tribe, while others were specialists who created outstanding objects that were meant to be preserved and cherished, like special carved totems, for example. From a young age, these specialists were apprenticed to master artists. Women had a different tradition. Although women did not share membership in this select artistic group, many wove baskets and textiles. Many became specialists in their own right in the artistic forms that were traditional to women: basketry, weaving, clothing design, and the creation of ceremonial regalia. Haida women, for example, were renowned for their amazing basketry made from the bark of the huge coastal cedars. While the role of the male artist was more visible in traditional northwest coast Aboriginal culture, both genders had a role in artistic development of the community.

Mode: _____

PARAGRAPH 3 Fish hawks, or ospreys, and bald eagles have some interesting differences. Both birds are predators, although bald eagles are much larger, reaching a wingspan of 1.8 metres. Ospreys, while smaller, are swifter when attacking prey. The two birds vary in size. Ospreys have crested heads, while bald eagles have smooth, white head feathers. Nesting habits also differ. Both birds build their nests out of sticks, but bald eagles tend to return to the same nest site year after year. Thus, the nests of bald eagles are built up over the years and can become huge. The two birds have distinctly different feeding behaviours. Ospreys feed exclusively on fish. Bald eagles, however, include fish like salmon in their diet along with other small prey such as ducks, rabbits, snakes, and even turtles. Ospreys are much more cosmopolitan birds than bald eagles; ospreys with their piercing cries can be seen hunting in and around waters close to human settlement. Bald eagles tend to be somewhat wary of people. Finally, the two birds vary in their migration habits. Ospreys migrate to South America in the winter months, but bald eagles remain in residence year round. For many reasons, ospreys and bald eagles, two of Canada's largest avian predators, have striking distinctions.

Mode: _____

PARAGRAPH 4 If you are a hiker who likes to find adventure along the forest trails of southern Canada, you are probably already familiar with a native plant that can cause great discomfort to you if you touch it. A member of the sumac family having shiny leaves and whitish berries, poison ivy grows along the gravelly or sandy slopes of forests. The plant prefers to grow in lime-based soils, but it can thrive virtually anywhere in woody habitat. Poison ivy causes a painful contact dermatitis to a hiker anywhere it touches bare skin. This rash results in watery skin blisters, which tend to last several days. Of course, poison ivy causes tremendous itching, and scratching a poison ivy rash will spread it.

Mode: _____

PARAGRAPH 5 Significant changes during the 1970s in North America can be said to have transformed attitudes. First, views of marriage changed. Marriage and birthrates fell, but there was a sharp rise in the number of unwed couples of all ages. Gay couples began to rally for the same rights as those in opposite-sex marriages. Therefore, the public began to think about the traditional view of marriage almost as a thing of the past. In addition, customary views of religion changed because some say there was a "loss of faith." Many young people renounced the faith of their parents, and many priests forsook pulpits. Yet as the decade came to a close, churchgoing was on the rise again. Some explain this reconnection with faith in the late 1970s as the expansion of the moral majority and the attempt to re-establish what were called "family values." Although the 1970s have been referred to as the time of the "me generation," many strong grassroots movements were formed that protested social injustice and corporate expansion and development.

Thousands of gays and lesbians went public to demand their rights; other groups espoused the causes of minority groups—immigrants, senior citizens, environmentalists, non-smokers, and women. All in all, the 1970s in North America was a strange blend of conflicted values and a compilation of forces impacting one another.

Mode: _____

PARAGRAPH 6   Experts divide rumours into two species: spontaneous and premeditated. Most spontaneous rumours appear in periods of stress, such as in a fuel crisis. They seem to thrive in an atmosphere of anxiety, mistrust, repression, or chaos and spread quickly. The second type, premeditated rumours, do not develop in an unprompted fashion. Instead, they are often planted for dubious purposes, particularly in highly competitive business environments. Both types of rumours die when they become irrelevant or when stressful conditions do not prevail.

Mode: _____

Exercise 3   Group Activity: Finding Examples of Rhetorical Modes

Form a group of three to five people who want this extra practice. Each of you should find an example of each rhetorical mode from newspaper, magazine, or internet writing. One group member can find an example of contrast; another person can find an example of comparison, and so forth. Your group will meet to share the pieces of writing and to discuss the mode of development. Your group should discuss what each method of development is and why it is effective or not. Be prepared to share your answers with the whole group.

CHECKOUT

To develop paragraph compositions, you can use the following five rhetorical modes of development as a tool for arranging ideas:

1. time-order, or process

2. comparison and contrast

3. classification and division

4. cause and effect

5. definition

As a writer, you will use different methods to suit different circumstances. You learn to use these methods to help map out your thinking, so that your writing becomes clear for you and your readers.

chapter 3

Analyzing Detail Organization

Chapter Objectives
After completing this chapter, you will be able to
- understand a paragraph's organization
- find topic sentences in paragraphs
- write effective topic sentences, showing the rhetorical mode
- add points and supporting details to paragraph compositions
- write concluding, or wrap-up, sentences to paragraphs

INTRODUCTION

In Chapter 2, you examined five rhetorical modes—tools to use when you think about *how* to develop your ideas. Once you have decided on rhetorical mode, however, you must then consider what points you want to talk about, what details you will use to support your points, and what arrangement to use. In other words, you discover a paragraph is organized around its topic sentence, main ideas or major points, and supporting details. It is important to recognize that writers may choose different arrangements. By reading other writers' work, you examine how they have arranged their ideas. Doing so will help make you both a better writer and a better reader.

LOCATING THE TOPIC SENTENCE

As you read the following paragraphs, you will see that the topic sentence can be located in various places in paragraphs: at the beginning, middle, or end. Sometimes, the topic sentence may be implied and not directly stated. Often writers locate the topic sentence at the beginning of paragraphs because they find it easier to develop ideas.

Using a clear topic sentence is vital to you as a developing academic writer. *Spotlight on Paragraph and Essay Skills* recommends you place your topic sentences at the beginning of your paragraphs. As you gain more confidence, experience, and skill in your writing, you may place topic sentences in other positions.

Exercise 1   Locating the Topic Sentence

Underline the topic sentence in each of the following paragraphs. Remember: the topic sentence contains the main idea of the paragraph. Bear in mind that, in some cases, a writer may leave out the topic sentence entirely: in such cases, readers must infer the topic sentence. Check your answers in the Answer Key.

PARAGRAPH 1 F.H. Varley was a member of the Group of Seven. He was born in 1881 and died in 1969. In 1912, he emigrated from England to Canada where he found work in commercial art. Varley was celebrated as a Canadian portrait painter. His most famous works include illustrations of the war in Europe in 1918 and many portraits. He spent years travelling between points in Canada and in the Arctic, sketching, photographing, and painting dramatic landscapes. He worked mostly in watercolours and oils. Many of his works now hang in prominent galleries in Canada and throughout the world and in the homes of art collectors as far away as Hong Kong.

PARAGRAPH 2 The United Nations was established in 1945, with its headquarters in New York City, New York, USA, and Geneva, Switzerland. Its mandate is to promote world peace and economic and social justice, along with the development of human rights and freedoms. The UN has some new concerns since 1945—science and technology. It is extremely difficult for the UN to resolve problems within nations because, in order to do so, all member nations of the UN must pull together in a diplomatic manner on a given agenda; in other words, all member nations must agree. Though the UN has suffered some severe financial problems in the past 15 years, it is beginning to regain world respect and confidence. Surprisingly, Canada is one of the largest contributors to the finances of the UN.

PARAGRAPH 3 In the first days of lumbering, the tree trunks on first-growth trees were huge, and cuts had to be made higher up on the trunk. Doing such cutting was a dangerous business. Before the introduction of the crosscut saw, lumbermen used the timber axe, a heavy, awkward tool. Lumbermen stood on a platform or springboard that was built around the tree, one man on either side of the tree. The progress in cutting was slow, and three times the usual number of oxen, and, later, horses, were used to haul the timber from difficult inland terrain. Skid roads had to be built out of logs to get the timber out of the forests. Tree cutters and the lumber industry in Canada have had to cope with many technical problems throughout their history.

PARAGRAPH 4 Rowing is a sport that is gaining in popularity. In Canada, rowing events have been reported as early as 1816 in St. John's Harbour. In the 1840s, rowing clubs began in Quebec and Ontario. In 1867, four Canadian rowers won a race in Paris, France. Between 1954 and 1960, Canadian rowing became even more commonplace because of the Commonwealth Games. In 1976, several Canadian rowers took medals at the Olympics. In the milder southern Canadian climate, hundreds of people now enjoy rowing as the major sport in their lives, and several key areas have become the training grounds for future Canadian champion rowers.

DEVELOPING AN EFFECTIVE TOPIC SENTENCE

Paragraph compositions are relatively short pieces of writing. Therefore, you should choose a topic that you can handle effectively—one that does not require a lengthy development. Because you cannot deal with complex issues in a single one-paragraph composition, you should begin by selecting a topic that seems appropriate to a composition of 150 to 250 words. Once you decide on a suitable topic, you shape a topic sentence having the following two purposes:

1. to contain the main idea or focus of the paragraph

2. to show the rhetorical mode you will use to work through your ideas: time-order, comparison or contrast, cause and effect, classification and division, or definition.

After you have shaped this important topic sentence, ask yourself the following questions:

1. Is my topic sentence "too big"? Is it too broad? Am I trying to deal with too much in a limited number of words? Is my statement so general I wander around my topic?

2. Is the topic sentence "too small"? Is it too narrow? Am I only going to be making one point? Am I restricting myself so much that I will be left with too little to say?

3. Is the statement "just right"? Does it show my general direction without being too ambitious or too restrictive? Does it indicate what method I will be using to organize my ideas? Does it seem interesting enough?

If your topic sentence seems "just right," you are ready to begin. Practise by doing some work in shaping topic sentences.

Exercise 2   Shaping Topic Sentences

Read the topic sentences and decide if they are too broad, too narrow, or "just right." If someone had given you each of them as a topic sentence for a paragraph composition, would you be able to use them effectively? Why or why not? Some possible answers appear right after the exercise.

1. His dog is disgusting.

2. I failed my computing test.

3. Green is Melanie's favourite colour.

4. Scientists are discovering new ways of treating cancer.

5. Highways are dangerous.

6. The criminal was a 15-year-old from Saskatchewan.

7. Puppy love can be divided into three types.

8. Email programs consist of seven basic features.

9. Children, unlike adults, should not play contact sports.

10. Swimming and hockey have certain similarities.

Read the explanations below to see how your answers compare.

1. This statement is too narrow. It is really an opinion—someone's dog is disgusting. It does not invite discussion. The writer does not indicate how he or she will handle the topic: there is no clear rhetorical mode indicated.

2. This statement is also narrow. It says that a person has failed a computing test, but beyond that, it does not indicate what the discussion will be about. Had the writer suggested that there were "four reasons for failing my computing test," then he or she would have more to talk about. The writer could generalize and discuss why people fail tests or why some people fail tests and others don't.

3. This sentence is too narrow to be an effective topic sentence. Although green may not be someone's favourite colour, this fact cannot provide enough to write about. Secondly, there is no clear mode indicated by the statement. Not having a clear mode can lead to just as many problems as not having enough to say.

4. At first glance, this topic sentence seems "just right"; however, you can see it is too broad—it tries to take in too much. Remember that a paragraph composition is short. This topic might make a good thesis statement for an essay, but in a short composition, you cannot explain it well enough to satisfy any purpose.

5. This statement is too broad. Everyone knows that some highways can be dangerous, but it does not indicate which ones and why. It might be effective for the writer to discuss the different dangers on two highways (contrast) or the types of dangerous highways (classification). The topic sentence lacks focus because it does not direct the development of ideas.

6. The statement is too narrow. It is a fact that the criminal is 15 years old, but unless the topic sentence is opened up for more discussion, there is little left for the writer to say. Besides, youth and crime is too complex a topic to try to deal with in a short paragraph composition. You see no clear development of ideas indicated by this statement.

7. This topic sentence seems "just right." The writer uses a clear mode—*classification*—to discuss the topic of puppy love. The topic also seems manageable and suitable for a shorter piece of writing.

8. This topic sentence seems "just right." The writer uses a *division* method—what seven parts make up an email program. The topic seems suitable for a shorter composition.

9. This topic sentence seems "just right." The writer indicates a *contrast* mode. He or she will explain the differences in the suitability of contact sports for the two age groups. The topic is manageable in a one-paragraph composition.

10. This topic sentence seems "just right." The writer uses comparison. He or she will discuss in what ways swimming and hockey are the same. The topic is suitable for a shorter composition.

How did you manage in your answers? As a writer, you will find the topic sentence is very important to your writing task. You will use the topic sentence as an obvious starting point. You will have a clear direction because a good topic sentence provides it. You can then sketch out what your paragraph will be about. Then you can move to the body of your discussion.

Exercise 3   Group Activity: Recognizing Patterns in Topic Sentences

Effective topic sentences may show one of the following five modes:

1. time-order, or process
2. comparison and contrast
3. classification and division
4. cause and effect
5. definition

Form a group of three to five people. Read each of the topic sentences below. Decide what rhetorical mode you think the writer might use. Write your group's answer after each sentence. Be prepared to share answers with the class.

1. Foreign-made cars are more economical to operate than North American-built vehicles. _____

2. A garage sale can be easy to organize if a person follows a few simple steps. _____

3. Adult learning is different from youth learning. _____

4. When I was 17, I learned what love meant. _____

5. The history of computers is entertaining to read about. _____

6. Some elderly drivers can cause accidents on the road. _____

7. Television commercials are unlike advertisements in magazines. _____

8. Canada's climate may be divided into five regional types. _____

9. The wetlands of Ontario and Manitoba are unique in four ways. _____

10. Here's how to restore an antique chair. _____

11. Both card games and chess can be educational. _____

12. Repairing a bicycle tire is easy to do. _____

13. Judging others can lead to some serious problems. _____

14. How can someone learn to keep a secret? _____

15. What is a bargain? _____

Exercise 4   Group Activity: Developing Topic Sentences Together

Form a group of three to five people to complete this activity. Choose one person to lead the group and another to write down the group's responses. Choose a third person to report responses to the class. Agree on each topic sentence you construct.

After each topic you will see a suggested rhetorical mode. Choose 10 of the following topics. Write a topic sentence for each according to the mode requested. You may use any aspect of the topic. For example, if the topic is "driving," you may discuss an aspect such as ambulance driving, professional driving, highway driving, and so forth.

1. a festival (time-order)
2. pets (definition)
3. parenting (contrast)
4. shopping (classification)
5. safety (division)
6. fashion (time-order)
7. stress (cause and effect)
8. recreation (comparison)
9. condominiums (contrast)
10. travel (division)
11. marriage (definition)
12. radar traps (time-order, or process)
13. hockey (classification)
14. bread making (division)
15. beer (classification)
16. photography (comparison)
17. diets (cause and effect)
18. camping (time-order or process)
19. happiness (cause and effect)
20. jokes (classification)

Exercise 5   Group Activity: Finding Effective Topic Sentences

Form a group of five people. Each member of the group is responsible for finding a single paragraph in a magazine or newspaper that has an effective topic sentence. Group members will come together to share the paragraphs they have found. Group members should be prepared to discuss why paragraphs have been selected and why the topic sentences are effective. If the group disagrees, the members should set aside those paragraphs. The instructor may want to collect the paragraphs and distribute them.

THE BODY OF THE PARAGRAPH

The explanation part of the paragraph composition makes up the content of the writing. Often called the **body** of the paragraph or essay, the explanation is made up of points. Each point has support or evidence for it, too. You establish points that follow from the topic sentence. Then you give proof for each point. The proof might be an example, a reason, a statistic, an anecdote, an explanation, or an illustration.

The paragraph below comes from Exercise 1. Read it again, paying attention to how the writer develops the body of the paragraph.

In the first days of lumbering, the tree trunks on first-growth trees were huge, and cuts had to be made higher up on the trunk. Doing such cutting was a dangerous business. Before the introduction of the crosscut saw, lumbermen used the timber axe, a heavy, awkward tool. Lumbermen stood on a platform or springboard that was built around the tree, one man on either side of the tree. The progress in cutting was slow, and three times the usual number of oxen, and, later, horses, were used to haul the timber from difficult inland terrain. Skid roads had to be built out of logs to get the timber out of the forests. Tree cutters and the lumber industry in Canada have had to cope with many technical problems throughout their history.

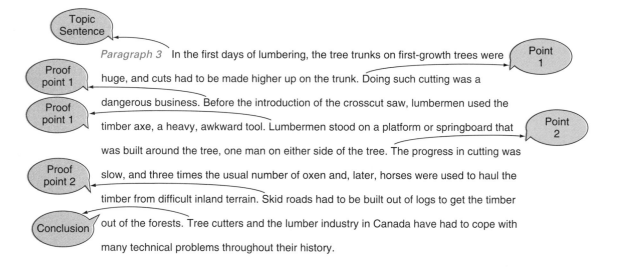

Exercise 6   Finding the Points in the Body

Read each of the following paragraph compositions. Underline the topic sentence. Then number each point the writer is making. Indicate what the proof is for each point. Write *proof* over these sentences. Be prepared to share your answers with the rest of the class.

PARAGRAPH 1 Papier mâché is a fun and inexpensive craft for children of all ages. The materials are cheap and easy to come by. Collect a stack of old newspapers, a square pan with sides that are about 25 cm high, about 500 ml of all-purpose flour, string, a small paintbrush, poster paint, and bits of wire to make a form. The steps are simple. Tear the newspaper into long, thin shreds. This is a job most young children love to do! Place the paper shreds into the square pan and cover them with water. Let the mixture soak for several minutes until the paper is soft and pliable. Add the flour and blend the ingredients together until all of the flour has been well incorporated into the strips of paper. Children will love this step, too, because they can dig in and enjoy the fun. Let the mixture rest for about 30 minutes. While the mixture is curing, shape a form with the wire. String may be added as well. Children can choose to make masks, jewellery, baskets, boxes, toys, or whatever pleases them. After 30 minutes, apply the first layer to the form. Keep adding more layers and wetting the mixture down if it becomes too dry or stiff. Let the shape dry overnight. The next step—decorating—holds lots of creative potential. More layers can be added if needed. The piece should be perfectly dry before paint is applied. Mix bright colours of poster paint and then decorate the piece. Use string or plastic beads or small objects to add interest. Paint over these so that the piece has texture. You can add glitter or lacquer to make the piece glossy. Children will proudly display their creations for everyone to see. So, with a few simple steps and materials, anyone can have fun making papier-mâché projects.

PARAGRAPH 2 Commuting can be relaxing. First, commuters can enjoy watching the scenery while someone else does the driving. Many people do not enjoy driving themselves from home to work and back again because they hate battling the traffic and the rush-hour grids. Another reason commuting can be enjoyable is the cost. It is much cheaper to take public transit than to pay for car insurance, gas, and maintenance on a vehicle. Commuters can save money. Finally, many find commuting fun. They enjoy meeting new people, reading a book, or just calming their nerves while they occupy themselves with their own thoughts. Some people even claim that commuting is the only time of the day they have to themselves. All of these reasons provide convincing evidence that commuting can be a positive experience.

Exercise 7 *Adding Points*

Add three major points to each of the following topic sentences. Identify each mode. Remember: you want to add ideas that relate to the topic sentence. Your ideas should be convincing.

1. Vacations can be a disaster.

   a. _____

   b. _____

   c. _____

2. Rabbits and skunks have three main differences.

   a. _____

b. _____

c. _____

3. Car accidents can have serious effects on young drivers.

a. _____

b. _____

c. _____

4. What makes a good listener?

a. _____

b. _____

c. _____

5. Doing laundry is easy if you follow these steps.

a. _____

b. _____

c. _____

Exercise 8   Group Activity: Providing Proof or Evidence

Form a group of three to five people. For each of the following points, provide proof. You can use examples, facts, reasons, statistics, or more explanation. Be prepared to share your answers with others in the class.

1. Working and going to school can be challenging.

a. Time management

Proof: _____

b. Getting enough rest

Proof: _____

c. Getting to know others isn't easy.

Proof: _____

2. Women are better at some sports than men.

a. Synchronized swimming

Proof: _____

b. Floor gymnastics

Proof: _____

c. Figure skating

Proof: _____

3. What makes up a nutritious diet?

a. Whole foods

Proof: _____

b. Fresh ingredients

Proof: _____

c. Careful preparation

Proof: _____

THE CONCLUSION OF THE PARAGRAPH

The **wrap-up** concludes the single paragraph composition. It is often called the **conclusion**, but this name can be deceiving. A conclusion in this sense is not always something that logically concludes from a written argument. For example, a narrative paragraph tells a story and does not necessarily have a logical conclusion. Rather, a conclusion, or wrap-up, in a paragraph composition completes the paragraph, so that the reader feels satisfied that it has ended.

Concluding, or wrap-up, sentences will depend on the rhetorical mode and the writer's purpose. In the case of a paragraph composition that uses a time-order method of development, for example, the paragraph composition may not actually have a conclusion: it may simply require a closing statement of some sort, telling the reader the process description is complete. A comparison or contrast mode may require a wrap-up sentence that mentions similarities or differences. On the other hand, a cause–effect mode will call for a statement that draws a probable conclusion from the points presented. In this case, the conclusion should follow from the arguments—points and evidence—presented in the composition. If you do not provide a clear and logical conclusion, then you might not convince the reader.

In your paragraph composition writing, you should leave the reader with a sense of satisfaction: each piece should end reasonably and clearly. The wrap-up sentence should help the paragraph come to a logical and pleasing ending.

Exercise 9   *Adding Wrap-Up Sentences*

On the line provided, add a good wrap-up sentence to each of the following paragraphs. Your instructor may want to see your work, or may want you to share your answers with others.

PARAGRAPH 1 Kitchen magnets became a fad in the early 1960s. They came about because refrigerators became widely available in the 1950s, when most people wanted to switch from the traditional iceboxes to major electric appliances. As householders began to use the fridge door as a place to post notes for members of the family, marketers noticed that the fridge had become a kind of bulletin board. They invented and developed "fridge magnets" in charming shapes and colours.

Wrap-up sentence: _____

PARAGRAPH 2 Foxes will eat anything. Foxes have become raiders of more than just the chicken houses in farmyards. They love junk food like noodles, potato chips, and jam, but are equally at home with cattle feed or mash. They seem to be hungry constantly and are always on the search for new edible delights. Half-grown pups, too small to hunt real game, forage in the woods for berries and roots, beetles, grubs, or even flying insects. The larvae in a dead stump or a wasp's nest can provide them with an ample meal.

Wrap-up sentence: _____

PARAGRAPH 3 Everyone enjoyed watching the first 3-D movies in the 1950s. At the door, patrons were handed strange-looking cardboard glasses. Viewers wore the glasses when they were watching the movie. The glasses were included in the price of the admission ticket. One eyeglass was red-tinted plastic; the other, green. In the theatre, all viewers, young and old, put on their weird equipment in order to see the spectacular visual effects that were advertised on every billboard.

Wrap-up sentence: _____

PARAGRAPH 4 According to psychologists, taking a short nap is good for you. When you feel sleepy in the afternoons or after eating, you should lie down for a short snooze. You should not sleep more than 20 minutes because you do not want your body to reach deep REM sleep, the deepest of the sleep stages. It can be startling to be pulled out of the REM stages of sleep. After all, you want to feel refreshed after a nap, not groggy and grumpy.

Wrap-up sentence: _____

Form a group of four or five people to complete the exercise below. Be prepared to share your answers with the rest of the class.

1. Underline the topic sentences; indicate if no topic sentence is given.

2. Indicate the rhetorical mode used: time-order; comparison, contrast; cause and effect; division; classification; or definition. Although the organization may seem to have a mixed pattern in some paragraphs, try to find one that seems dominant.

3. Number the points provided in each paragraph.

PARAGRAPH 1 Blood pressure, the force exerted by blood against the inner walls of the blood vessels, fluctuates as the heart beats. The highest pressure, occurring when the heart contracts, is called systolic pressure; the lowest pressure, when the heart dilates, is called diastolic pressure. Blood pressure is designated as a ratio, with systolic pressure over diastolic. In humans, blood pressure can vary according to a person's age, the level of exertion being applied to the body, and the level of excitement someone is feeling.

PARAGRAPH 2 Among the most insidious hazards is that of smoking during pregnancy. In 1976 more than 36% of Canadian women in the childbearing ages of 15 to 44 years were smokers. Yet a study by Quebec's Laval University found that smoking in pregnancy increased the risk of prenatal death by 24%, and 12 studies cited by the Public Health Service have revealed a "significant elevated mortality risk among the infants of smokers." Today in Sweden, which has the lowest infant mortality rate in the world, researchers have computed the "total death risk" in stillbirths, and in deaths occurring before one year of age, as an astonishing 60% higher for babies of smoking mothers. Despite these startling findings, many women continue to smoke while they are pregnant.

PARAGRAPH 3 What is the history of printmaking in Canada? Printmaking is the art of making images using several techniques. Woodcuts were the first printmaking images made, and these images were used mostly for advertising purposes in the 18th century. Then artists' sketches were etched or engraved on copperplates, and these prints became a popular art form. A rolling press, or intaglio press, was first brought to Canada in 1790, and prints became more sophisticated. The next development came with the intaglio press and aquatint etchings. For many years after that, lithography became the main form of printmaking. Finally, colour-screen printing, or serigraphy, became the predominant form of printmaking.

PARAGRAPH 4 The Thunderbird is an important being in Aboriginal mythology. First, the Thunderbird is a powerful, supernatural creature that produces and controls lightning and thunder. The Aboriginal stories say that when the Thunderbird flaps its wings, it produces thunder. When the Thunderbird opens and closes its powerful eyes, it produces lightning. Furthermore, the power of the Thunderbird as a hunter is told in many Aboriginal stories and songs. This wonderful bird is said to hunt whales and shoot arrows, using its wings like arms. It is said that humans can inherit the gifts of the Thunderbird. A person who is hit by lightning and survives becomes the shaman of the tribe; it is believed the person then has the power of the Thunderbird. In many Aboriginal legends, the Thunderbird is described as one of the most powerful beings.

CHECKOUT

Provide full, clear answers to the following review questions.

1. What is a paragraph?

_____

_____

_____

2. What does a topic sentence do?

_____

_____

_____

3. Where can you find topic sentences in paragraphs?

_____

_____

_____

4. If readers cannot find a topic sentence, what do they usually do?

_____

_____

_____

5. Name five methods by which you can organize details in paragraphs.

_____   _____

_____   _____

_____

6. Why is knowing about paragraph organization important?

_____

_____

_____

chapter 4

Time-Order, or Process, Development

Chapter Objectives

After completing this chapter, you will be able to

- recognize time-order, or process, development by reading paragraphs
- shape topic sentences using time-order, or process, development
- write a paragraph composition using time-order, or process, development
- set up a title page for presentation

INTRODUCTION

To write about how to do something, use time-order, or process, development, often called **chronological** order. Outline and then clearly explain each step of the process. The order in which you present the steps is critical because you are describing a sequence. Let's suppose, for example, you wish to tell the reader how to make a perfect breakfast for someone on a special day. The order of preparation is important so that the food can be ready and hot at the same time. Your reader doesn't want to have to back-track to do a step.

You can use time-order to report on a series of events. For instance, you might tell a story from your life, describe an incident you witnessed, tell someone else's story, or relate a chronicle from history. In these examples, you are reporting a narrative or story, having a chronological order. Using time-order effectively, you make a story sensible to readers. You may also wish to use time-order to explain a process. Perhaps you are taking a nursing course and have to write about how the body produces and uses insulin. A time-order mode would be the most appropriate way to explain the process.

Time-order is a relatively easy mode to adopt, because you are working with experience and observation as the content of your writing. You do not need to rely strictly on abstract ideas; instead, you can go through the events as you observe or remember them.

USING TRANSITIONS IN TIME-ORDER, OR PROCESS, DEVELOPMENT

Transitions are words or phrases that act as connectors between ideas. Transitions show a reader that a new point is coming next. They are cues for the reader: they signal a turn in the explanation. You might want to think about them as connecting bridges between ideas.

Different rhetorical modes of development use different transitions. When you use time-order, or process, development, you should use specific transitions that show a chronological or step-by-step relationship.

Useful Time-Order Transitions

first	secondly, thirdly
to begin with	following that
in the first place	next
before	after that
presently	in due time
now	then
meanwhile	soon
when	until
after a while	later
afterward	finally

READING TIME-ORDER DEVELOPMENT

Analyzing ideas and studying the use of devices such as transitions can help you develop your writing.

Exercise 1   Time-Order Development

Read the following paragraph, paying attention to the specific transitions the writer uses.

My friend Paula plans and organizes picnics that are inexpensive and entertaining for family and friends. To begin with, she decides how many people she will invite and what they like to eat. Next, she calls her closest friends to help with food preparation and expenses. She includes the children at this stage, too. Her picnics include two types of potato salad—one for vegetarians and one for meat-eaters—roasted chicken legs, green salad, corn salad, bean salad, hot dogs for the children, potato chips, and devilled eggs. We all show up the day before the picnic with a number of selected food items. We form a production line of cooks, each of us having several tasks to perform. For example, someone peels and cooks the potatoes, another person chops vegetables, usually two people chop onions for the salads and hot dogs, and another friend devils the eggs and puts the salad ingredients together. Paula usually roasts the chicken legs in her special sauce. Then we each take something home to store in our refrigerators. Paula also appoints people who are non-cooks to do other things: one person brings games and sports equipment, another brings a couple of large coolers, another gets together blankets, napkins, paper plates, and plastic cutlery. Someone else might arrange the entertainment at the picnic. Paula's "last-minute person" brings or buys whatever we need that we have forgotten when we get to the park. Groups usually bring their own beverages because it is difficult to please everyone when it comes to what we want to drink. On the day of the picnic, we all show up at the designated place and time, ready to dig in and have a good time. Without Paula's organizational skills and energy, all her friends and family would miss some great summer festivities.

First, notice that the topic sentence implies that a process, or some steps, will be described: "My friend Paula *plans* and *organizes* picnics that are inexpensive and entertaining for family and friends." The two words in italics tell you some sort of arrangement will be explained.

Next, notice the transitional words and phrases the writer chooses to introduce the ideas and shape the mode. *To begin with*, *next*, *the day before the picnic*, *then*, and *on the day of* all show time-order, or sequence. Inside the paragraph, you will also see other transitions, such as "for example" and "also": these help add one idea to another. Such expressions not only assist in developing ideas by a time-order method, but they also help the ideas to be coherent, clear, and fluid. They also signal the reader.

Finally, look at the wrap-up, or closing, sentence of the paragraph. Does it bring the writer's ideas together? Write an effective wrap-up sentence, and you leave your reader with a feeling of closure and satisfaction.

Exercise 2   Reading Time-Order, or Process, Development

Read the following paragraph. Pay attention to the topic sentence, the wrap-up sentence, and the transitions. Then examine how many steps or stages in the process the writer provides. Let the example above guide you in your analysis. Be prepared to share ideas with others.

With the costs of food going higher and higher, many people are banding together to learn to organize neighbourhood food cooperatives. The first step is for a group of interested people to get together. Usually one or two people get the idea and start talking to neighbours and friends to see if there are enough people who want to make worthwhile plans. Organizers can place notices on bulletin boards in shopping centres, nearby schools, community centres, and public libraries. The group might decide to take advantage of the free advertising cable companies and small, local newspapers offer. Then, after a number of people show interest in the project, the group can set the first meeting. They decide the scope of their cooperative and begin to discuss the policies and practices their association would like to have. There are numerous questions to sort out—How large should their cooperative get? Should the group work out of someone's home, or should they rent a small space somewhere? Should the group hire some part-time help? Are there legal problems to consider? After these decisions have been made, they can discuss how to finance the co-op, what the ongoing responsibilities of each member should be, who should be in charge of various duties, and where to buy the goods and produce. After the initial planning stages, the new co-op can begin its work of saving money for its members and providing an excellent service at the same time.

TOPIC SENTENCES REVEAL DEVELOPMENT

Your topic sentence should indicate what rhetorical mode—time-order, comparison and contrast, classification and division, cause and effect, or definition—you will use when you are developing your paragraph composition. Of course, you don't say, "I will use time-order to develop this topic." Instead, key words or phrases in your topic sentence show the manner in which you will develop your paragraph.

However, shaping a topic sentence takes practice. The following exercise will help you develop clear topic sentences based on a **time-order** mode.

Exercise 3   Writing Time-Order Topic Sentences

Read the topics below. For 12 of the topics, develop a topic sentence that indicates a time-order, or process, mode of development. You may use any aspect of the topic for your topic sentence. Your assignment should be on a separate paper and show your name, the date, and the assignment number at the top of the page. Your instructor may want you to hand in this assignment.

Topics for Time-Order, or Process, Topic Sentences

fires	gambling
laundry	photography
decisions	skateboarding
the internet	meditation
travel	shopping
parks	wines
pizza	the workplace
baseball	neighbours
parties	toast
bikes	apartments

ORGANIZING YOUR IDEAS CLEARLY

Rhetorical modes such as time-order can help you develop the ideas of your paragraph. However, you must still arrange your ideas clearly. A simple six-step method of setting up your ideas in a time-order mode is as follows:

1. Establish each step in a separate sentence. Tell the reader what the step is. Use transitions to help you.

2. Discuss the step. In a sentence or two, tell why the step is important, or explain what you think is important information connected to the step.

3. Establish your next step in a separate sentence. Use a transition to introduce the next step. The transition lets your reader know you are bridging one idea to the next.

4. Discuss the next step in a separate sentence. Provide relevant information about the step in another sentence or two.

5. Continue establishing steps and discussion.

6. Wrap up the discussion in the last sentence. Provide closure to the piece for the reader.

Exercise 4   *Following the Writer's Organization*

Go back to the paragraph about Paula and the picnic. Using the six-step formula above, trace how the writer developed points in the paragraph.

THE DRAFTING PROCESS

Because writing is a process, you will learn to produce several attempts, called **drafts**. Your first draft should never be your final draft; in other words, you should find ways you can improve your first draft. Perhaps you will detect problems in the organization. Perhaps you will see that a point has not been clearly established. You will probably also notice errors in proofreading—that is, errors in spelling, punctuation, grammar, and usage.

Your instructor may ask to see your first draft. He or she will make comments on the draft and then ask you to make revisions, clean up errors, improve the style, and so forth. In the second draft, you will be expected to pay closer attention to such details. In addition, your instructor may ask to see you for a **writing conference**, a short meeting between you and your instructor to discuss your draft.

Your instructor will mark and make comments on your paper. Furthermore, he or she may provide you with a marking scheme sheet. This sheet shows you what your instructor will be looking for in your paper.

Writing Assignment 1   Time-Order Paragraph

Choose a topic from the following list and write a paragraph composition using a time-order or process method of development. To complete the assignment, use the following three points:

1. The assignment should be 150–200 words long and double-spaced.

2. Check over spelling, grammar, and punctuation before you hand in your assignment.

3. Use a computer to complete the assignment. If you are unable to comply with this requirement, please talk to your instructor.

More Topics for Time-Order Paragraphs

how to plan a wedding	how to dye your hair
how to change the oil in a car	how to prepare for a test or exam
how to make a complaint	how to build a go-cart
how to set up a tent	how to catch a mouse without a trap
how to wallpaper a room	how to pickle eggs
how to apologize to your lover	how to buy a used bicycle (or car)
how to use the internet	how to organize a meeting
how to stop someone from snoring	how to purchase a computer
how to hold a garage sale	how to overcome shyness
how to play a game (or sport)	how to be an effective negotiator
how to use a fax machine	how to write a song
how to shop for bargains	how to start a small business

how to can peaches	how to stop gossiping
how to ask someone to marry you	how to catch trout
how to saddle a horse	how to investigate your credit rating
how to decorate a basement room	how to polka
how to stop a fight	how to play a trick

SETTING UP THE FINAL DRAFT FOR PARAGRAPH COMPOSITION ASSIGNMENTS

Presentation is very important in assignments for academic courses. Presentation means the following:

1. You have clearly typed (word-processed) the assignment on clean paper using a serif font of 11 or 12 points. Do not use smaller or larger fonts.

2. You have edited the assignment carefully and read it several times for errors (proofread). In other words, you have gone over the organization and content, along with spelling, punctuation, and grammar, before handing in the paper.

3. You have used standard white bond and not a coloured paper that is difficult to read.

CHECKOUT

1. Appropriate transitional words and phrases can indicate a time-order, or process, mode.

2. You can use key words and phrases in a topic sentence to show which mode of writing development you are using.

3. The drafting process will give you essential writing practice and sharpen your editing skills.

4. The time-order, or process, mode is quite easy to use because you can use your experience and real-life situations.

chapter 5

Comparison and Contrast Development

Chapter Objectives

After completing this chapter, you will be able to

- recognize the comparison and contrast mode through reading paragraphs
- work with similarities and differences between two ideas
- recognize and use a block form or point-by-point arrangement of ideas
- write a paragraph composition using comparison and contrast development

INTRODUCTION

You use the **comparison and contrast** mode to write about the similarities (comparison) and differences (contrast) between two things, ideas, people, or places. When you **compare** two items, you look for ways in which the items are the same. When you **contrast** two items, you look for differences between them. You can also combine these approaches and use both comparison and contrast in your development. For example, suppose you wanted to discuss visiting your hometown after several years of being away. You decide to begin your discussion with a comparison, looking at the way the town has stayed the same. You then move your analysis to a contrast—what is different about the town then and now. Using a comparison and contrast mode helps you discover new ideas and the relationship of ideas.

ARRANGING YOUR IDEAS AND SUPPORTING DETAILS

In the comparison and contrast mode, you will notice two main ways of arranging your points and supporting details: **block form** and **point-by-point**. In block form, you arrange all the ideas about each item in a block and then discuss the ideas in that block. For example, to discuss bees and wasps, you might arrange all your ideas about bees together in one block and place the ideas on wasps in another. If you choose a point-by-point arrangement, you could arrange your discussion by points and discuss the two items in relation to each point. For example, for the topic of bees and wasps, you might decide to talk about these three points: methods of food gathering, flight mechanisms, and body structures. In a point-by-point arrangement, you write about the method of food gathering in bees and then wasps. You discuss the next point—the flight mechanisms of both insects. Finally, you talk about your last point in connection with both—the features of each insect's body structure.

Block or Point-by-Point Format: Bees and Wasps

Block format

First part of the paragraph:

Bees

1. food gathering

2. flight mechanisms

3. body structure

Second part of the paragraph:

Wasps

1. similarities to or differences from bees in food gathering

2. similarities to or differences from bees in flight mechanisms

3. similarities to or differences from bees in body structure

Conclusion

Point-by-Point

Point 1. The food gathering behaviours of bees and wasps—their similarities and differences. This point could take several sentences to discuss and explain.

Point 2. The flight mechanisms of bees and wasps—their similarities and differences. This point could take several sentences to discuss and explain.

Point 3. The similarities and differences in body structure between bees and wasps. This point could take several sentences to discuss and explain.

Conclusion

EXPLORING THE COMPARISON AND CONTRAST MODE

A comparison and contrast mode can be effective if you plan your composition carefully. You must spend time thinking about how the two items are different and how they are the same. Try to think of ways that are interesting because it is easy to point out the obvious about the two items. Do not tell the reader what everyone already knows about the two items; instead, think about distinguishing features that will be appealing.

Working through an example may help to clarify the use of the mode. Suppose, for example, you want to contrast your peewee hockey experiences as a child with your adult experiences. It would be too obvious simply to say, "As a child, there was not as much violence in the game of hockey." Readers would probably already know that most kids' hockey games have fewer fights in them. What could you say that would be more interesting to read about?

As you think hard about your experiences, try to select what has particular meaning to you. Then ask yourself a question: what makes the experience different? Which points are most significant?

Use a Chart to Generate Ideas

Sometimes, drawing a chart with one item on one side and the other item on the other side can help you think more clearly. You can then consider what the two items have in common and what sets them apart in your experience or in your interpretation.

For example, how does age relate to sport?

Example of a Comparison and Contrast Chart

Peewee Hockey	Adult Hockey
physical skill developing	physical skill developed
players just learning	players experienced, but sometimes out of shape
reason for playing to develop skill & prowess	reason for playing is for sociable & fitness purposes
in leagues	often associated with community events
supervised by adults	unsupervised
fantasy of being in the NHL	acceptance of personal level of skill

---

You can see that laying the two lists side by side may help you to think creatively. Using this "chart" method can also help you generate new ideas. Think about particular aspects of two things and tease out what makes them the same or different. Then you can decide whether you wish to use block form by discussing the peewee ideas first and then discussing the adult experiences, or a point-by-point arrangement in which you take three of your strongest points and discuss peewee and adult experiences regarding each point.

TOPIC SENTENCES WITH COMPARISON AND CONTRAST

Your topic sentences must be focussed so that it is clear you are going to develop ideas using comparison or contrast, or a combination of the two. Study the examples below.

- The Canadian federal government viewed unemployment in the 1960s differently from the current view, and that difference has created a significant shift in training policies. (contrast only)

- Since the 1960s, federal unemployment policies have remained largely intact, and this consistency has protected Canadian workers. (comparison only)

- Although some federal unemployment policies have remained largely intact since the 1960s and have provided some protection for Canadian workers, the current Canadian federal government views unemployment differently, and this new definition has impacted training policies significantly. (comparison and contrast)

Exercise 1   Writing Comparison and Contrast Topic Sentences

In a small group, choose three of the topics below and write topic sentences according to the directions. Write your answers on poster paper, on the board, or on a computer so that your answers can be easily shared with the rest of the class.

1. training young teachers and developing professionalism in older teachers (contrast)

2. writing an email and writing a letter (comparison)

3. studying at home and studying at school (comparison and contrast)

4. coaching amateur sports and coaching professional sports (contrast)

5. being a volunteer and being a paid worker (comparison and contrast)

6. cooking Cantonese-style and cooking Szechuan-style (comparison and contrast)

7. designing a home office and designing shared workspaces in a company (contrast)

8. identifying the role of a technical director and the role of a regular director in theatre (contrast)

9. purchasing an HD television or a plasma television (comparison and contrast)

10. using natural hair dyes and using chemical hair dyes (comparison)

11. using wooden-shafted clubs and using fibreglass clubs in golfing (contrast)

12. arranging flowers and arranging a party (comparison)

When you use a comparison and contrast method of development, you consider what two items have in common and what differences seem to exist between them. The next section will discuss comparison and contrast separately.

COMPARISON PATTERNS OF DEVELOPMENT

Comparisons are useful when you wish to consider what is similar between two things, ideas, processes, and so forth. Often you can learn a good deal about something when you juxtapose it, or place it side by side with another item. Remember: in a comparison development, you are looking for how two items are similar.

Consider an experience from your life in which you actually use comparison development. Let's suppose, for example, you go out for a meal with your friends. Perhaps you choose an Italian restaurant for your dinner. After the meal is over, you begin to discuss what you think of the food. You might find yourself comparing the food you just ate with another favourite restaurant's, with your own cooking, or with a family member's recipe. You might use examples from your own experiences to help convince your listeners, or you might use what you have read in a food review. You are using a comparison and contrast mode to develop ideas about your experiences.

Examining similarities is a useful tool to enrich your understanding. It can provide a different perspective. For example, you may wish to examine what features two writers have in common. You could start with themes that appear in both authors' works. You then begin to investigate why these themes are of interest to each author. As you begin your comparative study, you may recognize ideas or facts that you had not discovered previously. Looking over the similarities helps you classify or organize information in a way that highlights features. Perhaps you gain a greater knowledge of each writer's works by examining what makes his or her works the same as the other's. Your investigation provides you with new ideas.

Use Analogies to Compare

Comparisons of one special kind are **analogies**. You might use analogies in situations in which you want to make an association between two items that do not seem to have much in common. Placing two items together in an unusual relationship and then considering what is similar about them is an interesting and revealing way of thinking. Analogies help you to examine things in a manner that varies from your normal way of thinking. Consider this statement, for instance: "Preparing a term paper is like going for a visit to the dentist."

Suddenly, you are asked to think, "How in the world can these be the same?" You might choose to organize your analysis in new ways and ask, "What parts of each process could be associated with the other—the anticipation, the ordeal itself, the evaluation, the relief of tension?" Before long, you find yourself analyzing one idea in relation to the other through examining the commonalities.

Make your analysis convincing. In academic writing, your interpretations must be reasonable, clear, and effective to convince your readers.

Your ideas in comparison development should cohere, or "stick together." Use transitions that show comparison to bridge ideas and make them flow.

Useful Transitions for Comparison

similarly	in the same fashion
also	still
likewise	like
in the same way	both

Exercise 2   *Finding Similarities*

Look at each pair of items in the following list. Think of how these two items can be related. Write down at least three links between the two that are common to both.

a candle and a flower

a comic book and a greeting card

a Canadian and an American

the games bingo and lotto

deer and mice

goblins and devils

values and judgments

a coat and a shawl

lacrosse and ice hockey

pennies and diamonds

CONTRAST PATTERNS OF DEVELOPMENT

On the other hand, you may want to use the **contrast** mode to consider the differences between two things or ideas. You can also use this mode as a tool for analysis to help expand and develop your thinking and writing.

In the contrast mode, you think in terms of what makes two things different. You must have some knowledge of each item. For instance, to contrast modelling with clay to modelling with paper, you would have to be acquainted with each type. Often this how-to knowledge comes from experience, but you can know about something in many ways.

You may also be able to talk in more abstract, interpretive terms when you speak of concepts. Wisdom, for example, is defined differently in different cultures. It might be said that living in one culture may help you to understand what it is like to live in another. You quickly become aware of the differences in practice or tradition between cultures. You gain knowledge that you do not even recognize you have until you need to call upon it or interpret it. In this way, writers often discover what they know about something when they write about it. Differences may be invisible, deeply set ideas that require the light of good, analytic writing to make them visible.

Consider an example to clarify. Although there are differences between you and your father or mother, you may not have thought about what they might be. In fact, you have knowledge of the differences, although you may not have articulated that knowledge in any way. If someone were to ask you, "How are you different from your mother or your father?" you might have to stop for a few minutes to think it over. Before long, though, you are able to provide some answers. In fact, you might be surprised by your own response. This experience is probably familiar. You have been asked a question and then have answered. Afterward you may have said to yourself, "I didn't know I knew that." In a similar way, writing can be an act of recognition.

You can use a contrast method of development to assist you to sort out what you know. You can consider two things that you think typically share many similarities: contrast will force you to consider their qualities in detail to determine if the two items really are alike at all. In fact, the examination may highlight differences. For example, you might think that two items—"school" and "education"—are alike, but are they? If you stop to think more deeply about the two items, you might find they have striking differences.

You could argue that school is unlike education because it is compulsory, whereas education could be seen as embracing all learning. In addition, you could imagine that education is a process that brings you some kind of wisdom, unlike school, which works from a set of social and curricular standards. These school standards may not bring you wisdom in the same sense. You could continue to think about how the two things are sharply distinct from one another, and you would be sorting out what you think and what you learn from your investigation.

Searching for differences helps you discover ideas. You must think intensely in new ways. It will take some practice and research on your part because deep learning involves engagement and intellectual work.

Exercise 3   *Group Activity: Thinking of Differences*

Form a group of three to five people. Choose five of the paired items below. List as many differences between each pair of items as you can invent. One group member records the group's ideas. Another group member reports on the group's imaginative ideas at the end.

Topics for Thinking of Differences

adult students and child students	gates and fences
unemployed and employed workers	teachers and parents
misdemeanours and crimes	driving a car and driving a motorcycle
jealousy and envy	bats and birds
theatre and film	tea and coffee
hobbies and work	flattery and glibness
order and authority	mysticism and the supernatural
apprehension and fear	collecting and hoarding
apricots and peaches	good and evil

Use Transitions of Contrast

When you use the contrast mode, remember to add transitional words or expressions of contrast to help your ideas cohere in your paragraphs:

Useful Transitions for Contrast

although	however
on the other hand	unlike
even so	despite
yet	nevertheless
on the contrary	though

A WEAK EXAMPLE OF A COMPARISON PARAGRAPH

Read the paragraph below. Although the paragraph is technically correct, it is ineffective. Read it; then explain why it doesn't work as a good paragraph composition.

Knitting and crocheting are very similar. Both crafts use techniques that are easy to learn. Someone who has never learned to crochet or knit can learn within a few minutes by watching someone else or by following basic instructions from a book or the internet. Besides, materials for both hobbies are very much the same: they require yarn and tools like needles or hooks. These supplies are available at department stores, craft or hobby shops, and specialty stores. Perhaps the most significant similarity is that the items created from knitting or crocheting are relatively inexpensive and are most useful. Sweaters, hats, gloves, mittens, and scarves, easily produced by these crafts, are always welcomed by family or friends. Homemade items are often cherished and passed from one generation in a family to another. All in all, since knitting and crocheting are quite easy to learn, share similar equipment, and produce useful and economical items, either can be easily adopted by any handcrafter or hobbyist.

Some experts refer to this type of paragraph as a "so-what?" composition. In other words, why would a writer bother telling us this information about knitting and crocheting? Clearly, the paragraph states the obvious. The writer does not introduce new ideas or present readers with something to think about.

Hint

When you write using a comparison or contrast mode, have a clear purpose in mind. Do not simply re-state obvious facts. Use the mode to discover something new or to explore connections between two items or ideas.

READING COMPARISON AND CONTRAST PARAGRAPHS

Exercise 4   *Reading for Comparison and Contrast*

Each of the four paragraph compositions below uses either comparison or contrast development. Read each, paying attention to the development: point-by-point or block form. If the paragraph uses comparison, think about the similarities it discusses. If the paragraph uses contrast, think about the differences it discusses. Also notice the structure of the topic sentence in each paragraph. Finally, look at the wrap-up sentences. In other words, read these examples analytically.

PARAGRAPH 1 Ecofeminism is the critical investigation of the women-to-Mother-Nature link of the relationship of body, fertility, and spirituality. Ecofeminists believe these views linking women to nature are oppressive because they justify the subjugation of women. Spiritual ecofeminists suggest because Mother Earth gives life and nurtures life, and because of the reproductive and caring link, women are viewed as closer to nature than men. These Western feminists have utilized Aboriginal beliefs, views, and teachings on nature to support their position. However, many critics argue spiritual ecofeminists have appropriated and misinterpreted many indigenous beliefs for their own purposes, which is another form of exploitation of Aboriginal cultures. Andy Smith (1997) says that when "they seek Indian spirituality in a book or a $300 sweat lodge, they are treating Native spirituality as a commodity" (qtd. in Warren, p. 31). Social ecofeminists, on the other hand, repudiate the perspective of the woman's link to nature based on pure biology. They claim this women-to-nature connection has created a gender-classed society in which gender stereotypes of "woman as life giver" supports a patriarchal structure.

Smith, Andy. "Ecofeminism through an Anticolonial Framework." *Ecofeminism: Women, Culture, Nature.* Bloomington: Indiana University Press, 1997, pp. 21–37.

PARAGRAPH 2 Plant cells and animal cells have important differences. First, plant cells have a rigid, non-living wall made from a material called cellulose. Animal cells, on the other hand, have walls made from a living, thin membrane. Furthermore, plant cells have small green bodies called chloroplasts, which help to manufacture food. Yet chloroplasts are absent in animal cells. Finally, plant cells have pouchlike bodies called vacuoles that retain water, whereas animal cells do not possess these features. These structural distinctions make plant and animal cells easily distinguishable under the microscope.

PARAGRAPH 3 Do only children feel differently about their upbringing than children from larger families? Some adults who were only children report a feeling of isolation. These adults said that as children they felt lonely because they did not have brothers and sisters to relate to. Others said that they felt their parents' expectations of them as only children were too high. They felt that their parents were putting all their hopes into them alone. At times, they saw this expectation as a difficult burden to carry. Some adults also reported that in later life they felt somewhat cheated because they would have liked to have had brothers or sisters to share or play with. Yet others reported being an only child as a positive experience because they did not have to share and thus received many more privileges than they would probably have gotten in a larger family. Although the evidence is still being gathered, it is clear that sharing and expectations are different for only children.

PARAGRAPH 4 Since viral meningitis, a serious but non-threatening form of the disease, and bacterial meningitis, a rapidly moving deadly strain, can at the onset of the disease mimic one another, physicians must pay strict attention to symptoms in order to save young lives. Since 95% of bacterial meningitis cases occur in children under the age of five, doctors cannot rely on patients' ability to articulate their symptoms and feelings. At first, the two types of meningitis display similar symptoms. Patients have high fevers and muscle aches.

They experience loss of appetite and, within a short duration, begin to feel lethargic. However, in cases of bacterial meningitis, other more serious signs develop very swiftly. Vomiting occurs, along with some internal bleeding. Fluid builds up on the brain as patients begin to lose consciousness. They may suffer shock and seizures. As fluids increase in the brain, patients may suffer irreparable brain damage. Death can occur within 24 hours if bacterial meningitis is not treated promptly with strong antibiotics.

Exercise 5   Group Activity: Similarities and Differences

Part A

Each student brings two objects from home. Students form groups of three to five people. Each student displays the items he or she brings from home. The group discusses what is the same about each set of items and what is different. The group then selects one pair of items and lists the similarities or the differences.

Part B

The same groups get back together. Using the list of similarities or differences, each group constructs a comparison or contrast chart. One member of the group is the recorder. The group then composes a paragraph together, and the recorder gives a copy to the instructor.

Part C

The same groups get back together. The instructor provides each group member with a copy of the paragraph that the group wrote in Part B. Now, the group looks over the paragraph and discusses how to improve it. The group corrects errors in spelling, punctuation, and grammar. One group member should be the recorder. The group supplies the instructor with a final, corrected copy of the group's paragraph composition.

Writing Assignment 1   Comparison Paragraph

Choose one of the topics below to write a paragraph composition using comparison development. If none of these topics appeals to you, you may choose your own after discussing it with your instructor. To complete the assignment you must

- write 150–300 words

- use double spacing

- check for correct spelling, grammar, and punctuation

- use a computer. If you are unable to word process this assignment, please talk to your instructor.

   This assignment may require a title page, so check with your instructor.

Topics for Comparison Paragraph

friendship and work	oysters and mussels
novels and life	seesaws and careers
winning and losing	cameras and eyes
video games and trees	bogs and swamps
punishment and discipline	yesterday and today
playing a musical instrument and walking a duck	wish and want
killer and beluga whales	hockey and football
drawing with ink and with graphite	desserts and dreams
bicycling and hiking	antiques and gardens
committees and networking	sisters and brothers
pomegranates and oranges	swallows and finches

Writing Assignment 2   Contrast Paragraph

Choose one of the topics below to write a paragraph composition using contrast development. If none of these topics appeals to you, you may choose your own after discussing it with your instructor. To complete the assignment you must

- write 150–300 words

- use double spacing

- check for correct spelling, grammar, and punctuation

- use a computer. If you are unable to word process this assignment, please talk to your instructor.

    This assignment may require a title page, so check with your instructor.

Topics for Contrast Paragraph

father and grandfather	heartbreak and frustration
workers and employers	watching videos and going to a movie
baseball and soccer	lacrosse and soccer
dreaming and fantasizing	morning and evening
cars and trucks	pears and apples
writing and talking	jokes and tricks
spending and saving	quails and partridges
oak and willow trees	toads and frogs
homemade and commercial ice cream	produce and create
comfort and love	mother and grandmother
reading and watching television	

CHECKOUT

1. You can use the chart method to examine similarities (comparison) and differences (contrast) to generate writing ideas.

2. Transitional words and expressions in a piece of writing are clues to its method of development.

3. The analogy is one special kind of comparison.

4. You can improve your ability to spot the type of writing development by reading and analyzing the work of other writers.

chapter 6

Classification and Division Development

Chapter Objectives

After completing this chapter, you will be able to

- recognize the classification and division mode by reading paragraphs
- practise working with the concept of classification and division
- write a paragraph composition using classification and division development

INTRODUCTION

A more complicated pattern for developing ideas in academic writing is **classification and division**. Classification and division are linked because they have some commonalities. Use a **classification** method of organization when you wish to *group* or *categorize* ideas or things. For example, if you want to discuss the game of soccer, you could cluster ideas—styles of play, home countries of players, or levels of skill. You would give readers a view of soccer by classifying some important aspects of it, perhaps achieving a new way of looking at the topic.

Classification is a tool used to organize human knowledge. In the natural sciences, such as biology or zoology, experts use systems of cataloguing. Scientists cluster plants or animals from the particular to the largest groups: species, genera, families, orders, classes, phyla, and kingdoms. Geologists classify the earth's layers according to specified time periods, or earth history. Other scientists, like physicists, use laws to categorize matter and energy. Social scientists classify and divide human knowledge according to the structure of human societies and communities. Psychologists, anthropologists, educators, and sociologists look at human behaviour, culture, history, and artifacts using either one or a combination of more than one method of organizing. Classification, therefore, provides a way of looking at something, whether complex or simple, by grouping or clustering, helping you to manage a way of seeing and understanding.

Use a **division** method when you wish to *partition* a topic into component parts. For example, you might want to study and discuss what makes up a good transit system in a large Canadian city. You would consider the parts of the system and then discuss each part: you might decide that a good transit system must be attractive, accessible, and friendly to the public. You could discuss each component and how the component contributes to the whole.

Division is a method of organization in philosophy, literary criticism, anthropology, sociology, linguistics, economics, history, and art. In these disciplines, scholars are interested in systems, fields, operations, meanings, concepts, representations, and so forth. They find division a powerful tool in their analysis.

USING CLASSIFICATION AND DIVISION IN ACADEMIC WRITING

As a writer in an academic program at a college or university, you have to understand and use classification and division to organize your thinking and writing. You'll be surprised at how much information from one area in your studies will intersect with another.

Knowledge in language studies might cross into history, sociology, psychology, or ethics. Literature study might be grouped by genres or types, historical context, region, date, author, theme, or in other ways. It is important to recognize how and why these categories have been established. Let's consider an example.

Suppose you take a course in Canadian literature. The course syllabus might show Canadian literature as social artifact through stories, poems, and novels that centre around important social issues or events: perhaps WW I and WW II, women and suffrage, Aboriginal land claims, industrialization in Canada, agrarian issues, or the relationship between communication and development. Generally speaking, the process of classification or division will depend on the course designer's perspective or purpose. So, for example, suppose the course designer wants students to recognize some of the social practices in Canada and selects literature pieces that might represent some of those practices. Then he or she might arrange them in a chronological order to facilitate the idea of development of such practices. How you classify or divide a topic depends on your purpose.

Transitions in Academic Writing

Choose transitions that convey a mode of classification and division to your reader. Transitions also help your writing flow and make your paragraphs more coherent. Here are some common transitions you can use.

Useful Classification and Division Transitions

for example	specifically
besides that	the first type
another part	one category
accordingly	a further category
in addition to	for instance
one component	to illustrate
next	another group
furthermore	also
as well as	such as

Exercise 1   *Classifying and Dividing*

Look at the page below. One side shows how an idea can be classified into types or groups. The other side of the page shows how the same idea can be divided into component parts. Complete the page with a classmate. Be prepared to share answers with other members of the class.

Classify:	**Divide:**
What types or groups?	What component parts?

1. Subject: Health food

   Types: non-fat; organic; not modified; locally grown

1. Subject: Health food

   Parts: no additives; organic ingredients; clear labelling; no trans fat or by-products

2. Subject: Fishing

   Types: _____

2. Subject: Fishing

   Parts: _____

3. Subject: Music

   Types: _____

3. Subject: Music

   Parts: _____

4. Subject: Cooking

   Types: _____

4. Subject: Cooking

   Parts: _____

5. Subject: Jokes

   Types: _____

5. Subject: Jokes

   Parts: _____

6. Subject: Outdoor recreation

   Types: _____

6. Subject: Outdoor recreation

   Parts: _____

7. Subject: Computers

   Types: _____

7. Subject: Computers

   Parts: _____

8. Subject: Shopping malls

   Types: _____

8. Subject: Shopping malls

   Parts: _____

READING CLASSIFICATION AND DIVISION DEVELOPMENT

Today, information technology is flourishing. When you are researching in the library or on the internet, you will recognize how ideas have been classified or divided often in relation to perspective and purpose. Methods of organizing are powerful tools.

Exercise 2	Reading for Classification and Division Patterns

Read each of the following paragraphs. Decide whether the paragraph is a classification pattern, a division pattern, or a combination of the two patterns. Be prepared to share your answers.

PARAGRAPH 1   Sea slugs, or nudibranchs (NOO-da-branks), are common in the northwest Pacific Ocean, but three types are of interest. The first type is the red sponge nudibranch. It blends in easily with the colour of the sponge on which it sits and eats. It actually takes the pigment of the sponge into its own body and camouflages itself. Another type is the sea lemon. It gets its name from its shape and colour and has bumpy skin with black dots like pepper. The sea lemon lays long strings of yellow eggs, which can be found on the moist undersides of rocks. The third type of sea slug is called the frosted nudibranch. This animal is beautifully decorated and can be seen in the intertidal zone. It feeds on sponges and sea anemones and can store the stinging cells of its prey for its own defence. While these sea slugs may not be as showy as other marine life, they are fascinating and gorgeous in their own way.

PARAGRAPH 2   Most bean salads are made up of three particular types of beans because they are nutritious and relatively cheap. The first main bean ingredient is a popular dried bean called the *kidney bean*. Kidney beans, which get their name from their shape, provide some protein and vitamins. These beans can be soaked and cooked before using. The second main dried bean has a number of different names. Some people use the term *garbanzo*, while others call them *chickpeas*. Garbanzos are not peas at all, but are special beans used by millions of people on Earth because of their high nutritive value. These beans are round and, when cooked, rather chewy. As well as adding nutrition to the salad, they are visually appealing with an interesting texture. The last bean ingredient is a snap bean like a green or a yellow wax bean commonly grown in the garden for freezing or canning. These snap beans add a delicate flavour all their own. They are best when they are fresh, lightly cooked, and added to the bean salad right away. Beans comprise a nutritious alternative ingredient for salads and provide an economical and welcome change.

PARAGRAPH 3   Of particular interest to Canadian biologists is the work being done by their American counterparts in the wildlife management of wolves. Wildlife biologists are monitoring wolf mortalities in Yellowstone National Park in the United States to determine what makes up the mortalities. They developed a study of the numbers of wolf deaths within the packs in the park from 1995 to 1998. In total, 44 wolves died: 13.6% died of natural causes; 29.5% were shot, mostly illegally within the park's boundaries; 13.6% were killed by vehicles on the road; and two, or 4.5%, died in natural disasters—one in an avalanche and the other in a thermal accident. The causes of the remaining wolf mortalities are unknown. Without this careful monitoring, scientists would not be able to determine how and why the wolf population is growing or decreasing in Yellowstone. At the same time, Canadian biologists consider how this study will have an impact on their work with wolves within Canadian national parks.

PARAGRAPH 4 What are the symptoms of concussion in an athletic injury? An athlete may display one or more of these symptoms. First, he or she may have a vacant stare and be slow in responding to questions or following directions. Next, the person may have incoherent or slurred speech. He or she may report feeling sick to the stomach and having waves of nausea. Also, the athlete may experience some temporary memory loss or deficits. He or she may be unable to recall simple information such as the score, the team's name, a person's name, and so forth. The injured athlete may also have blurred or double vision and describe not being able to focus clearly on an object in the distance. Ringing in the ears, loss of consciousness, and headache are also significant symptoms. Concussion is serious, and everyone involved in team sport or management should be aware of the telltale signs.

PARAGRAPH 5 Almost all drivers want a good sound system in their car. Basically there are two types of stereos: the factory radio and the aftermarket stereo. Factory radios are usually adequate for most purposes and perform well. They offer reasonably good sound quality, but the drawback is that there are no connections for enriching the bass. A special line-output converter must be purchased to add bass and deepen tone. The aftermarket stereo is a car stereo that is manufactured by a different company from the automobile manufacturer. These stereos must be purchased separately, from companies such as Sony, Alpine, Pioneer, and so on. Deciding which sound system to choose will depend on the owner's taste and budget.

Exercise 3   *Investigating Classification and Division Mode*

Part A

You can improve your classification and division method of development by discussing your ideas with another person. Work in pairs as you use the internet to research one of the following topics. You will learn either what groups or categories exist in the field (classification) or what parts make it up (division).

Topics for Research

anthropology	Canadian literature
astronomy	hockey
botany	dogs

chemistry	physics
marketing	early childhood education
soil science	shellfish
computing	retailing

Part B

Present your findings to the class and be prepared to answer questions. Say whether you discovered a classification or division pattern in your research, and what you discovered about the method.

Writing Assignment 1   Classification Paragraph

Choose one of the topics below and write a paragraph composition in a classification pattern. If none of these topics appeals to you, you may choose your own after you have discussed it with your instructor. To complete the assignment, keep in mind the following:

1. The assignment should be 150–200 words long and double-spaced.

2. Check spelling, grammar, and punctuation before you hand in your assignment.

3. Use a computer to complete the work. If you are unable to comply with this requirement, please talk to your instructor.

Topics for Classification Paragraph

weddings	theatre
cooking	reunions
contact sports	renovations
birds	desserts
hobbies	restaurants
movies	games
construction	magazines
childhood problems	crafts
travel	festivals
internet searches	skiing
cars	beer
fashion	lotteries
gardening	money

Writing Assignment 2   Division Paragraph

Choose one of the following topics and write a paragraph composition using a division method of development. To complete the assignment, keep in mind the following:

1. The assignment should be 150–200 words long and double-spaced.

2. Check spelling, grammar, and punctuation before you hand in your assignment.

3. Complete the work using a computer. If you are unable to comply with this requirement, please talk to your instructor.

Topics for Division Paragraph

relaxation	a good boss
driving	a good worker
a good cook	a good movie
a successful small business	a good book
family	an unusual habit
a joke	personal style
a union	an enemy
an excellent workplace	a habit
a relationship	marriage
a friend	partnership

CHECKOUT

1. Classifying ideas sets them into groups or categories; dividing ideas breaks them into component parts.

2. A chart is useful for organizing ideas for classification and division writing.

3. A method of writing organization can advance the perspective and purpose of your writing.

4. Before handing your writing assignment in for evaluation, follow the conventions of presentation that your instructor recommends.

chapter 7

Cause and Effect Development

Chapter Objectives

After completing this chapter, you will be able to

- recognize cause and effect by reading paragraphs
- practise working with the idea of cause and effect
- write a paragraph composition using cause and effect development

INTRODUCTION

Use **cause and effect** development when you wish to discuss how *something influences or affects something else*. You may also use this mode when you are considering *the causes of something*. The cause and effect mode establishes the relationship between ideas, making it necessary for you to think about how ideas are connected or why they might be connected in particular ways.

To consider what other relationships may be possible, you may have to *predict possible connections*. Think about this example. During the past few years, communities have become concerned over the safety of their water supplies. Thinking as a writer and using a cause and effect mode, you might begin to link what has happened to make people so cautious about their drinking water, what people are doing because of water safety scares, and what predictions can be made about water in local communities in the not too distant future.

Often cause and effect development is used in the natural sciences, particularly in environmental studies. For instance, you may read about how some natural phenomenon occurs and what effects the phenomenon might have on its surroundings. Let's suppose, for example, that a biologist wants to think about the impact of lack of rainfall on particular wildlife in a region. He or she might study how the animal's behaviour changes, how its life cycle changes, or how its new behaviour impacts other animals in its community or environment. Much scientific writing is either process oriented or causally related (cause and effect).

THREE CAUSE AND EFFECT TECHNIQUES

As a writer, you can use three cause and effect techniques:

1. You might analyze by describing an event or some occurrence. Then you might express the effect or effects the event has had or may have in the future.

2. You might describe an event and then, afterward, write about the possible causes of that event.

3. You might consider two events and then write about how they may relate in a cause and effect manner; for example, is one the cause of the other, or is one the effect or result of the other?

Each technique demands that you pay strict attention to your arguments, observations, and conclusions. Some events are complicated and cannot be explained simply. Some events have several effects. Some effects are not yet known or recognized. In all cases, you must work to make the link between relationships plausible for readers. You must pay even closer attention to naming causes.

If you use cause and effect to develop your ideas, you might find you need to research your topic. Since this book does not ask you to write long essays or research papers, you will not necessarily be expected to research your topic. However, if you choose a complex topic, check with your instructor to be sure you have enough information to structure a reasoned cause and effect piece.

Examples of Cause and Effect Relationships

Consider the statements below:

> Being late for work constantly, being uncooperative with other employees, and not following directions led to Elmer's firing. (Technique 1)

> Inhaling 20 or more cigarettes on a daily basis can lead to irritation of the lining of the nose, throat, and lungs; shortness of breath; heart overstimulation; emphysema; lung cancer; or heart attacks. (Technique 2)

> Learning to drive at an earlier age may help make you a better driver. (Technique 3)

The first statement uses the first technique. It describes possible reasons or causes for one effect—Elmer's firing. The second statement describes the possible results of one behaviour—smoking (inhaling 20 cigarettes daily). The third statement suggests a link between learning to drive early and becoming a better driver. It uses the third cause and effect development technique: it considers two events and discusses how they may be linked. It will require evidence or proof (research).

TIPS FOR CONSTRUCTING CAUSE AND EFFECT ORGANIZATION

Here are some hints to help you when you use cause and effect:

A. Watch out for oversimplification. Don't say that just one cause leads to just one effect—that could lead to some faulty conclusions. Consider the following example:

> Watching television creates violence.

In this statement, the writer has overgeneralized in two ways. First, he or she has said that sitting in front of a television and just watching the programs, anything from the news to cooking shows, leads to some sort of violence. Secondly, the writer claims a single cause for violence. How can the writer say that such a complicated thing as violence can come from a single cause—television viewing? Is this probable?

B. Do not connect two unrelated events together to form a wrong conclusion. Don't jump to the wrong conclusion after something has happened. Consider the following statements:

I failed the course because someone hates me.

Buying an SUV is a stupid thing to do because my friend bought two, and he said they were both lemons.

I had a horrible day today because it was Friday the 13th.

Can you see how illogical these statements are? Did all who failed the course fail because someone "hated them"? Is buying an SUV stupid because only one person says it is? Is it probable that the date caused a bad day?

C. Examine the causes and effects. Start by asking, "Why?" Frame your topic or subject into a why question; then you can begin to trace or unravel some of its essential ideas.

Once you begin to investigate possible reasons for why failure may occur in school, you begin to uncover the topic's complexity. No one answer is better than another. Furthermore, you may not be able to elaborate all possible reasons.

You may ask a different type of question: "What changed because of something else?" In other words, you may want to examine the impact of something on something else. You can discover many examples of such examinations: sociologists and lawyers frequently want to consider what influence a particular law is having in the courts; governments may want to study the impact of a new policy; a college or university may want to investigate

---

Examining Causes and Effects

Topic: Failure in school

Refined Topic: Failure of younger children in school

Why *Question:*   Why do some young children fail in elementary school?

Possible Causes and Effects:

1. cannot read and understand printed materials—leads to—confusion and inaccuracy—called "failure" of the student

2. cannot understand written directions—leads to—doing wrong things—getting wrong answers—called "failure" of the student

3. cannot follow teacher's directions—may have a first language interfering with understanding a second language—teacher may use a different vocabulary—teacher may be unclear in giving specific directions—teacher may speak too softly or may not get the child's attention—leads to—confusion—the child's doing the wrong thing at the wrong time or not following directions at all—called "failure" of the student

4. may have a learning disability—may not perceive the same as others—leads to—misinterpretation—called "failure" of the student

5. may be bored with materials or task—child may already be able to perform the task—already understands the concept or skill—leads to confusion and inaccuracy—called "failure" of the student

what influence new admissions policies are having on its student population. Every day experts study the influences of something on something else to determine what is working effectively and what is not and to examine unexpected outcomes.

USING TRANSITIONS IN CAUSE AND EFFECT MODE

In using the cause and effect mode, pay strict attention to transitions. They are key to helping your reader follow your reasoning. They are critical to coherence, too.

Useful Cause and Effect Transitions

as a result	hence
consequently	since
for these reasons	due to
because	then
therefore	as a consequence
thus	so

Reading Cause and Effect Patterns

Read each of the following paragraphs that develop ideas using a cause and effect pattern. Notice the transitions. Examine what effects or what causes the writer is discussing. Be prepared to share your analysis with the rest of the class.

PARAGRAPH 1 Young children today are very conscious of their appearance. First, young children tend to watch many long hours of television. They are bombarded with advertising that tells them what to wear and how to look. Children may then ask their parents to buy particular clothes or shoes that will make them look just like the "kids on TV." In turn, others see how their peers are dressed and then want to look like their classmates who look like the television advertisements. Another reason for the sudden interest in personal appearance is the influence from the schools themselves.

PARAGRAPH 2 Many teachers today are instructing children in personal hygiene. Dental care, bathing, and grooming may actually be taught in the daily curriculum. Because these instructions come from an "official" like a teacher or a public health nurse, children tend to treat these instructions seriously. They may not want to disobey the school or teacher, but instead, they want to fit in and be pleasing to others. For these reasons, young children today seem concerned about how they look.

PARAGRAPH 3 Cutting down large tracts of forest indiscriminately has disastrous results. First, the soil is lost. Trees have deep roots that help to anchor other small plants and the soil.

As trees are cut down, this anchoring is lost. Heavy rainfall then carries off the top layer of soil, which is often the richest. Along with this soil erosion, banks of streams and rivers where large numbers of trees have been harvested begin to wash away. Moreover, the plant and animal life are destroyed in the forested region. The natural homes for many creatures are gone or diminished with the trees. Plants that require the shade and benefits of the forest can no longer grow. Brutal logging practices can leave the land sterile and incapable of sustaining new life. The government is now becoming aware of these terrible consequences and is demanding that logging companies change their methods of tree cutting and removal.

Exercise 1   Group Activity: Structuring Causes and Effects

Form groups of three to five people and develop answers for five of the following. Write down your answers and be prepared to report on four of the topics to the rest of the class. You do not need to research any of the topics.

1. What are three causes of insomnia?

2. What are three effects of gambling?

3. What are three causes of overachievement?

4. What are three effects of stealing?

5. What are three causes of tooth decay?

6. What are three causes of homelessness?

7. What are three effects of homelessness?

8. What are three causes of forest fires?

9. What are three negative effects of erosion?

10. What are three causes of computer crashes?

11. What are three beneficial effects of stretching?

12. What are three causes of obesity in young children?

Exercise 2   Group Activity: Finding the Cause and Effect Mode

Part A

First, find a short article to bring to class that contains a paragraph or two using a cause and effect development. All of the paragraphs will be placed on one table. Form a group of three students. Select one of the articles. Read the article and discuss how the author develops his or her ideas by cause and effect. Then, as a group, write a one-sentence answer for each of these five questions.

1. What is the topic sentence (or main idea sentence) of the paragraph?

2. Does the author write about causes or effects?

3. What relationship does the author say exists between the ideas?

4. Name the effects or the causes mentioned.

5. Does the author convince you by the cause and effect development? Why or why not?

After completing the questions, staple your group's answers to the article. Your instructor will collect the answers from each group.

Part B

At the next class session, your instructor places all of the answers and articles on a table. Work in pairs and select one of the articles. Be sure you find a set of student answers stapled to the article you select.

Read the article and the student answers. Do you agree or disagree with the answers on the student sheet? The class will share responses in a larger group session.

Writing Assignment 1   Cause and Effect Paragraph

Choose one of the topics below to write a paragraph composition using a cause and effect development. If none of these topics appeals to you, you may choose your own after discussing it with your instructor. To complete the assignment, keep in mind the following:

1. The assignment should be 150–200 words long and double-spaced.

2. Check spelling, grammar, and punctuation before you hand in your assignment.

3. Use a computer to complete the work. If you are unable to comply with this requirement, please talk to your instructor.

Topics for Cause and Effect Paragraph

1. Why is unemployment so high?

2. What are the causes of divorce?

3. What effects does cold have on hibernating animals?

4. Why are some things considered "pornographic"?

5. What effects is the digital camera having on photography?

6. Why is the internet so popular?

7. Why is stress considered a problem?

8. Why are some drugs outlawed in North America?

9. What influences our ideas of beauty?

10. Why are recreational vehicles so popular?

11. What effects do video games have on children?

12. Why do lovers quarrel?

13. What results can debt have on an individual?

14. Why do sports cars attract so many people?

15. Why are professional athletes paid so much?

16. What effects can you achieve with lighting?

17. Why does the military choose specific helicopters?

18. Why do many species of birds migrate each year?

19. What results do cuts to social security programs have in a small city?

20. Why are Canadian farmers in trouble?

CHECKOUT

1. The cause and effect method of writing organization establishes a special relationship between ideas.

2. Predictions of possible cause and effect connections can be supported by plausible argument and research.

3. By choosing appropriate transitional words and phrases, you help your reader see the cause and effect method of writing development.

4. Be sure the cause and effect relationship you suggest is reasonable.

chapter 8

Definition Development

Chapter Objectives

After completing this chapter, you will be able to

- work with definition development
- recognize the definition mode by reading paragraphs
- write a paragraph composition using definition development

INTRODUCTION

How is a definition pattern different from a division pattern? In formulating a division pattern, you have to think about what constitutes or comprises something; in other words, you must think about what parts make it up. A definition pattern is somewhat similar, but it differs in relation to its purpose.

A definition provides a necessary explanation of what something is. Definitions stipulate what a speaker or writer means by a word or term because the word can have multiple meanings or shades of meaning. For example, if you looked up *freedom* in any dictionary, it might say: "choice" or "independence" or "autonomy." If you wished to use the idea of freedom with an emphasis on a person's choice, then you would have to stipulate that sense in your definition. You would have to say to your reader or listener that you mean "freedom" in the sense of having choices. You would provide further explanation for your **stipulative definition**, one that specifies your sense of a term or idea.

Extended definitions are lengthy and take a lot more explanation and thought. To consider what something means to you, you are actually thinking about that idea or concept. You are analyzing in order to define. In writing a definition, answer the question, "What is it?"

USING A FORMAL DEFINITION

A formal definition has three parts:

1. the term or idea that you are going to define
2. the class of things the term or idea belongs to
3. the distinguishing characteristics (what distinguishes it from others in its group)

Examples:

     1   2   3

A peavey is a tool with a long handle with a sharp hook at one end used by loggers for handling logs in the water.

Part 1 names the term or idea (peavey).

Part 2 names the group it belongs to (tool).

Part 3 names distinguishing features (long handle, sharp hook, used by loggers, used for handling logs, used on logs in the water).

     1   2   3

A problem is a situation requiring action, but in which the required action is not known. (Nickols, 2000)

Part 1 names the term or idea (problem).

Part 2 names the group it belongs to (situation).

Part 3 names the distinguishing features (requires action, but required action is not known).

You can choose to use a formal definition as your topic sentence. You can discuss or explain your definition in the paragraph and discuss the distinguishing features. You should provide examples, too.

Exercise 1   Writing Some Formal Definitions

Work in pairs for this exercise. Write clear sentence definitions for five of the following terms. Be prepared to share your answers with the class.

hot dog	goat	party	elevator
model	pizza	spy	faith
work	guide	slave	tuna
duty	blueprint	profit	sled
shelf	sheriff		

The formal definition works well if you already have a fairly clear idea of what your definition will be. Sometimes, however, you must work through ideas to develop a definition.

GENERATING IDEAS FOR THE DEFINITION MODE

How do writers "get at" what they think something is? A useful way to begin is by asking a direct question and using it as a launch to thinking. For example, suppose you were doing a paper in a course on human behaviour. Perhaps you are interested in reading, researching, thinking, and writing about fear. Begin by asking, "What is fear?"

Attempt to define fear. Look at the parts that make it up (division) to help with the initial outline of ideas. Add or stipulate what sense of the word *fear* you will use.

Another approach is to look at what something is unlike. First consider what you think about the topic. Begin your thinking process by thinking about what fear is not like.

Look at the example below. The notes you see are "thinking notes"—what someone writes down as he or she works through an idea.

You build a progression of thought or a *chain of ideas* by investigating like this. You have created a *map* of the idea called *fear*.

At this stage, you can also begin to investigate and research what others have to say about fear. You might read poetry that expresses a fearful situation, articles in professional journals that discuss or describe fear, or texts written by experts.

How deeply and how long you investigate a topic depends upon the course you are taking, the nature of the assignment, your audience, your purpose, and how much time you have. Once you have decided the limits of your investigation, you can begin to write about what fear is.

Example of "Thinking Notes"

1. What is fear?

2. What is fear unlike?

It is unlike confidence. It is unlike certainty. It is unlike calmness. It is unlike happiness.

3. Why is fear unlike confidence?

Confidence is feeling secure about what will happen or what you know. Fear is not like that because fear seems to imply some sense of not knowing, not being able to tell what will happen.

4. Why is fear unlike certainty?

Certainty makes you think you know something. Fear makes you feel you do not know something. You trust certainty; you do not trust fear.

5. Why is fear unlike calmness?

Calmness means a relaxed state of mind and body. You feel in control when calm. Fear, on the other hand, makes your heart beat faster, your thoughts race, your palms sweat, and your feelings go out of control.

6. Why is fear unlike happiness?

Happiness makes you feel comfortable and accepting. Fear makes you feel alert and guarded.

What the "Thinking Notes" Revealed

unlike confidence

seems to imply some sense of not knowing

not being able to tell what will happen

unlike certainty

makes you feel you do not know something

do not trust it

unlike calmness

makes your heart beat faster, your thoughts race, your palms
sweat, and your feelings go out of control

If you continue your investigation in this way, you can write a paper that provides a
definition of fear. At any stage of the investigation, you stipulate the sense of the term.
You use your own experiences to give a special sense to it. You provide views of what fear
is by living, reading, and researching "in the world."

Exercise 2   Getting the Sense of a Word

For this exercise choose a classmate to work with. Look at the topics below. Take each
idea and in note form write down how each idea is unlike the topic. Follow the same procedure used in the investigation of fear. Be prepared to share your answers.

1. Topic: *school* (Start: What is a school?)

   a. home (Ask: How is a school unlike a home?)

   b. parent (Ask: How is a school unlike a parent?)

   c. friend (Ask: How is a school unlike a friend?)

2. Topic: *memory*

   Start: What is memory unlike?

   List three things or ideas memory is unlike.

   Take each idea and ask: How is memory unlike this? or that?

   List the ways in which they differ.

   Then, using your "thinking notes," write about what memory is like.

   The following transitions will help make your definition "stick together." In other
words, they will assist the coherence and flow of your writing.

Useful Definition Transitions

for example	in addition
furthermore	also
besides	for instance
further	moreover
specifically	accordingly
at the same time	in other words
certainly	indeed
of course	

READING SOME DEFINITION PARAGRAPHS

Read the definition paragraphs below. The topics selected are not as complex or abstract as those you will use for essays because paragraph compositions are shorter.

PARAGRAPH 1 What is a good car? A good car is reliable. There is nothing worse than getting in a car only to find out it will not start. Drivers must feel confident that, no matter the situation, their cars will get them to where they want to go—day or night. A good car is comfortable. Sitting in a car for long ferry waits or in traffic gridlock can be more unpleasant if the vehicle is cold and has hard seats. Finally, the key attribute of a good car is that it is economical. Because gas prices are rising day by day, some drivers may find they are not able to afford to run their own cars because they are too expensive to operate. A good car, then, besides being dependable and comfortable, is relatively cheap to own and operate.

What is the writer's definition of a good car? Name the points.

PARAGRAPH 2 What is a good hockey game? To answer the question, one needs to decide from whose point of view one is considering it. From the owner's point of view, a good hockey game is one in which the team wins. Winning means staying on top and being popular in the media. It also means getting the value the owner is paying for since some players make millions in their contracts. The owner might say a good hockey game is one that has high ticket sales. Making money might be the most important feature of a good game to a team owner. Fans might have different definitions. Some might say a good hockey game is exciting to watch, with plenty of fast skating, passing, and pressing in the end zones, along with excellent plays. Others might say a good game is based only on the excellent plays. Players, on the other hand, might see a good game differently. They may say that a defining element is how well the team worked together on offence and defence. They may also simply consider the number of errors made during play or the number of penalties their team committed. Since a game is viewed by people in different ways in order to decide on a good definition, one would have to consider more than one point of view.

How does this writer define a good hockey game? How does he or she develop the ideas?

PARAGRAPH 3 What is a good cup of coffee? To a Canadian, a great cup of coffee has a rich, full taste. It is strong, but not bitter. It has an aroma that can wake up the senses and say, "Hey—let me get you going!" To an American, to be good, the coffee has to be somewhat strong, very hot, and really fresh. Most Americans would agree that good coffee should be available from almost any location, whether it be from a service station, a restaurant, or an upscale coffee shop. To a Greek, a good cup of coffee must be very strong. It should be served in a demitasse that has a layer of sugar in the bottom. The coffee should never be served in a paper cup because good coffee has to be savoured. For a Greek, a good cup of coffee takes time to drink—it should not be gulped. It could be said, then, that the definition of a good cup of coffee becomes a matter of taste and tradition: no one culture seems to have the "right" answer.

What does this writer say about the definition of a good cup of coffee? How does the writer develop his or her definition?

For the purposes of this book, you will be asked to write a paragraph of definition. Since a paragraph composition is relatively short (compared to an essay), it is important to leave more complex and abstract topics for a definition essay. Use simpler, more manageable topics in your definition paragraphs.

Exercise 3   Collecting Ideas in the Definition Mode

From a newspaper or magazine, bring one or two articles to class in which a writer uses definition. Be prepared to discuss your selection.

Answer these questions:

1. Who is the writer?

2. What is the source?

3. What is the topic?

4. How does the writer define his or her subject? What points does he or she make?

5. Does he or she use a formal definition in his or her paragraph?

6. Do you agree or disagree with the writer's definition? If you disagree, why do you feel this way? How could you improve the definition?

Exercise 4   Writing More Definitions

Without using a dictionary or any other sources, complete each of the following. (Answer in three sentences.) Be prepared to share your answers.

1. In your opinion, what is a good teacher?

   _____

   _____

   _____

2. In your opinion, what is grace?

   _____

   _____

   _____

3. In your opinion, what is greed?

   _____

   _____

   _____

4. In your opinion, what is a mystery?

   _____

   _____

   _____

5. In your opinion, what is a good student?

   _____

   _____

   _____

6. In your opinion, what is a good job?

   _____

   _____

   _____

7. In your opinion, what is a miracle?

   _____

   _____

   _____

Writing Assignment 1   Definition Paragraph

Choose one of the following topics and write a paragraph composition using a definition method of development. To complete the assignment, bear in mind the following:

1. The assignment should be 150–200 words long and double-spaced.

2. Check over spelling, grammar, and punctuation before you hand in your assignment.

3. Use a computer to complete the work. If you are unable to comply with this requirement, please talk to your instructor.

Topics for Definition Paragraph

1. What is a good chef?
2. What is a poor writer?
3. What is a good party?
4. What is an excellent wine or beer?
5. What is a perfect pet?
6. What is a fun movie?
7. What is a good kindergarten?
8. What is a good witch?
9. What is a good burger?
10. What is a peer?
11. What is a shooting star?
12. What is a tourist?
13. What is safety?
14. What is a tall ship?
15. What is a disaster?
16. What is an actor?
17. What is an Ipsos-Reid poll?
18. What is duty?
19. What is a delicacy?
20. What is a glacier?
21. What is a good joke?
22. What is a bad joke?
23. What is a good piece of furniture?
24. What is relaxation?
25. What is the perfect game of golf?
26. What is a mistake?
27. What is a partnership?

CHECKOUT

1. There are similarities between division and definition modes; however, each serves a different purpose.

2. An extended definition may comprise several written pages.

3. Asking yourself useful questions about your definition topic can be a helpful way to start writing.

4. You can create "thinking notes" that, like a map of your ideas, can help you navigate through a preliminary investigation of your topic.

chapter 9

Beginning Essays

Chapter Objectives

After completing this chapter, you will be able to

- recognize the basic parts of an academic essay
- shape thesis statements
- use transitional devices to connect ideas in essays
- structure a simple outline for an essay
- apply the principles of paragraph writing to essay writing
- write a beginning essay (optional)

INTRODUCTION

What is an essay? An **essay** is a written composition centring around one idea or theme. It presents a particular point of view, attempting to inform, convince, or persuade the reader. A short essay can be 500 words long, but typically college or university students write essays from 800 to 1500 words in length. Essays can be much longer, however. The principles you have learned about writing paragraphs in the previous chapters will apply to writing paragraphs in your essays, too. Well-organized, well-developed, and focussed paragraphs are essential to develop first-rate essays. This chapter will provide you with information about how to develop body paragraphs as elements of an extended piece of writing.

Writers have inherited the form called "the essay." It has been accepted as a writing "convention," but there are points of disagreement. Some English instructors prefer a specified structure; others allow a more flexible form. Some instructors demand that the thesis statement be in a particular position in the introductory paragraph of an essay, while others do not make that request. Most instructors insist that writers take a particular stance and defend it through the essay. On the whole, instructors expect students to revise and proofread. All instructors expect to receive written work that is thoughtfully and carefully edited. Some instructors place less importance on mechanical skills and more on content. To some composition instructors, the form is just as important as the ideas. All in all, you should not count on all English instructors having the same expectations. Recognize that different instructors have their own preferences, expectations, and ideas. You should find out what writing requirements each instructor in each of your courses has.

ABOUT THE ACADEMIC ESSAY

Conventionally, academic essays have three parts: the **introduction**, the **body**, and the **conclusion**. Specifically, the introduction consists of one paragraph and a **thesis statement** *that focusses the whole essay*. The introduction is an important feature of the essay because it frames what the essay will be about and opens the topic for your reader.

The **body** of a basic academic essay consists of *a minimum of three separate paragraphs*. It can, however, have more than three body paragraphs; in fact, it can have as many as a writer wants it to have. However, it must have at least three body paragraphs to be considered a basic essay. Each body paragraph discusses a major idea of the thesis, and develops points and gives evidence to support claims made by the thesis. An essay has a **conclusion**, which sums up major ideas in the essay and leaves the reader with a general thought on the topic.

Essentials of the Essay

An academic essay must have the following:

- Introductory paragraph containing a thesis statement (focus idea)

- Body paragraphs (at least three that support the claims of the thesis)

- Conclusion (summing up and providing a general thought)

- Strong evidence

- Effective transitional sentences

- Excellent editing

- Clear presentation (word processed with title page, 11- or 12-point font, good spacing)

WHY AM I ASKED TO WRITE AN ESSAY?

Some students would argue that writing an essay has only two purposes—to please an English teacher and pass a course. This claim may be partially true; however, there is more to it than that. Writing an essay helps develop thinking and assists in other ways.

An essay can provide you with opportunities. First, it can be a challenge. An essay can test skills of written expression and organization. It can become a test of your intellectual powers and your abilities to use language effectively. Moreover, it provides the chance to work with abstraction, using language. It provides the prospect of working through an intellectual puzzle like nothing else can. In fact, as college or university students know, being able to write good arguments is often crucial to passing courses in the humanities.

Next, an essay can be a tool. You can use it to convince or persuade someone of a particular point of view. It is writing that unwraps a writer's opinions to public view. An essay can be discovery. Essays and other forms of writing help you to discover your thoughts on a subject. It is true that you sometimes do not know what you think about something until you try writing about it. As a writer, you learn what you think about a specific topic or idea as you work your way through the writing process. In addition, your reader may learn from what you have to say.

Finally, an essay can entertain. Good discussion is entertaining, after all. You may choose a particular tone—light, casual, serious, amusing, and so forth—to create a mood in a reader. You may actually have fun doing the writing, too.

In all of these ways, essay writing allows you many learning opportunities. You probably are aware, of course, that it is only through the drafting and writing stages that you can develop as a writer. You can read a lot about essay writing, but it is through your writing experiences that you will learn the most.

AN OVERVIEW OF THE PARTS OF AN ESSAY

The Introduction

The introduction of an essay is a paragraph by itself. First, try to make the introduction interesting to read. Begin in the most engaging way you can imagine. Next, provide some background that helps to restrict the topic in some way. This is called the **controlling idea** because it helps narrow the focus of discussion. Lastly, the introduction should contain a sentence that indicates what the essay is going to be about. This sentence, called the **thesis statement**, shows the reader where you are going to take the discussion. It distills the narrowed topic, the controlling idea, to discuss a specific aspect. Then the thesis statement angles the particular aspect to show your point of view and the method, or mode, of development.

Although the thesis statement may, in fact, be anywhere in the introductory paragraph, *Spotlight on Paragraph and Essay Skills* suggests that you place the thesis statement as the last sentence of your introduction. As you become more experienced and confident in your writing, you may decide to place it in other positions.

The Body of the Essay

The body of an essay contains the points and discussion of the points you want to establish. The body should contain *a minimum of three paragraphs*, but it can contain more. Each paragraph should contain a topic sentence that controls the ideas in each paragraph. The discussion for each point should be thorough. You should set out a point; then you should provide proof and explanation for the point. This process is called *elaborating your ideas*. When you elaborate ideas, you make them full and convincing. The proof or support you provide could consist of examples, quotations, illustrations, or specified reasons. You may provide some commentary as well. Furthermore, paragraphs throughout the body of the essay should be balanced; that is, they should be roughly the same length.

Most writers will use sentences called **transitional sentences**. These lead-in sentences, found at the ends of body paragraphs, help bridge ideas between paragraphs. They review ideas and then suggest new ones in the next paragraph. Unlike the last sentence of a paragraph composition, transitional sentences in body paragraphs are not concluding sentences. They do not sum up or conclude anything. Instead, they are sentences with a dual function: they look back and draw a key word or phrase from the paragraph, and then they look ahead to draw a key word or phrase from the next paragraph. In so doing, they develop coherence between the body paragraphs. Transitional sentences are particularly useful in lengthy essays.

The Conclusion

The conclusion *wraps up the ideas of an essay*. First, you may restate or rephrase your thesis statement. Next, you can summarize the points in the essay to refresh the ideas for the reader. Then, you end the essay by leaving the reader with a general thought on the topic. Try to have a forceful ending that eases the reader out of the topic. Flat endings leave flat impressions. Do not introduce new ideas in the conclusion, but use the conclusion to tie up the ideas in the essay.

Exercise 1   The Terms of Essay Writing

Essay writing has a vocabulary of its own. Here are some of the terms used in connection with essay writing. As you think of each term, write down a definition. Work in pairs. Each pair should then check their answers with another pair in the class.

essay	introduction
body	conclusion
support	controlling idea
thesis statement	topic sentence
unity	organization
expository	balance
mode of development	editing
draft	transitional sentence
coherence	persuasive
elaborating ideas	

GETTING STARTED

One of the most difficult activities for all writers is getting started. Even the most experienced writers can have trouble just putting the first words down on the page. You, too, may find this happening when you write, but you should not worry. Have a course of action to follow. Try some of the prewriting strategies mentioned in Chapter 1 of this book. You can also use questions to get started:

1. What do I know about this topic?

2. What do I like about this topic?

3. What do I dislike about this topic?

4. What aspects of the topic seem clear?

5. What aspects of the topic seem unclear?

6. Where have I read about this topic before?

7. What sources proved useful after I searched the internet?

8. Do I have any strong opinions on this topic?

Try writing answers to these questions. You will find by writing to a focus—the questions—you may suddenly start to "unblock" a lot of ideas. Remember: just the act of writing helps us write. Getting something on the paper, even writing your responses to the previous eight questions, is much more useful and satisfying than writing nothing at all.

THE CONTROLLING IDEA

Once you have settled on a satisfactory topic, you are ready to consider the **controlling idea**, a narrower aspect of the topic. You must think your way through to getting something that can work as a controlling idea.

You can use some of the prewriting strategies you learned in previous chapters. Although these strategies were set out for paragraph compositions, they are also useful when you are preparing to write essays. You might begin with brainstorming.

After you have selected your topic, take a few minutes and brainstorm for ideas. As you recall, to brainstorm simply means to jot down whatever occurs to you. Do this activity for five to ten minutes, and then stop to read what you have written. Using your notes, try writing one or two more narrowed ideas. You are looking for a controlling idea in the topic. Consider the following example.

Suppose early childhood education is your topic. The topic is far too broad to handle. Think about what aspect of early childhood education you wish to discuss. You can brainstorm for a few minutes and then recognize an aspect of the topic that appeals to you. To illustrate, perhaps you identify gender-related issues. You can put together early childhood education and gender issues to develop a controlling idea.

Broad Subject	**Controlling Idea**
early childhood education	gender issues in early childhood education

Do you think this controlling idea can help you narrow your topic so that a clear and effective thesis can emerge?

Exercise 2   The Controlling Idea

Choose five of the following topics. Develop a more specific aspect of the topic, but do not work out a thesis statement. Write down your controlling idea. Be prepared to share your answers.

Topics for Developing the Controlling Idea

comic books	apartments
travelling	poverty
movies	books
essays	jokes
recreation	cars
music	celebrations
media	art

THE THESIS STATEMENT

Most written assignments will include some **expository** writing. In other words, you will be asked to *explain* something to your readers or *inform* them about a topic. When you do research papers, you will investigate a topic that may be unfamiliar. In most composition courses, though, you will have the opportunity to write from a large selection of topics. Therefore, select a topic that interests you and that you know something about.

After you have a controlling idea, you can then think about a specific aspect of the controlling idea—the thesis statement. Remember: a **thesis statement** is a sentence that shows what aspect of the topic you will discuss; it shows your particular view.

The thesis statement should be clear and concise. To develop your thesis, use your brainstorming notes. Some of the notes you made in your brainstorming session will be useful. Look over your notes. Are there any that could be included in your essay? Which ones are useful? Why?

It is also important to recognize that your thesis statement may be overgeneralized. **Overgeneralizations** are statements that, although appearing to be factual, are unsupported conclusions. For example, "Women love shopping" is an overgeneralization. Not all women love shopping. In fact, some hate it. Overgeneralizations should be avoided, particularly in thesis statements.

Exercise 3   Examining Overgeneralizations

Read each of the following statements. Each is an overgeneralization. Write down what in particular makes the statement an overgeneralization. Be prepared to share your answers.

1. Foreign students spend too much money.

2. In Canada children are independent by age 12.

3. Everyone in Canada loves hockey.

4. Left-handed people are more intelligent.

5. All Canadian teenagers watch too much television.

6. Women are more verbal than men.

7. Snack foods are bad for your health.

8. Playing sports develops character.

Exercise 4   Group Activity: Recognizing Effective Thesis Statements

Form a group of three to five people. Read each of the following thesis statements. Then decide if each statement could be a workable thesis statement. Tell why the thesis statement is effective or ineffective. Is it too broad or narrow in scope? Is it an overgeneralization? Does it seem manageable for a basic essay? Also decide what rhetorical mode you might expect the writer to use. Someone in the group should record your answers. Be prepared to share your responses with the rest of the group.

1. The world is a cruel place.

2. Sparring is an important part of the martial arts.

3. Names reveal everything about a person.

4. One aspect of reading literature is analyzing characters.

5. The fishing industry on the east coast of Canada needs revitalization.

6. Cable television has changed the way viewers watch television.

7. Women play hockey differently from men.

8. The CFL should be closed down for three reasons.

9. Unions should support women's groups.

10. Younger parents make better parents.

11. Not everyone should be protected by the law.

12. Fashion design has a surprising history in Canada.

13. Children should be seen and not heard.

14. Today credit unions are very much like banks.

15. The Olympic games are a waste of money.

Exercise 5   Shaping Thesis Statements

Suppose each of the following topics will be developed for an essay. Your task is to take each topic and shape it into a clear thesis statement. Your thesis statement should show the rhetorical mode it will follow. Your instructor may wish to see your work or have you share answers in your class.

Topics for Thesis Statements

skiing	magazines
curing snoring	biking
part-time jobs	communication
networking	clubs
family recipes	gifts

PARAGRAPHS IN ESSAYS

In the previous chapters, you learned the following about paragraph compositions:

• Paragraphs should start with topic sentences to show what the paragraphs are about.

• Paragraph compositions have topic sentences, major points, support for the major points, and wrap-up sentences or conclusions.

• You can use the following five different rhetorical modes or combination of modes to develop paragraph compositions:

1. time–order, or process

2. comparison and contrast

3. classification and division

4. cause and effect

5. definition

- Transitional words and phrases enhance the flow of ideas and help establish the rhetorical pattern in paragraph compositions.

- Writers should establish clear points in paragraph compositions. Some composition instructors say that every body paragraph should have three major points.

- You should elaborate on major points in paragraph compositions and provide proof. Support points by specific evidence through examples, reasons, statistics, anecdotes, or explanations.

Body Paragraphs in Essays

The body paragraphs of essays have major points and supports, but they differ in one important way: each body paragraph of an essay is part of a larger structure. The function of each body paragraph is to discuss a particular aspect of the thesis. Each body paragraph contributes to developing a line of thinking or reasoning in the essay that links with the thesis statement. Each body paragraph relates to the paragraph before it and the one following it.

USING TRANSITIONAL SENTENCES

Transitional sentences are used at the end of body paragraphs (except the last body paragraph of the essay) in essays, especially longer pieces like research essays or papers. Transitional sentences help the flow of ideas and the development of the line of reasoning. By hinting at what will come in the next body paragraph, they assist in keeping the focus for both the reader and the writer of the piece. They provide coherence in the essay by making the essay feel like a whole, consistent unit.

Look over the following diagram of the basic academic essay. Pay particular attention to how the parts relate to the whole essay.

Writing the Introduction of an Essay

The introduction has three purposes. It gets your reader interested in the topic, provides some background information to your reader, which leads to the controlling idea of the essay, and provides the thesis statement for the whole essay. The introduction should be at least five sentences long. If it is too short, it will not fulfill the three purposes.

Start the introduction with an interesting statement of some sort: a "grabber." Next, in a general way, provide some background information about the topic that helps to narrow the discussion: the controlling idea. Finally, shape your thesis statement and place it as the last sentence of your introduction. Be sure that the thesis statement shows a clear method of development or rhetorical mode. Your reader should be able to tell what your paper is going to be about and how you will develop it simply by reading your thesis statement.

The Basic Academic Essay

The Introduction

An interesting opener

Background moving to the controlling idea

The thesis statement

Body Paragraph 1

Topic sentence

Major point 1

Elaboration with specific support for point 1

Major point 2

Elaboration with specific support for point 2

Major point 3

Elaboration with specific support for point 3

Transitional sentence to body paragraph 2

Body Paragraph 2

Topic sentence

Major point 1

Elaboration with specific support for point 1

Major point 2

Elaboration with specific support for point 2

Major point 3

Elaboration with specific support for point 3

Transitional sentence to body paragraph 3

Body Paragraph 3

Topic sentence

Major point 1

Elaboration with specific support for point 1

Major point 2

Elaboration with specific support for point 2

Major point 3

Elaboration with specific support for point 3

Conclusion

Wrap-up of ideas

Follows logically from the line of reasoning in the essay

Closes discussion

No new points

Remember: student academic writing usually means writing for a course. Instructors and markers do not want to wade through cluttered introductions. They do not want to struggle to find out what the thesis is or where you have placed it. In short, be clear, direct, and interesting in the introductory paragraph of your essay.

Writing the Body of an Essay

When you write essays, you try to convince your reader. To be convincing, you must have organized and clear ideas.

First, you want to show your reader that you have thought ideas through, in other words, you have given thought to your topic. Your reader can tell when an essay has been slapped together without attention to detail, good evidence, conventional essay format, or clear organization. You want your essay to be thoughtfully and carefully arranged for best presentation.

Next, you must work to connect ideas to convince your reader. Ideas should not appear to be "splashed" onto the page nor to fit randomly with the topic. You must establish the relationship between ideas. You must make the "fit." The reader depends on that connection.

Furthermore, you must select your evidence or arguments wisely. The examples or pieces of evidence you select must support the point you are establishing. This proof must be convincing; otherwise, your reader will not take your ideas seriously.

Consider an analogy. Writing an essay is somewhat like playing a card game. When you have decided what topic to write about and when you have formulated a thesis, it is like the first approach to the card table. You know basically what the game is that you are about to play. You understand the ground rules of the game, just as you understand the ground rules of essays, but you do not know precisely how the game will work out, just as you do not know exactly how your essay will turn out. You are dealt a hand just as you deal yourself ideas. To win a hand, you must use your best cards. To win a point or to convince your reader, you must use the best ideas or strongest examples you can find. If you play the first hand you get without thinking it through, you will lose the hand, and you may lose the game. You may lose the reader and suffer the consequences.

Essentials for the Body of the Essay

The body of the essay should have these characteristics:

- a clear organization

- points that are clearly established and laid out in separate sentences

- points that are supported by strong examples, reasons, or facts

- arguments that are convincing

- transitions that are used selectively

- a confident style, convincing but not arrogant

- a concise sentence structure.

Let's consider what makes up a good argument.

Choosing Evidence to Make a Good Argument

Think about how a person wins an argument. Imagine a convincing person. What situation is this person in? How does the person behave? What sort of language does the person use? How does the person win?

Think of salespeople as examples of those who can win when they want to. Most effective salespeople and most effective sales training courses use a great deal of psychology in the process. Salespeople are taught to be clear in their own objectives. They are taught that they can sell anything to anyone if they are clear about their purpose. So, first of all, as a writer, you must use the same technique. When you are establishing a point, ask yourself, "What am I really trying to write about? What point is it that I am trying to establish?"

The next thing salespeople might be taught is how to get the customer to buy the product. In other words, how can the goal be reached? You, too, must think of how you are going to achieve your purpose. As a writer, once you have established the point you are trying to make, you should ask yourself, "How am I going to convince someone that my point could be true?"

Making something convincing lies in selecting powerful examples. Think of at least two reasons why your point may be valid. Three reasons are even more attractive. Good salespeople can think of a whole flock of reasons why you should buy their product. In sales, they are taught not to waste a customer's time while they desperately try to think of good reasons the customer should buy something. They will rehearse dialogue with an imaginary customer many times and may even have anticipated possible arguments or questions the customer may have. In a similar way, when you construct an argument, you must also anticipate questions and arguments. You must think of or find several real examples, illustrations, or facts to support the point you are trying to establish. Here are some tips to help you construct the argument.

TIPS FOR CONSTRUCTING AN ARGUMENT

1. **Establish a point.** For example, if you are writing about television program content, you might begin with a point like this:

   Most television programs have poor content, and viewers become insulted.

2. **Provide proof or evidence for your point.** You might use examples, statistics, explanations, anecdotes, or facts. For example, you might say this:

   A good example of such programming is the "reality show" and the "challenge" that many networks now broadcast. These shows depict people doing utterly stupid things for money. Most of the time the characters' behaviour displays the worst in people. In one show, one character was asked to cheat and steal from another to "knock the person out of the game."

3. **Explain how the proof connects with your point.** After you describe your example, tell how you think it relates to the major point.

4. **Keep the point you are trying to establish separate from the proof.** Do not mix the two in the same sentence, because doing so confuses issues.

The news anchor, the "hero" of the supper hour, is a person who is not really genuine because he or she must create a persona for the camera and the viewers, pretending to be an expert in all things and at all times.

Notice that the writer has mixed the point being established with the proof. What is the point the writer wants to make? What is the proof he or she uses?

The point: "The news anchor is really not genuine."

First piece of evidence to support the point: "He or she must create a persona for the camera and the viewers, pretending to be an expert in all things and at all times." The reader will find this statement confusing because it blends the point with an example.

5. **Choose the most convincing evidence you can find or think of.** A strong or compelling example is very important. It can sway your audience.

6. **Be confident in your statements.** Say things such as, "The politician was selfish in his actions, causing the ruin of several important people in his life." Don't say, "Some may not agree with me, but I sort of think that the politician might have been just a little selfish." Make a bold, clear statement as your point. Then find good evidence to back up your claim. Then comment to make the connection.

7. **Use transitional devices (a word, a phrase, or a whole sentence) to bridge ideas.** Transitions indicate to the reader that you are adding to the idea, contrasting it, comparing it, or modifying it in some way, or that you are changing to a new point. Transitions assist the flow of ideas. You will find more about transitional devices in the next few pages.

8. **Write freely.** As Henriette Anne Klauser tells us in *Writing on Both Sides of the Brain: Breakthrough Techniques in Writing* (Toronto: HarperCollins Canada, 1987):

When you edit and write at the same time, the result is often a disaster: a disaster for you as a writer and eventually for your reader. Purple patches come from the unrestricted pen. Go back and edit later. Later is when you invite the logical sequential strength side of you to come forward and apply all the techniques of good grammar and construction that have been drilled into you since the beginning of your school days.

Exercise 6   *Evaluating Evidence*

Find another person in the class to work with. Together evaluate each pair of statements. Statement 1 is supposed to provide a clear point. Statement 2 is supposed to provide evidence or proof for the point.

After Statement 1, write **C** for clear if you believe the statement clearly establishes a point. Write **O** if you think the statement is an overgeneralization. Write **P** if you think the statement is an opinion and not a fact. Write **V** if you think the statement is too vague.

Then consider Statement 2. Does it provide good supporting evidence? If it does, write **YES.** If it does not, write **NO.** Be prepared to explain and share your answers.

Pair A

Statement 1:   Owners of pets are irresponsible people.   _____

Statement 2:   The other day I noticed a dog owner
                      who did not pick up after his dog.   _____

Pair B

Statement 1:   Some safety features of our roadways
                      need to be improved.   _____

Statement 2:   According to a survey in *Safe Driving*,
                      62% of drivers do not shoulder check
                      when they pull out from the curb.   _____

Pair C

Statement 1:   All math anxiety stems from poor
                      self-esteem.   _____

Statement 2:   Practising positive "self-talk" can
                      improve math scores on tests.   _____

Pair D

Statement 1:   Something needs to be done about
                      the crime rate in this city.   _____

Statement 2:   Crimes are on the increase.   _____

Pair E

Statement 1:   I believe Tanya is the best person
                      for president of the student council.   _____

Statement 2:   She is well organized and a hard worker.   _____

Pair F

Statement 1:   Children should be protected from
                      violence on television.   _____

Statement 2:   My children get aggressive after
                      they watch cartoons.   _____

CONCLUDING AN ESSAY

The last paragraph of your essay is called a **concluding paragraph** or a **conclusion**. The conclusion is an important paragraph because it is the last section your reader will see. You want to leave the reader feeling satisfied after he or she has read your essay, feeling "eased out" of the writing effectively.

Your concluding paragraph should provide three things for the reader:

1. **It should restate the thesis.** Write the thesis again, but use different words. This technique reminds the reader of what you had set out to discuss in your essay. In long essays, such a restatement is particularly useful.

2. **It should highlight the main points of the essay.** Look at each body paragraph and summarize each in a few words. Your summary statement may be only one sentence long, but in a lengthy essay, you may need two or more sentences to recap the major points you have made.

3. **It should end by leaving the reader with a general thought on the topic.** Instead of simply summing up your ideas and leaving the reader there, add a global thought on the topic. This general thought provides closure in the reader's mind. However, do not add new ideas to the essay in the conclusion. A conclusion is not the place to introduce new ideas or points that have not been mentioned previously in the essay. Instead, the last paragraph is the closing stage of a presentation—a place where you as a writer sum up and then uplift the reader. You want the reader to finish reading, thinking about what you have said.

Keep these hints in mind when you write. Review them from time to time. Remember: the work you do in advance of the actual writing will make the writing itself a much easier task.

TRANSITIONAL DEVICES

When you write, you must show connections or relationships between ideas. Words, phrases, and sentences called **transitions**, or **transitional devices**, help make connections between ideas in sentences, between sentences, and between paragraphs.

Which transitional devices you use depends on which rhetorical mode you have chosen. For example, if you contrast ideas (a contrast mode), then you use transitional devices showing contrast. If you choose cause and effect, you select transitions that convey a cause and effect relationship.

In a paragraph, you use transitional words between major points and between examples or explanations. At the end of a body paragraph, place a sentence that quickly summarizes the main gist of the paragraph and opens up ideas in the next paragraph. This transitional sentence bridges ideas from one paragraph to the next. However, it is not necessary to place a transitional sentence at the end of the last body paragraph because you do not require a link to a conclusion.

Examples of Transitional Words and Phrases

To add ideas

furthermore	in addition
another	moreover
also	and

To show process

first	next
when	to begin with
finally	during
second	before
as soon as	initially
while	afterward
third	after
then	at last
after that	until

To add examples

for instance	for example
a case in point	to illustrate

To show cause/effect relationships

of course	for
thus	hence
therefore	due to
consequently	as a result
since	then

To show differences (contrast)

on the other hand	whereas
although	unlike
in contrast	but
yet	conversely
however	a differing

To show similarity (comparison)

similarly	the same
just as	also
in addition	as well as
like	in the same way

EXAMPLE OF A PROCESS, OR TIME-ORDER, ESSAY

Read the following student essay that Kerry-Anne wrote under timed conditions in the classroom. It uses a process mode. As you read, pay attention to the parts of the essay. Look at how Kerry-Anne has structured her introduction. Notice how clearly she lays out each stage of the process.

Settling an Argument

Kerry-Anne Doole

When we argue or disagree with a friend, it can take time to come to a peaceful resolution, but it is well worth the effort. Settling an argument involves admitting to not being perfect. Most of the time we can find a resolution, but sometimes more help is needed. Settling an argument includes three major steps.

The first step to settling an argument is talking one-on-one with the other person. Do not to go to anyone else at this point. When we tell another person about our argument, we cause people to take sides. The person we talk to is going to tell others about the problem, leading to rumours. As the rumours spread, the story can become twisted: our words may end up being misunderstood. The person we originally argued with may find out through the grapevine that we are upset with him or her. Hearing such a story second-hand can lead to hurt feelings and a possible end to a great friendship. We risk breaking up long-established relationships if we do not try to deal with issues more directly. Often we may find the problem more easily resolved by going to the person involved first. In fact, most of the time, going to anyone else can cause greater problems in the relationship. The second reason meeting face-to-face is important is to try to clear up misunderstandings. It is crucial to go back to the person we argued with and ask for clarification on any issues that we do not understand. We may have heard the person say one thing, when in reality he or she said something entirely different. Furthermore, the friend we argued with may not realize that we are upset with him or her. Meeting face-to-face also allows for apologies on both sides. The third reason for a meeting is common courtesy. The polite thing to do is to talk to the person who has offended us. If we do not go back to the original person, how can the relationship be repaired? If we go to that person, it eliminates the number of other people who can take sides and reduces possible misunderstandings. However, it can sometimes be difficult to meet another person when both parties feel angry or hurt.

If the person refuses to listen, the second step is to take someone else with us. This person must be neutral and not take sides in the argument. A neutral person is like a mediator who has no connection with either party. The person must be neutral because nothing productive will be accomplished at a meeting if he or she starts to take sides. Moreover, the purpose of having someone else go with us is to allow for reasonable, calm conversation. The mediator can help to keep tempers under control. When things start to get out of hand, he or she can stop the discussion until everyone has cooled down. In addition, the mediator allows each party to have a say, eliminating the possibility of one person taking over the conversation. Both people in the conflict feel as if their version of the argument has been heard. The mediator, therefore, creates the space where each party has a voice and where neither person feels frustrated by not being able to express their side of the story. In these ways, the mediator helps to bring the two opposing sides to a peaceful resolution, but the mediator's work still involves one last stage.

The final step involves a plan of action. The mediator helps the people involved to draft a plan of action indicating what the parties are willing to do to work out their differences. To draft such a plan, they need to sit down with the mediator and put in writing what they will do to solve their disagreement. They must agree to follow through, or the plan will not work. One example of following through is getting together once a week to talk about their differences. Furthermore, there must be a desire to change or the reconciliation will not succeed. If one of the people involved in the argument refuses to make an effort, the relationship will not succeed. The two parties need to stay focussed on their goal of friendship. If the parties have agreed to work together, then they must be committed to what they need to do. The plan of action makes clear what needs to be done to get the relationship working again; more importantly, the plan of action is a negotiated agreement between the two people—each one must make a commitment to move forward in a positive way.

The steps to solving an argument can be painful and difficult. Participants must be willing to be direct with one another, get the assistance of a neutral person or mediator, and draft a plan of action that both parties agree to follow. Negotiating a conflict between friends is a risky business. It may mean losing a friendship. It may also mean that a stronger relationship develops. No one really knows for certain. If the people involved in the argument are willing to work together, their relationship has a fighting chance. If they are not capable of working out their differences, it may be time to go their separate ways. However, learning to settle an argument in a reasonable fashion using clear steps may be one of the most important lessons any person can have.

Exercise 7   Analyzing Kerry-Anne's Essay

Re-read Kerry-Anne's essay, and then complete the following outline. Use note form if you wish. In completing the outline, you will begin to understand how Kerry-Anne organized her essay. After you have finished, go to Exercise 8 and answer the questions.

Settling an Argument

Introduction:

Background and controlling idea:

_____

_____

_____

Thesis statement:

_____

_____

Body paragraph 1:

Topic sentence:

_____

_____

Major point 1: _____

Evidence or support: _____

_____

Major point 2: _____

Evidence or support: _____

_____

Major point 3: _____

Evidence or support: _____

_____

Transitional sentence: _____

_____

Body paragraph 2:

Topic sentence:

_____

_____

Major point 1: _____

Evidence or support: _____

_____

Major point 2: _____

Evidence or support: _____

_____

Major point 3: _____

Evidence or support: _____

_____

Transitional sentence: _____

_____

Body paragraph 3:

Topic sentence:

_____

_____

Major point 1: _____

Evidence or support: _____

_____

Major point 2: _____

Evidence or support: _____

_____

Major point 3: _____

Evidence or support: _____

_____

Conclusion

Restatement: _____

_____

General thought on the topic: _____

_____

Exercise 8   Questions on "Settling an Argument"

Completing an outline can also help you to evaluate a writer's argument. Answer the following questions. Be prepared to share your answers.

1. Has Kerry-Anne provided enough clear evidence? If not, what evidence might she provide?

2. Why is Kerry-Anne's argument convincing or not convincing?

3. How are the ideas Kerry-Anne has provided useful?

4. Comment on the following features of the essay:
   • essay balance
   • writer's choice of words
   • sentence style
   • use of transitions

5. How have you settled arguments in the past? Has your technique worked? Why or why not?

Writing Assignment 1   A Beginning Essay (Optional)

Your instructor may ask you to write a basic essay. Choose one of the following topics. Write an essay of about 500–600 words that has an introduction, three body paragraphs, and a conclusion. Your first essay will use a clear rhetorical pattern to help organize your ideas effectively.

Instructions:

1. Double space your work.

2. Check spelling, grammar, and punctuation before you hand in your assignment.

3. Use a computer to complete the assignment. If you are unable to comply with this requirement, please talk to your instructor.

4. Check with your instructor regarding a title page.

Topics for a Time-Order, or Process, Essay

how to make a celebration feast
how to teach a dog a trick
how to make downtown living more enjoyable for residents
how to make the morning commute more pleasant
the process of selecting a university or college
the process of reading for enjoyment
how to win an argument
how to order books from the internet
how to curl
how to manage a restaurant
the process of losing weight
how to become a vegetarian

Topics for a Comparison and Contrast Essay

differing views on discipline and teenagers
conflicting views on censorship and the internet
differing views on playing video games
similarities in managing personal and work time
similarities in choosing partners and leisure time
similarities in sport management and fitness beliefs

Topics for a Classification and Division Essay

types of contests
what makes up a good contest
types of television hosts
what makes up a good television host
types of conversations
what makes up good conversation

Topics for a Cause and Effect Essay

the relationship between consumerism and personal image
the relationship between dating and happiness
the relationship between travel and food
the relationship between office gossip and morals
the relationship between fitness and nutrition

CHECKOUT

1. Academic essay writing has specific requirements and follows useful conventions.

2. Essay writing offers many intellectual opportunities.

3. Taking action can help overcome the difficulties of getting started writing an essay.

4. With the help of your instructor, you can formulate an organizational plan before beginning to write an essay.

5. Developing a workable thesis statement before beginning to write an essay helps avoid wasted effort.

6. Clear writing organization, rational arguments, and convincing supporting evidence will invite the reader to take your writing seriously.

chapter 10

The Beginning Research Paper

Chapter Objectives

After completing this chapter, you will be able to

- distinguish what a research paper is
- identify the MLA style of formatting a research paper
- identify the APA style of formatting a research paper
- recognize plagiarism when you are researching
- recognize the parts of a research paper
- make use of steps to plan and write a beginning research paper.

INTRODUCTION

The most common paper you will write at college and university is the research paper, sometimes called the **research essay**. This chapter will introduce you to some basic ideas about a beginning research paper. The first part of the chapter will explain what a research paper is. You will then learn about the two most common styles of formatting your research paper: Modern Language Association (MLA) style, a style used mostly in the humanities, and American Psychological Association (APA) style, a style used mostly in the social sciences. Next, you will learn about avoiding plagiarism in academic writing. After that, you will examine the parts of a research paper, using a sample paper in APA style. At the end of the chapter, you will read two examples of research papers, one in MLA and one in APA style.

It is important to note that this chapter is an introduction to research paper writing. It contains only basic information. So, for more specific, detailed, or advanced ideas on the subject, you may want to visit some of the excellent education sites on the internet. Almost every college or university library, learning centre, or writing centre provides extensive information on research paper writing. On these web pages, you will also find various helpful links to other sites dealing with research writing. You can also visit the official MLA and APA web sites; they contain up-to-date information. In addition, you can purchase valuable English handbooks that contain comprehensive material on research writing and the use of MLA and APA style. Your college or university bookstore also carries copies of different English handbooks.

Your English instructor may recommend a particular handbook to accompany your course. Or, if you choose not to purchase one yourself, you will find a useful selection of English handbooks in your campus library.

WHAT IS A RESEARCH PAPER?

According to the Online Writing Lab from Purdue University, "A research paper is a piece of academic writing that requires a more abstract, critical, and thoughtful level of inquiry than you might be used to" (http://owl.english.purdue.edu/workshops/hypertext/ResearchW/what.html). When you write a research paper, you are attempting to persuade or analyze a particular aspect of a topic using expert sources as your evidence. When you write a research paper, you do not merely report on what authorities have said on the subject. Instead, you examine what they have to say, which will help you explore or argue your own position. In other words, you will use expert sources in your paper, but your research question, in conjunction with those sources, will make the construction of your paper distinctive. You will choose a formatting style according to the conventions of the discipline you are studying. As examples, if you are a nursing student, you will choose APA style because that is the standard for nursing papers. Or if you are an English major, you will choose MLA style because that is the accepted convention for English papers.

Deciding on a specific topic and doing research are both a part of the preparation for writing your paper. To begin, decide on your topic and develop a **research question**—a question that formulates the specific area of inquiry connected to your topic. When researching and reading about the topic, you will use books, internet sources, Canadian newspapers, scientific and sociological journals, respected magazines, interviews, films, broadcasts, or podcasts for your sources. As you work through the material, you begin to understand your own position as it connects to your research question. The sources you use, the quotations, figures, statistics, facts, and evidence you choose to use, and how you put it together will all be unique to you. No one else will develop and craft a research paper quite the way you do.

Developing a plan for, and then writing, a research paper will make demands of you. These demands will include researching a topic, thinking critically about new information, analyzing new data, working out an outline for writing, managing your time effectively, creating a longer paper, and using essay format and a particular style of documentation.

A typical research paper contains the following:

- an exploration of a specific aspect of a topic

- longer essay format

- appropriate sources of research and information

- references inside the body of the paper using a specified style, usually MLA or APA

- a last page showing all sources quoted in the paper called the **Works Cited** sheet (MLA) or **References** sheet (APA)

MLA OR APA STYLE OF DOCUMENTATION

If you are a student whose work in postsecondary studies will be in the humanities—English, art history, linguistics, philosophy, or classics studies—then you should choose MLA (Modern Language Association) style when formatting your research paper. If you are planning to do major work in the social sciences, education, or nursing, you should choose the APA (American Psychological Association) method of formatting. In some cases, your instructor will designate the style you are to use in

MLA Style	APA Style
The title page: MLA has no title page: the first page of the paper provides the title of the paper, the author's name, the date, and a header at the top left of each page.	**The title page:** APA uses a title page. It has a running head, the title of the paper, the author, the course name and section, the instructor's name, and the date of submission.
The body of the text: in-text citations The author's name and the page number are placed in parentheses after the quotation. Example: (Morton 453)	**The body of the text: in-text citations** The author's name, the date of publication, and the page number are placed in parentheses after the quotation Example: (Morton, 2008, p. 453)
Headings in the paper: MLA does not generally show headings.	**Headings in the paper:** APA uses different levels of headings. Level 1 headings include the title of the paper. Level 2 headings show the broadest category of discussion. Level 3 headings are a sub-category of Level 2. Most undergraduate papers do not use more than three levels of headings. For specific information on headings, check an English handbook or writing centre web site from a college or university.
Source Sheet All of the sources you quote in your paper must be listed in alphabetical order and placed on a separate sheet as the last page of your paper. This is called the "Works Cited" sheet. The author's last name and complete first name is placed at the edge of the left margin. No date is placed after the author's name. For detailed information, please look up this reference in your English handbook or on a writing centre web site from a college or university. Date of retrieval of information from a web site may be given. Check with your instructor.	Source Sheet All of the sources you quote in your paper must be listed in alphabetical order and placed on a separate sheet as the last page of your paper. This is called the "References" sheet. The author's last name and initial of his or her first name is placed at the edge of the left margin. The date of publication follows the author's name. For detailed information, please look up this reference in your English handbook or on a writing centre web site from a college or university. The date of the retrieval of information from a web site is given.

your papers since there are more than seven different styles available. MLA and APA are the most commonly used.

There are important differences in format between MLA and APA. It is important to use an authoritative reference such as an English handbook or educational web site to check out how to document using these two styles. The above chart shows you some main differences between the two styles.

AVOIDING PLAGIARISM

The University of Toronto web site provides a clear, direct definition of plagiarism: "The word 'plagiarism' comes from a Latin word meaning 'kidnapper' because a plagiarist is one who makes off with another person's ideas. Whether intentional or unintentional, it is a breach of professional or academic trust, in which a person takes credit for someone else's work" (http://www.ecf.utoronto.ca/~writing/handbook-plagiarism.html).

The internet has made it tempting for students to copy and paste ideas directly from a web page, online article, e-newspaper, or electronic magazine. After all, it seems that "liberal borrowing" from original sources occurs more often now than ever before, with individuals downloading music, movies, or newscasts from pirated copies on the internet. To do so, however, breaches copyright and is against the law.

Similarly, colleges and universities have policies governing plagiarism and copyright infringement. Postsecondary institutions are well aware of increasing plagiarism and are devising ways to address it. Many have purchased site licenses for software packages like Turnitin, which checks for plagiarism by reviewing thousands and thousands of papers stored in its databanks, along with millions of sites on the internet. Most plagiarism policies are harsh.

If you plagiarize and are caught, you will be subject to the plagiarism policy of your school. In other words, you will be charged with cheating or academic misconduct of the worst order. This incident could lead to your failing the course or the complete term. It could also bring about dismissal from your college or university.

Sometimes it is difficult to know when you are plagiarizing. However, most of the time, you can tell. *If you use someone else's words or ideas without crediting your source, even if you summarize or paraphrase them in your own words, you are plagiarizing.* In order to keep your work honest while respecting the right of ownership of others, *cite* your sources. To cite a source means to tell exactly who the author is, where you found the source, along with its date (APA) and page number (MLA and APA).

Remember: even if you are **summarizing** (condensing the ideas into your own words), or **paraphrasing** (giving the ideas in approximately the same number of words as the source but using your own words), you *must cite your source.* Keep careful records of where you found the information, along with *citation information*:

- For books, magazines, journals, and newspapers, you need the title of the work, the name of the author or authors, the date of publication, the city of publication, and the publishing company.

- For internet sources, you need the URL and the name of the author or authors of the web page. If there is no author, you need the name of the organization and the company or corporation that the web site represents.

THE PARTS OF A RESEARCH PAPER IN APA STYLE

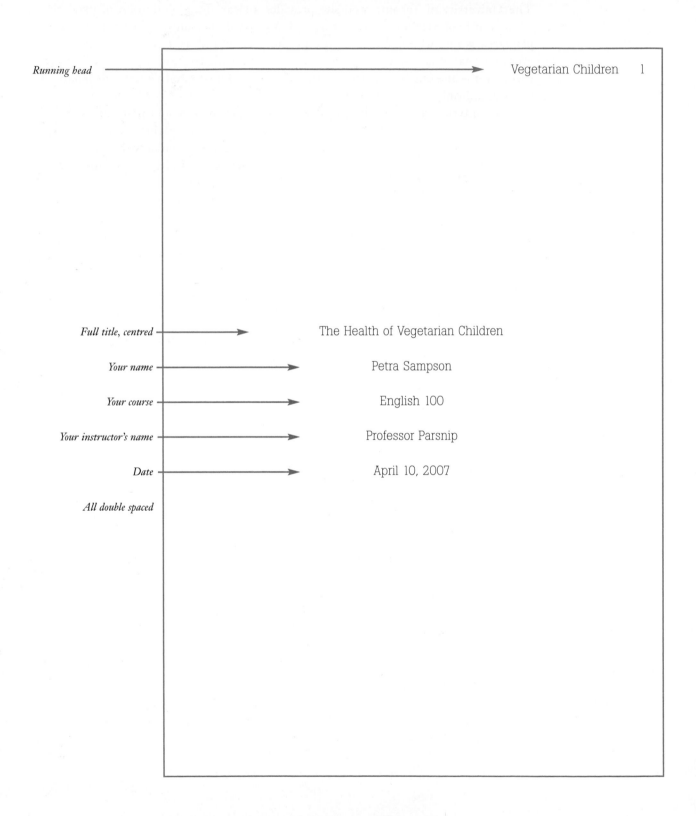

Running head ————————————————→ Vegetarian Children   1

Full title, centred ————————→ The Health of Vegetarian Children

Your name ————————→ Petra Sampson

Your course ————————→ English 100

Your instructor's name ————————→ Professor Parsnip

Date ————————→ April 10, 2007

All double spaced

Running head ————————————————▶   Vegetarian Children   2

Heading in bold and centred ————▶ **Growing Up in the Garden: The Health of Vegetarian Children**

Introduction ———▶   Vegetarians are people who for some reason avoid the consumption of
meat or products made from animals. A healthy vegetarian diet incorporates a
variety of foods—fresh fruit, vegetables, and whole grains. Sixty years ago,
vegetarians were an almost invisible group in Western civilization—only 0.25% of
British people claimed to avoid eating meat during World War II (Sabaté, 2001,
p. 8). Vegetarianism is now gaining popularity, and more young people and
families are switching to a meat-free diet (Sabaté, 2001, p. 9). This is causing
alarm in people who claim a vegetarian diet cannot support healthy growth in
Thesis statement ———▶ children (Sabaté, 2001, p. 174). However, properly planned, a vegetarian diet can
be as healthy for children as an omnivore's diet.

Heading in bold and centred ————————▶ **Characteristics of a Vegetarian Diet**

Development paragraph ———▶   People usually adopt a vegetarian diet due to concerns about their health,
a belief in animal rights, or from the influence of people close to them (Sabaté,
2001, p. 8). Many religions endorse vegetarianism, such as Zoroastrianism
(Sabaté, 2001, p. 511), Hinduism (Sabaté, 2001, p. 518), and certain parts of
Seventh Day Adventism (Sabaté, 2001, p. 63). There are many different variations
on the vegetarian diet (Sabaté, 2001, p. 5). Pesovegetarians eat fish, but avoid
other kinds of meat. A lacto-ovo vegetarian does not consume meat, but does eat
eggs and milk products. According to Chen (1991), "approximately 90–95% of
vegetarians in North America include dairy and/or eggs in their diet" (qtd. in
Sabaté, 2001, p. 5). Lacto vegetarians exclude egg products, but drink milk and
eat milk products, while ovo vegetarians will not consume milk products, but do
eat eggs. Vegans avoid consumption of any animal products. A macrobiotic diet
is usually classified as vegetarian, but depending on the strictness of the diet, it
will sometimes include fish (Sabaté, 2001, p. 5). The most restrictive of macrobiotic diets require the dieter to avoid fruits and vegetables, replacing them with
"unpolished rice and other whole grain cereals, seaweeds, soya products, and
miso soup" (Sabaté, 2001, p. 75). With the exception of the macrobiotic diet, most
vegetarians aim for a large variety of fresh fruits and vegetables in order to
acquire essential nutrients from non-animal sources.

Heading in bold and centred ————————▶ **The Vegetarian Population**

Development paragraph 2 ———▶   Vegetarianism has been growing in popularity for years. While the
average age of vegetarians is still higher than among omnivores (Sabaté,
2001, p. 9), more young people and families are taking up vegetarianism.

Forty-eight percent of vegetarians in the United States report being married, and 37% of all vegetarians have children under the age of 18 (Sabaté, 2001, p. 7). Many children are choosing to adopt a vegetarian diet without influence from their parents, out of concerns for animal rights and the environment (Hussar qtd. in Anderson, 2006), and some medical doctors are promoting vegetarianism as a weight-loss tool (Tunick, p. 77).

Heading in bold and centred ————————————▶   **Childhood Nutrition**

Development paragraph 3 ——▶   It is important for children to consume sufficient minerals and vitamins while they are growing, in order to aid proper development and prevent future medical problems. If a vegetarian does not take the proper precautions by eating foods that provide good sources of vital nutrients, he or she could eventually develop health problems (Sabaté, 2001, p. 301). For that reason, many parents are hesitant to allow their children to take on a vegetarian diet. In a few cases children have died from nutritional deficiencies—usually when following a macrobiotic diet (Sabaté, 2001, p. 301)—and a study on British preschool-age children found that "Nutrient intakes and status [are] generally adequate in preschool children who did not eat meat" (Thane & Bates, 2000).

Development paragraph 4 ——▶   Any diet can be unhealthy if it does not include different sources of nutrients essential for normal growth. Depending on its strictness, a vegetarian diet can be healthier for a child than an omnivorous diet because "vegetarian diets are generally high in fibre, low in cholesterol, and low in saturated fats . . . [and] may lead to a lower risk of obesity, heart disease, high blood pressure and Type II diabetes" (Vegetarian Diets for Children, 2003, p. 23). However, parents and caregivers must ensure vegetarian children consume enough calories for their age group, and receive adequate amounts of protein, iron, zinc, calcium, and vitamin B12 (Sabaté, 2001).

Heading in bold and centred ————————————▶   **The Obesity Epidemic**

Development paragraph 5 ——▶   Obesity rates are rising all over the world. According to the U.S. Federal Institute of Medicine, "17.1% of American children and teenagers 13 to 19 were obese and an additional 6.5% were at risk of becoming obese" (qtd. in Murdock, 2006). This is a worrisome trend, since "approximately half of obese school-age children become obese adults" (Sabaté, 2001, p. 92), and childhood and adult obesity are linked to Type II diabetes, increased chance of stroke, sleep apnea, heart disease, and other life-threatening ailments (Sabaté, 2001, p.92).

Running head

Development paragraph 6

According to the director of nutrition at the Physicians Committee for Responsible Medicine, childhood obesity is on the rise because "kids are much more sedentary than ever before, and they're overconsuming . . . nutrient-poor, calorie-dense foods" (Lanou, qtd. in Tunick, 2004, p. 173). Studies have found that young vegetarian children have lower body mass indexes, and evidence suggests older vegetarian children do as well (Sabaté, 2001, p. 99). Joan Sabaté speculates that vegetarians are less likely to be obese because of other healthy lifestyle practices associated with vegetarianism, and the nutritional differences between a vegetarian diet and an omnivorous one (Sabaté, 2001, p.101). Despite the studies showing vegetarian children to be leaner than their omnivorous peers, and the lower-calorie food most vegetarians eat, some studies have found that vegetarianism does not guarantee a lower body mass index. In a study released in the *Journal of Paediatrics & Child Health* in 2001, S.S.F. Leung et al. reported that the "prevalence of obesity among the studied [vegetarian] children was 25% in boys and 13% in girls, which was higher than the local population (4–13% in boys and 4–11% in girls, aged from 4 to 14 years)" (Leung et al., 2001, p. 252). The study attributed this to the fact that over half of the children spent less than two hours per week being physically active (p. 252).

Heading in bold and centred

Conclusion

Conclusion

As the vegetarian movement grows, more studies will become available offering definitive information about the effects of a low-fat, meat-free diet on young children. Using the evidence currently available, vegetarian children appear as healthy, or healthier, than their omnivorous peers. In some cases, they do not grow at the same rate, but that could be due to the different groups studied, as many vegetarian children in the studies follow different dietary plans that do not represent most other vegetarians (Sabaté, 2001, p. 181). Sabaté mentions that other studies of vegans report growth rates similar to those of omnivores, but lower average height and weight (2001, p. 184). A vegetarian diet is linked to a longer lifespan (Sabaté, 2001, p.267), lower cancer rates (Sabaté, 2001, p. 74), and less likelihood of obesity (Sabaté, 2001, p. 99). Conversely, an unplanned vegetarian diet can lack the calories, minerals, and vitamins needed for healthy growth during childhood (Sabaté, 2001, p. 20); and there is no proof that a vegetarian diet actually promotes a healthy body mass index (Sabaté, 2001, p. 101). However, if a vegetarian diet combines exercise, sunlight, and nutritious foods (Sabaté, 2001, p. 324), a vegetarian child will grow to be just as healthy as his or her peers.

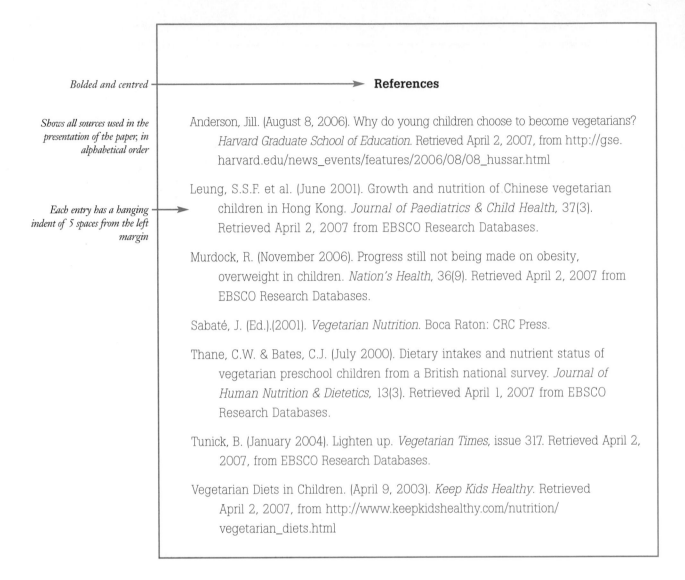

Bolded and centred ⟶ **References**

Shows all sources used in the presentation of the paper, in alphabetical order

Anderson, Jill. (August 8, 2006). Why do young children choose to become vegetarians? *Harvard Graduate School of Education*. Retrieved April 2, 2007, from http://gse. harvard.edu/news_events/features/2006/08/08_hussar.html

Each entry has a hanging indent of 5 spaces from the left margin ⟶ Leung, S.S.F. et al. (June 2001). Growth and nutrition of Chinese vegetarian children in Hong Kong. *Journal of Paediatrics & Child Health*, 37(3). Retrieved April 2, 2007 from EBSCO Research Databases.

Murdock, R. (November 2006). Progress still not being made on obesity, overweight in children. *Nation's Health*, 36(9). Retrieved April 2, 2007 from EBSCO Research Databases.

Sabaté, J. (Ed.).(2001). *Vegetarian Nutrition*. Boca Raton: CRC Press.

Thane, C.W. & Bates, C.J. (July 2000). Dietary intakes and nutrient status of vegetarian preschool children from a British national survey. *Journal of Human Nutrition & Dietetics*, 13(3). Retrieved April 1, 2007 from EBSCO Research Databases.

Tunick, B. (January 2004). Lighten up. *Vegetarian Times*, issue 317. Retrieved April 2, 2007, from EBSCO Research Databases.

Vegetarian Diets in Children. (April 9, 2003). *Keep Kids Healthy*. Retrieved April 2, 2007, from http://www.keepkidshealthy.com/nutrition/ vegetarian_diets.html

STEPS IN WRITING A RESEARCH PAPER

You must plan a research paper carefully because it requires several preparatory steps before you begin to organize and write your paper.

1. Select a topic that is appropriate. Check with your instructor or professor if you are not certain that the topic you have picked will be workable and acceptable.

2. Develop a research question to guide you.

3. Develop a rough or sketch outline that includes the broad categories you will discuss in your paper.

4. Research your topic, using a variety of sources.

5. Take careful notes, including all citation information you will need.

6. Slot the notes into the correct categories in your sketch outline.

7. Write your first draft, using MLA or APA format for in-text citations.

8. As you write the first draft, also prepare the Works Cited (MLA) or References (APA) sheet as you incorporate your sources.

9. Revise and edit the first draft.

10. Prepare your final draft for presentation, paying attention to the accuracy of your formatting in MLA or APA style. Use a checklist to ensure you have all the parts of the paper and have checked specifics.

Below is an example of the process you might go through on your first research paper.

Let's suppose you choose a topic related to the environment. You may choose to persuade your reader, or you may simply want to analyze a topic in order to discover what can be learned from the analysis. If you wish to talk about the negative impact of scientific exploration on the delicate environment of the North, for instance, then your paper will try to persuade the reader that doing such research has its price. On the other hand, you might decide to investigate how Canada's North has been experiencing development in scientific exploration over the past 20 years.

You formulate a research question, for instance, "How has scientific exploration of Canada's North over the past 20 years impacted the indigenous people living there?" Remember: a **research question** is a question that formulates the specific area of inquiry connected to your topic. The research question is narrow enough so that you can handle a particular area of your topic. If you began your research by thinking about Canada's North in general terms, then you will find your topic is *too broad*. You will find you will quickly lose focus in your project because so much material is available. In order to handle the topic so that your paper talks in some depth, you will need to concentrate on a definite aspect. You shift your attention from the general to the more specific in order to narrow your topic so that it is manageable. The illustration on the top of the next page represents how the shift helps you gain focus and clarity.

In your research writing, you will need to learn about two types of **citations**: the ones you place *inside your paper* (**in-text**) and the ones you include at *the end of your paper* in a **source sheet** (**Works Cited** for MLA and **References** for APA).

Canada's North

Time period of 20 years

Aboriginal peoples living in the North

The scientific investigations

Impact

What is the impact on Aboriginal peoples over 20 years
of scientific investigations in Canada's North?

Tips:

- As soon as you find a source in a text, journal, or magazine that you will use in a paper, write down everything you will need for the citation: the author, precise title of the article or book, the volume number, the date of publication, the page number, the publisher, the city of publication.

- If you are using an internet source, write down everything you will need for the citation: the URL address of the web site, the author of the web site if available, the date of the web site, and the date you retrieved the information. If there is no author given on the web site, cite the name of the company, group, organization, or corporation instead of the author.

Include the author's name and page number after your quotation in the body of your paper (MLA style), or include the author's name, date of publication, and the page number after your quotation in the body of your paper (APA style).

A sketch outline is a rough plan of the categories in your paper. For the research question, "What is the impact on Aboriginal peoples over 20 years of scientific investigations in Canada's North?" you might divide your topic into these sections:

- what part of the Canadian North has had the most scientific exploration

- who the Aboriginal peoples are living in that area

- the types of scientific research done over the past two decades

- the impact of this research on communities

Thus, your paper will have four broad sections in it that can make up the sketch outline. As you read and gather research, you can plug the information into the appropriate spot. You will find this method useful because you will know if a section is "lighter" than the others. In other words, you may find you cannot find enough reliable research on some sections. In this case, you can decide to delete that category in favour of another.

You should set clear time limits for each step of the paper. Begin by setting a timeline—one that shows start to finish with dates assigned to each step. See the example below that uses the steps from page 108.

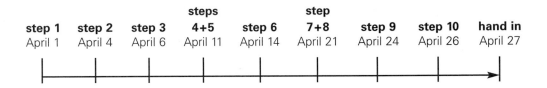

			steps		step			
step 1	step 2	step 3	4+5	step 6	7+8	step 9	step 10	hand in
April 1	April 4	April 6	April 11	April 14	April 21	April 24	April 26	April 27

When you prepare your final draft, use a checklist such as the one below to ensure you have completed all necessary steps and components of the paper:

Checklist for Final Presentation

1. My thesis statement is clear and effective. ✓_____

2. My introduction is interesting and appealing. ✓_____

3. My APA paper has headings to show categories. ✓_____

4. The body of my paper discusses specific aspects of my thesis. ✓_____

5. My in-text quotations, summaries, and paraphrases follow APA or MLA conventions. ✓_____

6. I have included a Works Cited (MLA) or Reference sheet (APA) at the end of my paper. ✓_____

7. I have included a title page (APA). ✓_____

8. I have included a correctly formatted first page (MLA). ✓_____

9. I have edited for spelling, grammar, and punctuation. ✓_____

10. I have kept a copy, just in case of loss. ✓_____

SHORT SAMPLES OF APA AND MLA STYLE

The last section of this chapter provides two sample papers: one uses MLA format, the other APA. Read through the papers. Your instructor may ask you to analyze the papers, so be prepared to answer questions.

SAMPLE PAPER #1: MLA STYLE OF DOCUMENTATION

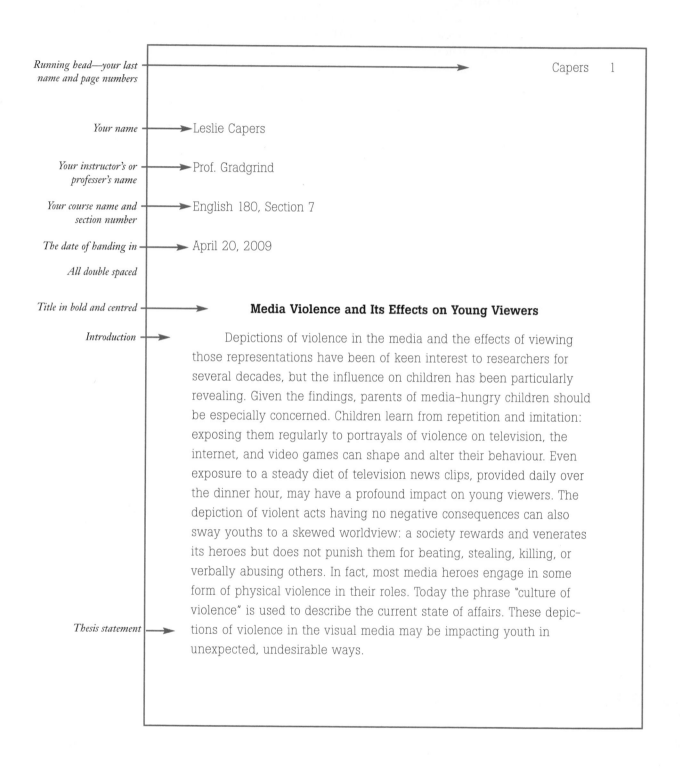

Running head—your last name and page numbers → Capers   1

Your name → Leslie Capers

Your instructor's or professer's name → Prof. Gradgrind

Your course name and section number → English 180, Section 7

The date of handing in → April 20, 2009

All double spaced

Title in bold and centred → **Media Violence and Its Effects on Young Viewers**

Introduction →   Depictions of violence in the media and the effects of viewing those representations have been of keen interest to researchers for several decades, but the influence on children has been particularly revealing. Given the findings, parents of media-hungry children should be especially concerned. Children learn from repetition and imitation: exposing them regularly to portrayals of violence on television, the internet, and video games can shape and alter their behaviour. Even exposure to a steady diet of television news clips, provided daily over the dinner hour, may have a profound impact on young viewers. The depiction of violent acts having no negative consequences can also sway youths to a skewed worldview: a society rewards and venerates its heroes but does not punish them for beating, stealing, killing, or verbally abusing others. In fact, most media heroes engage in some form of physical violence in their roles. Today the phrase "culture of violence" is used to describe the current state of affairs. *Thesis statement* → These depictions of violence in the visual media may be impacting youth in unexpected, undesirable ways.

Running head →   Capers   2

Development paragraph 1 →   It is important to define what violence in the visual media is. Physical contact is not always considered violence. In sporting events, such as hockey or football, physical contact is considered part of the game. However, physicality can be abusive, even in game playing, particularly the type of gratuitous violence shown in video games. Kimberly Thompson's study "Violence in E-Rated Video Games" suggests that different types of games have varying levels of violence. She says the difference "may be explained by how the authors defined violence, which they described as 'acts in which the aggressor causes of attempts to cause physical injury or death to another character'" (Harvard Public Health Now 8). Therefore, most physical acts represented on television, on the internet, in video games, or in movies tend to be aggressive and reactive, and can be classified as "violent" images, according to this definition.

Development paragraph 2 →   Tolerance for depictions of violence is increasing. Michael Rich of the Harvard School of Public Health and Harvard Medical School "believes that exposure to violent images in the media—television, movies, video games, and music videos—has led to an increasing tolerance for violence by young people" (Research Matters, "How media violence touches children" (¶ 1). Other researchers claim that the increased tolerance for violence is due to viewers' desensitization toward it (Bandy ¶3). Being desensitized to depictions of violence means that producers must make films with more shock effects to gain attention for their movies or programs. Douglas A. Gentile and Craig A. Anderson refer to this outcome as "the bystander effect," in which viewers become "more callous, and less sympathetic to victims of violence" (134).

Development paragraph 3 →   Parental supervision is slowly being removed by the media. Parents ought to have the right to control what their children watch on television or see on the internet. Some argue that governments should support parents in their roles. The Chair of the House of Representatives, Subcommittee on Courts, the internet, and Intellectual Properties said in his opening remarks to the hearing for the *Family Movie Act* of 2004 that he was prepared to put forward this legislation "to protect the right of parents to shield their children from violence, sex, and profanity" (Family Move Act 2). Similarly, Canadian legislators have argued for parental controls.

Running head

Development paragraph 4

Specific negative behaviours are being modelled in cartoons and in other children's programming. Cartoons depict characters taking part in real-life activities, which many would find undesirable or offensive. Fumie Yokota and Kimberly Thompson "found nearly half of all G-rated animated feature films showed alcohol and tobacco use as normal behaviour and offered no warnings about the health consequences of using the substances" (cited in Harvard Health Now ¶ 16). Cartoon characters often carry weapons and use them indiscriminately to solve problems. Such representations can lead some viewers to copy what they see because "viewing violent portrayals may also lead to imitation of violent acts in real life" (Bandy ¶ 4).

Development paragraph 5

The length of viewing time may increase the negative impact. As children's time in front of a television or video screen increases, their time for physical activity decreases. Zero to Three, the web site for the National Center for Infants, Toddlers, and Families, states that obesity in preschoolers may go up for every hour of television or videos watched on a daily basis ("What the Research Tells Us About the Impact of Media on Young Children" (¶ 9). In addition, young children learn through sustained repetition. Even very young children can reproduce a behaviour like rattling a baby rattle if they observe the activity on video over a long period of time ("What the Research Tells Us About the Impact of Media on Young Children" ¶ 8). In fact, children's viewing times have increased significantly. Aletha Huston and her co-authors advise that by the time children are 18, they will have observed 200 000 acts of violence with 40 000 murders on television programming ¶ 8). The Senate Committee on the Judiciary, 1999, concluded that children who spend significant time viewing media are likely to demonstrate some aggressive behaviours and hold antagonistic values and attitudes.

Conclusion

Many media experts argue that sustained watching of representations of violence by young viewers influences their worldview, values, physical development, and attitudes. Parents fight for more control over what their youngsters are watching, while some government officials attempt to legislate control of the airwaves. Although scholars report young viewers are affected negatively by violent depictions in the media, they claim that how these effects will influence cognitive and social development is as yet not clear.

Title in bold and centred →

Works Cited

Set at margin →
Indent 5 spaces →

Bandy, Elizabeth. "Heroes and Villains: When is Media Violence Justified?" Stanford
Research Communication. 4 May 2001. http://www.stanford.edu/group

The Family Movie Act. House of Representatives, Subcommittee on Courts, the
Internet, and Intellectual Property, Committee on the Judiciary, Washington,
D.C. 17.14 Jun. 2004. [transcript]

Gentile, Douglas A. and Craig A. Anderson. Media Violence and Children: A Complete
Guide for Parents and Professionals (Advances in Applied Developmental Psychology). New York: Praeger Publishers, 2003.

Harvard Public Health Now. "Thompson Finds Some Video Games Rated 'Suitable
for Everyone' Contain Violence." Press release 2001
http://www.hsph.Harvard. edu/now.

Huston, Aletha. et al. Big World, Small Screen: The Role of Television in American
Society. Lincoln, NE: University of Nebraska Press, 1992.

Research Matters. "How media violence touches children."
http://www.researchmatters. harvard.edu.

Senate Committee on the Judiciary. "Children, Violence and the Media: A Report
for Parents and Policy Makers." 14 Sept. 1999.

"What the Research Tells Us about the Impact of Media on Young Children". Zero
to Three: National Center for Infants, Toddlers and Families.
http://www.zerothree.org 23 May. 2006.

SAMPLE PAPER #2: APA STYLE OF DOCUMENTATION

Running head

Canadian Innovation Leading to Victory   1

Title in bold and centred

Canadian Innovation Leading to Victory at Vimy Ridge

Your name

Chris Cownden

Your course name and section number

English 100 Section B

Date handed in

12 April 2007

All double spaced and centred.

Running head → Canadian Innovation Leading to Victory   2

Title in bold and centred → **Canadian Innovation Leading to Victory at Vimy Ridge**

Introduction → On 9 April 1917, 35 000 men of the Canadian Corp went "over the top" to try and take German positions on Vimy Ridge. The positions had been held by the Germans since 1914 and were among the most heavily fortified on the Western front. It is often wondered how the Canadian Corp managed to drive the Germans back almost 8 km in three days, the farthest Allied advance to that point in the war, when tens of thousands of French and British could not even get from their positions to the Germans 1000 metres away. General Arthur Currie introduced several radical innovations into the Canadian Corp prior to

Thesis statement → Vimy: their organization of the platoon unit being perhaps the most radical. It was this reorganization that can be credited with giving the Canadians the advantage they needed to overrun the German positions on Vimy Ridge.

Heading in bold and centred → **The Way Things Were**

Development paragraph 1 → The conversion in warfare up to and including the first half of The Great War was to have an army's platoon units consist entirely of one type of soldier. There would be a platoon of riflemen, one of machine gunners, another of grenadiers, and one of sappers, essentially grouping types together. Doctrine also dictated a straight ahead advance on the enemy along a linear front. For the types of war being fought at the time, this was effective enough as it would allow the various platoons to support each other in their operations and advances against the enemy. In The Great War, however, this method, while still used, became outdated because of the manner in which the war was fought. With the two sides dug in and fortified in their respective trenches, the machine gun became a primarily defensive weapon; therefore, the machine-gun platoons were left in the trenches and unable to effectively support advances against enemy positions without shooting their comrades in the back. Likewise, the segregation of grenadiers into separate platoons made it impractical for them to support riflemen who were pinned down by enemy machine-gun fire. Currie decided that "an infantry platoon had virtually none of the weaponry, and consequent tactical flexibility, needed to meet the peculiarities of trench fighting" (Greenhous & Harris, 1992, p. 58). This shortcoming was illustrated throughout the early war. The Entente continually hurled tens of thousands of infantrymen at the Germans only to have them cut down by machine-gun fire. This is chronicled well by Lewis (1918) who, writing about the first 30 minutes of the Battle of the Somme says, "By this time we had lost not only Major Delancy, but Lieuts. Hallesy, Sheriff, Feindel, Barber, as well as other officers wounded, and some 1200 men both killed and wounded" (p. 54). His

Running head

battalion began the day with a strength of 1500 men. So, Currie had identified what he believed to be his chief problem; now he had to fix it.

Heading in bold and centred

The Innovation

Development paragraph 2

To address this basic shortcoming in the armies of the Entente, General Arthur Currie decided to reorganize platoon units throughout the Canadian Corp prior to the assault on Vimy Ridge (Judson, Nielson & Haig, 1997). In the winter of 1916, Currie did just that. He decreed, "Henceforth, each platoon will consist of rifle, rifle grenade, bombing and machine gun sections" (as cited in Greenhous & Harris, 1992). The easy part now taken care of, Currie next had to see if his newly organized platoons would work; it is one thing to shift men around, but another entirely to make them work together as a cohesive unit. For two months prior to the battle, the newly organized Corps trained thoroughly. Currie also decided that the standard attack doctrine needed to be revised. Instead of the regulated charge ahead in an evenly spaced straight line, Currie's doctrine called for two much rougher lines of uncertain spacing (as cited in Duffy & Halpern, 2007), the idea here being that with the rougher two-line formation, the German machine guns would not be able to simply strafe down the advancing line and inflect horrific casualties. Currie now had his plan in place, and all that remained was to see if it would work.

Heading in bold and centred

The Results

Development paragraph 3

The Canadian Corp, with its new organization and doctrine in place, launched the attack on Vimy Ridge at 0530 hours on Easter morning, 1917. It was now time to see what effect General Arthur Currie's innovations would have on the battle. The advance on the German positions was swift and for the most part successful. By 1330 hours, every battalion save one had reached, and secured, its objectives. The new formations and tactics worked very well. A given platoon's machine-gun component was able to provide cover fire for the advancing infantry and the grenadiers were able to engage and neutralize German machine-gun nests with alarming effectiveness. These two factors enabled the riflemen and bombers to easily reach the enemy trenches; from that point there was little problem overcoming the fire teams and blowing up the dugouts. There were setbacks, as inherent to any military operation, but they, too, were swiftly and decisively overcome by selfless acts of bravery. Here, the after-action report of the Third Brigade illustrates several such acts, "and of the four hostile machine guns which attempted to hold up their advance, two were put out of action by mills bombs, one was attacked and put out of action by a party led by Lieut. Davidson, while the remaining gun was

Running head Canadian Innovation Leading to Victory   4

captured personally by CSM Hurley who bayoneted the crew" (as cited in Green-hous Harris, 1992, p. 88). Another such act is shown in the accounts of Lieutenant M.M. Lewis (1918) who wrote that "Private Milne sprang up from a gun nest . . . he crawled within bombing distance of it, and with his grenades had put it out of action" (p. 68). Private Milne was killed later that day while neutralizing another gun position; he was awarded the Victoria Cross posthumously.

Heading in bold and centred

Conclusion

Conclusion

    In the aftermath of Vimy Ridge, it can be concluded that General Arthur Currie's innovations in unit composition and tactical doctrine were as successful as the assault itself. The implementation of Currie's plans had allowed the Canadians to drive the Germans back an average of 7.5 kilometres along a 6-kilometre front that had been held for three years, since the beginning of the war. At some points, the Germans had been moved back only 9 kilometres. This was the farthest advance of Entente armies to this point in the war. Another key point on the relative success of the battle was that in four days of combat, there were 10 500 total Canadian casualties and only 3250 dead. While any loss of life is abhorrent, this figure is astounding since over 100 000 British and French soldiers had died trying to take the very same ridge. All in all, it appears that the idea of a Canadian General, who prior to the war was a Nanaimo real estate agent, was the key factor in the success of this pivotal battle of The Great War; so much so that now, the platoon compositions in modern armies are almost identical to those implemented by Currie in 1917.

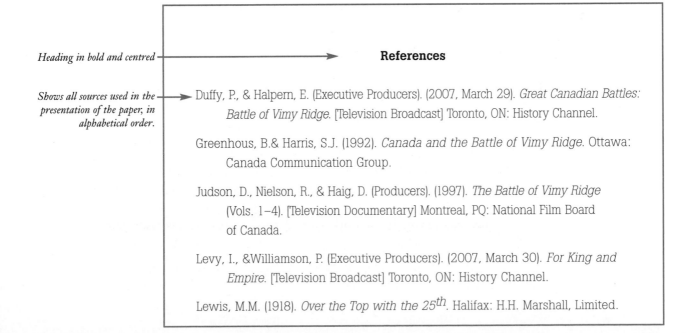

Heading in bold and centred

References

Shows all sources used in the presentation of the paper, in alphabetical order.

Duffy, P., & Halpern, E. (Executive Producers). (2007, March 29). *Great Canadian Battles: Battle of Vimy Ridge*. [Television Broadcast] Toronto, ON: History Channel.

Greenhous, B.& Harris, S.J. (1992). *Canada and the Battle of Vimy Ridge*. Ottawa: Canada Communication Group.

Judson, D., Nielson, R., & Haig, D. (Producers). (1997). *The Battle of Vimy Ridge* (Vols. 1–4). [Television Documentary] Montreal, PQ: National Film Board of Canada.

Levy, I., &Williamson, P. (Executive Producers). (2007, March 30). *For King and Empire*. [Television Broadcast] Toronto, ON: History Channel.

Lewis, M.M. (1918). *Over the Top with the 25th*. Halifax: H.H. Marshall, Limited.

chapter 11

Nouns, Pronouns, and Verbs

Chapter Objectives
After completing this chapter, you will be able to
- recognize some basic grammatical terms
- classify words according to their function
- distinguish between the object of a verb and the object of a preposition
- distinguish between action and non-action verbs
- identify and use the correct forms of nouns, pronouns, and verbs

INTRODUCTION: LEARNING ABOUT GRAMMAR

Grammar is a set of rules or guidelines applied to a language that enables you to understand the relationship between words in sentences. Studying grammar is an exercise in thinking. Your study of grammar will help you analyze and solve problems, using words as the tool.

Go step by step through this grammar study so that you understand each idea. Remember: always be sure you understand everything clearly. Chapter 11 will teach you about terms and functions regarding nouns, pronouns, and verbs.

Each grammar chapter contains a variety of exercises at the following three different levels of difficulty:

- Level of difficulty 1: introductory

- Level of difficulty 2: intermediate

- Level of difficulty 3: advanced

Choose level 1 of difficulty if you feel you will need to do a lot of work on the topic. Choose level 2 of difficulty if you have some knowledge of the topic and simply need to refresh your understanding of the ideas. Choose level 3 of difficulty if you feel you have mastered the ideas and want to challenge your knowledge.

In the following section, you will find a self-test that asks questions about the grammar ideas in Chapter 11. Each of the grammar chapters that follows also begins with a self-test to help you to determine what you know about grammar. Try writing the self-test before you do the work in the chapter. In this way, you will begin to understand how the tests can help you learn what you need to study. You will find the answers in the Answer Key.

Chapter 11: Self-Test

Part 1: Nouns, Level of Difficulty 2

Underline all nouns in the following sentences. (10 points)

1. Dr. Alonzo developed an understanding with her clients.
2. The representative has left the office, but he will be back in a moment.
3. In protest, several workers did not sign the petition.
4. The doctor gave them pills for their depression.

Part 2: Nouns as Subjects or Objects of Verbs, Level of Difficulty 2

All nouns are underlined. Write **S** above the nouns that work as subjects in the sentences. Write **O** above the nouns that work as objects of verbs in the sentences. Be careful: some nouns are acting as objects of prepositions and not objects of verbs. (10 points)

1. Eunsook and Pierre are planning to be married in the spring.
2. A fax machine sat in the hall.
3. Malcolm invited Bob to the club dinner.
4. High in the trees noisy crows squawked at us.
5. The group ordered French fries, sandwiches, and coffee for their meeting.

Part 3: Verbs, Level of Difficulty 1

Underline all verbs in the following sentences. (5 points)

1. We had been waiting for over two hours for our plane.
2. Marcus will be singing a duet with Patty.
3. Have you ever worked for the government?
4. The cornerstone of city hall is granite, polished bronze, and marble.
5. His uncle started the business several years ago.

Part 4: Verb Tenses, Level of Difficulty 1

Write **P** if the verb shows present action. Write **PT** if the verb shows past action. Write **F** if the verb shows future action. (10 points)

1. Oatmeal makes a nutritious and wholesome breakfast. _____
2. Will my dating improve by seeking professional advice? _____
3. Several chickens were wandering on the road. _____
4. Am I too direct when I talk? _____
5. Grumpily, Walter emptied the trash into the large container behind the store. _____
6. Butterflies are beautifully patterned. _____

7. Jocelyn hates snakes and treats them with disgust. _____

8. Had Rob forgotten his promise? _____

9. My supervisor was lecturing the new employee on appropriate dress for the office. _____

10. Ernest seemed to know everything about computer viruses. _____

Part 5: Verb Forms, Level of Difficulty 1

Give the correct form of the verb in each set of parentheses. (2 points each, 20 points)

1. The youngest children have _____ (eat) their lunches.

2. The man had _____ (swear) under his breath.

3. Yesterday I _____ (see) a golden eagle.

4. Five weeks ago they _____ (begin) their new jobs.

5. Rodd has _____ (do) something wonderful: he has created a family album.

6. No one had _____ (bring) any paper cups for the picnic.

7. We were _____ (choose) a bright wallpaper for the bathroom last week when we saw Rosie.

8. Clare has _____ (work) for the mobile phone company for 15 years.

9. Helen and Norm have _____ (write) a report to the Ministry of Education.

10. I may _____ (drive) to Port Townley on the weekend.

Part 6: Identifying Nouns, Pronouns, and Verbs, Level of Difficulty 2

Identify whether each underlined word is a noun, pronoun, or verb. Write your answers in the spaces. (½ point each, 5 points)

1. They were afraid of being publicly humiliated. _____

2. The union was upset by the offer, so they rejected it without hesitation. _____

3. I am flying to Reno, but I don't intend to gamble. _____

4. Were you interested in the meeting, or did you think it was a waste of time? _____

5. Does Bennie like kale because it is high in calcium? _____

6. The officer gave her some advice: don't speed in a school zone. _____

7. The garden lost its colour after the first fall frost. _____

8. Ivan is mixing the dough for three giant pizzas. _____

9. Carmelita loves dancing and has been a competitor for 12 years. _____

10. We gave it to Nicole when she returned from maternity leave. _____

Part 7: Identifying Action and Non-Action Verbs, Level of Difficulty 2

(5 points)

A. Underline all verbs. (½ point)

B. Identify whether each verb is action or non-action. Write your answers in the spaces. (½ point)

1. Ray decided to leave after he received the terrible news. _____

2. The tourists are too hot in the Mexican sun. _____

3. The cyclists stopped for a break under a wooden bridge by the coolness of a stream. _____

4. I thought about it and became calm. _____

5. Leslie is certain she will win the design contest. _____

Part 8: Identifying Verb Tenses, Level of Difficulty 3

Underline the verbs in each of the following sentences (½ point). Then identify the specific tense of each verb (½ point).

1. After the coroner has examined the victim, we will be expecting the chief investigator's office to issue a new set of charges.

2. When you are packing a cooler, put your most perishable goods like meat, poultry, or salads with mayonnaise on the bottom, and then pack your food in reverse order so that those items you expect to use first will be on top.

3. "Eating a little bit of chocolate or having a drink of hot cocoa as part of a regular diet is probably good for personal health, as long as people don't consume too much of it," Dr. Becker said.

4. We are now moving into the part of the fire season where human activities mainly cause outbreaks that become difficult to contain in rough terrain.

5. The passenger should have been wearing his seatbelt; had he done so, his injuries would have been less severe.

Exercise 1   Classifying, Level of Difficulty 1

In order to understand grammar, you must first be aware of how words are classified. Then you can begin to look at how classes of words function in sentences. Classify the following terms. You can check your answers in the Answer Key.

Example: wrench, pliers, screwdriver, hammer, chisel   <u>tools</u>

Terms   **Class**

1. poodle, cocker spaniel, German shepherd, Doberman pinscher   _____

2. knife, fork, spoon, scoop, spatula, pie lifter, chopsticks   _____

3. Volkswagen, Chevrolet, Chrysler, Mazda, Honda   _____

4. chair, table, stool, couch, bookshelf, bed   _____

5. mouse, rat, rabbit, bear, wolf, kangaroo, iguana   _____

How did you classify? What process did you go through? To understand classes of things, you recognize the characteristics or traits that the things have in common. Then you think of the name of the class.

Grammar consists of much the same sort of classifying. You will most often be able to determine the class of words in grammar not by shape, colour, or size as you did with some of the items above, but rather, by what each class of words does. In grammar, then, it is important to remember the term or **part of speech** (the name of the class of words) and **function** (what the words in this classification do in sentences).

NOUNS

A word is a noun if you can place the determiner *the*, *a*, or *an* in front of it, and if the addition makes sense. A noun names a person, place, or thing. It can be a **common noun**, such as actor, city, or queen, or a **proper noun**, such as Brad Pitt, Mumbai, or Queen Elizabeth.

Exercise 2   Nouns, Level of Difficulty 1

Underline all the words below that can be classed as nouns. Check your answers in the Answer Key.

foot	wagon	rum	rare
apricot	joke	sauce	examination
planet	magnificent	create	hate
main	love	moist	harbour
end	paint	retire	community
law	tent	hero	sit
hours	kip	person	
television	kitchen	ghetto	

Concrete and Abstract Nouns

In grammar, we use the words **concrete** and **abstract** to classify nouns. The term *concrete* designates the class of nouns that names tangible material things. Words like *gate* or *truck* are concrete nouns. Here are some examples of concrete nouns:

cigarette, building, barn, dinner, pen, Andy

The term **abstract** designates the class of nouns that names such things as ideas, emotions, and situations. A word like *safety* is an abstract noun because it refers to a state or condition. An abstract noun like *anger* refers to an emotion. Here are some examples of abstract nouns:

> fear, tension, accident, argument, worry

Exercise 3   Concrete and Abstract Nouns, Level of Difficulty 1

Underline all the nouns in the following sentences. Write **A** above every noun that is abstract. Write **C** above every noun that is concrete. Check your answers in the Answer Key.

             C   **A**   **C**

The small **child** toddled off in the **direction** of its **mother**.

1. The passengers waited for the bus in the pouring rain.

2. Ronnie bought two more models for his collection.

3. The artist used coloured paper, scissors, glue, and a soft pencil.

4. Many children hate games if they cannot be the boss.

5. The rusty ship waited for a new coat of grey paint.

6. The smiling prince bowed to the guests at the dinner party.

7. Outside the hotel gunshots and cannon fire broke the silence.

8. The carpenter pounded finishing nails into the trim around the window.

9. The eggs fell to the pavement and smashed.

10. The television program was too long.

11. The company will send the order by delivery van.

12. The baby skunk wandered out of the bushes and stood on the path to the shed.

13. The wasp stung the old woman without warning.

14. Paul brought his father's truck back to the farm.

15. The fight in the bar was over a rule in hockey.

Exercise 4   Concrete and Abstract Nouns, Level of Difficulty 1

List 10 concrete nouns and 10 abstract nouns. Do not use any from the lists or your practice exercises. Ask another class member to evaluate your answers.

Concrete Nouns   **Abstract Nouns**

    1. _____   1. _____

    2. _____   2. _____

    3. _____   3. _____

    4. _____   4. _____

5. _____	5. _____
6. _____	6. _____
7. _____	7. _____
8. _____	8. _____
9. _____	9. _____
10. _____	10. _____

Nouns as Subjects and Objects of Verbs

A noun names a person, place, or thing. However, that definition does not clarify how a noun functions in a sentence. For example, nouns can function as subjects or as objects of verbs in sentences. To figure out how a word functions, you have to study the whole sentence in which the word is found.

The subject of the sentence is the *doer of the action* or *who or what the sentence is about.*

The frog hopped across the path. (*Frog* is the subject because it did the action.)

To determine what the subject in a sentence is, think about who or what the sentence is all about. If you consider that the sentence above is about a frog, you can then say that the subject of the sentence is the word *frog*.

Exercise 5   Subject Nouns, Level of Difficulty 1

Write down which noun is the subject noun, or the doer of the action. All nouns are underlined, but not all nouns are functioning as subject nouns. Check your answers in the Answer Key.

1. Marie prepared a fresh, green salad for the community school buffet. _____

2. The small dog barked at the postal carrier on the street. _____

3. The boxer threw a left-handed punch at his opponent's jaw. _____

4. Terry erased her math mistakes with a large, pink eraser. _____

5. Sylvia interrupted the meeting to announce some news. _____

6. The workers noticed an enormous opening in the earth near the gravel bed. _____

7. Wally scrubbed the deck with an abrasive cleanser. _____

8. Seven dancers entertained people in the streets. _____

9. The wolf hunted the shaggy, sick moose. _____

10. The car skidded from the intersection and into the path of the oncoming tour bus. _____

11. The soccer team won the match, but the captain felt disheartened by the crowd's jeers. _____

12. The train halted near the tunnel as the snowplough cleared the tracks. _____

All of the subject nouns performed the action in each of the sentences in the exercise above. How can you tell which noun is the subject if a sentence shows no action?

If a sentence does not express action, it is a sentence of description. The subject noun in this type of sentence will be the main noun that is described; in other words, it is best to begin by asking, "What is this sentence all about?"

There is a girl in the hallway.

This sentence has no action word. So you must figure out which noun the sentence is mainly about. Is this sentence about a hallway or about a girl? Because the sentence is all about the girl, *girl* is the subject noun of the sentence.

Exercise 6   Subject Nouns, Level of Difficulty 2

All of the sentences below show no action; they are sentences of description. All nouns are underlined. Write down which noun is the subject noun. Check your answers in the Answer Key.

1. Many <u>times</u> during the Shakespearean <u>festival</u>, the <u>actor</u> was absent for <u>rehearsal</u>. _____

2. For 24 <u>years</u>, <u>Margaret</u> was a <u>secretary</u> at the local elementary <u>school</u>. _____

3. The <u>paper</u> was dotted with <u>specks</u> of <u>paint</u>. _____

4. My <u>dog, Kady</u>, loves to play with a tennis <u>ball</u>. _____

5. <u>Yesterday</u> at nine o'clock, <u>Tom</u> was in the <u>cafeteria</u> for the early bird <u>special</u>. _____

6. <u>Yogurt</u>, a nutritious <u>treat</u>, is easy to find at any food <u>store</u>. _____

7. The <u>soup</u> was made from fresh <u>vegetables</u> and <u>chicken</u>. _____

8. The <u>lawn</u> near the swimming <u>pool</u> was healthy and green. _____

9. There are <u>cookies</u> on the <u>shelf</u> in the <u>pantry</u>. _____

10. The <u>lamp</u> from <u>Sears</u> is not suitable for the <u>playroom</u>. _____

11. <u>Philip</u> was in the <u>library</u> at <u>lunchtime</u>, preparing for his economics <u>exam</u>. _____

12. <u>Children</u> under 9 <u>kg</u> must be secured in a rearward-facing child safety <u>seat</u>. _____

Nouns can also function as objects of verbs in sentences. An object is the *receiver of the action* of the verb. It answers *what?* after the action verb.

Annie bought some beautiful yellow roses.

Annie is a noun and functions as the subject of the sentence; *Annie* did the action of buying *roses*. The word *roses* is also a noun, but it is not functioning as the subject of the sentence. Roses are what Annie bought. *Roses* receive the action; roses are the object of the verb "bought."

The following examples illustrate how nouns can be the objects of action verbs. Remember to use the action word and then ask *what?* or *who?* or *whom?*

The cook fired the sous-chef for insubordination and tardiness.

The cook is the subject noun.
Ask: The cook fired whom?

Answer: the *sous-chef*, so sous-chef is the object of the action verb *fired*.

China has lifted its ban on poultry and poultry products from Canada.

China is the subject noun.
Ask: China has lifted what?
Answer: *its ban*, so *ban* is the object of the action verb *lifted*.

Exercise 7   Subject Nouns and Object Nouns, Level of Difficulty 2

All nouns have been underlined. Write **S** above every noun that acts as a subject. Write **O** above every noun that is functioning as an object of the verb in the sentence. Some sentences can have more than one object; others may not have any at all!

Do not write **O** above objects of prepositions. Look at sentence 1 below. In phrases like "with a light motion," *with* is a preposition or word of direction. *Motion* is the object of the preposition *with*. If you ask the question "With what?" *motion* is the answer. Therefore, *motion* is the object of the preposition *with*; it is not the object of the verb. It is not what got sanded. After you complete the exercise, check your answers in the Answer Key.

1. <u>Rodd</u> sanded the <u>plywood</u> with a light <u>motion</u>.

2. The <u>students</u> set the <u>rules</u> for the psychology <u>classroom</u>.

3. The greedy <u>man</u> hid his <u>money</u> underneath the <u>floorboards</u>.

4. The <u>puppy</u> grabbed the <u>rag</u> on the <u>floor</u> and tugged.

5. Mrs. <u>Pobsby</u> rolled up the <u>rug</u> in the living <u>room</u> and began to rumba.

6. The <u>chef</u> tossed the <u>salad</u> into the <u>air</u> in order to entertain his <u>guests</u>.

7. The young <u>boy</u> sprained his <u>ankle</u> in the <u>fall</u> from his <u>skateboard</u>.

8. Her <u>cousin</u> ate a whole, giant <u>pizza</u> last <u>night</u>!

9. <u>Ozzie</u> collects <u>rocks</u> and <u>stones</u> from the <u>beach</u>.

10. Last March <u>Madame Lem</u> predicted a <u>disaster</u> in <u>California</u>.

You will learn more about nouns as objects of prepositions later in this chapter.

Exercise 8   Subject Nouns and Object Nouns, Level of Difficulty 1

Underline all nouns; write **S** above all nouns that work as subjects, and write **O** above all nouns that work as objects of the verbs. You can check your answers in the Answer Key.

       S   **O**
The **tourists** bought **souvenirs** from the **pedlars** near the **wharf**.

1. The child drew a picture of his new home in the subdivision.

2. The coffee from the restaurant tasted sour and burned.

3. A crow was digging our garbage from the bins.

4. Near the stream beside an old oak a girl was reading a novel.

5. The supervisor threw a surprise party for her staff.

6. On the weekend the family had a picnic at Fairview Hill Park.

7. Francis bought a parrot from a travelling salesman.

8. Charlie spent too much time on his project.

9. The gentleman ordered a ham sandwich and a beer.

10. Harvey cooked a delicious spaghetti sauce for last night's supper.

Nouns can be of two types: *concrete* and *abstract*. Nouns can function as *subjects* or *objects* within sentences. You should also know that a sentence can contain more than one subject or more than one object. This means that two or more people or things could be doing the action. In grammar, you call having more than one subject a **compound subject** and having more than one object a **compound object**.

Alexander, Phillip, and Terry were rowing the boat.

Three people are the subjects or doers of this sentence; therefore, this sentence contains a compound subject.

Jessie bought scissors, fabric, bias tape, and a pattern for her new summer outfit.

Notice that Jessie bought a number of items. In other words, *scissors*, *fabric*, *tape*, and *pattern* are all functioning as objects of the verb—a compound object.

Exercise 9   Subject Nouns and Object Nouns, Level of Difficulty 2

First underline all nouns. Then find all subjects and objects in the sentences below. Write **S** above subject nouns and **O** above object nouns. Be careful: not all sentences contain objects. Do not write **O** above objects of prepositions.

1. The real estate agent and the owner negotiated the price of the land.

2. Maxwell built a small, wooden bridge over the ravine.

3. The astronauts measured the temperature of the atmosphere outside the module.

4. The kittens were abandoned in the old house.

5. Several pilots were removed from active duty.

6. Many people like smaller foreign cars and trucks.

7. Gasoline and water do not mix.

8. Hot blueberry muffins are delicious with butter.

9. The players and the coach were overjoyed with the victory.

10. Four teenagers pushed the dune buggy to the service station.

11. Stella's eyes were irritated by the dust.

12. Sound and light travel in waves.

13. The early explorers reached the coast of Canada hundreds of years ago.

14. The honeybee landed on a bright, purple wildflower.

15. The students and teachers of Halifax Elementary visited Gloaming Park.

PRONOUNS

Pronouns are another class of words in grammar. Because pronouns can *take the place of nouns*, they can do the same work as nouns (*pro = for*); in other words, they can work as subjects or objects, in sentences.

Any noun can have a pronoun substitute. Instead of saying a person's name, you might say *he* or *she*, or *you*. Consider the two sentences below. The first one contains all nouns; the second sentence substitutes pronouns for the nouns.

Iris told Bill that Iris was wrapping the gift for the teachers.

She told him that she was wrapping it for them.

Pronouns take on the same functions in sentences as nouns.

      subject   object of verb
The young **supervisor** was finishing the **project**.

However, there is a difference between noun use and pronoun use. The subject form of a pronoun is not the same as its object form.

In the following examples, consider what happens to the subject form of the pronoun when it becomes the object of a verb.

subject   object of verb
1. **I** left **him** alone in the gym after school.

subject   object of verb
2. **He** left **me** alone in the gym after school.

The subject form of the pronoun *I* in sentence 1 changes to *me* in sentence 2 when used as an object. Notice, too, that the subject form of the pronoun *he* in sentence 2 changes to *him* when used as an object in sentence 1.

In the following examples, consider what happens to the subject form of the pronoun when it becomes the object of a preposition.

subject   object of preposition
1. **She** gave the assignment to **them**.

subject   object of preposition
2. **They** gave the assignment to **her**.

The subject form of the pronoun *she* in sentence 1 changes to the form *her* in sentence 2, when used as the object of a preposition. Notice, too, that the subject form of the pronoun *they* in sentence 2 changes to *them* when used as the object of a preposition in sentence 1.

Pronoun Changes of Form

Subject Case	Object Case
I	me
he	him
she	her
it	it
we	us
you	you
they	them

Exercise 10 *Pronouns, Level of Difficulty 2*

Substitute pronouns for nouns. Check your answers in the Answer Key.

Noun	Pronoun Substitutes
1. the watch	_____
2. Mark and Jane	_____
3. the dog	_____
4. an instructor	_____
5. the government	_____
6. the television	_____
7. Mr. Feldman	_____
8. children	_____
9. The worker drank the tea.	_____
10. Mrs. Grabowski and Mr. Fisher are here to see Mrs. Gallant.	_____
11. The chicks and hens were pecking for worms.	_____
12. The landlady talked to the city councillor.	_____
13. Ross doesn't mind work, so his family appreciates Ross.	_____
14. Ruth's son went to see the show.	_____
15. The books sold quickly, a surprise to Robyn.	_____

Exercise 11 Subject and Object Nouns and Pronouns, Level of Difficulty 2

Underline all nouns. Put all pronouns in parentheses. Write **S** above the nouns or pronouns that are working as subjects, and write **O** above the nouns or pronouns working as objects of the verbs. Check your answers in the Answer Key.

    S   **S**   **O**   **O**
Valerie and **Stan** enjoy their **children** and their **home**.

                 S
(They) received a **call** about the **shipment**.

      S
The **trees** in the **forest** have been attacked by spruce **budworm**.

1. We whipped the cream for the icing.
2. Rhonda wrote a poem about Daisy's childhood.
3. The mayor opened the new art gallery in downtown Calgary.
4. After the meeting, he took the reports to his home.
5. I watched the parade for two hours.
6. Books and papers were missing from the room, but nothing of value was taken.
7. During the night, we heard voices in the backyard.
8. John and I will investigate the charge immediately after the hearing.
9. She broke it.
10. Al left the meat on the counter, and it spoiled.
11. You caught a cold and the chills from the rainy, freezing weather.
12. I taught Joe and her to play tennis.
13. We broadcast the program; however, the audience hated it.
14. The dogs and the cat chased the squirrel up the tree.
15. He shut the window to his office and closed the door for the evening.

Exercise 12 Review of Nouns and Pronouns, Level of Difficulty 2

Use separate paper. Clearly label the exercise. Your instructor may ask to see this review.

1. Write three sentences. Each sentence should contain at least one concrete noun. Underline each concrete noun.

2. Write three sentences. Each sentence should contain at least one abstract noun. Underline each abstract noun.

3. In three separate sentences, use the following three words as nouns working as subjects.

   1. Mark   2. the designer   3. cheating

4. In three separate sentences, use these three words as nouns working as objects of verbs.

   a. cash   b. doctor   c. nails

5. Make up two sentences of your own that have compound subjects. Underline the compound subjects.

6. Make up two sentences of your own that have compound objects of verbs. Underline the compound objects.

7. Use three pronouns working as subjects in three clear sentences.

8. Use three pronouns working as objects in three clear sentences.

VERBS

Verbs are another class of words in grammar. You can see how verbs function in sentences by considering what the subject does or by viewing how the subject is linked to the rest of the sentence.

There are two types of verbs, each having a different task.

1. **Action verbs tell what subjects do in sentences**. They tell what action the subject performs.

   The judge <u>marked</u> the score on the official form.

2. **Non-action verbs link the parts of the sentence together**. They do not tell what subjects do. Instead, they tell about the state of the subject by describing or renaming it.

   Michael Ondaatje <u>is</u> a Canadian writer who <u>was</u> born in Sri Lanka.

Action Verbs

Think of an action verb as a word that shows what someone or something can do; ask yourself: "Could I do this?"

Actions can be either mental or physical.

I <u>walk</u> to work. (physical action)

I <u>think</u> about it. (mental action)

I <u>annoyed</u> him. (mental action)

I <u>laughed</u> at the joke. (physical action)

Exercise 13   *Action Verbs, Level of Difficulty 2*

Underline the action verbs in the sentences below. Remember that some verbs do not show action. Check your answers in the Answer Key.

1. Much to my surprise, the alarm clock rang at six this morning.

2. Sparky caught a mouse and carried it into the house.

3. My son is very tall for a 14-year-old.

4. Monique swims every Saturday, although she is 80 years old.

5. The gardener seeded the lawn carefully and tamped the ground gently.

6. Since it was Wednesday, we cooked hamburgers for supper and then went out for dessert.

7. Each year for seven years we drove to Long Beach to camp.

8. Eleanor traded in her stereo and bought an MP3 player.

9. I understood his meaning when he winked at me.

10. They wrote the tragic story of their grandfather's imprisonment.

Non-Action (Linking) Verbs

Some verbs do not show action. If a sentence describes, it contains a non-action, or linking verb. It links the subject with the words that describe it. Here are some sentence examples of linking verbs:

I **am** tall.

The ice cream **tastes** great.

The book **was** thrilling.

Non-action verbs are called linking verbs when they appear alone in sentences. Linking verbs link the parts of sentences together; they also tell about the state of the subject. The subjects in these sentences do not do anything; the sentence merely describes them.

Monica is afraid.

In this sentence, Monica is being described. She is not performing any action.

Examples of Non-Action Verbs

am	appear
look	become
is	was
taste (no object)	are
were	feel
seem	smell (no object)
sound (no object)	

Exercise 14   *Action and Non-Action Verbs, Level of Difficulty 2*

Underline all verbs in each sentence. Write **ACT** above those showing actions, and write **NO ACT** above those showing no action. Check your answers in the Answer Key.

1. The dog lay in the sun and panted heavily.

2. Ralph is my brother, and he is 11 years older than I am.

3. The student had $40 for the book, but she discovered the cover price was more.

4. The dinner smells spicy, and the music sounds romantic.

5. We were in the store for a few minutes only when two burglars entered.

6. The teacher said, "Grammar is fun!"

7. The newspaper reporters interviewed the president of France.

8. Here are the missing sets of keys to your luggage!

9. The couple purchased a tent trailer for their mountain vacation.

10. Yin will be on time for his wedding, despite his repeated lateness.

11. Susan was afraid of bugs if they crawled on her bed.

12. The English instructor is absent from class, so today's session is off.

Non-Action (Auxiliary) Verbs

You can combine non-action verbs with action verbs to be very exact about the time or condition of the action. Non-action verbs used with action verbs are **helping verbs** because they help the action to be complete or exact. They are also referred to as **auxiliary verbs**. Together they form **verb phrases**.

We will be sewing our own clothes this fall.

Sewing is the action verb. *Will* and *be* are the non-action, or helping verbs. These helping verbs show that the action will take place in the future. The words *will be sewing* are a verb phrase.

Nora should be earning a good wage.

Earning is the action verb. *Should* and *be* are the helping verbs. These helping verbs help to set the condition on earning: Nora ought to be earning a good wage. In another sense, you might be wondering how much money Nora is making these days, and saying that at this time in her working life, "Nora should be earning a good wage."

Notice that some auxiliary verbs indicate time, while others indicate condition.

He can walk. (meaning he is able to—shows condition)

She might sing. (she hasn't quite decided yet—shows condition)

I was paddling the canoe. (shows time—was indicates the past).

You can add non-action verbs to action verbs to make a *verb phrase*. The non-action verbs are called *auxiliary* verbs.

NA   AV
I **am walking** to work.

Typical Helping or Auxiliary Verbs

can	am	did
has	might	would
been	be	had
must	may	does
were	are	shall
was	could	do
will	have	
should	is	

    NA   AV
She **was bending** the rules.
    NA   AV
Rod **has swept** the garage.

Sometimes auxiliary verbs show time in sentences. In the following examples, verbs have been underlined.

He <u>is sleeping</u>. (*Is* shows that the action of sleeping occurs in the present.)

I <u>am falling</u> in love. (*Am* shows that the action of falling occurs in the present.)

He <u>did know</u>. (*Did* shows that the action of knowing occurred in the past.)

The cat <u>was creeping</u> along the ground on its belly. (*Was* indicates past.)

They <u>were choosing</u> a colour for the bathroom. (*Were* indicates past.)

We <u>are leaving</u> for Ottawa. (*Are* indicates present.)

I <u>did knit</u> this sweater by myself. (*Did* indicates past.)

Mark <u>will steer</u> the boat. (*Will* indicates future.)

I <u>am beginning</u> a new book. (*Am* indicates present.)

Sometimes helpers set up a special condition for the action verb. These verbs are called **modals**, or **modal auxiliaries**. In the following examples, verbs have been underlined.

I <u>can skate</u>. (*Can* shows that you have the ability to do the action of skating.)

Fran <u>may leave</u> now. (*May* shows that there is permission to leave.)

The welder <u>might quit</u> his job. (*Might* indicates a choice.)

He <u>must stop</u>. (*Must* shows no choice.)

The baby <u>should sleep</u> well tonight. (*Should* indicates a condition—the baby ought to sleep well. *Should* often indicates a prediction.)

The social worker <u>would know</u> what to do. (*Would* indicates a condition—this person will probably know. *Would* is often used in reported speech.)

The puppy <u>could learn</u> quickly. (*Could* is the past of *can*; it indicates a subject knows how to do something.)

Exercise 15   Action and Non-Action Verbs, Level of Difficulty 2

Underline all the verb phrases in the following sentences. Look for both action and non-action (linking or auxiliary) verbs. Include modals as well.

1. We feel honoured because Borys is coming to dinner tonight.

2. Although she has seen you before, she will not admit it.

3. The flowers and vegetables have grown well this season, so our harvest should be abundant.

4. Will you be needing the car, or will you be taking a taxi?

5. Adding detergents to washing water will produce grey water.

6. I was going to develop my vocabulary through crossword puzzles.

7. Must you snore so loudly?

8. Did they teach you anything at tennis camp?

9. Would we prefer not to answer the questions on the survey?

10. The women were losing some benefits on the job and were protesting their losses as cutbacks.

11. Machiko can stay here tonight until she can locate a new apartment.

12. Could you ever strike it rich on Lotto 6/49?

Basic Verb Tenses

The form of the verb that expresses time is called the **verb tense**. Verbs can have three basic tenses: present, past, and future.

Simple Tense

I walk to the college campus. (*Walk* indicates **simple present** tense. The sentence indicates the speaker walks to campus often and that he or she continues the habit of walking.)

I walked to the college campus. (*Walked* indicates the **simple past** tense. The sentence means the speaker has just finished walking. It may be that the speaker walks to campus once in a while; we are not certain, but we do know that the speaker has completed the action for the time being.)

I will walk to the college campus. (*Will walk* indicates the **simple future** tense. The sentence means the speaker has the intention of walking. He or she has not yet done the action; the speaker is telling us of an action that will take place in the future.)

Note that the simple tenses usually contain only one verb.

I run to the bus each day. (simple present)

I ran to the bus each day. (simple past)

I will run to the bus each day. (simple future)

Progressive and Perfect Tenses

PROGRESSIVE TENSES

I am walking to the college campus. (*Am walking* indicates the **present progressive** tense. The sentence means that the speaker is in the process of walking. The action is in progress: the action continues over a period of time.)

I was walking to the college campus when I saw a deer. (*Was walking* indicates the **past progressive** tense. The sentence means the person was in the process of walking in the past when he or she noticed a deer.)

I will be walking to the college campus this week. (*Will be walking* indicates the **future progressive** tense. The sentence means the person will perform the action of walking in the future. The sentence indicates the action will happen over time—one week.)

Here are more examples of the progressive tense:

I am learning to play the guitar in the evenings. (present progressive)

Esther is waiting for her partner right now. (present progressive)

The neighbour was painting his garage door during the weekend. (past progressive)

My friends are having coffee with their supervisor from three until four today. (present progressive)

Our chickens were escaping from their pen when I saw them in the morning. (past progressive)

We will be expecting you for dinner at seven o'clock. (future progressive)

PERFECT TENSE

I have walked to the college campus every day for five years. (*Have walked* indicates **the present perfect** tense. The sentence means that the action you started five years ago continues to this day. Notice "have" or "has" is in the present tense.)

Sometimes the present perfect tense is used when you do not know exactly when an action happened in the past. For example, you could say, "His brother has resigned from his position," indicating an action occurred at an unspecified time. You are not exactly sure when his brother did the action.

However, if you use the past perfect tense, it means that an action you started in the past is now over. Another action or habit might begin after that.

I had walked to the college campus before I moved away. (*Had walked* indicates the **past perfect** tense. An action you started in the past no longer continues today.)

Generally speaking, when you use a past perfect verb in a sentence that contains another action, the past perfect happens first.

Sheila had wanted some peace and quiet, so she wandered off by herself. (Sheila's wanting peace and quiet occurred before she wandered off.)

When you use the future perfect tense, it means that you expect an event to conclude before a specified time.

I will have walked to the campus by eight o'clock. (*Will have walked* indicates the **future perfect** tense. This sentence means that you predict an action to be completed by a certain future time; it also implies another future action will take place.)

Here are more examples of the perfect tense:

He <u>has wanted</u> to marry her for a long time. (present perfect)

They <u>have tried</u> to convince him to quit smoking. (present perfect)

Marvin <u>had peddled</u> his invention at trade fairs before he applied for a patent. (past perfect)

Note the difference in meaning between these two sentences:

Eagles <u>have nested</u> in that tree for four seasons. (present perfect—The eagles started the habit of nesting in a particular tree and are expected to continue their habit of nesting there.)

Eagles <u>had nested</u> in that tree for four seasons. (past perfect—The eagles no longer nest there. Their habit of nesting in that particular tree is over.)

PERFECT PROGRESSIVE TENSE

When the perfect tense is placed with the progressive tense, the form is called the *perfect progressive*. This form is used when you want to emphasize an action over time.

Tyron has been practising his karate since he was six. (*Has been practising* is the **present perfect progressive** tense. It indicates that Tyron's activity has occurred over a long period of time and is continuing into the present.)

Tyron had been practising his karate since noon when he was interrupted by a phone call. (*Had been practising* indicates the **past perfect progressive** tense. It indicates that Tyron was completing an action over time in the past; now the action is over.)

Tyron will have been practising his karate for the Olympic tryouts. (*Will have been practising* indicates the **future perfect progressive** tense. The sentence indicates that Tyron will perform an action over time in the future. The future perfect progressive tense emphasizes a length of time over which an action occurs. Usually a second action or a reason for the first action is implied. In this case, Tyron will practise in order to compete.)

Exercise 16   *Identifying Verb Tense, Level of Difficulty 2*

Read each sentence and underline the verbs. Then write whether the verb is
- simple present, past, or future
- present, past, or future progressive
- present perfect progressive, past perfect progressive, or future perfect progressive.

Check your answers in the Answer Key.

1. Olivia has been wanting to buy a house in Calgary for several years now.

2. Several of the voters had left before the candidate arrived.

3. Have you been standing there all this time?

4. Montrose had loved the opera all his life.

5. If the bus is not running on time, Marcella expects to be late.

6. No one knew the handsome stranger who was drinking alone at the bar.

7. Twelve kittens had been sold before we selected one.

8. Mannequins can be so lifelike that customers will often ask them for directions.

9. Were the restaurant owners fighting the new ban on smoking?

10. The Count de la Roy will have written his book by the time we arrive at his castle.

11. Have Daniella and Peter ever gone out on a date together?

12. The chief of police suspected the person who was sitting next to him at the banquet.

Regular and Irregular Verbs

Verbs are called **regular verbs** if they form the past tense by adding a *d* or *ed* to the base form of the verb. Verbs are called **irregular** if they do not end in a *d* or *ed*. Their spellings are different in the past tense.

Some Regular Verbs

Present	Past
work	worked
talk	talked
look	looked
fix	fixed
hope	hoped

Some Irregular Verbs

Present	Past
become	became
begin	began
break	broke
bring	brought
catch	caught
choose	chose
come	came
do	did

(continued)

Present	Past
draw	drew
drink	drank
drive	drove
eat	ate
fall	fell
feed	fed
fly	flew
forgive	forgave
freeze	froze
give	gave
go	went
grow	grew
know	knew
ride	rode
ring	rang
rise	rose
run	ran
see	saw
sing	sang
speak	spoke
spin	spun
steal	stole
swear	swore
swim	swam
take	took
throw	threw
wear	wore
write	wrote

Exercise 17   *Verb Forms, Level of Difficulty 1*

A. Fill in the form of the verb that is required in each sentence.

B. Then at the end of each sentence, indicate if the verb is in the past, present, or future. Be prepared to share your answers.

I was <u>reading</u> (read) a book all day. (past)

1. The young birds are _____ (feed) from our backyard feeder this morning. _____

2. She must _____ (write) a note to her old friend who is very ill. _____

3. Because of her viral infection, we _____ (worry) about the baby last year. _____

4. Last week Tamas _____ (fly) to Kamloops to join his brother's firm. _____

5. Did she _____ (freeze) the fish he caught, or did she prepare it for smoking? _____

6. I will _____ (forgive) Arnold soon, but for the time being, my feelings are hurt. _____

7. Please _____ (speak) louder; I have a slight hearing loss. _____

8. Marvin _____ (take) lots of chances with his clients' money. _____

9. They were _____ (donate) the old flat screen TV to the charity auction. _____

10. Every winter I _____ (catch) a cold no matter what I do. _____

11. Tina does _____ (drive) a truck for a living. _____

12. The children will _____ (become) cranky if they get too tired. _____

13. The crew _____ (stop) filming at eleven last night when the storm _____ (break). _____

14. The advisory committee _____ (meet) to collaborate on the task. _____

15. Last October my elderly neighbour _____ (fall) on an icy patch and _____ (break) her hip.

16. The sailors are _____ (wear) dress uniforms for the presentation ceremony. _____

17. Someone who has a concussion should not _____ (participate) in any physical activity for two weeks. _____

18. Mrs. Upton _____ (rise) each day at 5 a.m. and _____ (feed) the swans at the pond's edge.

19. The clerk _____ (swear) under his breath, but the customer did not _____ (hear) him.

20. The Clarks _____ (go) to the prairies last summer and _____ (visit) Head-Smashed-In Buffalo Jump in Alberta.

Has, Have, and Had as Auxiliary Verbs

When you add *has*, *have*, or *had* to some verbs, they form an irregular past participle. Choose the correct form when you are writing.

Irregular Past Participles

Present	Past	Past Participle
become	became	has, have, had become
begin	began	has, have, had begun
break	broke	has, have, had broken
bring	brought	has, have, had brought
catch	caught	has, have, had caught
choose	chose	has, have, had chosen
come	came	has, have, had come
do	did	has, have, had done
draw	drew	has, have, had drawn
drink	drank	has, have, had drunk
drive	drove	has, have, had driven
eat	ate	has, have, had eaten
fall	fell	has, have, had fallen
feed	fed	has, have, had fed
fly	flew	has, have, had flown
forgive	forgave	has, have, had forgiven
freeze	froze	has, have, had frozen
give	gave	has, have had given
go	went	has, have, had gone
grow	grew	has, have, had grown
know	knew	has, have, had known
ride	rode	has, have, had ridden
ring	rang	has, have, had rung
rise	rose	has, have, had risen
run	ran	has, have, had run
see	saw	has, have, had seen
sing	sang	has, have, had sung

(continued)		
speak	spoke	has, have, had spoken
spin	spun	has, have, had spun
steal	stole	has, have, had stolen
swear	swore	has, have, had sworn
swim	swam	has, have, had swum
take	took	has, have, had taken
tear	tore	has, have, had torn
throw	threw	has, have, had thrown
wear	wore	has, have, had worn
write	wrote	has, have, had written

Exercise 18   Adding Verb Forms, Level of Difficulty 1

Add the correct form of the verb to each of the following sentences. Check your answers in the Answer Key.

1. Cecilia has _____ (write) a cheque for a down payment on the car.

2. Has he _____ (forgive) you for the damage to his bike?

3. Ming had _____ (take) out a loan to go to business school.

4. Have the students _____ (break) the plagiarism policy?

5. We have _____ (throw) out our old bad habits and _____ (replace) them with positive ones.

6. I had _____ (know) him for only a short time when he suddenly _____ (pass) away.

7. We _____ (see) the premier last week, but she _____ (fail) to notice use.

8. Raisins and almonds had _____ (give) me energy, so I _____ (swim) an extra 500 metres.

9. Have you ever _____ (ride) a camel?

10. Last night it _____ (begin) to get chilly, and we _____ (light) the woodstove.

11. Rajit and Elsie have _____ (speak) to me about the strange arrangements.

12. The children _____ (become) silent because they were afraid.

13. Have they _____ (choose) their new class president?

14. How many times have you _____ (write) your essay?

15. The RCMP have _____ (give) out some information about the missing German tourist.

Combined Review Exercise 19 Level of Difficulty 3

Complete this combined exercise that is a bit more challenging. Check the Answer Key for some sample answers.

1. Write a sentence that contains one subject noun, one object noun, and a verb in the simple progressive.

2. Using the future perfect tense, write a sentence containing two subject nouns and a form of the verb *fly*.

3. Write a sentence that contains three verbs; one of the verbs should be in the past perfect progressive. Use a form of the verb *steal*.

4. Using the past participle of *spin*, write a sentence that contains a compound subject and a compound verb. The verbs should be in the past perfect tense.

5. Using the past participle of *freeze*, make up a sentence that contains two objects and two verbs. Use the past in both verbs.

Chapter 11: Review Test

Your instructor may want to see your test.

Part 1: Nouns, Level of Difficulty 1

Underline all nouns in the following sentences. (10 points)

1. Clifford bought junk food from the convenience store.

2. The investigator will generate a special report.

3. Several chips of wood flew off the saw.

4. Her anger interrupted her concentration.

Part 2: Nouns as Subjects or Objects, Level of Difficulty 2

All nouns have been underlined. Write **S** above the nouns that work as subjects in the sentences. Write **O** above the nouns that work as objects of verbs in the sentences. (10 points)

1. The demonstration lasted for 20 minutes.

2. The hill was too high for the cyclist.

3. Neil searched the cupboards for the missing box of chocolates.

4. Our <u>group</u> will miss <u>Julie</u> when she leaves our <u>company</u> for <u>England</u>.

5. <u>Mistletoe</u> and <u>holly</u> are used at <u>Christmas</u>, and we can trace their origins to the 11th <u>century</u>.

6. <u>Tanya</u> wore a red <u>vest</u> to the <u>opera</u>, which attracted the <u>attention</u> of the first <u>violinist</u>.

Part 3: Verbs and Verb Phrases, Level of Difficulty 1

Underline all verbs and verb phrases in the following sentences. (5 points)

1. The fish were swimming to the shallow end of the pond.

2. I did see Wayne yesterday, after the match was over.

3. How were they going to recover their losses in the stock market?

4. First aid treatment is important to administer promptly.

5. My friend Ameeta customized her new van.

Part 4: Simple Verb Tenses, Level of Difficulty 2

Write **P** if the verb shows simple present tense. Write **PT** if the verb shows simple past tense. Write **F** if the verb shows future action. (10 points)

1. Floods cause enormous damage in parts of the prairies during the spring. _____

2. Will Mike repair the motorcycle for us? _____

3. The floorshow was boring even though tickets were pricey. _____

4. Am I expected to attend, or do I have the option to stay in my office? _____

5. The shortstop threw the ball, but the pitcher could not make the catch. _____

6. Had you made a mistake on your income taxes? _____

7. Furniture costs a lot of money but much of it is junk. _____

8. The microbes mutate so rapidly that chemical intervention becomes impossible.

9. The copy was hard to read, and the edges of the page were curling. _____

10. She was telling me about her ordeal, and I was feeling sympathetic. _____

Part 5: Verb Forms, Level of Difficulty 1

Give the correct form of each verb in parenthesis. (2 points each, 20 points)

1. The townspeople have _____ (give) time to the festival every summer.

2. Ruby has _____ (wear) her red shoes to the party.

3. My neighbour and I were _____ (freeze) several dozen cobs of corn from her garden.

4. Today the sun has _____ (rise) at 5:20 a.m.

5. The artist had _____ (draw) a sketch of the rocks.

6. Most of the children did _____ (swim) in the new pool yesterday.

7. The first-base player is _____ (catch) the throw from left field.

8. Mila has _____ (fly) on Air Japan previously.

9. The neighbourhood children had _____ (grow) some sunflowers last summer.

10. Has Brad _____ (feed) the ducks, the fish, and the goats?

Part 6: Identifying Nouns, Prounouns, and Verbs, Level of Difficulty 1

Identify whether each underlined word is a noun, pronoun, or verb. Write your answers in the spaces. (½ point each, 5 points)

1. Sheila called <u>them</u> about it. _____

2. The <u>examination</u> was difficult, but all students passed. _____

3. Rose <u>felt</u> happy and comforted. _____

4. The house <u>seemed</u> too quiet and damp. _____

5. Marvin gave <u>him</u> a ride, so we paid Marv for the gas. _____

6. <u>Coriander</u> is a spice, which is popular in Asian cooking. _____

7. The class <u>took</u> a break by stepping out into the sunshine. _____

8. Marnie has <u>been</u> sick for over two years. _____

9. Unfortunately, the rescuers <u>are</u> unable to come, and we will have to fend for ourselves. _____

10. <u>It</u> was apparent that Sherlock could solve the case. _____

Part 7: Identifying Verbs and Their Tenses, Level of Difficulty 3

(5 points)

A. Underline all verbs.

B. Identify the tense of each verb.

1. They had been climbing the small mountain in India when their equipment failed. _____

2. Will arguing over the matter help us resolve the issue? _____

3. The coach was instructing the team while the manager prepared the roster. _____

4. Several owls had roosted on the highest beam of the barn. _____

5. Writing off your debts is not always the best tactic you should be taking. _____

CHECKOUT

1. Grammar enables us to understand the relationship between words in sentences.

2. The study of grammar can sharpen thinking skills.

3. If a sentence does not have an action word, then the sentence is a description.

4. Words are classified in grammar according to their function.

5. The members of a class of words have characteristics in common. For example, some auxiliary verbs indicate time, while others indicate condition.

chapter 12

Subjects and Verbs

Chapter Objectives

After completing this chapter, you will be able to

- understand grammatical terms by looking at their context
- decide what part of speech a word is by noting its function
- spot modal verbs
- know the correct forms of *to be* and *to have*
- make subjects and verbs agree
- distinguish verb phrases and prepositional phrases
- identify compound subjects and compound verbs
- recognize subjects that are understood in commands

INTRODUCTION

To understand what grammar terms mean, consider the context in which they are used rather than a definition you have memorized. By looking at how a word functions, you will understand its part of speech.

This chapter focusses on **subject and verb agreement**, since many students often have difficulty matching subjects and verbs in number and gender when they write. First try writing the self-test below to determine what you remember about subjects, verbs, and their agreement. Check your answers in the Answer Key.

Each grammar chapter contains a variety of exercises at the following three different levels of difficulty:

- Level of difficulty 1: introductory
- Level of difficulty 2: intermediate
- Level of difficulty 3: advanced

Choose level 1 of difficulty if you feel you will need to do a lot of work on the topic. Choose level 2 of difficulty if you have some knowledge of the topic and simply need to refresh your understanding of the ideas. Choose level 3 of difficulty if you feel you have mastered the ideas and want to challenge your knowledge. You will find the answers in the Answer Key.

Chapter 12: Self-Test

Part 1: Subject and Verb Identification, Level of Difficulty 2

Write **S** above each subject. Write **V** above each verb. (½ point each, 10 points)

1. Sasha and Lowell booked a flight to Toronto for the holidays.

2. The druggist filled the prescription and then left for lunch.

3. Lucinda comes from a very small African country.

4. The flies were buzzing around the fruit salad.

5. Several of the customers were upset by the poor meal.

6. The child seemed afraid of the water when we took him to the beach.

7. When the economy is slow, many companies view outside influences as beyond their control.

8. Under the sign, we spotted our missing keys.

9. Chocolate ice cream is too rich for me; however, many people choose it as their favourite dessert.

Part 2: Subject–Verb Agreement, Level of Difficulty 2

Make the verbs agree with their subjects. Underline the correct verbs so that they agree with their subjects. (10 points)

1. Kimberly or Mitchell (want, wants) a new video game.

2. Crumpled paper and dirty plastic (was, were) rolling in the windy street.

3. The mayor or his secretary (is, are) going to speak on television tonight.

4. A steady stream of customers (pour, pours) into the new supermarket.

5. The choirmaster and his students (perform, performs) on Thursdays.

6. The tax on tobacco products (is, are) high.

7. Gilbert and Roy (is, are) going to cater the party.

8. A bowl of soup and a slice of fresh bread (make, makes) a wholesome lunch.

9. (Are, Is) Janice or Maureen going to answer the phone?

10. (Has, Have) the truckers formed a blockade?

Part 3: Identification of Subjects, Level of Difficulty 1

Write **S** above each subject in each of the following sentences. (10 points)

1. Dawn and her niece will take a course together.

2. One of the students wasn't feeling well.

3. A case of fresh peaches fell from the truck and rolled into the open doorway.

4. The manager of the theatre spoke to the attendant.

5. Do Marcus and Leo take karate lessons here?

6. The hoot of an owl came from the tall Douglas fir.

7. After a long semester, the instructor felt exhausted.

8. Only one of those chairs is a genuine antique.

Part 4: Subject–Verb Identification, Level of Difficulty 3

Write **S** above each subject in each sentence; write **V** above each verb in each sentence. (24 points)

1. During arrivals and departures, several air traffic controllers direct planes that are heading to or away from the runway.

2. Having little to say on the matter, Rafella and her lawyer left the reporters who had clustered on the steps of the courtroom.

3. There were few places the lovers could meet, except in the small park near the factory.

4. Tons and tons of waste plastic are found floating on the oceans' waters, and while most of it comes from garbage that has fallen from barges, a large percentage originates from boat and ship traffic.

5. In her article, "Smog Sleuth," Marci MacDonald says, "Air pollution is blamed for 1900 premature deaths, 9800 hospital admissions and 13 000 emergency room visits from respiratory distress in Ontario each year."

Part 5: Subject–Verb Agreement, Level of Difficulty 2

Read each sentence carefully. If the sentence contains a subject–verb agreement error, circle the error, and write the correction in the space provided. If the sentence does not contain a subject–verb error, write **CORRECT** in the space provided. (30 points)

1. Each of the tomatoes were ripe for making fresh salsa.

2. Here is the newspaper and the magazine from the drugstore. _____

3. Have Marilyn or Cheryl ever sung a solo before? _____

4. One of those kittens are promised to my neighbour. _____

5. Where is the answer key for my math questions? _____

6. Vanessa or her sister go water skiing on Clear Lake. _____

7. The toast and the jam was tasteless. _____

8. There is the set of legal papers that Solomon lost from his briefcase. _____

9. Each of the girls were trying to get the job. _____

10. One of the men in my department own a farm. _____

11. The group of campers were too noisy last night. _____

12. The supervisor or the clerk check for errors in accounting. _____

13. Nina and Peggy has chosen an interesting hobby—flying kites. _____

14. An appointment book and a calculator is missing from her desk. _____

15. Each of the colours in the garden harmonize with those of the house. _____

THE FUNCTIONS OF GRAMMATICAL TERMS

Understanding what various grammatical terms do, that is, how they function in a sentence, requires you to analyze their context, usually the sentence in which they occur. Look at the following four sentences:

1. The *rock* fell onto the road.

2. I will *rock* the baby to sleep.

3. He enjoys *rock* music.

4. The child threw a *rock* at the shed.

To understand what part of speech *rock* is in all four sentences, you must determine how it functions in each sentence. Is *rock* a noun in the second sentence? Is it a noun in the third sentence? If it is a noun in the first sentence, how does it function?

> The *rock* fell onto the road.

In this sentence, *rock* is the subject. Because the sentence states *the rock*, you know it refers to a noun.

> I will *rock* the baby to sleep.

In this sentence, on the other hand, the subject is not *rock*. The subject of the sentence is the pronoun *I. Rock* is an action verb; it tells what the *I* (subject) is about to do—*rock*.

> He enjoys *rock* music.

He is the subject of the sentence, and *enjoys* is the action he does—the action verb. *Music* is the thing he enjoys—it is an abstract noun. Because *music* tells what he enjoys and is the receiver of the action, it is a noun functioning as the object. Now, how does *rock* function?

Rock describes what sort of music he enjoys. Thus, *rock* functions as an adjective because it describes the noun *music*.

> The child threw a *rock* at the shed.

In this sentence, the subject of the sentence is *child*, a noun. The action the child performed is *threw*. But how does *rock* function in this sentence? *A rock* indicates a noun, and it is what the child threw. Therefore, it functions as an object.

Use a step-by-step breakdown of each sentence to know how the parts of the sentence function together. You will deepen your understanding of the meaning of the sentence. *Using analysis* is what grammar study is all about.

Grammar study may pleasantly surprise you by sharpening your problem-solving and thinking abilities. As you hone your powers of analysis, you can benefit by an improvement in your reading and language performance. Besides these benefits, you will learn to become a better editor of your own and others' writing.

Remember, read each sentence carefully. To gain meaning from the sentence, think of **S-V** (**subject–verb**: a subject is doing something) or **S-V-O** (**subject–verb–object**: a subject is doing something to an object). Then analyze the sentence to figure out how words function in relation to one another.

SUBJECTS AND VERBS

A subject of the sentence is the *doer*, or *performer*, of the action or what the sentence is about. The previous chapter explained that a verb can *show action or link parts of the sentence*. Sentences should have *both subjects and verbs* and *complete a whole thought*.

> The mule kicks hard.

Mule is the subject, and *kicks* is the action the mule expresses.

> The mayor is rich.

This sentence is a description telling what the mayor (subject) is. The linking verb shows no action and links *mayor* to *rich*.

Exercise 1   *Subjects and Verbs, Level of Difficulty 1*

Write **V** above each verb. Some verbs show action; some are linking verbs. Write **S** above each subject. Check your answers in the Answer Key.

1. The children are at the movie all afternoon.
2. We whispered to each other about the secret email.
3. Her daughter is tall for a girl of six.
4. Maxwell worked for the insurance company during the late 1990s.
5. I phoned for an appointment with the orthopedist.
6. She is nervous because of the noise of the fireworks.
7. You should not make the assumption that you will receive immediate benefits.
8. Pat's friend was an architect from western Ontario.
9. They drank iced tea in the shade of the rose trellis.
10. Margaret lives in St. John's only during the weekends.

TO BE AND *TO HAVE*

The forms of the verb *to be* do not show action; they tell what something is. The forms of the verb *to have* do not show action either; they tell what something or somebody has.

Forms of the Verb *To Be*	Forms of the Verb *To Have*
I am a person.	I have a cold.
He is an electrician.	He has a Firebird.
She is a carpenter.	She has two sisters.
We are on campus.	We have a garden.
You are my friend.	You have made a mistake.
They are excited.	They have coffee at ten.
She was in Winnipeg.	She had a fever.
We were at the beach.	We had a fight.

Some non-action verbs are called *linking verbs* or *state-of-being verbs*.

Linking Verbs

am	sound	appear
is	grow	smell
were	are	remain
become	was	

Remember: when non-action verbs are placed with action verbs, they are called *auxiliary* (*helping*) verbs; together they make *verb phrases*.

My father *is* an alderman. (linking verb)

Ronald *has* four children. (non-action verb)

Their mother *has planned* a party for them. (auxiliary with action verb)

The crowd *was gathering* outside the arena. (auxiliary with action verb)

Exercise 2   *Subjects and Verbs, Level of Difficulty 2*

Write **V** above each verb. Write **S** above each subject.

1. The monk in the red cloak is the leader of the group.

2. Several students were at the office of the registrar early this morning.

3. The team and their coach have lunch at 12:30 each day of practice.

4. The antique buttons are not in the box, nor are they in the sewing kit.

5. He was the manager of the theatre for over 11 years and then became the regional supervisor of an entertainment company.

6. First Nations peoples have opinions about what should become of their cultural artifacts.

7. Surprisingly, the sack of jelly beans was on the bedroom bureau.

8. Male frogs are territorial and protect their part of the pond from male intruders.

9. Last week Tom had the flu, a cough, and chills, so he remained at home in bed.

10. The bird in that rare Japanese painting is stunningly beautiful.

MORE ABOUT VERB PHRASES

A **phrase** is a group of two or more words working together to perform a function in a sentence. There are many different types of phrases. A **verb phrase** works to show the complete action or state of the subject and contains one or more auxiliary (helping) verbs and often one action (main) verb.

Here are some examples of verb phrases. Notice how the verbs in the phrases work together.

> Ted *will be waiting* a long time for his cab.
>
> You *could have been studying* for your exam.
>
> The employees *may have left* the office early.
>
> Mr. Mallory *will be checking* on the baggage.
>
> *Does* Arlene *want* another cup of coffee?

Other Common Auxiliary Verbs

am	was	has
had	*could*	*would*
might	*may*	*can*
be	do	is
were	have	*should*
will	*must*	been
did	does	

Sometimes a helping verb is called a **modal** because it sets a specific mode, or condition, on the action verb. Modals are shown in italics in the above group.

> He *could* work harder.

Could is the modal; it implies the subject has the ability to work harder if he so wishes.

The professor *might* visit France.

Might is the modal; it indicates that the professor has not yet decided. There is the possibility of going.

I *must* remember to change the baby soon.

Must is the modal; it indicates a duty or obligation.

Exercise 3   Verb Phrases, Level of Difficulty 2

Underline each verb phrase. Check your answers in the Answer Key.

1. Joesph is working for the candy company from Sault Ste. Marie.

2. He has been driving the same car for 10 years and has enjoyed having few repair bills.

3. Patrick Roy has won four Stanley Cups and three Conn Smythe Trophies.

4. Alex must write to her father before the deadline date, or she will lose privileges.

5. I should go with you to the opening of the new theatre since my company will be staging a play there.

6. They are deciding what to do about their son's disability insurance.

7. The raccoon was noisily picking through our garbage and chewing on old bones.

8. The rookie police officer can leave soon, but you will have to remain on duty.

9. Marta has had bad luck for the last few years until she met Henrik a few months ago.

10. Because we may have been writing to the wrong person about the complaint, we must visit the office in person.

Exercise 4   Verbs, Verb Phrases, and Subjects, Level of Difficulty 3

Underline each verb or verb phrase. Write **S** above each subject. After you have completed the exercise, check your answers in the Answer Key.

1. Being a general means one must review the troops and then dismiss them.

2. The hikers and the guide were fearful of the coming storm and prepared for the worst.

3. The television networks should have been broadcasting the terrible images of the tsunami and making the world aware of the disastrous results.

4. His current approach to solving budget problems in his department leaves some supporters wondering if college history is about to repeat itself.

5. My mother worries about me and always gives me advice that I seldom follow.

6. The country's leading environmentalists have called for a halt to any further development in the sensitive region where ecosystems have established themselves over the millennia.

7. Alarmed by the test results, the research biologist and her assistants might have been coerced into silence.

8. The article suggests that eating lightly on a hot day may prevent the onset of headache, fatigue, and dehydration.

9. Adriana and her mentor had entered the cooking contest before they completely understood the contest rules.

10. Norman Spector says in one of his columns that, " No price is too high and no effort should be spared to save the lives of our loved ones, but few of us are willing to pay the level of taxes necessary to guarantee the same for people we've never met" (*Vancouver Sun*, June 17, 2005, A19).

PREPOSITIONAL PHRASES IN SENTENCES

Remember that a phrase is a group of words that works together to do a specific job. One type of phrase that you have examined is a verb phrase. Another type of phrase is a phrase that works to show particular detail in a sentence. This type of phrase is called a **detail**, or **prepositional, phrase**. The job of the prepositional phrase is to give details of *how*, *where*, *when*, *what sort*, or *why*.

Most prepositional phrases begin with a little word of direction called a **preposition** and end in a noun or sometimes a pronoun. They have objects called **objects of the preposition** because they answer *what* after the preposition.

Consider these examples:

Karena ate her lunch and read her book in George Hill Park.

Karena is the subject of the sentence. *Ate* and *read* (compound verbs) are the action verbs. *Lunch* is an object of the verb—what she ate. *Book* is an object of the verb—what she read. *In George Hill Park* is a prepositional phrase telling where she completed the action. *George Hill Park* is the object of the preposition *in*. (in what? In George Hill Park.)

His team had won the hockey tournament in last year's winter games.

Team is the subject of the sentence. *Had won* is the verb phrase. *Tournament* is the object of the verb—what the team won. *In last year's winter games* is a prepositional phrase that tells when the team won the tournament. *Games* is the object of the preposition *in*.

Jasbir went to the store for some onions.

Jasbir is the subject of the sentence. *Went* is the action verb. *To the store* is a prepositional phrase telling us where Jasbir went. *Store* is the object of the preposition *to*.

For some onions is a prepositional phrase telling us why Jasbir went in the first place. *Onions* is the object of the preposition *for*.

PREPOSITIONS AND PREPOSITIONAL PHRASES

Following is a list of common prepositions.

Common Prepositions

about	despite	over
outside	above	down
through	across	during
to	after	except
toward	against	for
under	along	from
underneath	around	in
until	at	inside
with	before	into
within	behind	near
without	below	of
beneath	off	beside
on	between	
by	out	

Prepositional phrases end in nouns or pronouns. Sentences can contain several prepositional phrases. Here are some more examples of prepositional phrases.

Some Prepositional Phrases

without happiness	around it
above the crowd	toward them
except Freddy	between classes
on the tray	against you
by the rocks	for the children
through the window	underneath the bridge
off the record	near her

Prepositional Phrases Separating the Subject and Verb

Do not choose the prepositional phrase as part of the subject. Often the prepositional phrase separates the subject from the verb, as in these examples.

> The members of the board are meeting tonight.

Members is the subject of the sentence. *Are* is the linking verb. *Of the board* is a prepositional phrase describing which members are meeting. *Of the board* is not part of the subject.

> The flock of starlings was circling the large tree.

Flock is the subject of the sentence. *Was circling* is the verb that agrees with *flock*. *Of starlings* is a prepositional phrase describing what was in the flock. *The tree* is the object; it is what the flock was circling.

Notice that you could easily make a mistake in subject–verb agreement by selecting *board* as the subject of the first sentence and *starlings* as the subject of the second sentence. Thinking that these sound "right," you might mistakenly write the following:

> The members of the board is meeting tonight.

> A flock of starlings were circling the large tree.

These two sentences contain *subject–verb agreement errors* because the verbs do not match their true subjects. Watch for sentences that contain prepositional phrases, separating subjects from verbs.

Exercise 5   Prepositional Phrases, Level of Difficulty 1

Underline each prepositional phrase. Check your answers in the Answer Key.

1. Across the valley lies a beautiful ranch.
2. The family had a picnic along the river near some rocks.
3. A group of bears was eating wild berries at the park gate.
4. We searched the horizon for the flock of snow geese.
5. He shouted in a foreign language.
6. The dancers on the stage are part of the show.
7. The runner won the race against the odds.
8. Near the swamp beside a clump of weeds the dog rested.
9. The couple walked through the crowd of protesters.
10. The cups behind the counter are valuable antiques.

Prepositional Phrases and Subjects

Most often the prepositional phrase in a sentence comes after a subject, but occasionally, the prepositional phrase is found at the beginning of a sentence.

> *During the storm on that hot August night,* the baby was born.

The subject of the sentence is *baby*. The linking verb is *was*. *During the storm* and *on that hot August night* are two prepositional phrases that tell when the baby was born.

Between the two towns the government built a new bridge.

Note that *between the two towns* is a prepositional phrase that begins the sentence. *Government* is the subject of the sentence. *Built* is the action verb. *Bridge* is the object—what was built.

> ## Exercise 6   Subjects, Verbs, and Verb and Prepositional Phrases, Level of Difficulty 2

Underline each verb or verb phrase. Write the letter **S** above the subject(s) of each verb. Place each prepositional phrase in parentheses ( ).

1. In the middle of the third act, the author of the play left the auditorium.

2. The doctor will be performing the operation on Mrs. Lambert this evening or tomorrow morning.

3. During the morning, someone entered the garage and took several sets of tools.

4. From the front balcony of the professor's house, he could see the entrance to the bank.

5. The earthquake destroyed most of the buildings in the town and caused considerable damage to nearby farms.

> ## Exercise 7   More about Prepositional Phrases, Level of Difficulty 1

Prepositional phrases tell us *when, why, where, how,* or *what.* Underline each prepositional phrase. Over each phrase write *when, where, how, what,* or *why.* Check your answers in the Answer Key.

        where   **when**
Come **to my house after seven.**

1. He bought the boat from a dealer in Edmonton.

2. The Boy Scouts pitched their tents in the woods.

3. This wallet is made of snakeskin.

4. Wayne and Reeves walked against the strong winter wind.

5. After the game, the students drank beer.

6. Sheila's aunt from Jamaica is visiting until Sunday.

7. The jacket on the floor was extremely dirty.

8. A flock of magpies chattered high in the trees.

9. My monkey knocked over the tall vase of flowers.

10. The man and his dog slept under the bridge.

Exercise 8 — Verbs, Verb Phrases, Subjects, and Prepositional Phrases, Level of Difficulty 2

Underline each verb or verb phrase. Write **S** above each subject. Place parentheses ( ) around the prepositional phrases. Check your answers in the Answer Key.

1. At the party, I met an old friend from Yellowknife who talked about white water rafting.

2. One of the horses escaped from the corral and ran onto the highway.

3. The driver of the commercial truck fell asleep at the wheel.

4. His raise of $300 was quite a surprise to him.

5. A bunch of flowers arrived for you today by special delivery.

6. The winners of the race stayed at the racetrack for a photograph in the winners' circle.

7. His marks for his mechanics exams were not very high, so he hired a tutor for extra help.

8. After the storm, the baseball game continued while the fans sat on soggy benches.

9. The ducks and the loons were feeding near the shore.

10. The master of ceremonies tripped on his way to the podium.

Exercise 9 — Subject–Verb Agreement and Detail Phrases, Level of Difficulty 2

Underline the verb that matches each subject. Place parentheses ( ) around the detail (prepositional) phrase. Check your answers in the Answer Key.

1. There (is, are) two pens on the desk.

2. The key to the doors (is, are) on the wall.

3. Marvin from Flin Flon (drive, drives) home each weekend.

4. The group of men (is, are) expecting a raise in pay.

5. All of the students (has, have) left the campus.

6. There (is, are) some cupcakes in the fridge.

7. Up the hill and over the bridge (was, were) a long hike.

8. In the mornings she (prepare, prepares) breakfast for her family.

9. The odour of cigarettes (irritate, irritates) me.

10. The prices of those items (go, goes) up weekly.

COMPOUND SUBJECTS

Sometimes sentences may contain *two or more subjects* that share in the "doing" of the action.

Todd and *Ralph* are working on their car in the garage.

In the above sentence, two subjects are doing the action.

Frieda or *Jim* is working at the garage.

In the above sentence, one or the other subject is doing the action. Notice that a compound subject may be connected by *and* or by *or*. If *and* is used as the conjunction, or joiner, both subjects are the doers of the action. If *or* is used as the conjunction, then both subjects are given, but only one is the doer of the action. The conjunction *or* indicates a choice. The verb must agree with one or the other.

Roger or *his girlfriend* is going to be in charge of the show tonight.

Use *is* as the verb because it agrees with *Roger* or *his girlfriend*—not both.

Exercise 10   Verb Phrases and Compound Subjects, Level of Difficulty 1

Underline each verb or verb phrase. Write **S** above each subject.

1. Janet or Tina goes out each Wednesday for choir practice.

2. Kibibe and her cousin love to rent foreign videos.

3. The postman and the insurance agent have stopped by today with special documents.

4. Hawaii or Miami is an excellent vacation spot during January and February.

5. Mr. and Mrs. Tully are leaving for Quebec for at least two months.

6. The magazine and the dictionary belong to Marie.

7. The girls or their mother should be visiting you soon.

8. The wrench or the screwdriver is missing from my tool box.

9. The movies and live theatre are interesting forms of entertainment.

10. The class and the instructor will go on a field trip to the art gallery.

UNDERSTOOD SUBJECTS: COMMANDS

Find the verb in the following sentence, and then try to figure out what the subject is in the sentence.

Give Mrs. Jenkins a copy of this book.

The verb in the above sentence is *give*. The sentence is a *command*. The sentence is actually saying, "You" give Mrs. Jenkins a copy of this book. However, when you give orders, you leave out the word *you*. The word *you*, which is the subject of the sentence, is understood by the reader or listener. Here is another sentence. Find the verb; then figure out what the subject is.

Bring me a cup of coffee.

The verb in the above sentence is *bring*. The subject is *you* (understood).

Exercise 11   *Verbs and Commands, Level of Difficulty 1*

Write the letter **V** above each verb. Write the subject of the sentence. Check your answers in the Answer Key.

     V
Return the book to the library. (*You* is understood.)

1. Stack the empty cartons by the garbage cans in the backyard.

2. After dinner, offer the guests coffee and liqueurs.

3. Distribute copies of these letters among the members of all departments.

4. Before the end of the week, remove all signs from the walls of the building.

5. After sweeping the floor, arrange the books on the shelf.

6. Please stop the guests at the door and introduce yourself.

COMPOUND VERBS

Sentences express more than one action when they contain compound verbs.

Pete washed and waxed his car.

Pete has done two actions—*washed* and *waxed*.

The teacher was talking to the class, (was) writing notes on the board, and (was) laughing.

The teacher has done three actions—*was talking*, *writing*, and *laughing*.

When you are considering sentences, remember that they may contain more than one subject or more than one verb—compound subjects or compound verbs.

SUBJECT–VERB AGREEMENT

Written English can be more formal than verbal English. You cannot always rely on what you might use in your speech. When you use written language, especially formal written language, you must be certain that what you have written is regarded as standard, correct English. Generally, an academic student is expected to avoid use of informal, non-standard English in her or his assignments.

In English grammar, subjects of sentences must match or agree with their verbs. For example, you would not say: "They is coming to the party." You know that *they* and *is* do not go together. It is important, then, to practise making subjects agree with their verbs.

Subject–Verb Agreement with Pronoun Cases

You will recall that pronouns *take the place of* or *can substitute for nouns*. *Case* refers to the number and gender of pronouns.

Case (Pronoun Number and Gender)

I refers to a single or singular person—first person.

She refers to a singular female person—third person singular.

He refers to a singular male person—third person singular.

It refers to a singular thing or animal—third person singular.

We refers to more than one person—first person plural.

You refers to one or more than one person—second person singular or plural.

They refers to more than one person—third person plural.

Here are examples of alternative pronoun subjects:

The teachers (they) are at a conference.

Randy (you), please close the door.

The gerbil (it) gets new toys each week.

Yolanda (she) works as a realtor.

The technician (he) is training at the local community college.

Subject–Verb Agreement: *One* and *Each*

The *indefinite pronouns one* and *each* are singular. They are called *indefinite* because they do not refer to a specific person. These pronouns are often used as the subjects of sentences. When they are used as subjects, they are frequently separated from the verbs by other words or prepositional phrases. Remember: *always make the verb agree with the subject.* Do not be confused by words that come between the subject and the verb.

One of those books *is* mine. (not *are*)

One of my brothers *plays* hockey. (not *play*)

Each of those glasses *is* cracked. (not *are*)

Each of the guests *wants* more wine. (not *want*)

Exercise 12   One and Each, Level of Difficulty 2

Write the correct word in the blank. Check your answers in the Answer Key.

1. (goes/go) One of those buses _____ to Prince George.

2. (was/were) Each of the contestants _____ given five minutes to work out the answer.

3. (gives/give) One of these books _____ information about summer vacations in Europe.

4. (is/are) One of those houses _____ for sale.

5. (needs/need) Each of the workers _____ new safety boots.

6. (has/have) One of her children _____ a cold.

INVERTED ORDER: THE SUBJECT IS NOT ALWAYS FIRST

Most of the time the subject comes before the verb. Sometimes, however, the verb can come before the subject in particular circumstances.

SITUATION 1

There is, there are, there were, here is, here are, here were, where is, where are, or *where were* begin the sentence:

> *There are* two chambers in the human heart.

The subject is *chambers*, not *there*. Try changing the sentence around and saying: *Two chambers are there in the human heart.*

> *Here is* your timetable.

The subject is *timetable*, not *here*. Try saying: *Your timetable is here.*

> *There are* some cookies on the table in the kitchen.

The subject is *cookies*. Say: *Some cookies are there on the table in the kitchen.*

> *Was there* some money in his wallet?

The subject is *money*. Try this as a statement: *Some money was there in his wallet.*

> *Where was* the truck parked?

The subject is *truck*. The verb is *was parked*. Say: *The truck was parked where?*

SITUATION 2

Prepositional phrases start the sentence and the subject comes last:

> In the middle of the forest was an old cabin.

The sentence starts with two prepositional phrases: *in the middle* and *of the forest*. Say: *An old cabin was in the middle of the forest.*

> In the top drawer of his desk was a photograph of his former wife.

Say: *A photograph of his former wife was in the top drawer of his desk.*

SITUATION 3

In questions, the subject will often come between an auxiliary verb and the main verb.

> Has he finished his work?

The verb is *has finished*. The subject *he* is between the auxiliary verb *has* and the main verb *finished*.

> Will she be seeing him today?

The subject is *she* and the verb is *will be seeing*.

Have her parents sold their house?

The subject is *parents*; the verb is *have sold*.

Did you watch the program about South America?

The subject is *you* and the verb is *did watch*.

Exercise 13   Subjects and Verbs, Level of Difficulty 2

Write the letter **S** above each subject and the letter **V** above each verb (including auxiliary verbs).

1. Will he be running for election this fall?

2. There are two books by this author in the library on William Avenue.

3. Were there any pineapples in the last shipment of fruit and vegetables?

4. Where is the stapler that I just bought?

5. Here are his coat, gloves, and scarf.

6. In a paper bag at the bottom of the trunk was an old revolver.

7. During the past few weeks, there have been several accidents at the intersection.

8. Have Mrs. Pepin and Miss Meredith been working on their report?

9. Where were those birds flying?

10. Has the manager cancelled his appointment with Dr. Ross?

Exercise 14   Subject–Verb Agreement, Level of Difficulty 2

Underline the correct verb for each sentence. Be careful to match subjects with verb forms when you are making your selection. Check your answers in the Answer Key.

1. Edna or Sharon (is, are) typing the minutes from the meeting.

2. The papers and the folders (was, were) sitting on the filing cabinet.

3. The author of the book or her publisher (is, are) speaking there tonight.

4. Verna or her friend (go, goes) to the school to do volunteer work.

5. A monkey or a dog (make, makes) a good pet but (demand, demands) attention.

6. Smoking and eating too much (is, are) bad for your health.

7. Christopher and I (have, has) been going to sales.

8. The cat and the dog (have, has) fleas and (need, needs) a bath.

9. The child and his brother (was, were) watching the firemen.

10. The library or city hall (is, are) closed on Mondays.

Exercise 15   Subject–Verb Agreement, Level of Difficulty 2

Write the correct word in the blank.

1. (play/plays) Their three sons _____ softball.

2. (make/makes) That colour _____ the room seem larger.

3. (visit/visits) Logan or Jasmine _____ the museum every summer.

4. (make/makes) Loud noises _____ him feel nervous.

5. (cost/costs) A bucket of ice cubes _____ $6.

6. (enjoy/enjoys) My sister and her husband _____ their children.

7. (was/were) Allen or Sally _____ elected to student council.

8. (goes/go) My mother and father _____ to visit my brother in Toronto.

9. (was/were) The fruit and the vegetables _____ not fresh.

10. (look/looks) His mother or his brother _____ after his children.

11. (visits/visit) Friends or relatives _____ every summer.

12. (needs/need) The curtains in this room _____ to be washed.

13. (has/have) Another shipment of electrical parts _____ just arrived.

14. (receive/receives) The workers at the Fairmont _____ good wages.

15. (are/is) The hotels or the restaurants _____ popular in Charlottetown.

16. (goes/go) A bag of potato chips _____ well with a bottle of cold beer.

17. (was/were) A carton of cigarettes _____ missing from our order.

18. (is/are) The weight of those stones _____ too heavy for the floor.

19. (is/are) The cupboards in the kitchen and the large chair in the dining room _____ made of maple.

20. (agrees/agree) The members of the legislature _____ on very few topics.

Exercise 16   Review, Level of Difficulty 3

Read each of the following sentences carefully. If the sentence contains an error, underline the error and write the correction. If the sentence does not contain an error, write the word **CORRECT.**

One of those bicycles <u>are</u> hers.   <u>   is   </u>

David and Consuelo commute to Richmond by bus.   <u>correct</u>

1. The man with all the cats lives next door to my aunt's best friend.   _____

2. With the party going on in the street, there is too many distractions
   for the baby to settle down comfortably tonight.   _____

3. Over the breeze float the irresistible aroma of doughnuts, pizza, and bread. _____

4. The survey, based on 20 colleges in five provinces, reveal students' attitudes to learning has become career-oriented. _____

5. On the back of my old school gymnasium were several photographs of my winning basketball team back in 1996. _____

6. Both Alexei and Jansen has earned a spot on our college's hockey team. _____

7. A career that contains high "people contact" have greater potential for personal and professional growth than individual contract work on home-based projects. _____

8. Among the many books on Hespeth's shelves, the housekeeper or her assistant have noticed a small revolver. _____

9. One of the premier's many talents are talking to the press and fielding questions from the gallery. _____

10. The annual activities of the bird fanciers club appears to be cancelled due to the threat of forest fire in the designated area. _____

11. Of the two products advertised, here are the better bargain. _____

12. One of the queens of England was known for her hatred of strong smells and ghastly-coloured foods. _____

13. In the cool evening after a hard day's work in the restaurant Marla or her cousin barbecue seafood on the deck. _____

14. One of the elements of the play that contribute to the overall tension was the sudden appearance and the dreadful words of the ghost. _____

Exercise 17   Review of Errors in Sentences, Level of Difficulty 2

If the sentence contains an error, underline the error and write the correction in the space provided. If the sentence does not contain an error, write the word **CORRECT** in the space provided.

One of those computers <u>are</u> hers. <u>is</u>

The twins work at the fast-food restaurant. <u>correct</u>

1. Mrs. Magnum or he are generally in the office by 8 o'clock. _____

2. Uncle Bo and Aunt Martha feel happy to be home again. _____

3. One of your sisters resembles my cousin. _____

4. Is there any crackers left in the box? _____

5. These writing pads was all that he ordered. _____

6. There are the shovel and the rake that I was looking for. _____

7. Don't the faucets in the bathroom work properly? _____

8. Has the plumbers gone on strike? _____

9. Each of the members of our club were given a complimentary ticket. _____

10. Here is the dictionary and the novel that you ordered. _____

11. The noise of those engines have given him a headache. _____

12. Has the instructor finished writing his report? _____

13. He and she usually walks to work. _____

14. The waiters in this hotel were trained by an expert. _____

15. Jerry Johnson, his wife, or his sister works at the community club on Saturday morning. _____

Chapter 12: Review Test

Part 1: Subject and Verb Identification, Level of Difficulty 2

Write **S** above each subject. Write **V** above each verb. (½ point each, 10 points)

1. The sportscaster and the producer are going to Montreal for the World Series.

2. A throng of customers was waiting for the doors to open.

3. Put the stamps and the letter on the kitchen counter.

4. My travel agent will make all the arrangements for us.

5. The hero of the play was only 11 years old.

6. Will you need a bus pass this month?

7. Yvonne and Russ celebrated their 10th wedding anniversary this weekend.

8. One of the executives of the company has been talking to the journalist.

9. A sting from a bee can be quite painful.

Part 2: Subject–Verb Agreement, Level of Difficulty 2

Make verbs agree with their subjects. Underline the correct verbs. (10 points)

1. Rudolph and Comet (is, are) expected to win the favourite-reindeer contest this Christmas.

2. The target and the scores (was, were) taken down after the shooting tournament was over.

3. A basket of plump plums (is, are) sitting out on display.

4. (Was, Were) Joe or Bob supposed to hose down the horse stalls?

5. The trail and the climb (was, were) too difficult for a novice.

6. The plane and the crew (was, were) grounded by the terrible windstorm.

7. The cashier and the clerks (work, works) late shifts to get the stock ready for the annual sale.

8. A boatload of tourists (stop, stops) at the village to see the artisans' work.

9. (Has, Have) the children put their duffel bags into the school bus?

10. (Do, Does) Lee or Jill take minutes at the meetings?

Part 3: Identification of Subjects, Level of Difficulty 2

Write **S** above each subject in each of the following sentences. (10 points)

1. Women and children in colourful clothing filled the fields near the festival grounds.

2. Each of the computers needed to be serviced.

3. One of the old bicycles belonged to the old gentleman from Halifax.

4. The winner of the snooker tournament gave an interview to *City Magazine*.

5. Do Freddie and Arlette shop at Superstore or Loblaws?

6. The sound of the dentist's drill made me nervous.

7. Kathleen or Anne will plan the trip to England.

Part 4: Subject–Verb Identification, Level of Difficulty 3

Write **S** above each subject in each sentence; write **V** above each verb in each sentence. (17 points)

1. Most of the people in the crowd were booing the speaker and from the sidelines tossing insults that were harsh and personal.

2. Pretending to be reading lines, the actor and her lover exchanged glances with the technician who was hanging lights over the main stage.

3. One of the tragedies of modern living is isolation and alienation, despite the fact that most people live in crowded urban areas.

4. Richard Hawley, a dean of students, wrote, "Television has a way of intruding into lives, and last year it intruded into my life and into the life of the school where I work in a way that many of us will never forget."

5. According to tradition, nothing should be said to the person who loses the contest since only the elder can approach the person.

Part 5: Subject–Verb Agreement, Level of Difficulty 2

Read each sentence carefully. If the sentence contains a subject–verb agreement error, circle the error, and write the correction in the space provided. If the sentence does not contain a subject–verb agreement error, write **CORRECT** in the space provided. (30 points)

1. One of the photocopiers contains coloured paper. _____

2. There are three astronauts on the space mission. _____

3. Have Donna or Stephen found a good campsite? _____

4. Each of those cars sell for $50 000. _____

5. Where is the calculator and briefcase from my office? _____

6. Yona or her sister love to share an apartment. _____

7. The fireworks and the music were thrilling. _____

8. There are the bunch of grapes. _____

9. Each of the animals appear frightened. _____

10. One of the trainees was afraid to ask questions. _____

11. The organization are arranging a conference in Victoria. _____

12. The electrician or the apprentice wire each house according to the code. _____

13. Del and Gabriella wants to create a piñata. _____

14. The witness and the prosecutor were both out of order in the courtroom. _____

15. Each of the tourists were given a small flag of Canada. _____

CHECKOUT

1. Reduce memorization; analyze the whole sentence to determine how terms function.

2. Complete sentences contain both subjects and verbs.

3. Auxiliary verbs help action verbs.

4. Verb phrases contain two types of verbs.

5. Modals set conditions on the action verb.

6. Compound subjects and compound verbs appear in some sentences.

7. Academic students must know the conventions of standard English.

8. Grammar study improves critical thinking, reading, and writing.

Modifiers

Chapter Objectives

After completing this chapter, you will be able to

- distinguish between the forms of adjectives used to compare things
- recognize adverbs that tell *how, where, why,* or *when*
- use adjective and adverb prepositional phrases
- avoid misuse of *good, well, bad, badly, real,* and *really*

INTRODUCTION

Modifiers are words that describe other words. They provide detail in sentences. You can use them to describe the noun you are discussing or when, where, why, or how something occurred. Basic modifiers in English are *adjectives, adverbs,* and *prepositional phrases.*

To check out your knowledge of modifiers, try the following self-test. Check your answers in the Answer Key.

Each grammar chapter contains a variety of exercises at the following three different levels of difficulty.

Level of difficulty 1: introductory

Level of difficulty 2: intermediate

Level of difficulty 3: advanced

Choose level 1 of difficulty if you feel you will need to do a lot of work on the topic. Choose level 2 of difficulty if you have some knowledge of the topic and simply need to refresh your understanding of the ideas. Choose level 3 of difficulty if you feel you have mastered the ideas and want to challenge your knowledge. You can check your answers in the Answer Key.

Chapter 13: Self-Test

Part 1: Finding Adjectives, Level of Difficulty 2

Read the following sentences. Underline all adjectives. Note: not all sentences contain adjectives. (1 point each, 18 points)

1. They were ashamed of the fact that they had been very greedy.

2. The impatient customer left the convenience store in a huff.

3. I recommend fresh lemons for the recipe and not lemon extract.

4. The historic lighthouse had the most wonderful view of the beautiful bay at sunset.

5. Hubert warned the excited tourists about the light-fingered thieves that roamed the bustling streets of Cairo.

6. Madelaine quietly spoke to the young children as they entered the imposing doors of the dinosaur exhibit.

7. He cut himself a thick slice of blueberry pie.

8. A shaggy moss partially covered the stone statue.

9. Turpentine has a very strong odour.

10. He usually waits until seven in the evening.

Part 2: Finding Adverbs, Level of Difficulty 2

Read the following sentences. Underline all adverbs. Note: not all sentences contain adverbs. (1 point each, 20 points)

1. With a shy smile, the supervisor quietly thanked his workers for the retirement gift.

2. Today we are expecting Joanne to bring the green salad to the potluck supper because she usually does.

3. The rescue team desperately tried to save the hikers who had fallen quite dangerously close to the rapids.

4. Anna is intensely watching the skating competition because her daughter is performing now.

5. He will certainly call you if a position unexpectedly opens tomorrow.

6. The hockey announcer talks excitedly when he is not on the air.

7. Many students are extremely happy with just one course in English; however, I believe students need more work than a single course provides.

8. The opposite page has clear diagrams.

9. She tied her hair tightly into a ponytail; then she began her exercise routine.

10. A tiger lily is a commonly grown plant that can do rather well in poor soil.

Part 3: Finding Prepositional Phrases, Level of Difficulty 2

Read the following sentences. Put parentheses ( ) around each prepositional phrase. (1 point each, 12 points)

1. Despite the weather, the ball game continued in the rain.

2. We were worried about the exam on Monday, but we did not discuss our fears with anyone.

3. Can you find fresh fish at the farmers' market on Blunt Street?

4. Helen did not appreciate the joke in the lunchroom, but I found it funny.

5. The workers invited their old supervisor for a beer at the hotel.

6. Please relax; the flight will be over in a short time.

7. A crowd of students gathered just as the speaker arrived on the platform.

Part 4: Identifying Adjective and Adverb Prepositional Phrases, Level of Difficulty 3

Read the following sentences. Put parentheses ( ) around each prepositional phrase. Then write **ADJ** above the prepositional phrase if it is an adjective prepositional phrase. Write **ADV** above the prepositional phrase if it is an adverb prepositional phrase. (1 point each, 10 points) (½ point for finding, ½ point for identifying **ADJ** or **ADV**)

1. The woman from Brazil talked to immigration officials.

2. A container of pumpkins and a large vase of sunflowers decorated the stage of the hall.

3. One of the planks is missing from the deck.

4. They wandered through the mall while the children talked about their plans.

5. Maria gathered the clothes in her arms.

Part 5: Using Comparisons, Level of Difficulty 1

Underline the correct comparative form of the adjectives or adverbs in parentheses. (1 point each, 10 points)

1. The circus ride we had at the exhibition was (good, better, best) than the ferris wheel at the fair.

2. Ron was the (more, most) ambitious engineer I have ever met.

3. The (bad, worse, worst) film we saw was *Freddie Got Fingered*.

4. Of the two flavours, grape is the (good, better, best).

5. That job is the (little, less, least) complicated of the four I have to do.

6. Carey was the (much, more, most) energetic of the recruits in the class.

7. That is the (more, most) sensible of the two solutions.

8. Sol is (good, better, best) at cooking than his wife is.

9. (Many, More, Most) tourists visited the display than the organizers had expected.

10. This restaurant is (good, better, best) at presenting food than the average place.

Part 6: Your Own Sentences, Level of Difficulty 3

Follow the instructions carefully as you make up your own sentences. (2 points each, 10 points) Your instructor may want to correct your work.

1. Use the word *sell* in a sentence that contains one adverb prepositional phrase. Underline the adverb prepositional phrase.

_____

_____

2. Use the word *pretty* in a sentence that contains two adverbs. Underline the adverbs.

   _____

   _____

3. Use the word *game* in a sentence that contains one adjective prepositional phrase.

   _____

   _____

4. Use the word *party* in a sentence that contains two adjectives. Underline the adjectives.

   _____

   _____

5. Use the word *child* in a sentence that contains one adjective and one adverb.

   _____

   _____

Part 7: Usage, Level of Difficulty 2

Correct the following sentences by crossing out the adjective or adverb that is incorrectly used. Write the correct form above the incorrect form. (5 points)

1. Monique is a real talented actor who recently arrived in Ottawa from Montreal.

2. The puppy was behaving bad, but we knew terriers had that reputation.

3. Francis and Rob danced good together; the couple was a crowd pleaser.

4. Several loaves of bread were not baked good enough.

5. Stella felt badly about telling her boyfriend their relationship was over.

ADJECTIVES

Creating Interesting Sentences

Every sentence contains at least one subject–verb (S–V) set or subject–verb–object (S–V–O) set.

S   V
The boy studies.

S   V
Dogs growl.

S   V   V
A woman is reading.

S   V   O
The child builds models.

S   V   O
Hillary knits tams.

The sentences above are "bare bones"; they have no detail. To make sentences more interesting to read and more exact in meaning, you can add words of description. Suppose you described every noun in each of the sample sentences below. The sentences then might look like this:

                 N
The redheaded boy studies.
   describer

          N
Wild dogs growl.
describer

                   N
A tall, young woman is reading.
   describers

           N   **N**
The energetic child builds interesting models.
   describer   **describer**

   N   **N**
Hillary knits crazy, colourful tams.
         describers

The added describer words help to distinguish what kinds of nouns you are talking about. *Words that describe nouns* are called **adjectives**.

Exercise 1   *Group Activity: Adjectives, Level of Difficulty 1*

Form a group of three to five people to complete the following activity. Below is a list of nouns. Add two adjectives before each noun. Place a comma between your adjectives. Be prepared to share your answers.

Example: a tiny, efficient kitchen

1. a _____, _____ beach

2. the _____, _____ restaurant

3. some _____, _____ geese

4. a _____, _____ course

5. two _____, _____ children

6. the _____, _____ dessert

7. a _____, _____ dog

8. one _____, _____ apple

9. the _____, _____ bus

10. some _____, _____ sentences

11. several _____, _____ people

12. the _____, _____ shoes

13. a _____, _____ liquid

14. _____, _____ garbage

15. the _____, _____ horse

Exercise 2   Sentences with Adjectives, Level of Difficulty 2

Work in pairs. Use each of the following nouns in sentences. Use three adjectives in each of your sentences. Be prepared to share your answers.

1. friend _____

_____

2. game _____

_____

3. furniture _____

_____

4. ocean _____

_____

5. breakfast _____

_____

6. park _____

_____

7. garden _____

_____

8. inspector _____

_____

Comparative and Superlative Forms of Adjectives

Adjectives are often used to compare things.

Eunice makes a *good* hamburger; Arnie's is *better*, but Mel's is the *best*.

In the sample sentence, you see three *adjectives of comparison—good, better,* and *best.*
Good is used to describe one item. *Better* talks about the differences between two things. *Best* refers to the differences among three or more things.

Using Regular Adjectives to Compare

Positive (One)	Comparative (Two)	Superlative (Three+)
tall	taller	tallest
great	greater	greatest
happy	happier	happiest
friendly	friendlier	friendliest

Using Irregular Adjectives to Compare

Positive (One)	Comparative (Two)	Superlative (Three+)
good	better	best
bad	worse	worst
little	less	least
much	more	most
many	more	most

ADJECTIVES USING *MORE* AND *MOST*

Generally speaking, you can show comparison with adjectives by simply adding *more* or *most*. Below are some examples.

Some adjectives are not regular in their formation of the comparative. You would never say "beautifulest" or "gratefuller," for example. For these adjectives, you simply add "more" or "most" to the positive (root) form.

Examples

more beautiful	most beautiful
more grateful	most grateful

Often if the adjective has a suffix (a part added to the root word), you add "more" or "most" to construct the comparative form.

Examples

worthless	more worthless	most worthless
possible	more possible	most possible
agreeable	more agreeable	most agreeable
natural	more natural	most natural

ordinary	more ordinary	most ordinary
helpful	more helpful	most helpful
feminine	more feminine	most feminine

You may use *more* or *most* with regular adjectives, too, particularly if you wish to add emphasis to your idea.

Using *More* or *Most* to Compare

Positive (One)	Comparative (Two)	Superlative (Three+)
fortunate	more fortunate	most fortunate
silly	more silly	most silly
heavy	more heavy	most heavy
shady	more shady	most shady
graceful	more graceful	most graceful
plump	more plump	most plump
satisfied	more satisfied	most satisfied

Mixed Adjective Forms

You can make comparisons in different ways:

Instead of saying: plump—more plump—most plump

You could say: plump—plumper—plumpest

Do not mix adjective forms when using adjectives that compare. A common mistake is to mix *more* and *most* with the regular adjective form; the following error results:

Incorrect: more friendlier

Incorrect: more better

Incorrect: more drier

Exercise 3   *Adjectives That Compare, Level of Difficulty 2*

From the lists on the previous pages select adjectives that correctly complete the following sentences. Check your answers in the Answer Key.

1. Although this year's statistics for child poverty are _____, last year's were _____.

2. I think Valerie's is the _____ restaurant in town.

3. Tom felt horrible because he thought he had given the _____ speech of his life.

4. Of the two arguments, the first is _____.

5. Chieko remarked that the new hotel had the _____ service in the city, and she would not return to the place.

6. Uncle Clifford said, "That was the _____ enjoyable time I ever had!"

7. It is _____ important of all that you check the pressure gauge.

8. The movie was _____ interesting than the book.

9. Cougars are _____ dangerous when food is scarce.

10. Today's announcement was _____ welcome than last week's.

11. Of the two brothers, Quigley is the _____ charming.

12. I seldom think about which are the _____ exciting fashions today.

13. Has she become _____ serious about her work than she used to be?

14. That house plan is _____ expensive than this one.

15. The baby's cold is _____ today than yesterday.

ADVERBS

Adverbs describe *verbs, adjectives,* or *other adverbs*. Adverbs tell *why, when, where, how,* or *how much*.

      adv   **V**
Carrie **suddenly** stopped for a break.

Suddenly is an adverb; it describes the verb *stopped*. The adverb tells how Carrie stopped.

        adv **adj**
Manuela was **perfectly** happy with the idea.

Here *perfectly* is an adverb; it describes the adjective *happy*. The adverb tells how happy Manuela was.

        adv adj
The supervisor was **very** ill.

Here *very* is an adverb; it describes the adjective *ill*. *Very* tells how ill the supervisor was.

Exercise 4 Adverbs, Level of Difficulty 2

Adverbs usually end in *-ly* (suffix). Here are some typical adverbs.

nervously	finally	stubbornly
silently	basically	rapidly

frankly	financially	happily
coldly	immediately	truly
hopelessly	discreetly	unusually

Form a group of three to five people and use each of the above -*ly* adverbs in good sentences. You should end up having 15 separate sentences.

Many adverbs do not end in -*ly*. Here is a list of some of them.

Some Adverbs Not Ending in -*ly*

not	somewhat
just	soon
then	there
so	almost
less	always
very	too
also	much
here	quite
now	never
often	seldom
rather	

Exercise 5   *Adverbs, Level of Difficulty 2*

Underline the adverbs in the following sentences. Check your answers in the Answer Key.

1. Often Giorgio speaks really freely at public meetings.

2. My dog sleeps lazily in the sun whenever she can position herself just right.

3. My wife and I seldom go to restaurants because we find the food is too greasy.

4. The teenagers sadly said goodbye, parted slowly on the steps, and then waved weakly.

5. On very damp Saturdays, Marco usually sleeps in, happily snuggled in his warm bed.

6. The politician never swears unless he is quite alone.

7. The family usually goes camping there almost every holiday in the summer.

8. Walter and Frieda often dance in contests, but they are somewhat shy about it.

9. Fried mushrooms always taste very good with pepper and lemon sprinkled generously on top.

10. We scarcely know her, yet she seems strangely familiar to us.

11. Ada understands German perfectly, but she is unable to speak it fluently.

12. Luke was unhappily married for 12 years and was just too miserable in the relationship.

13. They shook their heads furiously at the suggestion and then agreed.

14. Cacti grew beautifully in his sunny backyard although he almost never tended them.

15. Francisco was somewhat dismayed that he had gotten rejected so loudly.

Adverbs Telling When

Adverbs tell us *how*, *where*, *why*, or *when*. Here is a list of some of the adverbs that tell the frequency of an action. Adverbs are often used to describe people's habits.

Some Adverbs Telling When		
always	usually	often
hardly	sometimes	frequently
never	scarcely	occasionally
hardly ever	rarely	seldom

Here are a few of these adverbs used in sentences:

He usually reads before he goes to sleep.

The children seldom eat fish.

He is often at the office by 7 a.m.

The elderly frequently rest after meals.

Adverbs of Time

Other adverbs refer to time specifically. Here are some examples: *then, yesterday, tomorrow, today.*

Exercise 6   *Adverbs, Level of Difficulty 2*

Read each sentence and underline each adverb. Check your answers in the Answer Key.

1. Alvin did his assignments really carefully yesterday.

2. They discovered the neatly folded note outside.

3. The children fought noisily over there in the playground.

4. The colt clumsily stumbled to its feet.

5. The most beautiful cake at the fair was Sabrina's.

6. Here are the reports recently received by our department.

7. Seldom will Donald respond unless he is provoked intentionally.

8. The angry bear ferociously charged the two hunters.

9. Yesterday the baby slept quietly on the sun porch while Cheryl happily read her latest magazine.

10. Sean rarely goes anywhere.

11. Bravely, the boy fought back his tears.

12. We will leave early, but we will call you later to hear the news.

13. The two children smiled shyly at one another.

14. Immediately, you must apologize for your rude remark.

15. Slowly, Fernie opened his eyes, and quietly, he spoke in a low, but steady voice.

16. Heather is a less experienced secretary than Estelle.

17. Today the sun shone brightly over the lake.

18. The tiny deer is too frightened to move.

19. They were more afraid of the water than the wasps.

20. His coach was extremely suspicious of the player's excuse.

21. Honestly, Jans did not take advantage of the situation; he rarely does.

22. What was more upsetting to the teacher was the parent's insistence that the child was always right.

23. Please sit down, and tell me calmly and clearly what happened.

24. A young salesman was arguing softly with the resident of the old building.

25. Tomorrow we will be quite happy to help you.

26. The back door banged loudly, and Kerry stomped angrily through the kitchen.

27. She was so worried about the car that she stared blankly at the service manager.

28. Is the management completely sorry that you strongly disliked your meal?

29. He casually informed her that she was fired immediately.

30. We hardly recognized him when he was extremely well dressed.

Exercise 7   Finding Adverbs, Level of Difficulty 2

Underline the adverbs in the following sentences. Note: some sentences also contain adjectives. Do not underline adjectives.

1. The restless students were really anxious about the test results from yesterday.

2. The work went smoothly today except for one small delay.

3. Some toffee is too chewy for my old fillings.

4. A red snapper tastes delicious when it is lightly baked with lemon sauce and fresh dill.

5. The city workers systematically tore up the pavement in front of the park.

6. The librarian helpfully directed me to the DVDs on the second floor.

7. Indian corn, called maize, is used extensively in Mexican cooking.

8. Sometimes drug companies add codeine to cough syrups.

9. Yesterday there was an outburst of anger from a taxpayer's group.

10. Mandy seldom takes a taxi, but tomorrow she plans to take one to the airport.

11. The examination went poorly for Clark because he had not studied thoroughly.

12. Do you always do as you are instructed?

13. Frequently, André was too late to get any real bargains.

14. The circle of friends was suddenly broken by an unexpected death.

15. Bacon and eggs are rather high in fat, but surprisingly, they remain a popular breakfast food.

PREPOSITIONAL PHRASES

Phrases are groups of two or more words working together to perform a certain task. One type of phrase mentioned earlier in this book is called a detail phrase or a **prepositional phrase**.

A prepositional phrase works in the same way as an adjective or an adverb. The phrase adds detail to a sentence. Like an adjective, a prepositional phrase can describe a noun, as in this sentence:

The girl *in the white hat* is my cousin.

In the white hat is a prepositional phrase. It describes the girl. Since *girl* is a noun and adjectives describe nouns, the phrase works just like an adjective.

The cake *on the bottom shelf of the fridge* is stale.

On the bottom shelf and *of the fridge* are two separate prepositional phrases. The first phrase, *on the bottom shelf*, describes the cake. The second phrase, *of the fridge*, describes the shelf. Both phrases describe nouns; therefore, both phrases are *adjective prepositional phrases*.

A prepositional phrase *can also work like an adverb to tell how, where, when, or why an action takes place.* These sample sentences show prepositional phrases acting like adverbs:

He was working *for better grades.*

For better grades is a prepositional phrase. It adds why the person was working. The prepositional phrase describes working (a verb); the phrase works like an adverb.

She faced her opponent *with a snarl.*

With a snarl is a prepositional phrase. It describes how she faced her opponent. The phrase works like an adverb.

Hugh swims *in his neighbour's pool.*

In his neighbour's pool describes where Hugh swims. It is a prepositional phrase, working like an adverb.

We eat *at six.*

At six tells when we eat. This small prepositional phrase works like an adverb. Prepositional phrases often come between the subject–verb set.

S   **V**

The **president** *of the corporation* **was** only 30.

Of the corporation is a prepositional phrase that interrupts the subject–verb set, *president—was.*

Prepositional phrases begin with words of direction called prepositions. You can review these words in Chapter 12.

Prepositional phrases end in nouns or pronouns: these are *the objects of the prepositions.* They answer *what?* after the preposition.

Here are some examples of prepositional phrases.

Examples of Prepositional Phrases

without a trace	except Bernice
on the campus	above the people
by the main building	near them
around the city	through the ordeal
between meals	against me
off the edge	toward her
underneath the deck	inside the crater

Exercise 8   Group Activity: Prepositional Phrases, Level of Difficulty 2

Form a group to complete this exercise. Fill in the blanks by adding prepositional phrases to the following sentences. Be prepared to share answers.

1. _____ the dog barked _____.

2. The teenager _____ is my cousin.

3. The van _____ was customized _____.

4. _____ I read a book _____.

5. _____ the girl sewed a skirt _____.

6. The animals _____ are hungry.

7. Several crows landed _____.

8. The clamp _____ broke.

9. _____ Michael worked _____.

10. A painting _____ sold _____.

11. We roamed _____ and _____.

12. The cathedral _____ holds mass _____.

Exercise 9   Prepositional Phrases, Level of Difficulty 3

Read the following sentences. Put parentheses ( ) around all prepositional phrases. Check your answers in the Answer Key.

1. Between you and me, I think Molly and Rich are planning a special dinner in honour of their parents' wedding anniversary.

2. The volcano was an inferno of flames and melted rock.

3. Traditional forms of embroidery can be found in many cultures of the world.

4. A rare wasp was discovered in a bog near Copetown, Ontario.

5. In case of an emergency, call 9-1-1, and then wait beside the patient.

6. Have you ever seen any killer whales in the waters around Vancouver Island?

7. Kindergarten is a special time for children because they leave the security of their homes and parents behind them.

8. Inside the tunnel, the workers could see a light that was coming from beneath them, but they could not locate its source.

9. Peacocks are loved for their great beauty, despite their irritating voices.

10. The potter plopped the lump of clay in the centre of her wheel and then kicked the pedal with her foot.

11. Along the edges of the field, we found deposits of a red-brown mineral.

12. The pouch of jewels disappeared without a trace.

13. Across the open meadows and through the thickets and forests, the travellers hiked to safety.

14. I have written in my notebook that there will be an exam on Wednesday.

15. Below the surface of the water was a school of tiny blue fish.

16. We all took an interest in the scene except Vicki, who was bored with the nature hike.

17. Please uncork this bottle of wine for me.

18. The crane was caught in a tangle of old fishing lines below the wharf.

19. She is prying into my business and asking my neighbours questions about me.

Exercise 10   Adjective or Adverb Prepositional Phrases, Level of Difficulty 3

Prepositional phrases can function like adjectives (describing nouns) or adverbs (describing verbs, adjectives, or other adverbs). Read the following sentences. First, underline the prepositional phrases. Then write **ADJ** above the phrase if you think the prepositional phrase describes a noun, or write **ADV** if you think the prepositional phrase describes a verb, adjective, or another adverb. Check your answers in the Answer Key.

1. On Sunday afternoon, the family gathered on the grounds for a reunion.

2. Several of the dogs were running loose in the playground and terrifying two small girls on tricycles.

3. Workers in the city were striking for better wages.

4. The woman in the sun hat just won a prize for the finest carnations.

5. Inside the house the cats were yowling around the kitchen and asking for their dinner.

6. Thousands of salmon were dying from the chemical spill of garden fertilizer.

7. Mrs. Lum, who was seated at the large, decorated table, was happy about the celebration of her 80th birthday.

8. The sailors from the American ship visited several shops and a large restaurant on Government Street.

9. People from that region of the globe do learn the customs of their new Canadian home.

10. The weapons had been tested during the Gulf War by various countries.

11. We saw Shanice on the upper deck of the large ferry.

12. Help us with this heavy couch; we want it moved to the other side of the room.

13. Joshua was not frightened by the other man's threats, but he left within a few minutes.

14. The baby in the little blue sneakers is eating his first bowl of chocolate ice cream.

15. That tin of biscuits is imported from Britain.

16. On an evening during the winter, the scientist saw the asteroid in the fourth quadrant of the galaxy.

17. On Laugh Night on Tuesday at the downtown bar, a young comedian nervously told his bad jokes to a silent audience.

18. The group of campers wandered along the beach at low tide.

19. A flock of blackbirds was singing high in the treetops.

20. The fat puppy ate his plate of crunchies with a large saucer of milk.

21. Take this box of books up the stairs, down the hall, and into my room; put it on the shelf over my bed.

22. He sent his girlfriend a basket of roses; inside the basket, he had tucked a small box of chocolates.

23. Despite my protests, Charlotte went on the trip.

Exercise 11   Group Activity: Sentences with Adjective or Adverb Prepositional Phrases, Level of Difficulty 3

Form a group to compose sentences according to the directions below.
Be prepared to share your answers.

1. Use the word *treasure* in a sentence that contains at least one adjective prepositional phrase.

2. Use the word *recording* in a sentence that contains at least one adverb prepositional phrase.

3. Use the word *party* in a sentence that contains at least one adjective prepositional phrase.

4. Use the word *trapped* in a sentence that contains at least one adverb prepositional phrase.

5. Use the words *melt* and *lab* in a sentence that contains one adjective prepositional phrase and one adverb prepositional phrase.

6. Use the word *expert* in a sentence that contains one adjective prepositional phrase and one adverb prepositional phrase.

7. Use the word *expense* in a sentence that contains two adjective prepositional phrases.

8. Use the words *shoe* and *rip* in a sentence that contains one adjective prepositional phrase and two adverb prepositional phrases.

9. Use the words *sleep* and *fly* in a sentence with one adverb prepositional phrase and two adjective prepositional phrases.

10. Make up a single sentence that contains as many adjective or adverb prepositional phrases as you can think of!

Exercise 12   Mixed Practice, Level of Difficulty 3

The following sentences may contain adjectives, adverbs, or prepositional phrases. Follow the instructions below. Check your answers with others in the class.

A. Underline all adjectives.

B. Highlight all adverbs.

C. Put all prepositional phrases in parentheses ( ).

D. Write **ADJ** above all adjective prepositional phrases.

E. Write **ADV** above all adverb prepositional phrases.

1. The sound of a distant drum rolled across the valley as the soldiers slowly advanced through the forest.

2. The adventurous boys intercepted a letter in an official-looking envelope and excitedly imagined that it had arrived from a master spy.

3. The inventive young cook used a mixture of raisins, bread crumbs, and nuts for the stuffing, and blended cucumber, chervil, white wine vinegar, and olive oil for the dressing.

4. Despite the heavy rain, the enthusiastic players continued in their designated positions.

5. A very tired employee finished the last of the financial reports that her demanding boss had requested earlier.

6. He inherited a string of stables from his mother and a chain of drugstores from his father.

7. The pure water originated from springs that collected in mountain hollows.

8. Their huge mortgage created a terrible burden in their busy lives and made them so anxious about the payments that the young couple sold the property.

9. Uncle Wilfred is a distinguished musician who really enjoys giving benefit concerts to sick or elderly residents of the city.

10. The border collie herded the reluctant sheep back to their pens for the night.

ADVERB AND ADJECTIVE USAGE

Place an adverb as close as possible to the word it describes; otherwise, the meaning of the sentence might be different from what the writer intends.

Consider these examples using the adverb *only*.

Only Lucia loved Nestor. (Only one person loved Nestor.)

Lucia only loved Nestor. (Perhaps she really did not like him but loved him.)

Lucia loved Nestor only. (At this time, Lucia is concentrating on Nestor alone.)

Here are some examples that show how meaning in sentences is changed if the adverb is misplaced.

He got almost killed. (The statement is illogical. A person is killed or not killed; he cannot be "almost killed.")

They fell just into the river. (*Just into the river* implies they did not fall anywhere else.)

He walks his dog hardly down this street. (*Hardly* is misplaced. It should not be modifying *down this street*; instead, it should modify *walks*.)

Peggy spends money seldom on herself. (*Seldom* is misplaced and appears to be modifying *on herself*. Instead, *seldom* should modify *spends*.)

Morton ate just the pizza. (Placing *just* in this position implies that Morton only ate the pizza and nothing else.)

Just Morton ate the pizza. (Placing *just* in front of *Morton* makes it seem that no one else ate pizza except Morton.)

Good and Well

Good is an adjective; you should use it to describe nouns. *Well* can be either an adjective or an adverb.

Incorrect use:	Delbert sings good.
Correct use:	Delbert sings well.
Incorrect use:	Baldev is doing good after his operation.
Correct use:	Baldev is doing well after his operation.
Correct use of *well* as an adjective:	I visited your aunt; she is well. (*Well* describes the aunt.)
Correct use of *well* as an adverb:	The performer danced well in the play. (*Well* describes how the person danced.)

Real and Really

Real is an adjective. *Really* is an adverb.

Incorrect use:	Sheila is a real good friend.
Correct use:	Sheila is a really good friend.
Incorrect use:	This cake is real sweet.
Correct use:	This cake is really sweet.
Correct use of *real* as an adjective:	He has never seen real snow.

Bad and Badly

Bad is an adjective. *Badly* is an adverb.

Incorrect use:	The accident victim is hurt bad.
Correct use:	The accident victim is hurt badly.
Incorrect use:	Melissa plays tennis bad.
Correct use:	Melissa plays bad tennis.
Correct use:	Melissa plays tennis badly.

However, if a sentence contains a linking verb (no action), you use the adjective form *bad* in the sentence.

Aaron felt bad about the news.

The food was bad at the restaurant.

My puppy is being bad in the playroom.

The soup tasted bad to me.

Those flowers smell bad.

Some new music sounds bad.

The weather looks bad.

Some Linking (Non-Action) Verbs

feel	was	being	is
taste	smell	am	were
be	are	sound	look
seem	appear	become	

Exercise 13   *Adjective and Adverb Usage, Level of Difficulty 2*

Add *good, well, real, really, bad,* or *badly* to each of the sentences below. Check your answers in the Answer Key.

1. The dockyards have been _____ disturbed by recent cutbacks.

2. Indra loves creating with stained glass; her works are _____ beautiful.

3. Those cupboard doors fit _____; I think we should call the contractor back and let him have a _____ look at them.

4. The meeting went _____; fights broke out over the least contentious issues.

5. My feet feel _____ after I had that long walk when I wore those tight shoes.

6. The choir sang _____ at the concert.

7. Did you know she got a _____ offer to act in that Hollywood film?

8. The _____ tooth was _____ aching.

9. Dylan has a _____ good friend who helps him with his essays.

10. A pack of dogs was making a _____ mess of the garbage in the cans in the back alley.

11. Behind our hedge we saw a nest full of _____ small, speckled hummingbird eggs.

12. The goalie played _____, but I think the team's defence was poor.

13. Are you a _____ expert cook, or are you a novice whose meals usually turn out _____?

14. Don tried making a _____ box kite, but it flew _____.

15. The young fellow felt so _____ about the incident that he offered to do some _____ community work.

16. The graph indicates that car sales have gone _____ in the summer months.

17. The soldiers were not treated _____ during the hostage taking.

18. How _____ can you ride a horse?

19. A true friend will help in times of _____ trouble.

Intensifiers

When *adverbs* (adv) *describe adjectives* (adj), they tend to *heighten or intensify the qualities* of the adjectives.

   adv   adj
   very polite

   adv   adj
   too weary

     adv   adj
   extremely upset

    adv   adj
   happily married

When *adverbs describe other adverbs*, they tend to *heighten or intensify the qualities of how something was done.*

   Wendy works quite well under stress.

Quite is an adverb that describes another adverb, *well*. *Quite* tells how well the subject works.

Exercise 14   *Mixed Practice for Review: Dividing Sentences into Parts of Speech, Level of Difficulty 3*

Identify the parts of speech in each sentence by writing

N above all nouns

P above all pronouns

S above nouns or pronouns that are subject nouns or pronouns

O above object nouns or pronouns

V above all verbs

A above action verbs

L above linking, or non-action, verbs

ADJ above all adjectives and **ADV** above all adverbs

Enclose preposition phrases in parentheses ( ).

1. That range of mountains runs along the coast of British Columbia and Alaska.

2. Mr. Feldman conducted the symphony orchestra with a great deal of style and flourish.

3. Suddenly, the ridiculous actor burst into tears, and the audience broke into applause.

4. The shrewd criminal is secretly devising a clever scheme of escape.

5. In the winter, Austin walks through heavy snows and seldom misses days of work.

6. They were happily camping on the banks of the rushing river.

7. The hotel is serving sugar-coated doughnuts, hot coffee, and buttered toast in its main foyer.

8. One of the pigeons can do cute tricks for tasty snacks.

9. In the morning, we will take Edgar to the Victoria International Airport.

10. Mary Jane was carefully washing the cotton fabric for the patchwork quilt.

11. Surprisingly, no one suspected Richard of the petty theft despite his motive.

12. We are quite sorry about the unfortunate incident; however, we cannot compensate you for your loss.

13. In the frigid darkness, the soldiers waited impatiently for their orders.

14. The umpire ejected the veteran ballplayer during the last inning of the game.

Chapter 13: Review Test

Part 1: Finding Adjectives, Level of Difficulty 2

Read the following sentences and underline all adjectives. Be careful: not all sentences contain adjectives. (1 point each, 21 points)

1. Alexander seemed sorry about the missing report.

2. We remembered the funny incident that had happened when we were silly children.

3. The toasted marshmallows and hot chocolate certainly tasted wonderful around the fire.

4. The negligent driver was speeding like a maniac through a school zone.

5. The raspberry juice thoroughly stained Jessica's favourite cotton dress.

6. The autumn months can be chilly and gloomy, but I rather enjoy the rain.

7. Duncan prepared baked apples with ginger sauce for our dessert tonight.

8. We were somewhat afraid to enter the darkened basement, especially with scraping sounds emanating from it.

9. The patient cannot eat solid foods while he is slowly recovering from surgery.

10. Sharon will adapt quickly to the changes in her office since she hopes they will lead to improved service.

Part 2: Finding Adverbs, Level of Difficulty 2

Read the following sentences and underline all adverbs. Note: not all sentences contain adverbs. (1 point each, 20 points)

1. The scientist carefully conducted the delicate experiment.

2. Yesterday they were anxiously calling the newsroom and talking confidentially to the seasoned reporter.

3. The most recent study proves conclusively that the virus is deadly.

4. There at the edge of the very old forest a stately Douglas fir grew.

5. The young man was not closely related to the victim, but he knew her very well.

6. The most experienced skydiver warned the nervous beginners who were tightly gathered in a small group.

7. Her uncle exported specialty food products that were made in Canada.

8. The speaker was visibly upset by the damaging remarks that had been recently printed in the local newspaper.

9. The party was quite successful and was surprisingly economical.

10. Miles is a rather respected writer who certainly can become argumentative about neutral topics.

Part 3: Finding Prepositional Phrases, Level of Difficulty 2

Read the following sentences. Put parentheses ( ) around every prepositional phrase. (6 points total)

1. During the campaign, the candidate lost his best friend.

2. The bowl of fresh flowers filled the room with a sweet, spicy scent.

3. For 15 years, the satellite had been making its orbit around the earth.

4. They were certainly happy that the budget cuts had not affected any of the departments in their institution.

5. Montgomery had been elected to Parliament when he was about 30 years old.

6. In a fury, Greg turned on his heel and was gone.

7. A herd of Canadian elk blocked the Yellowhead Highway.

Part 4: Identifying Adjective and Adverb Prepositional Phrases, Level of Difficulty 3

Read the following sentences and put parentheses ( ) around each prepositional phrase. Then write **ADJ** above the prepositional phrase if it is an adjective prepositional phrase. Write **ADV** above the prepositional phrase if it is an adverb prepositional phrase. (1 point each, 10 points) (½ point for finding, ½ point for identifying it as **ADJ** or **ADV**)

1. An excited group from Morioka arrived on the Seattle ferry.

2. A bouquet of red roses and a bottle of wine arrived by special messenger on Friday.

3. The reel of fishing line cost $14 and included a box of waterproof matches.

4. At the beep, please leave your message for Gail or Tanya.

5. Surprisingly, Richard swims at the new Commonwealth pool when it is open late in the evenings.

Part 5: Using Comparisons, Level of Difficulty 1

Underline the correct comparative form of the forms in parentheses. (1 point each, 10 points)

1. The recipe we got from Gertie for tourtière is (good, better, best) than the one we have.

2. Marina is the (more, most) skilled dancer that I have ever seen.

3. The (bad, worse, worst) meal we had on our trip was in Washington state.

4. Of the two poems, yours is the (good, better, best).

5. That technician is the (little, less, least) experienced of the five new employees.

6. The *Belle Princess* is the (much, more, most) luxurious cruise ship in the whole fleet.

7. That is the (more, most) mature of the two plants, so use it in the display area.

8. Susan is (good, better, best) at finding out the truth than I am.

9. (Many, More, Most) applicants applied for the job than the company expected.

10. This cola is (good, better, best) tasting than that one.

Part 6: Your Own Sentences

Follow instructions carefully as you make up your own sentences. (10 points) Your instructor may want to see your sentences.

1. Use the word *repair* in a sentence that contains one adverb prepositional phrase. Underline the adverb prepositional phrase.

   _____

   _____

2. Use the word *angry* in a sentence that contains two adverbs. Underline the adverbs.

   _____

   _____

3. Use the word *mansion* in a sentence that contains one adjective prepositional phrase. Underline the adjective prepositional phrase.

   _____

   _____

4. Use the word *letter* in a sentence that contains two adjectives. Underline the adjectives.

_____

_____

5. Use the word *feel* in a sentence that contains one adjective and one adverb. Underline the adjective; circle the adverb.

_____

_____

Part 7: Usage, Level of Diffficulty 2

Correct the following sentences by crossing out the adjective or adverb that is incorrectly used. Write the correct form above the incorrect form. (5 points)

1. Lisa is a real honest friend.

2. The steak was burning bad.

3. Eileen and I travel good together.

4. The microwave does not work good on high power.

5. Jude felt badly about missing the opportunity.

CHECKOUT

1. To make sentences more interesting and more exact in meaning, you can add words of description: adjectives, adverbs, and prepositional phrases.

2. You can make comparisons in different ways.

3. Adjectives describe nouns; adverbs describe verbs, adjectives, or other adverbs.

4. Prepositional phrases work in the same way as adjectives or adverbs.

chapter 14

Punctuation and Capitalization

Chapter Objectives

After completing this chapter, you will be able to

- use punctuation correctly—commas, semicolons, colons, and apostrophes

- recognize conjunctive adverbs

- capitalize words as required

INTRODUCTION

Punctuation means the use of marks like commas, periods, semicolons, and so on in writing to make meaning clear. Punctuation can be a matter of style, but as an academic English student, you need to know about the use of standard rules of punctuation when you edit or proofread your written work. You also must know about the rules of capitalization for your academic writing. *English handbooks*, which deal with the rules of punctuation, capitalization, spelling, grammar, usage, and specific writing forms like the essay or research paper, will provide a useful reference for you when you are working on your writing.

Try the following self-test to see what you remember about comma, semicolon, colon, and capital use. Check your answers in the Answer Key.

Each grammar chapter contains a variety of exercises at the following three different levels of difficulty.

- Level of difficulty 1: introductory

- Level of difficulty 2: intermediate

- Level of difficulty 3: advanced

Choose level 1 of difficulty if you feel you will need to do a lot of work on the topic. Choose level 2 of difficulty if you have some knowledge of the topic and simply need to refresh your understanding of the ideas. Choose level 3 of difficulty if you feel you have mastered the ideas and want to challenge your knowledge.

Chapter 14: Self-Test

Part 1: Comma Use, Level of Difficulty 2

Insert commas wherever you think they are necessary in the following sentences. Some sentences may not require commas. (½ point each, 12 points)

1. The beaver the eagle the bulldog and the koala are all animals used as national symbols by four countries.

2. Before the play was finished Rita left the auditorium.

3. Ten of the horticulture students were turning the soil breaking up lumps and adding compost; four of the others were sorting seedlings checking labels and reviewing the garden plan; the last students were loading the plants into wagons moving them to the garden site and planting them in raised beds.

4. On November 10 1871 British Columbia joined the new federation of provinces called Canada.

5. Their wedding day will be 9 June 2010.

6. A loud bang I understand startled everyone in the movie theatre.

7. The last cigarette I had was in August 2007.

8. Walking briskly each day working in the yard and doing chores around the house improve a person's fitness levels.

9. Arlette joined the military on August 12 1988 and she left the service on October 16 1994.

10. Of course his remark was sarcastic stupid and rude.

Part 2: Semicolon Use, Level of Difficulty 2

Add semicolons wherever you think they are necessary in the following sentences. Some sentences do not require semicolons. (1 point each, 14 points)

1. The children's rabbit escaped from its hutch fortunately, the neighbour found him and brought him home.

2. The crow wanted the handout from the tourist however, it was afraid of the tourist's dog, which watched carefully.

3. We were afraid of the damage that the storm might do.

4. The clothes dryer was broken Monica had to hang the wash on the line.

5. During the heat, one of the workers was taken to hospital she was attended to immediately.

6. I think you look nice in green you may not agree with me about it.

7. Please allow me to introduce myself I am Count Dracula.

8. The family called the RCMP because they heard shots coming from down the street.

9. Sony is a well-known brand name in electronics it was the first company to develop a portable cassette player for individual use.

10. No one knew what had happened to the treasure everyone had a theory about it.

11. Many farmers prefer to work their fields at night they enjoy the peacefulness and the cool air.

12. *Pinocchio* and *Snow White* are two Disney classics my children love both of them.

13. The minister swayed in the pulpit the congregation sang a rousing hymn.

14. Do these packages include instructions for the software?

Part 3: Colon Use, Level of Difficulty 3

Add colons wherever you think they are necessary in the following sentences. Some sentences do not require colons. (1 point each, 7 points)

1. Be sure to order the following parts the halogen bulb, the bolts, and the tap fittings.

2. He told us his secret he cherished every moment of his life.

3. Paul and Francine received some lovely wedding gifts a DVD player, a new set of china, and a trip to Tahiti.

4. The reason the rocket had not launched was ridiculous the door of the module had been left open.

5. The remedy consisted of peppermint leaves, lemon, and stout.

6. City hall sent out the following material property tax notices, schedules of council meetings, and notification of new zoning laws.

7. He was told to obey the following orders check all passports, question travellers about their destinations, and inspect hand luggage for weapons.

Part 4: Commas, Colons, and Semicolons, Level of Difficulty 3

Add commas, colons, and semicolons wherever you think they are necessary in the following sentences. Some sentences may not require commas, colons, or semicolons. (1/2 point each, 10 points)

1. Grade 12 students met with first-year Mohawk College students they discussed courses at the postsecondary level demands of their schedules and careers in chemistry.

2. Steven was an energetic child who found every opportunity to get into mischief.

3. Having a car payment high rent and extra food costs stretched the family's budget to the limit no one had much extra personal spending money.

4. Most animals use some sort of communication exactly what the communication is how it functions and why a particular species uses it are questions scientists are trying to answer.

5. He on the other hand told the audience about his campaign platform however he forgot to tell them about his government's latest scandal.

6. Canadian poets like P.K. Page Margaret Atwood and Susan Musgrave still live and write in Canada other modern Canadian writers are leaving Canada to find opportunities in places like the United States Britain and France.

7. The children formed a circle the music began.

8. Sadi told Malva his secret he had never loved her.

Part 5: Capitalization, Level of Difficulty 1

Read each sentence carefully. Underline each letter that should be capitalized. (1 point each, 31 points)

1. Last monday uncle robert stopped at the four roads motel.

2. He consulted with several doctors in toronto.

3. The royal canadian mounted police were called in to investigate the robbery in port renfrew.

4. we ordered swiss steak and french fries.

5. The Alberta credit union is closed on saturdays and most evenings except Fridays.

6. mrs. walsh talked to a woman from the department of mines and resources.

7. Some of the students bought four safeway cheesecakes and a case of coke for the meeting at lansdowne junior high school.

PUNCTUATION

The Comma

The comma *separates* items or *encloses parts of a sentence* to clarify meaning. There are two main categories of comma use.

CATEGORY 1

1. **Commas to Separate Words, Phrases, Letters, or Figures in a Series**

   Separate distinct items in a series because doing so helps keep meaning clear. Use a comma between the last item and the word *and* or *or*.

   Unclear: The children played cat and mouse, snakes and ladders and cops and robbers. (The meaning is unclear because the last comma in the series was omitted.)

   More clear: The children played cat and mouse, snakes and ladders, and cops and robbers. (The meaning is made more clear because the last comma is included.)

   Unclear: The students bought red, green, blue, mauve and pink notebooks. (The number of categories of notebook is unclear because the last comma is missing. There could be four or five categories.)

   More clear: The students bought red, green, blue, mauve, and pink notebooks. (The meaning is made more clear because the last comma is included. You can now tell the students purchased five colours of notebooks.)

2. **Commas between Adjectives in a Series**

   Use commas to *separate adjectives in a sequence*. Be sure the adjectives are all describing the noun separately. If you can say "and" between the adjectives, you can use a comma.

Jared used an old, clean baby diaper to wash the windows. (Do not use a comma between the last adjective in a series and the item it describes. Notice you can insert "and" between the adjectives.)

3. **Semicolons with Commas**

   When items in a series contain commas already, use semicolons to separate the larger items or units of meaning.

   Some of the workers sorted letters, bills, and pamphlets; others called people from the voters' lists, survey list, and telephone book; several other people helped the volunteers, food vendors, and caterers set up tables.

4. **Commas in a Date**

   Use a comma to separate parts of a date.

   Sheila left for her new job on Thursday, March 27, 2005.

   The celebration was to be held in October 2009. (No comma is used between the month and year when the day of the month is missing.)

   They announced their engagement on 5 February 2008. (No comma is used when the day of the month is given first.)

   They visited us at Easter 2009. (No comma is used between dates and holidays.)

   Their trip was in spring 1912. (No comma is used between dates and seasons.)

5. **Commas and Place Names**

   Use a comma to separate names of places.

Calgary, Alberta	Moncton, New Brunswick
Hull, Quebec	Sarnia, Ontario

   She received mail at the Boxwood Hotel, Centennial Square, Yorkton, Saskatchewan.

   Mona will see him in Abbotsford, British Columbia, at Christmas. (Two commas are used to set off the name of a province after a city has been named.)

6. **Commas and Parts of Letters and Memos**

   Use commas to set off the greeting in letters or memos and the closings of letters or memos.

   Dear Luigi,

   Dear Cousin Hobnob,

   Sincerely yours,

   Yours truly,

7. **Commas after Introductory Phrases or Clauses**

   During the hockey game, a fan threw a beer can at the ref.

   By the way, never call me again.

   Because he felt sorry for himself, Spike pouted.

   In a flash, Superman was on the roof.

Exercise 1   Using Commas, Level of Difficulty 2

Place commas wherever you think they are necessary in the following sentences. Check your answers in the Answer Key.

1. At the largest music store in town Bob Dylan Leonard Cohen and Janet Jackson are all available on CD at sale prices.

2. After bathing the baby doing the wash returning some phone calls and cooking dinner Bob was exhausted.

3. She is looking for a copy of *National Geographic* from May 1998.

4. Election day in the province is 23 June 2012.

5. Alberta British Columbia Saskatchewan and Manitoba are considered the West in Canada.

6. Christmas 2008 and Valentine's Day 2009 were not as prosperous for merchants as was predicted.

7. Have you ever visited Santa Barbara California or Portland Oregon?

8. The students were planning to bring cakes cookies juice and pop to the picnic.

9. Each hospital patient got cream and sugar bread and butter and a cup and saucer on his or her dinner tray.

10. Amandeep prepared the dough batter and pastry; Stella shaped the buns breads and cookies; Alicia baked sorted and stacked all the items.

11. We knitted pink red orange blue and yellow scarves and toques for the children.

12. For breakfast Mr. Stanton ordered a boiled egg light toast sugarless jam and puffed rice with skim milk.

13. Maria worked in Baden Baden Germany from February 22 1997 to July 6 2003.

14. We will tour Winnipeg Manitoba then Edmonton Alberta and Swift Current Saskatchewan for the Small Business Association of Canada.

15. Rice whole wheat lentils and beans are all good sources of protein.

Exercise 2   Group Activity: Using Commas, Level of Difficulty 2

Form a group of three to five. Together agree where to place commas in the following sentences.

1. Amy Ann Jamie and Tan will of course help set up the tables for bingo.

2. On February 14 2012 Jane and Robert Tony and Maggie and Louis and Cheryl will all take a trip together to Banff Alberta.

3. Sidney puzzled over his writing assignment wrote down several ideas for his essay and then began to write the first draft.

4. Tomatoes oranges lemons grapefruit and limes contain large amounts of vitamin C.

5. Mrs. Allonzo on the other hand voted against the motion at the meeting.

6. Worried about her student loan tired after a hard day's work and frustrated in the traffic Shirley began to cry.

7. Ilsa bought two loaves of fresh bread several grams of salami dill pickles hot mustard and crispy lettuce for the picnic sandwiches.

8. Farley's quote which was from the Bible seemed appropriate.

9. The last time I saw him was spring 2007.

10. A terrible earthquake occurred in Lima Peru in March 1952.

11. Uncle Maxwell dozing in his chair during the meeting suddenly fell with a loud crash.

12. The long lonely cries of the pup attracted the small curious children to the cage.

13. The letter stated "As you are aware the rent is past due."

14. Sweet potatoes curly endive oyster mushrooms and Japanese eggplant seem like exotic vegetables to me.

15. Elmo painted the figures cut them out and pasted them; Sam arranged them on the layout sheet pasted them in place and tacked them down; Helen photographed them placed them in a pile and removed them from the studio.

Exercise 3   *Using Commas, Level of Difficulty 2*

Insert commas in the following sentences wherever you think they are necessary. Some sentences do not require commas. Check your answers in the Answer Key.

1. Ronald needed glue nails drill bits and wood for his woodworking project.

2. Many of the students worried about test anxiety low marks and peer pressure when they were youngsters in school.

3. Her relatives will arrive from Sydney Australia on Tuesday August 23 2009.

4. The article was published in January 2003.

5. Squirrels chipmunks rats and mice are all considered rodents.

6. The cafeteria offered eggs and ham eggs and bacon and eggs and hash browns on its breakfast menu.

7. Two of the children were playing with beads blocks and boxes; five children were drawing painting and colouring; others were whispering listening and watching.

8. Antonio wanted to study psychology philosophy and music in his further studies.

9. The test flight was scheduled for 7 May 2010.

10. We will buy onion and jalapeño salt and vinegar and cheddar and bacon potato chips for the party.

11. Sarah arrived in Hamilton Ontario in fall 2007.

12. He enjoys rock and roll rhythm and blues and jazz on his car stereo.

13. Do you take cream and sugar milk or sugar in your coffee?

14. Mo Alice Amanda and Terry are all applying for the job.

15. The new shopping mall will open on Saturday December 1 2009.

16. Don was born in Vancouver British Columbia; his son was born in Oshawa Ontario.

17. Apples quinces and crab apples are high in pectin content.

18. The book was interesting informative and current.

19. The puppy ran up the stairs into the bedroom through the patio doors and onto the deck.

20. He was concerned that we get a fair wage have good working conditions and know about safety on the job.

21. Poodles terriers spaniels and retrievers are popular breeds of dogs.

22. Arnold will fix the refrigerator repair the basement steps paint the fence and build a new deck this summer during his vacation.

23. The green grocer stocks Valencia Mandarin and Seville oranges.

24. November 11 1918 was a significant date in world history.

25. The employment agency helps clients write résumés prepare for interviews select appropriate interview techniques and do follow-ups.

CATEGORY 2

Use commas *to enclose information that explains, emphasizes, or interrupts.*

1. **Use commas to surround information that is non-essential.**

   Mr. Gaines, who is a coach, commented on the game for the radio listeners.

   He was worried, one might say, about his new position as manager.

   A clause that is not needed to define essential meaning is called *a* **non-restrictive clause**. The commas indicate it is non-essential information. In the above sentence, *who is a coach* is incidental information. You do not need it to identify the subject since his name is specifically given. It is information that may add interest, but it is *non-essential*. *Who is a coach* is called a *non-restrictive clause*. (A clause contains a subject and verb set.)

   One might say is called an *interrupter*, or **parenthetical expression**. It divides up the main idea, but it does not actually add information: it adds emphasis. It is considered a *non-restrictive*, or *non-essential*, element.

   Here are some common interrupters, or parenthetical expressions, used in sentences:

> **Common Parenthetical Expressions**
>
> | | |
> |---|---|
> | of course | therefore |
> | it seems | no doubt |
> | however | after all |
> | on the other hand | for example |
> | as a matter of fact | |

He will, after all, accept the new position.

Toni, on the other hand, does not agree with the policy.

Bears, as a matter of fact, are rather shy and solitary creatures.

The newscaster and the editor, it seems, were at odds over the issue.

2. **If the information is essential to the sentence, do not use commas.**

The woman who spoke with such passion impressed the audience.

Who spoke with such passion is needed to identify the speaker. If you use commas around the clause (a unit containing a subject and verb set), you will be saying that it is not needed (non-essential) in the sentence to identify the speaker. However, since the sentence requires the information for its intended meaning, you do not use commas. A clause that is needed to define or provide essential meaning is called a **restrictive clause**. *Who spoke with such passion* is a restrictive clause—no commas are used.

The student who invented the product won a prize.

Who invented the product is essential. You need to have the clause in order to identify which student won the prize. *Who invented the product* is a restrictive clause.

Exercise 4   *Using Commas, Level of Difficulty 3*

For this exercise, form a group of three to five people. Together, agree where to place commas in the following sentences.

1. Timothy Findley's only mystery novel *The Telling of Lies* is set in a hotel in a vacation spot.
2. A circus on the other hand might be more fun for the children.
3. The people who waited outside the classroom were studying intensely for their upcoming exam.
4. Mr. Jones who runs the hardware store has decided to seek a seat in the next provincial election.
5. His excuse as a matter of fact was ridiculous and insulting.
6. The older children however tend to want to play games that require more interaction.
7. The meeting you understand was cancelled because of her lateness.

8. The bank more importantly knew about the error for some time.

9. The couple who vacationed in Mexico became terribly ill on their return.

10. Her story was in my opinion simply silly.

11. The priest who was working with the farmers in the fields became faint from the heat.

12. His dog which waits for him by the gate is well trained and loving.

13. Anna who is in training in the RN program has always enjoyed helping others.

14. The television show dreadful as it was was loved by millions.

15. Hugmar becoming braver by the minute interrupted the director to give his own viewpoint on the matter.

USING COMMAS IN COMPLEX SENTENCES

Complex sentences are made up of two or more clauses. Each clause has a subject–verb set. One clause can stand alone; it is called the **main clause**, or **independent clause**. The other clause cannot stand alone; it is called the **dependent clause**.

main clause   **dependent clause**
Arnold won (because he was strongest).

    main clause   **dependent clause**
They slept in the tent (until a storm approached).

If a dependent clause comes first in a sentence, use a comma after it.

dependent
   clause   **main clause**
(If I am late,) I will miss the meeting.

Exercise 5   Complex Sentence, Level of Difficulty 2

Work in pairs to decide the answers to this exercise. Underline the main clauses. Put the dependent clauses in parentheses ( ), and then place commas wherever you think they are needed in the following sentences. Check your answers in the Answer Key.

1. Since he fought with his sister little Edward was sent to his room.

2. While Jens was baking the bread we prepared the salad.

3. You can clean the windows after you have your lunch.

4. Some of the animals of the forest were frightened because the wind was so strong.

5. Unless I win the chess game I will be disappointed.

6. She waited at the campus until her boyfriend picked her up.

7. As Mario opened the library book a $20 bill fell to the floor.

8. Since my uncle is a nervous fellow the doctor has advised him to avoid driving in rush hour traffic.

Chapter 14   Punctuation and Capitalization   207

9. The dog couldn't decide if she wanted to bury the bone or not.

10. While her parents were on vacation the teenager threw a wild party at the house.

11. The supervisor will call you if there is any work.

12. As Rodney turned to get the box of cereal from the store shelf a mouse scampered across the floor and disappeared under the bulk bins.

13. Because the snowstorm blew down some heavy trees and took out hydro lines power was lost in most of the city.

14. Max was elected president of the club because he is a tremendous organizer.

The Semicolon

A semicolon has *one main purpose*—to *join* two complete ideas (*independent*, or *main*, *clauses*) or simple sentences together.

John loves to watch hockey; he particularly enjoys the playoff series.

Notice that the semicolon joins one sentence—*John loves to watch hockey*—to another sentence—*he particularly enjoys the playoff series*. The semicolon in this example works like the conjunction *and*.

CONJUNCTIVE ADVERBS

Be sure that the word you think is a conjunction really is one. *However, moreover, otherwise, consequently, therefore, likewise, nevertheless, furthermore*, and *indeed* are weak conjunctions. They require punctuation assistance to join effectively. They are called **conjunctive adverbs**. Use correct punctuation, usually a semicolon, with these words.

Matthew was leaving for Europe; *consequently*, he felt rushed.

You must secure the lock firmly; *otherwise*, the door swings open easily.

The veterinarian warned the cat owner not to give the kitten feather toys; *nevertheless*, the owner disregarded the advice.

Conjunctive adverbs can be placed in different positions in sentences. However, if the conjunctive adverb is placed at the beginning of a clause in the middle of a sentence, you must place a semicolon in front of it and a comma after it.

Samuel wanted to buy a new car; *however*, the payments were too high.

Samuel wanted to buy a new car; the payments, *however*, were too high.

Notice that the semicolon joins the two main clauses together in both sentences.

Exercise 6   Group Activity: The Semicolon, Level of Difficulty 3

Form a group of three to five students. Together correct the semicolon use in the following sentences. If the sentence is correct, write **OK** after it. Check your answers with some of the other groups. You can also check your answers in the Answer Key.

1. Tony was afraid of dogs, therefore, he would not consider a job as a postal carrier.   _____

2. After a long night of tossing and turning, Elrod made up his mind about accepting the promotion; the decision made him happy.   _____

3. Arnold, a considerate person, offered to stay after the dance and help clean up the social director did not hear his kind offer and walked past him without speaking.   _____

4. He tried raising patio tomatoes; that was an expensive disaster.   _____

5. Please be seated; the doctor will be with you in a moment.   _____

6. The students worked very hard to complete the project, however, they were unable to meet the deadline.   _____

7. The contractor was unsure of removing the large tree from the front of the lot; and he consulted with an architectural landscaper to help sort things out.   _____

8. The dance pair was dazzling in their finery; as they swept across the floor to the beat of the samba.   _____

9. Unfortunately, Mr. Costanos cannot come to the phone; because he is in conference.   _____

10. The explorers dove into the icy waters; hoping to find examples of blue-green algae, they were determined in their quest.   _____

11. At three, call Mrs. Penman about the shipment of Crazy Glue; at four, call our Toronto office about the hula hoops.   _____

12. The Cat Fanciers' Club of Regina met in the basement of the church; and the meeting was to plan the annual cat show to be held in the Memorial Arena.   _____

13. The letter lay on the front porch; it seemed ominous to Teddy because it bore the seal of the RCMP.   _____

14. The small boy pouted and shouted his demands; moreover, he instructed his parents on what they were to order for him in the restaurant.   _____

15. California is a beautiful state, but it is running out of fresh drinking water.   _____

The Colon

A colon has two major uses. The most common use is to show your reader that you will be giving a list of some sort.

> Eleanor gathered her equipment: camera, tripod, lens case, and light meter.

Notice that when you choose to use a colon, you do not separate your verb and object with a colon.

Incorrect use of colon: Eleanor gathered: camera, tripod, lens case, and light meter.

Do not separate the verb *gathered* from its objects—*camera, tripod, lens case,* and *light meter.*

A second major use of the colon is to add a second sentence that explains the first sentence.

> Nat knew that the preparation work for the wedding cake was complicated: she had baked the fruitcake months in advance and had to ice it at least a week prior to the wedding.

Notice that the second idea is a complete sentence that adds explanation to the first sentence. Using a colon every now and then in your writing helps to enrich and enliven your writing style. However, don't overuse it because, like anything used too often, it can become boring and predictable.

Exercise 7   *Colon Use, Level of Difficulty 3*

Check the colon use in each of the following sentences. If you think the sentence is right as is, write **OK** after the sentence. If you think the sentence has a colon error, repair the error. Check your answers in the Answer Key.

1. The campers were told to bring: pots, tents, hatchets, and matches to the camp. _____

2. Several features of a successful relationship include: trust, humour, communication, and concern. _____

3. Being an engineer was not what he expected: the piles of paperwork he faced made him feel more like a clerk. _____

4. Please include the following in my order: toothpicks, live bait, six artichokes, a large can of whipped cream, and a bag of ice. _____

5. Her job consisted of: inspecting the site plan, reviewing the septic site, and checking perc tests. _____

6. We learn to give love: it is a gift that costs little but means a great deal. _____

7. Murphy, my crazy cocker spaniel, was known for: chewing furniture, messing on the rugs, stealing the children's toys, and barking at the drop of a pin. _____

8. Tell them to: open the mail, fax me important messages, and send out the orders to Waterloo. _____

9. Tina's anxiety attacks were worsening, she could hardly bring herself to go out in public or be in a room with more than two people in it. _____

10. The instructions on the work order were clear: do all repairs before four that afternoon. _____

Exercise 8   Adding Colons and Commas, Level of Difficulty 3

Add colons and commas wherever you think they are necessary in the following sentences. Some sentences may not require colons or commas at all.

1. His answer was always the same it protected him from the truth.

2. Many woodworking hobbies require expensive tools power saws electric drills lathes sanders and routers.

3. Meteorites are not stars at all they are pieces of metal or stone that fall toward the earth.

4. Yanni cancelled her dancing lessons she did not like her instructor.

5. Some languages are easier to learn than others although some are less commonly used.

6. Robins towhees and blackbirds are noisy birds that have a rich vocabulary of sound.

7. The group will discuss the following topics parenting nutrition discipline and games.

8. Since he had left his hospital job Norman had gotten a string of jobs car washer janitor dishwasher and hamburger chef.

9. Basket weaving is not as simple to do as people think it requires a great deal of patience finger dexterity and knowledge of patterns and materials.

10. The church committee elected the following people Mr. Biggs Mrs. Bannish Mrs. King and Ms. Merihue.

Exercise 9   Group Activity: Comma, Semicolon, and Colon Use, Level of Difficulty 3

Form a group of three to five people. Add commas, semicolons, or colons to each of the following sentences wherever the group thinks they are necessary.

1. South Korea sometimes called the Republic of Korea has a population of approximately 45 million.

2. No one listened to Rebecca's excuses they had heard them all before.

3. The college hired an ombudsperson who would hear the complaints of both students and faculty the ombudsperson would try to represent all issues without bias.

4. When you are sending your children to camp please include the following items extra socks extra underwear a flashlight with extra batteries rain boots and a raincoat.

5. Although we enjoyed the dinner expensive as it was we did not appreciate the humour of the stand-up comedian.

6. Rapée pie a favourite in Quebec contains simple ingredients chicken pork rabbit potatoes and onions.

7. The chairperson of the committee gave the following directives to the committee meet deadlines attend every meeting and refrain from smoking.

8. Wallace opened a small craft stand at the ferry terminal he sold many items handcrafted belts quilted goods seashell ornaments and handmade soaps.

9. At one time the Inuit used the igloo when travelling it was a dome-shaped shelter made from snow blocks which protected the traveller from biting winds.

10. Everyone arrived on time Terry Randy Maxine and Marge.

11. Because Irene was sick she missed three of her math classes.

12. Stop shaking the table I am trying to draw a picture!

13. Police dogs specially trained police and mediators were sent into the hostage-taking area.

14. The DVD player the television the stereo the computer and the answering machine were damaged by the power surge.

The Apostrophe

Use an apostrophe in two cases: when you want to show that someone owns something (**possession**) or when you are using a shortened form of two words, called a **contraction**.

SHOWING POSSESSION

Simon's dog, the children's lunches, the rabbits' warren, her friend's address

Rather than learning complicated rules for the use of an apostrophe, remember this: start from your meaning—the root word. For example, if you were going to write about a town and its decision to change its water protection policy, then work from the root word—*town*—out to the possessive form:

town $\longrightarrow$ town's $\longrightarrow$ town's policy

If, on the other hand, you intend to talk about several towns and their policies, start with the new root word—*towns*—and work out to the possessive:

towns $\longrightarrow$ towns' $\longrightarrow$ towns' policies

As you know, some nouns in English do not form their plural in a regular way. Look at these examples:

men, women, children, mice, deer, sheep, feet, curricula, antennae, alumni, analyses, teeth

In such cases, these are the root words. It would make no sense for you to add an additional -*s* or -*es* to each one like this: *mens, womens, teeths, deers,* and so forth because these are not the plural forms. To make irregular plural nouns possessive, use the same procedure: work out from the root word (which is already in the plural):

Correct: men's hats

Incorrect: mens' hats

(There is no root word *mens*. Always *look to the immediate left of the apostrophe for the root word*. You can see that immediately to the left of the apostrophe is *mens*, which is not a word.)

Correct: women's clubs

Incorrect: womens' clubs

Correct: children's toys

Incorrect: childrens' toys

A special situation arises in connection with two people and ownership. If you wanted people to share ownership of something, then you would write the last person's name in the possessive case by using an apostrophe. If, however, you wanted to show that each person owned something separately, you would make each person's name in the possessive case.

Bill and Sharon's restaurant (jointly owned—a single restaurant shared)

Bill's and Sharon's restaurants (Each person owns a restaurant.)

the cat and kittens' blanket (They share the same blanket.)

the cat's and kittens' blankets (The cat has a blanket. The kittens share one blanket.)

the cat's and kitten's blankets (The cat has a blanket. There is only one kitten with its own blanket.)

CONTRACTIONS

The second major use of apostrophes is in **contractions**—*when two words are shortened into one*. The apostrophe takes the place of the missing letters.

Common Contractions

here is	here's
you are	you're
he will	he'll
she is	she's
it is or it has	it's
there is	there's
I am	I'm
will not	won't
can not (or cannot)	can't
they will	they'll
I will	I'll

Exercise 10   Using Apostrophes, Level of Difficulty 2

Read each sentence. Think carefully whether you will need to use apostrophes or not. Add apostrophes wherever you think they are necessary. Check your answers in the Answer Key.

1. None of Zoes flowers survived the winter, and shes upset about it.

2. Two of the childrens socks are missing from the dryer.

3. One of the mens complaints was about overtime pay.

4. The golfers swing was so poor that everyone ducked to avoid being hit.

5. His cats name tag was missing from its collar.

6. Tom and Annas card shop was sold last week.

7. The ships whistle blew, and the passengers lunch was disturbed by the noise.

8. Theyll be over to talk with you in a minute.

9. The hospitals surgeon told us hed be assisting in Dads operation.

10. Were afraid youre too late to save the sheeps life.

CAPITALIZATION

Use 1

Always use a capital letter at the beginning of every sentence.

Mr. Woods lifts weights.

Fish are animals.

Use 2

Always capitalize a person's name and any title that goes with that name.

I watched Patty and Nell in the contest.

Have you met Professor Ko?

I introduced Dr. Brim.

Mrs. Wippinski is my aunt.

Do *not* use capitals to identify occupations or professional rank unless they are part of a person's title.

Wendy is an electrician.

Who is the new lawyer?

Bob is now manager of the department.

How pleased we were to meet Premier Allen!

Use 3

Always capitalize names of relatives when you are using them as a kind of title.

I decided to ask Mother.

Have you spoken to my mother? (You need no capital here. You are not addressing your mother by her title.)

I think Uncle Bob is a card.

My friend's uncle is a farmer.

Use 4

Always capitalize the word *I*.

I want to know why.

I can't go.

Exercise 11   Capitalization, Level of Difficulty 1

Put in capital letters where they are needed. Check your answers in the Answer Key.

1. has uncle fred taken the job with doctor robinson?

2. did i tell you that my mother knows your uncle seth?

3. the supervisor told mr. eng to talk to his doctor.

4. early in the afternoon the teacher talked to superintendent davis.

5. inspector gladeau discussed the incident with chief beckley.

Use 5

Always use capital letters to distinguish specific cultures, nationalities, and languages.

Do you speak French?

We are Canadian citizens.

Her friend is Jewish.

Use 6

Always use capital letters for days of the week, months of the year, and special holiday names.

I'll visit you on Boxing Day.

Ralph will be in Ontario on Monday.

Do *not* capitalize the names of seasons: fall, winter, spring, summer.

Use 7

Always capitalize the first word and the important words in the titles of books.

I enjoyed reading *A Bend in the River*.

Our English class is reading *The Fall of the Sparrow*.

Exercise 12   Capitalization, Level of Difficulty 2

Put in capital letters where necessary. Check your answers in the Answer Key.

1. *a whale for the killing* is the title of a book by farley mowat, the famous canadian author.

2. many indo–canadian members of the community will be visiting india this summer.

3. my mother and i will spend christmas together in halifax.

4. last tuesday the manager of the department told us that march and april would have spectacular sales in spring fashions.

5. did you know that gwen speaks fluent english, italian, and spanish?

6. mark read *twelve days to a better body*.

7. a well-known scientist talked to dr. johnson at the convention in red deer.

8. new year's day is a statutory holiday for canadian workers.

9. the notice reported free french lessons to the residents of the city of moncton.

10. chef schneider prepares delicious german dishes.

Use 8

Use capital letters in the names of places in addresses.

> They live at 22 Alder Way.
>
> The newest movie theatre is on Johnson Street near Broad Avenue.

Use 9

Use capital letters for geographical names.

> They canoed on the Sooke River.
>
> June moved to Swift Current, Saskatchewan, from Grande Prairie, Alberta.
>
> My sister-in-law used to live in Thunder Bay, Ontario.

Use 10

Capitalize words like *river*, *lake*, and *mountains* when they are part of the name of a place.

> North Saskatchewan River
>
> Lake Erie
>
> Rocky Mountains

Use 11

Use capital letters for the names of organizations or institutions.

> She works for the Ministry of Health.
>
> We went to Coldale High School.
>
> Mariette works for the Ontario Hydro Commission.

Use 12

Use capital letters for the names of specific buildings.

> They met at Oxford Towers.
>
> That building is the Dominion Hotel.

Use 13

Use capital letters for brand names or product names with registered trademarks.

Phillip organized a workshop with Microsoft technicians.

My aunt loves Diet Coke on ice in the summer.

Buy two boxes of Kleenex at the drugstore, please.

Exercise 13   *Capitalization, Level of Difficulty 2*

Put in capital letters where they are necessary.

1. the niagara peninsula is known by canadians and americans alike.

2. does the fraser river flow into the pacific ocean?

3. we attended a seminar at the holiday inn in nanaimo, british columbia.

4. morgan has a savings account at island credit union in the herald building.

5. while vivian was on james island, she met some people from montreal, quebec.

6. The union of public employees talked to representatives from the ministry of labour.

7. my aunt laverne sold her house on fernie street and bought a condominium in sydney, n.s.

8. i told her to talk to ms. macdonald, the minister of employment.

9. arlette bought the book *best restaurants in canada* at the gift shop.

10. the burlington recreation centre hosted hockey teams from across canada and the united states.

11. we will make polish potato salad for supper on saturday.

12. a german shepherd dog is an intelligent, trainable, and loyal breed.

13. i knew him when he attended mount royal secondary school.

14. on mother's day, i'll send my mother a bouquet of carnations and roses.

15. the students of edmonton college organized a skiing trip to the cascade mountains.

16. for the city, a french poodle or a welsh terrier makes a friendly family pet.

17. i bought a box of christie's cookies and a can of sunrype apple juice as treats for the kids i babysit in oak bay.

18. my honda lawnmower has lasted for more than six years.

19. the boy scouts had a carwash at the petrocan station on shelbourne street.

20. the university of victoria had a guest speaker in the clearihue building last thursday evening.

21. she wears jordache jeans, zany tee-shirts, and bongo shoes.

22. my brother-in-law is the manager of the toy shop on yates street.

23. uncle john's toyota corolla station wagon runs better than his volkswagen.

24. the president of the alberta government employees union was quoted in wednesday night's *calgary herald*.

25. the teenager bought a bottle of pepsi and a package of hostess chips.

Chapter 12: Review Test

Part 1: Commas, Level of Difficulty 2

Insert commas wherever you think they are necessary in the following sentences. Some sentences may not require commas. (1/2 point each, 12 points)

1. The dogwood the wild rose the crocus and the trillium are all flowers used as provincial emblems.

2. Maxwell left his shift early because he felt feverish.

3. Five of the employees were collecting the mail sorting the addresses and checking the postal codes; two of the others were checking addresses on parcels sorting packages and checking labels; one employee was feeding the letters into the scanner checking addresses and monitoring the computer.

4. On December 8 1991 the Soviet Union became the Commonwealth of Independent States.

5. The deadline for project proposals is 7 May 2009.

6. The meeting was of course interrupted by the same individual.

7. The last trip I had was in July 2007.

8. Chewing furniture stealing food and pestering the cat made the new pup rather unpopular.

9. Frederick Ormstead joined the college on February 17 1989 and he retired from teaching on August 26 2008.

10. For your information misunderstandings can be avoided by using clear communication focussed goals and understandable language.

Part 2: Semicolons, Level of Difficulty 2

Add semicolons wherever you think they are necessary in the following sentences. Some sentences do not require semicolons. (1 point each, 14 points)

1. Marilyn applied for the job as technician she believes her experience qualifies her for the job.

2. The teenagers longed to go to the concert therefore, they were prepared to spend the night in line waiting for tickets.

3. She was certain that his answer would be disappointing.

4. Mediterranean cooking is very flavourful and healthy many cooks are experimenting with some of the classic recipes.

5. After the summer storm, six of their rose bushes were broken Lewis has managed to save two of them.

6. The doctor made a decision you may not agree with her.

7. The master carpenter studied his blueprints he puzzled over a set of difficult stairs.

8. Martine was frustrated because she had not won the prize.

9. There are three rattlesnakes found in Canada one called the western rattlesnake can be found in the southerly parts of three western provinces.

10. Paulina and Vincent broke off their engagement no one is certain what happened between them.

11. Ruffed grouse are chicken-like birds of the woodlands the males make a distinct drumming sound.

12. Politics and government gossip don't interest Carla in the least.

13. Helmut coaches soccer at the university his son is on the team.

14. Her illness left her feeling restless and moody.

Part 3: Colons, Level of Difficulty 3

Add colons wherever you think they are necessary in the following sentences. Some sentences do not require colons. (1 point each, 7 points)

1. Don't make the mistake of giving out credit card numbers over the phone or telling strangers what your bank account number is.

2. Finally, the plan was revealed everyone was to get a cut in personal taxes.

3. The children received many gifts from their grandparents books, dolls, painting sets, and video games.

4. His excuse for arriving late for the important meeting seemed suspicious thieves had stolen his car.

5. Her recipe for good health was exercise, good nutrition, plenty of sleep, and lots of humour.

6. Jill and April made the following costumes for the play one platypus, three penguins, four cats, and one toad.

7. Good hockey players require certain skills and talents they must be fast on the ice, agile on skates, and quick-thinking.

Part 4: Commas, Colons, and Semicolons, Level of Difficulty 3

Add commas, colons, and semicolons wherever you think they are necessary in the following sentences. Some sentences may not require commas, colons, or semicolons. (1/2 point each, 10 points)

1. The captain of the lacrosse team met with management they discussed training time contract demands and endorsement rights.

2. Emile proved to be a wonderful juggler who could entertain crowds of all sizes.

3. Eating patterns family values and parenting skills may begin at home in our early years we continue to modify these beliefs during our lifetimes.

4. The reporter on the other hand would not reveal his sources he believed in protecting his informant.

5. We worried of course in spite of ourselves however, we did not reveal our anxiety.

6. Sports such as boxing kick-boxing and wrestling are considered to be too violent some groups are openly opposing them lobbying for new laws against them and speaking out against the sponsors.

7. Do not forget your dental appointment the dentist must check your sore tooth and repair the filling.

8. The rainy evening was to be different for Howard he was to meet the woman of his dreams.

Part 5: Capitalization, Level of Difficulty 1

Read each sentence carefully. Underline each letter that should be capitalized. (1 point each, 30 points)

1. Last tuesday aunt lisa stayed at the pacific princess hotel.

2. I converse with a group at mercy hospital.

3. the canadian cancer society sells daffodils every april to raise money for cancer research.

4. We prepared swiss fondue and german chocolate cake.

5. the bank of montreal is closed most evenings, except thursdays and fridays.

6. mr. eriksen talked about the situation with his neighbour, mr. yinh, who works for the department of fisheries.

7. Some of the parents brought thrifty's nacho chips, mexicale salsa and a case of coke for the ball game at spectrum high school.

CHECKOUT

1. Academic English students need to acquire and use exemplary writing skills.

2. An English handbook provides a useful reference to help with your writing work.

3. If a dependent clause comes before the main clause in a sentence, use a comma after the dependent clause.

4. *However, moreover, consequently, therefore, likewise, nevertheless, furthermore, otherwise,* and *indeed* are weak conjunctions. They are called conjunctive adverbs and are often accompanied by semicolons.

5. The correct use of standard punctuation and capitalization in academic writing helps to make meaning clear to the reader.

Patterns of Sentences

Chapter Objectives

After completing this chapter, you will be able to

- identify simple, compound, complex, and compound–complex sentences

- recognize how to connect independent clauses in compound sentences

- recognize coordinating conjunctions

- use dependent and independent clauses to create complex sentences

- decide whether the special relationship between ideas in a complex sentence is based on time or condition

- recognize subordinate conjunctions

- use relative clauses

- write various patterns of sentences

INTRODUCTION

English has the following four basic patterns of sentences:

1. simple

2. compound

3. complex

4. compound–complex.

You can recognize each sentence pattern by how many ideas it contains and how the ideas relate to one another.

Each sentence pattern contains at least one clause. A **clause** is a unit of meaning with a subject–verb set in it. What makes sentence patterns different from one another is how the clauses in each pattern relate.

Each grammar chapter contains a variety of exercises at the following three different levels of difficulty:

- Level of difficulty 1: introductory

- Level of difficulty 2: intermediate

- Level of difficulty 3: advanced

Choose level 1 of difficulty if you feel you will need to do a lot of work on the topic. Choose level 2 of difficulty if you have some knowledge of the topic and simply need to refresh your understanding of the ideas. Choose level 3 of difficulty if you feel you have mastered the ideas and want to challenge your knowledge.

Try the self-test to see what you remember about sentence patterns. Then check your answers in the Answer Key.

Chapter 15: Self-Test

Part 1: Identifying Patterns of Sentences, Level of Difficulty 2

Read each sentence carefully. Write **SIMPLE** after each simple sentence. Write **COMPOUND** after each compound sentence. Write **COMPLEX** after each complex sentence. (2 points each, 30 points)

1. Email me if you have time. _____

2. Several people were hurrying to catch the bus, but they were too late. _____

3. Hamsters are popular pets for kids. _____

4. The airport was crowded; I couldn't find my friend. _____

5. Is your brother-in-law a qualified electrician? _____

6. Please wait here until she returns. _____

7. Although he was young, he was wise for his age. _____

8. Gene tried to row across the lake, but he tired after an hour. _____

9. The supervisor wanted her staff to be more productive. _____

10. Many hours were spent in talking about the project, and, at last, the plans were finalized. _____

11. Because Latisha couldn't swim, she was not allowed to go. _____

12. She has been a member of the *Peel Regional Police Service* for 10 years. _____

13. The radio and the television were on at the same time. _____

14. While I got a haircut, my son read a book. _____

15. You can buy this used book from me, or you can pay a lot more online. _____

Part 2: Identifying Clauses, Level of Difficulty 2

Underline every main clause (simple sentence). Put parentheses around every dependent clause. (1/2 point for each part, 20 points)

1. While you were at the store, the office supervisor called you.

2. Although the wind was strong, no property was damaged.

3. Please ask Adara if she is coming with us.

4. Ronald played the violin until he was 12 years old.

5. Tell me when Christopher can meet at the conference.

6. We're having a celebration after our last exam is over.

7. Since she left, I've been lonely.

8. The fishers caught some whitefish when they went out yesterday.

9. As the child walked, he whistled.

10. When we were away last weekend, the power was off at our house.

Part 3: Combining Sentences, Level of Difficulty 3

Combine these simple sentences into one complex sentence. (5 points each, 20 points, to be marked by your instructor or a student marker.)

1. The soup was cold.

   The soup was salty.

   We complained about the soup.

   _____

   _____

2. She yelled at her son.

   She was sorry for yelling.

   She apologized to her son.

   _____

   _____

3. The green dress was expensive.

   The blue dress was cheaper.

   I bought the blue dress.

   _____

   _____

4. The sea was rough.

   We did not take the boat out.

   The boat was five metres long.

   _____

   _____

Part 4: Your Own Sentences, Level of Difficulty 3

Write your own sentences, in the spaces provided, but follow directions carefully. (5 points each, 30 points, to be marked by your instructor or a student marker.)

1. Write a compound sentence using the word *storm*.

   _____

   _____

2. Write a simple sentence using the word *desk*.

   _____

   _____

3. Write a compound sentence using the word *bank*.

   _____

   _____

4. Write a complex sentence using the word *magic*.

   _____

   _____

5. Write a compound–complex sentence using the word *violence*.

   _____

   _____

SIMPLE SENTENCES

A **simple sentence** contains *one complete idea, a single subject–verb* (S–V) *set*. It is a *one-clause sentence*. A clause that stands on its own can be termed a *principal, main,* or *independent clause*. It has one or more subjects or verbs.

    S   V

The **tree bends** in the wind. (The sentence has one S–V set; the single idea is that the tree bends.)

    S   V   V

The **tree bends** and **groans** in the wind. (The sentence has one S–V set (S–V–V); it is a one-idea sentence—a tree can bend and groan.)

    S   S   V

The **tree** and the **shrubs bend** in the wind. (The sentence has one S–V set (S–S–V); one idea is in the sentence—trees and shrubs can bend in the wind.)

COMPOUND SENTENCES

A **compound sentence**, on the other hand, is really a double sentence. It expresses *two simple, complete ideas*. It contains two separate S–V sets, two completely separate ideas or *independent clauses*. To create a compound sentence, write one simple sentence, and then add another simple sentence to it. Think of a compound sentence as one (independent clause) + one (another related independent clause) = compound.

The tree bends in the wind, but it does not break.

First simple sentence: The tree bends in the wind.

Second simple sentence: The tree does not break in the wind.

The two simple sentences have been joined with *but*. In addition, the noun *tree* in the second clause has been changed to the pronoun *it*, and the phrase *in the wind* has been dropped for smoother reading. Notice that you must use a comma in front of the conjunctions in compound sentences.

Joiner words, or *conjunctions*, join simple sentences to make compound sentences. Conjunctions that work in compound sentences are called **coordinating conjunctions** because they coordinate two independent clauses.

Coordinating Conjunctions

and	but	yet	
or	for	so	nor

A *semicolon* can join related clauses (the two independent clauses) to make compound sentences.

I love to eat ice cream; I buy it every shopping trip.

Exercise 1   Compound Sentences, Level of Difficulty 1

The following sentences are compound sentences. Write **1** above the first complete idea (simple sentence) in the sentence; write **2** above the second complete idea (simple sentence) in the sentence.

1. I studied hard, but I did not pass the test.

2. She must have left, or she would be in the office right now.

3. Helina wrote to the company, but she did not get an answer.

4. The newly hired accountant was tired, and she wanted to go home.

5. Most of the houses in our area were built in the 1950s, but some new ones are being built up on the hill.

6. The meeting was cancelled, but it will be rescheduled for next week.

7. Sherry filled in an application for the job, and she mailed it on her way to class.

8. Would you like to come with us, or would you prefer to stay here?

9. My mother won a contest last week, and she's delighted with the prize.

10. The boys did the dishes, and then they mowed the lawn.

Exercise 2   Compound Sentences, Level of Difficulty 2

Work in pairs. Add another complete idea (simple sentence) to each of the following simple sentences to form good compound sentences. Use one of the coordinating conjunctions *and, but, or, for, nor, yet,* or *so,* or use a semicolon to connect your ideas. Use commas correctly. Write the new compound sentences in the spaces provided. Check with other pairs to correct your answers.

1. Groceries are expensive today.

   _____

2. The movie was exciting.

   _____

3. His course was boring.

   _____

4. Some of the customers were angry.

   _____

5. I lost $20.

   _____

6. Arnie bought a new car.

   _____

7. Her daughter is a doctor.

   _____

8. It is raining hard.

   _____

9. The unemployment rate is high.

   _____

10. His wife attends Valley College.

    _____

Exercise 3   Compound Sentences, Level of Difficulty 2

Combine these simple sentences into compound sentences. Use *or, and, but, nor, so, yet,* or *for,* or use a *semicolon* to join the sentences. Rewrite your sentences in the spaces provided. Use commas correctly. Check your answers with other students in the class.

The day was sunny. (simple sentence)

The day was not hot. (simple sentence)

The day was sunny, but it was not hot. (compound sentence)

1. Dogs can be a tremendous nuisance.

   This fact does not prevent people from owning them.

   _____

   _____

2. The coffee is strong.

   The coffee is not hot.

   _____

   _____

3. My uncle owns a delicatessen.

   The delicatessen is not doing good business.

   _____

   _____

4. The back of the lawn chair is broken.

   The chair needs to be fixed.

   _____

   _____

5. A terrific storm blew down the shack.

   The greenhouse beside the shack was not harmed.

   _____

   _____

6. Several people were lined up at the bank.

   Several people seemed angry.

   _____

   _____

7. We could go to the theatre to see the movie.

   We could rent the DVD from Top Video.

   _____

   _____

8. Lightning flashed across the lake.

   A hard rain began to pour down.

   _____

   _____

Exercise 4   *Simple and Compound Sentences, Level of Difficulty 2*

Read the following sentences. Write **S** after each simple sentence, and write **C** after each compound sentence. Check your answers in the Answer Key.

1. Margot and Antonio make the best cappuccino coffee. _____

2. After driving through the storm, Michelle was tired, hungry, and nervous. _____

3. Certainly children need plenty of exercise and fun in their lives. _____

4. At the festival, a few merrymakers were swimming in the city fountain, and the police were called to remove them. _____

5. A clown was talking to the cashier in the beauty shop, and she was smiling and laughing at his remarks. _____

6. Nadia will have to go to the store to buy some anchovies for the Caesar salad. _____

7. Workers did not ratify the agreement; they decided to walk off the job at midnight. _____

8. Their cottage industry was making scented candles and soap. _____

9. We will drive through the Okanagan to pick up some peaches for canning, and we have also decided to tour around Kelowna at the same time. _____

10. The watch is broken, or it needs a new battery. _____

11. Collecting rare glass and old jazz records are two of Felicia's interests. _____

12. A student in my class, Lev, can speak four languages fluently. _____

13. The hostess had prepared for all eventualities, but she was not prepared for the Duke's sudden arrival at dinner. _____

COMPLEX SENTENCES

A *compound* sentence is really a double sentence made up of two simple (one idea) sentences and a coordinating conjunction (*and*, *but*, *or*, *so*, *nor*, *for*, or *yet*) that joins the two main clauses. **Complex** sentences are also two-idea sentences, but they have an important difference.

In a complex sentence, *how the two ideas relate to one another* is most important. *One clause* is called the *main* (or independent or principal) clause while the other is called the *dependent* (subordinate or fragment) clause. The *dependent clause* needs the independent clause to make sense.

He would not eat his Brussels sprouts because he hated the taste.

The first clause is *He would not eat his Brussels sprouts*. The second clause is *because he hated the taste*. Although the second clause contains a subject–verb set, it cannot stand by itself. It is a **fragment**. The first clause can stand alone; it is independent.

More about Clauses

The clauses in a complex sentence have a special relationship based on *time* or *condition*. The main clause is like a simple sentence, and the second clause is like a fragment or piece of a sentence. All clauses contain subject–verb sets.

He would not eat his Brussels sprouts because he hated the taste.

The second clause gives a reason why he would not eat the vegetables. The relationship between the two clauses is based on a *condition*—a causal one. The dependent clause serves as the condition.

You could keep changing the condition. Conditions and time factors change the meaning of sentences. The main clause can be kept the same, but by adding different times or conditions, you can change the meaning of the sentence.

main clause	dependent clause
(simple sentence)	**(adding a new condition)**

He would not eat his Brussels sprouts *until she ate hers.* (time condition)

He would not eat his Brussels sprouts *because they were overcooked.* (causal condition)

He would not eat his Brussels sprouts *although his parents threatened him.* (contrast condition)

He would not eat his Brussels sprouts *even if you paid him.* (condition)

He would not eat his Brussels sprouts *when suppertime arrived.* (time)

He would not eat his Brussels sprouts *before he went out.* (time)

He would not eat his Brussels sprouts *as he was watching TV.* (time)

All of the dependent clauses add a condition or time to the main clause.

Exercise 5   *Two Types of Clauses, Level of Difficulty 2*

Write **M** above the main clause. Write **D** above the dependent clause. Check your answers in the Answer Key.

1. Because we had a party last night, we're exhausted today.

2. A salesperson will help you if you ring the bell.

3. When Mrs. Singh was in Europe, she visited Rome.

4. The kids were watching television as we were playing cards.

5. Although Maxine is a qualified welder, she can't find work.

6. Before you go to bed, let the cat out.

7. After his family telephoned, Acton was depressed.

8. Since Aileen won't be able to be in class tomorrow, I'll collect the assignment for her.

9. If I tell you about it, will you keep it a secret?

10. Because her son had the measles, Dotti missed a week of classes.

11. When he went for the interview, he lost his glasses.

12. He twisted his ankle while he was water skiing.

13. If the baby cries, pick her up.

14. I wanted to go to Montreal, although I couldn't afford the trip.

15. The game was exciting because the two teams were very competitive.

16. After the new manager was appointed, the employees became suspicious.

Conjunctions

Subordinate conjunctions hook two clauses (ideas) together in a complex sentence. They show a time or conditional relationship. They are powerful because they control meaning.

Consider this complex sentence:

Wanda screamed *as* the dentist extracted her tooth.

The subordinate conjunction *as* shows a special time relationship between the two ideas. You get a picture in your mind of Wanda screaming just as the dentist is pulling her tooth. In other words, *as* shows ideas happening simultaneously.

Next, take the same two ideas, but change the conjunction.

Wanda screamed *after* the dentist extracted her tooth.

After shows a time relationship. Which idea happened first? First, the dentist extracted Wanda's tooth. Second, Wanda screamed.

Change the conjunction again.

Wanda screamed *because* the dentist extracted her tooth.

Because shows a reason and, therefore, it indicates a condition exists between the two ideas. Wanda screamed (why?) because the dentist extracted her tooth.

Recognize the meaning *through the relationship of clauses in a complex sentence.* To do that, you must consider whether time or condition plays a part. You'll notice, too, that reading with this awareness of how ideas relate will increase your overall reading ability tremendously.

Below is a list of subordinate conjunctions and their functions.

Subordinate Conjunctions

To establish a time relationship:	To establish a condition:
after	if
as	since
before	because
until	although
while	when

Here are example sentences using subordinate conjunctions:

After the concert, we went to Bob's Place for steak and beer. (time)

As Roland was working the tiller, we rowed the boat. (time)

Before the winner was announced, the contestant fainted. (time)

Until the old person got a seat, he had to stand on the bus. (time)

While I was boiling the pasta, you prepared the salad. (time)

When Stephanie finished singing, the audience burst into applause. (time)

If the fire alarm rings, leave by the nearest exit. (condition)

Since Jacob was a small boy, he wanted to fly a plane. (time)

Because rent is expensive in Toronto, she has decided to leave. (condition)

Although most people are cautious, accidents still happen. (condition)

The clauses can change position, too. All of the above sentences could start with the main clause and end in the dependent clause; meaning would remain the same. Let's take three of the above sentences and exchange the position of the clauses.

Jacob wanted to fly a plane since he was a small boy.

She has decided to leave because rent in Toronto is expensive.

Accidents still happen although most people are cautious.

The meaning of the sentences does not change; however, *when the dependent clause is placed first*, it is *followed by a comma*. When a main clause is placed first, the sentence does not usually require a comma.

Exercise 6   *Clauses and Complex Sentences, Level of Difficulty 2*

Work in pairs. Decide if a time relationship or a conditional relationship exists between the clauses. Write **TIME** or **CONDITION** after each sentence. Check your answers in the Answer Key.

1. Because Laurie can fix her own car, she saves a lot of money. _____

2. When the buzzer goes off, take the buns out of the oven. _____

3. Because he was too old, he was not accepted. _____

4. He wanted to stay in school until he'd achieved his goal. _____

5. Although they made a mistake, they didn't apologize. _____

6. If the plant gets too tall, pinch it back. _____

7. The hall looked colourful after it had been decorated. _____

8. Hockey is popular since fans find it an exciting game to watch. _____

9. As he plays the guitar, he sings in a soft voice. _____

10. After she came to Canada, she worked in a grocery store. _____

11. He kept on drinking until there was a crisis in his family. _____

12. After I cleaned the eavestroughs, I painted them. _____

13. Although he appeared to be calm, he was very angry. _____

Exercise 7   Clauses and Complex Sentences, Level of Difficulty 2

Make each dependent clause into a complex sentence by adding words to make it complete. Be sure to add at least one main clause along with your dependent clause. Use commas correctly. Check with others for correct answers.

since he was laid off

Tony has been very worried since he was laid off.

1. because Ari loves Hollywood movies

_____

2. when the tide comes in

_____

3. as we quickly prepared breakfast

_____

4. although the room was messy

_____

5. as the meeting was going on

_____

6. while I sleep

_____

7. because Mr. Beggs has a bad temper

_____

8. until the lights went out

_____

9. when Sal won't talk to me

_____

10. before the settlement was reached

_____

11. when he designs a stage set

_____

Sentence Fragments

A **sentence fragment** *is a piece of a sentence*. Although it may contain a S–V set, it does not make sense by itself. Here are some examples of sentence fragments:

Because I was sick.

Wendy dusting the shelf.

Dark and stormy clouds.

Since the coach was angry.

Forgetting my assignment on the table.

None of the above makes sense alone. Each fragment relies on the sentence before it or after it in order to complete its meaning.

Sentence fragments are errors in academic writing. They can make reading difficult and meaning ambiguous. Although you may use fragments when speaking with another person, fragment errors are *sentence-level errors in formal writing*. You should avoid writing them.

Exercise 8   *Recognizing Fragments and Sentence Patterns, Level of Difficulty 3*

Read each of the following word groups. If the word group is a fragment (piece of a sentence), write **FRAGMENT** after it. If the word group is a simple sentence, a compound or a complex sentence, write **SIMPLE**, **COMPOUND**, or **COMPLEX** after it.

1. Pamela was afraid to go to the job interview at Delby and Delby, Attorneys at Law. _____

2. Running too hard and breathing with difficulty. _____

3. Reuben wanted to keep track of his hours, but he forgot to write them down. _____

4. Unusual animals can be found in the tropics, and some species are particular to specific zones only. _____

5. After the celebration is over. _____

6. Tiffany is learning to operate a motorcycle. _____

7. Theo's painting has steadily continued in its development. _____

8. Although Allen is afraid of snakes, he won't admit it. _____

9. The restaurateur and the tax accountant jog every morning before work. _____

10. Many wonderful things to eat! _____

11. On a warm May afternoon we sang and paddled our canoe with a deep sense of camaraderie. _____

12. The young woman was a gifted pianist who played at the annual charity event for the homeless. _____

13. Since the water heater had broken. _____

14. The papers, blowing all over the floor. _____

15. Eating too many rich foods and sleeping too much can create
health problems. _____

A simple sentence contains a single idea, a compound sentence has two simple sentences or main clauses, and a complex sentence involves a special relationship between an independent and dependent clause. Identify each of the following sentences by writing **SIMPLE, COMPOUND,** or **COMPLEX** after each. Check your answers in the Answer Key.

1. The Belgian artist and the Swiss National have lived in the same
neighbourhood for 20 years. _____

2. I went to the concert alone because my friend wouldn't come with me. _____

3. Since Rita arrived in York, she's been really busy. _____

4. Unfortunately, Norman did not finish his thesis at Northwest University. _____

5. Many fish died in the river, but scientists could not find a cause. _____

6. The baby giggled and giggled while we snapped photos of her. _____

7. The postal workers went on strike since a settlement could not be reached. _____

8. Would you like to experience the trip of a lifetime this summer? _____

9. The music was low, but it bothered me anyway. _____

10. With hesitation and a slight stumble, the patient walked down the
corridor of the hospital. _____

11. The date of Picassco's blue period is memorable in the
history of Western art. _____

12. The door had sprung open with the force of the wind, or someone
had pried it open deliberately. _____

13. Add one cup of flour and two fresh eggs to the pancake recipe. _____

14. We talked, and then we took a long stroll along the beach. _____

15. The wedding party was a success; everyone enjoyed it. _____

16. The golfer made flamboyant gestures if he didn't make his putt. _____

17. When you drive south on Allan Road, turn left at Finch Avenue. _____

18. The office was closed, but I couldn't wait for it to open again. _____

19. For heaven's sake, stop lying to me! _____

20. Two of the students were discussing some of the difficulties of
coming back to college. _____

Relative Clauses

Relative clauses are *special dependent clauses in complex sentences*. They begin with *who, that*, or *which* and sometimes *whose* or *whom*. They are called *relative clauses* because they start with relative pronouns. You must place these clauses next to the words they describe. Relative clauses often split the main clause because they are often in the middle of the clause.

The man *who passed me* looks familiar.

The man looks familiar (main clause) who passed me. (relative clause).

Who passed me is a clause pointing out which man the speaker is talking about. The clause must be placed right after *man*.

If you do not place relative clauses next to the words they define, funny things can happen.

The little boy bought the dog who wore glasses and a Blue Jays baseball cap. (Where should the relative clause *who wore glasses and a Blue Jays baseball cap* go?)

The portrait belonged to the City of Halifax that was sold. (How would you fix this sentence to make it clear?)

The answer was found at the back of the book which was wrong. (Is it the answer or the book that is wrong?)

Mr. Altman that had fleas found an old, shaggy dog. (Who had fleas?)

Mike lost his cat in the park that was orange and three-legged. (Where should you place the relative clause?)

Cathy that was a brown tabby and wearing a blue collar lost her cat in the park. (Who is wearing a blue collar?)

These sentences sound ridiculous, don't they? You should place relative clauses next to the words they modify. Also if a dependent clause comes first in a complex sentence, place a comma after it.

Restrictive and Non-Restrictive Clauses

You learned about restrictive and non-restrictive clauses in Chapter 13. Do you recall what these two special cases of clauses mean? If a relative clause is *essential to the meaning* of a noun or the sentence itself, it is a *restrictive clause*. You would not place commas around it.

However, if a relative clause is *not essential to the meaning* of a noun or the sentence itself, it is called a *non-restrictive clause*. You would use commas around it.

Here is another hint for you: Use the relative pronoun *that, which*, or *who* to begin restrictive clauses.

None of the birds *that were found in that region* were infected by the West Nile virus.

The chairs *that had been sold to Mr. Tong* are missing from the storage area.

Several out-of-the-way places in Ontario, *which we enjoyed visiting very much*, are featured in the magazine *Travel Ontario*.

Exercise 10 Relative Clauses and Complex Sentences, Level of Difficulty 3

Use the following as relative clauses to make good complex sentences. Use separate paper. Your instructor may ask to see your work, or you may exchange your work with others in the class.

who worked at the department store (relative clause)

Sentence containing the relative clause: The woman who worked at the department store won the lottery.

1. that was incorrect

2. who invented the SnoreMaster

3. which was fun

4. who wore the leather jacket

5. which is being torn down

6. who is tall and thin

7. that we bought

8. which they are investigating

Exercise 11 Group Activity: Review of Complex Sentences, Level of Difficulty 3

Form a group of three to five students. Combine each of the following sets of simple sentences into one good complex sentence. Be prepared to share your answers.

The television was too loud.

The television belonged to my neighbour.

The television annoyed me.

The television that belonged to my neighbour annoyed me because it was too loud.

1. The students were busy.

   The students were finishing.

   The teacher talked to the students.

   _____

   _____

2. My uncle owns a horse.

   The horse is a champion.

   _____

   _____

3. Eggs are expensive.

   Cheese is expensive.

   Eggs are a good source of protein.

   Cheese is a good source of protein.

   _____

   _____

   _____

4. The house was for sale.

   The house was rundown.

   The house sold last week.

   _____

   _____

5. The man was a millionaire.

   The man owned property.

   The property was on Prince Edward Island.

   _____

   _____

6. The woman had an interview.

   The woman was nervous.

   The woman wore a red suit.

   _____

   _____

7. The farmer lost money on his crops.

   His crops were ruined by the drought.

   _____

   _____

8. The elevator door slid open.

   I heard music inside the elevator.

   _____

   _____

9. The mayor made an announcement.

   The citizens of the town were shocked.

   _____

   _____

10. Unusual patterns of stars can be seen.

    Unusual patterns of stars are best seen in the fall.

    In the fall the earth's atmosphere is clear.

    _____

    _____

11. He enjoys shopping.

    He enjoys buying items on sale.

    Sale items are often bargains.

    _____

    _____

12. The family bought a jeep.

    The family rented camping gear.

    The family went on a camping trip to Alaska.

    _____

    _____

Exercise 12   Main Clauses, Dependent Clauses, and Commas, Level of Difficulty 3

Underline the main clauses. Put parentheses ( ) around dependent clauses. Insert commas wherever necessary. Be prepared to share your answers.

1. Salvatore is the best Italian chef in town because he cares about the quality of food in his restaurant.

2. The actress answered the reporter's questions after the filming was over.

3. Since you decided to stop drinking have you noticed any change in your outlook?

4. Several students were from Argentina where they had been political prisoners.

5. While the teacher was reading a story to the class a student gave each child a book of cut-out valentines some scissors and some glue.

6. When he was in the navy Pedro learned many skills in electronics.

7. Because Rick prefers to work alone he is often assigned to the night shift.

8. Rose and her sister opened a ladies' fashion store in the small mall although neither had any experience operating a business.

9. Albertina stood on the deck watching the seabirds while her children played on the beach.

10. Red orange green and purple peppers were used in the salad because the colours looked scrumptious on the buffet table.

11. As the cat studied the bird in the tree the bird in the tree studied the cat.

12. Roger read the magazine article until it was time to go for the appointment.

13. Because the peddlar did not have a licence the police officer arrested him.

14. Cape Breton biologists report a drop in the number of songbirds because dangerous pesticides are getting into the food source and making the birds sterile.

Exercise 13   Review of Simple, Compound, and Complex Sentences, Level of Difficulty 3

Read each sentence carefully. Write **S** after all simple sentences. Write **C** after all compound sentences. Write **CX** after all complex sentences. Insert commas where needed. Check your answers in the Answer Key.

1. The Rangers have won most of their games but the Oilers are not far behind them. _____

2. Although the salesclerk tempted me into buying the new appliance I was not convinced it was a bargain. _____

3. Several lettuce heads and a few of the spinach plants had been damaged by insects. _____

4. Thirty dollars is not enough to buy a ticket but you may be able to get a better deal from the discount ticket booth. _____

5. Randolph worries about his looks and is concerned over his thinning hair. _____

6. The library is closed on Sundays and it is often closed holiday Mondays, too. _____

7. You can make delicious and nutritious meals for very little money if you are willing to spend the extra time on preparation. _____

8. Canada is a country made up of many cultures and beliefs with liberal immigration policies. _____

9. We travelled for three long hours but we were unable to find a motel. _____

10. Since he became president of the college he has been hard to contact. _____

11. Despite their best efforts the members of the jury could not reach a verdict in the difficult trial. _____

12. She described what she tried to do during her previous years at CIDA. _____

13. Some television shows are utterly stupid; they are often insulting to the viewers. _____

14. While the teams were on the field a fan threw a chicken at the umpire. _____

15. If you decide to invest in a condo determine how adequate the association's reserve fund is. _____

Exercise 14   Review of Simple, Compound, and Complex Sentences, Level of Difficulty 3

Follow the directions to complete this exercise. Be prepared to share your work.

1. Write a simple sentence using the word *refrigerator*.

   _____

2. Write a complex sentence using the word *flowers*.

   _____

   _____

3. Write a compound sentence using the word *honest*.

   _____

   _____

4. Write a complex sentence using the word *several*.

   _____

   _____

5. Write a compound sentence using the word *pamphlet*.

   _____

   _____

6. Write a simple sentence using the words *hot dog*.

   _____

   _____

7. Write a complex sentence using the word *terrifying*. Be sure the sentence has one restrictive clause.

   _____

   _____

8. Write a simple sentence using the word *chief*.

_____

_____

9. Write a complex sentence using the word *office*.

_____

_____

10. Write a compound sentence using the word *forecast*.

_____

_____

COMPOUND AND COMPLEX SENTENCES

The final sentence pattern is the **compound–complex sentence**. This sentence combines one or more dependent clauses with a compound sentence. This pattern of sentence is not as common as the other three mentioned earlier. However, as an academic reader, you will see the pattern. As an academic writer, you will use it.

The parents of the child who had been chosen for the part in the commercial were ecstatic, and they planned to celebrate with their family that evening.

Eating too much of a good thing could be harmful if you think about items like butter or cheese, and this excess could lead to heart disease.

In the first example, you see a compound sentence made up of two independent clauses or simple sentences:

The parents were ecstatic, and they planned to celebrate with their family that evening.

You also see a relative clause (restrictive, because it defines which child won).

who had been chosen for the part in the commercial

The combination of the compound sentence with the relative (dependent) clause makes up a compound–complex sentence.

In the second example, the two independent clauses in the compound sentence are *eating too much of a good thing could be harmful, and this excess could lead to heart disease*. The dependent clause is *if you think about items like butter or cheese*. The combination of a compound sentence with a dependent clause gives you a compound–complex sentence.

Exercise 15   Compound–Complex Sentences, Level of Difficulty 3

All of the following sentences are compound–complex. Underline the compound sentence. Put the dependent clause or clauses in parentheses ( ). Be prepared to share your answers.

1. After the terrible storm was over, the villagers assessed their buildings for damage, and they tried to rescue their animals.

2. Some of the people who were applying for the position were waiting in the main foyer of the building; they wanted to speak to the recruiting officer.

3. Neither Sheffield nor his partners would answer the enquiries that the government tax inspector was asking; moreover, they appeared to snub him in the hallway.

4. Of all the creatures on earth that she could want for a pet, why would she be interested in purchasing a boa constrictor, and where would she keep it?

5. The smuggler who was importing heroin was caught on an impaired driving charge, and he was also speeding at the time.

6. Work on this until you have completed it, and then you can go home.

Exercise 16   Group Activity: Writing Compound–Complex Sentences, Level of Difficulty 3

Form groups of three to five people. Write compound–complex sentences using each of the following words. Be prepared to share your answers with the rest of the class.

1. casino
2. the assumption
3. one player
4. believes
5. the parents
6. smiled
7. worries
8. the internet
9. stuffy
10. his dog

Chapter 15: Review Test

Part 1: Identifying Patterns of Sentences, Level of Difficulty 2

Read each sentence carefully. Write **SIMPLE** after each simple sentence. Write **COMPOUND** after each compound sentence. Write **COMPLEX** after each complex sentence. (2 points each, 30 points)

1. If I work hard, I'll pass the course. _____

2. The painter dipped his brush, and then he considered the canvas. _____

3. Too much sugar is not good for children's health. _____

4. He worked for the Red Cross; for 18 months, he was a volunteer. _____

5. Will you be over for supper tonight, or will you be eating out? _____

6. Beat this batter until it is smooth. _____

7. Because the flood had washed away the bridge, the road was closed. _____

8. The puppy tugged at the tablecloth, but he could not pull it out of the basket. _____

9. My sister-in-law and her friend took a trip to Greece last spring. _____

10. Many new techniques are used in medicine today, but many ways are still traditional. _____

11. The race was over although the fans were still cheering. _____

12. Electric charges have states: static or potential, and dynamic or flowing. _____

13. We rafted down the Thompson River and then explored a ranch in Clinton, B.C. _____

14. As the baby slept, the family played a board game. _____

15. He works out every day, and he feels better for it. _____

Part 2: Identifying Clauses, Level of Difficulty 2

Underline every main clause (simple sentence). Put parentheses around every dependent clause. (1/2 point for each main clause and 1/2 point for each dependent clause, 20 points)

1. After you read the book, give me your opinion of it.

2. Although we had chopped all the wood, we were too exhausted to stack it.

3. Orton does best when he works alone on a company project.

4. The kindergarten class gave a concert because they wanted to raise money for a field trip.

5. In 1805, William Clark and Captain Meriwether Lewis crossed the Rockies since few botanical expeditions had done so.

6. Wait until the digital camera has adjusted itself to the light.

7. If I watch the baby for you, will you buy me a coffee?

8. Before you camp on this site, dispose of your garbage in animal-proof trash receptacles.

9. The sailor wanted to know if he could buy me a drink.

10. Vincent Price acted in movies until he was 80 years old.

Part 3: Combining Sentences, Level of Difficulty 3

Combine these sentences into one complex sentence. (5 points each, 20 points, to be marked by the instructor or a student marker)

1. We cleaned the carpet.

   We painted the wall.

   We were exhausted.

   _____

   _____

2. The car was new.

   The car was expensive.

   We bought the car anyway.

   _____

   _____

3. She bought a lottery ticket.

   The lottery ticket cost $20.

   She wanted to win.

   _____

   _____

4. The bears were dangerous.

   The bears were getting into garbage.

   The wildlife workers moved the bears.

   _____

   _____

Part 4: Your Own Sentences, Level of Difficulty 3

Follow directions carefully as you write your own sentences in the lines provided. (5 points each, 30 points, to be marked by your instructor or a student marker)

1. Write a good complex sentence using the word *bicycle*.

   _____

   _____

2. Write a good simple sentence using the word *cigarette*.

   _____

   _____

3. Write a good compound sentence using the word *plane*.

   _____

   _____

4. Write a good complex sentence using the word *politician*.

    _____

    _____

5. Write a good compound–complex sentence using the word *photographer*.

    _____

    _____

CHECKOUT

1. What makes sentence patterns different from one another is how the clauses in each pattern relate to each other.

2. Place relative clauses next to the words they describe in a sentence.

3. Compound sentences contain two S–V sets joined by a coordinating conjunction.

4. Try varying your own writing style by using different patterns of sentences.

Sentence-Level Errors

Chapter Objectives

After completing this chapter, you will be able to

- identify and repair common sentence faults—run-on sentences, comma splices, sentence fragments, pronoun reference errors, parallelism faults, and faulty shifts

- use semicolons correctly in compound sentences

- identify conjunctive adverbs to aid punctuation

INTRODUCTION: SIX TYPES OF SENTENCE FAULTS

In this chapter you will find several types of common sentence errors: run-on sentences, comma splices, sentence fragments, pronoun errors, parallelism faults, and faulty shifts. These sentence-level errors are faults considered serious because they disrupt meaning.

These sentence-level errors are often subtle. In other words, as a writer you must keep them in mind when you edit, revise, and proofread. Here are some tips:

1. Think about what you want to say. Write your sentence and then re-read it carefully.

2. Concentrate on getting your ideas into words.

3. Read and re-read your sentences as many times as needed to make sure the sentences are saying what you want them to say. Read your sentences out loud to "hear" them.

4. Concentrate on the grammatical aspects of your sentence after you are satisfied the sentence means what you want it to mean.

5. Check for spelling and punctuation errors.

6. Now check for the subtle sentence-level errors discussed in this chapter.

7. It is important to refer to an English handbook from time to time. Look up a grammar issue when you are uncertain about it, because looking something up is a good way to learn.

8. Discuss structural sentence errors with others; you will find this method also enhances your learning.

9. You should be aiming constantly and consistently to improve the standards of your academic writing and to edit your own work better. Aim for improvement.

Each grammar chapter contains a variety of exercises at the following three different levels of difficulty.

Level of difficulty 1: introductory

Level of difficulty 2: intermediate

Level of difficulty 3: advanced

Choose level 1 of difficulty if you feel you will need to do a lot of work on the topic. Choose level 2 of difficulty if you have some knowledge of the topic and simply need to refresh your understanding of the ideas. Choose level 3 of difficulty if you feel you have mastered the ideas and want to challenge your knowledge.

Try writing the self-test on sentence-level errors that follows. Check your answers in the Answer Key.

Chapter 16: Self-Test

Part 1: Identifying Fragments and Sentences, Level of Difficulty 1

Read the following groups of words. Some are correct sentences; others are not. Write **S** after the groups of words that are correct sentences. Write **FRAG** after the groups of words that are fragments. (1 point each, 10 points)

1. Paid attention during the whole lecture. _____

2. Pamela battling a serious illness. _____

3. Because we noticed three seals on the beach. _____

4. An orchid is a delicate flower. _____

5. Thrifty's will be right over with the pizza. _____

6. With frustration and a heavy heart. _____

7. Interviews the clients for the company. _____

8. Donna locking the garage by remote control. _____

9. Since I picked up a *Globe and Mail* at the newsstand. _____

10. Learning to water ski can be fun. _____

Part 2: Identifying Run-ons and Sentences, Level of Difficulty 2

Read the following groups of words. Some are correct sentences; others are not. Write **S** after the groups of words that are correct sentences. Write **RO** after the groups of words that are run-on sentence faults. (1 point each, 10 points)

1. Hardly a word had been spoken during the dinner, everyone was deep in thought. _____

2. Owen was nervous on his first date with Kathy because it was the first since his divorce. _____

3. Some species of wildlife must be placed under protection, otherwise, their natural habitat would disappear with land development. _____

4. Marcie will write a proposal for starting a new program at the college, but she will have difficulty convincing the Ministry of Forests and Land Resources to give her funds. _____

5. The rescue attempt was set back because of the wind on the water; however, a crew will try again when the weather breaks. _____

6. The Engineering Department will set its exam for next week, consequently, students will be studying hard. _____

7. The carpenter measured the closet wall then he began making notes. _____

8. The TV movie was obnoxiously melodramatic; we couldn't bear to watch it. _____

9. Patchwork quilting can be done by anyone, however, a person has to have patience with the sewing. _____

10. Del's prescription was very expensive he said it cost over $100. _____

Part 3: Identifying Fragments and Run-on Faults, Level of Difficulty 2

Read each of the following word groups. If the word group is a correct sentence, write **S** after it. If the word group is a fragment, write **FRAG** after it. If the word group is a run-on, write **RO** after it. (1 point each, 10 points)

1. On occasion, Woo visits the museum, he is very interested in natural sciences. _____

2. Clark seems preoccupied with fixing his car this evening, therefore, he will not be going to class. _____

3. Several of the women were taking prenatal classes to help them with their first births; many were accompanied by their partners. _____

4. Having many preparations to make for the journey into space. _____

5. Our family does not enjoy packaged foods, and we rarely buy them at the grocery store. _____

6. There were more than 16 chess players in the room all were deeply concentrating. _____

7. Since she was elected to the legislature in Winnipeg. _____

8. Describing the treatment he had received as a hostage. _____

9. Jeremy, sick with the flu, stayed in bed all weekend. _____

10. The anxious group preferred to speak with the manager of the mall immediately, on the other hand, they were willing to make an appointment to see him. _____

Part 4: Finding and Repairing Fragments and Run-ons, Level of Difficulty 2

Read each of the following groups of words. If the word group is a fragment, write **FRAG** after it. Then correct the fragment error, and write the correction in the spaces provided.

If the word group is a run-on, write **RO** after it. Then correct the run-on error, and write the correction in the spaces provided. (1 point for each correct identification, 1 point for each correction of error, 20 points; your instructor may want to mark this section)

1. Worrying and having low self-esteem. _____

   _____

   _____

2. Madison really enjoying her summer at Lake of the Woods. _____

   _____

   _____

3. The pitcher bent down to pick up the ball, then he stretched a little and walked to the mound. _____

   _____

   _____

4. The committee decided the supervisor's action was not ethical, consequently, the group recommended his removal from the company. _____

   _____

   _____

5. Slow down when you come to the hospital zone the police monitor the area carefully. _____

   _____

   _____

6. Under the stars in the little tent the boy. _____

   _____

   _____

7. Tent caterpillars spin cocoons, then, in this state, they can safely and slowly change into adults. _____

   _____

   _____

8. Although the microwave was purchased last Tuesday. _____

_____

_____

9. Wondering whether she should brake or not. _____

_____

_____

10. Wade refinished the rocking chair, Mei built the futon frame. _____

_____

_____

Part 5: Repairing Sentence Faults, Level of Difficulty 3

The following sentences contain one of the following sentence faults: fragment, run-on, pronoun reference error, shift in person/number, or shift in verb tense. First, read each sentence. Then repair the error and write the corrected version of the sentence in the space provided. You do not need to tell what kind of error the sentence contains. (2 points each, 30 points; your instructor may want to mark this section)

1. Several of the girls at camp were missing her mother back home.

_____

_____

2. If one wants to argue, you should get your facts straight.

_____

_____

3. Tony looks upset, but he wasn't talking to anyone.

_____

_____

4. Artichokes a little hard to clean.

_____

_____

5. Because the bank is closed for the holiday.

_____

_____

6. She works out at the gym, then she goes to lunch with her friends.

_____

_____

7. Alexis was a wonderful stage actor. Who died at age 50.

_____

_____

8. All of the women enjoyed herself.

_____

_____

9. He completes the assignments, then he goes to Rome.

_____

_____

10. There was a huge mess and several complaints about the party, this made the land-lord angry.

_____

_____

11. Kevin is studying percentiles in his statistics class, however he doesn't understand it.

_____

_____

12. Wallace told Amrit that he was fired.

_____

_____

13. Because the staples don't fit the staple gun.

   _____

   _____

14. Everybody should vote according to his conscience.

   _____

   _____

15. Jennifer informed Georgia that she was the better singer of the two.

   _____

   _____

SENTENCE FRAGMENTS

A sentence is a whole idea. It carries meaning because it makes sense. A fragment, on the other hand, is incomplete. It does not express a whole idea. A fragment does not make sense on its own. Often sentence fragments begin with conjunctions like *because, since, as, although, when,* or *unless.* Here are some examples of sentence fragments:

Because he was not invited.

Worried after the long illness.

Her family in which there are two girls and one boy.

Since the weather has been cloudy.

Standing alone waiting for the bus.

Notice that pieces of information are missing from all of the above examples.

- Sometimes a main clause might be missing as in the first example.

- The subject may be missing, as in the second example.

- In the third example, the writer has not included a verb.

- In the last example, it is not certain who is standing alone; in other words, the subject is missing.

Some situations may allow for a writer's or speaker's use of fragments. In conversation, for example, listeners can complete the meaning of a speaker's fragment by simply asking the speaker what he or she means. Of course, many famous writers have used fragments in their writing, but in academic writing, *fragments are considered errors because they are imprecise and potentially confusing.* Sentence fragments are considered a type of sentence fault or sentence-level error.

Read the following piece of writing. Can you spot the many fragments that make the meaning difficult to follow?

Riding around in his new car last Saturday night. Bruno felt really happy. He had promised his friend, Frankie, to pick him up at seven. The thrill. The speed. Suddenly, arriving at his favourite Greek restaurant. Because he loved to go there every Saturday. Bruno remembered. Thinking Frankie was probably angry at him. After all. He has forgotten to pick up his best friend. Who had been waiting for two hours! Embarrassing!

Tips: How to Correct Fragment Errors

1. **If the subject or verb is missing, add one.**

Fragment:	Working all weekend.
Correction:	Marcel is working all weekend.

Fragment:	Mrs. Lomas on the escalator.
Correction:	Mrs. Lomas is on the escalator.

2. **If a fragment gives partial information, add the necessary information to make it complete.** Sometimes it is effective to join the fragment to the sentence in front of it.

Fragment:	A traffic jam occurred near the bridge. Because only one lane was open.
Correction:	A traffic jam occurred near the bridge because only one lane was open.

3. **Sometimes it works to join the fragment to the sentence after it.**

Fragment:	Although he had not spoken at the meeting. We knew he had something to say.
Correction:	Although he had not spoken at the meeting, we knew he had something to say.

4. **If the fragment does not closely relate to the sentence before or after it, place it in a separate and complete sentence by adding more words.**

Fragment:	Louis was always a musical person. Since he was three.
Correction:	Louis was always a musical person. Since he was three, he has played the piano and the violin.

SEMICOLON USE

Remember: compound sentences usually contain a semicolon.

Each part of the compound sentence is really like a simple sentence that makes sense on its own. Do not write a complete sentence on one side of the semicolon and a fragment on the other. For example:

	complete idea	fragment
Incorrect:	Mrs. McVitie lost her purse;	became frantic.

	complete idea	complete idea
Correct:	Mrs. McVitie lost her purse;	she became frantic.

	complete idea	fragment
Incorrect:	Children should be taught street safety;	knowing how to react to strangers.

	complete idea	complete idea
Correct:	Children should be taught street safety;	they should know how to react to strangers.

Exercise 1   Fragments, Level of Difficulty 1

Read the following groups of words. Some are complete sentences; others are not. Write **S** after the correct complete sentences. Write **FRAG** after the groups of words that are not complete. Check your answers in the Answer Key.

1. Golfing, a pastime enjoyed by many people. _____

2. Than leaving the class before the others. _____

3. Shopping for bargains is difficult in 2008. _____

4. Because he was unable to complete his project on time. _____

5. Fishing as a way of life is dying out. _____

6. Although the roads are slippery in the winter. _____

7. Because the teachers were on strike. _____

8. Liam found a part-time job in sales. _____

9. The police will investigate the matter over the next few weeks. _____

10. Soybeans are rich in protein. _____

11. Shivering, huddling together for warmth, the stranded hikers. _____

12. Stay calm. _____

13. Rocky is expert at diving and swimming. _____

14. The academy opening in the winter of 2009. _____

15. Despite the heavy protests and the threats of violence. _____

16. Some diseases are transmitted through the air. _____

17. She fought against depression. _____

18. With balloons and face painting in the main tent. _____

19. Do you think because he was caught? _____

20. Building boats is an expensive hobby. _____

Exercise 2   Repairing Fragments

Work in pairs. Find all sentence fragments. Rewrite each sentence in order to correct errors. Note: not all word groups in the following exercise are fragment errors. Some may be correct sentences. Use separate paper. Be prepared to share your answers.

1. A woman working for minimum wage in Canada today.

2. Three seals were spotted off Mervin's Point last night.

3. Then stopped to chat with his friend.

4. Under the tree near the old oak was a chest full of money.

5. The pony ridden only on Saturdays.

6. The unfriendly serviceperson sorting through the pile of bills.

7. Because she had forgotten her wallet, she could not pay for her groceries.

8. Since she was appointed to the position.

9. In the tool shed at the back of the yard.

10. Cruising along the highway, we saw many visitors who were taking pictures of the elk.

11. Did the pharmacist talk to the customer about the medication?

12. The dog under the porch of one of the old buildings.

13. Alex and Miki sitting on the lawn eating their lunches.

14. Cartons of beer were delivered to the wrong store.

15. All of the ingredients for the special cake.

16. Laurence and Caroline took their parents out for an Italian dinner. Lorenzo's the best Italian restaurant in the city.

17. Greeted her enthusiastically at the airport.

18. I used to be frightened of the dark when I was little; even had to have a night light in my room.

19. Children were running amok in the mall. Because Beepo, the clown was to arrive soon.

RUN-ON SENTENCES

A run-on sentence is a fault because the writer has written two, perhaps even three, sentences as a single sentence *without using the correct punctuation or correct conjunction to connect the sentences*. Once again, meaning becomes confused because of the sentence fault.

Run-on:	Their idea was to complete their computer graphics courses and get good jobs new hope was on their horizon.
Correction 1:	Their idea was to complete their computer graphics courses and get good jobs: new hope was on their horizon.
Correction 2:	Their idea was to complete their computer graphics courses and get good jobs; new hope was on their horizon.
Correction 3:	Their idea was to complete their computer graphics courses and get good jobs. New hope was on their horizon.
Correction 4:	Their idea was to complete their computer graphics courses and get good jobs for new hope was on their horizon.

Notice that in the example above the run-on fault has been corrected in four different ways.

- In the first correction, a full colon is used to join one sentence to the other.

- In the second, a semicolon is used to connect ideas.

- In the third, the sentence has been separated into two smaller sentences.
- In the fourth, the conjunction *for* is used to connect clauses.

All four repair methods are equally effective. You might be able to think of others, too.

Exercise 3   *Run-on Sentences, Level of Difficulty 2*

Read each sentence. If the sentence is a run-on fault, write **RO** after it. Then correct the error and rewrite your corrected sentence in the space provided. If the sentence is correct as given, write **CORRECT** after it. Check your answers in the Answer Key.

1. The young couple was arguing about the rent money, however, they seemed to settle their differences. _____

   _____

   _____

2. Two of the bank managers were fired from their positions the government inspectors had found serious errors in their accounting systems. _____

   _____

   _____

3. Daisy loves to play baseball in the spring her husband, Arnold, likewise loves the game. _____

   _____

   _____

4. The teacher wanted to encourage discussion about Chaucer many students on the other hand were more interested in Shakespeare. _____

   _____

   _____

5. I found the shoes very uncomfortable, however, I could not return them because the store had gone out of business. _____

   _____

   _____

6. On election night, the crowd gathered around the favoured candidate, they cheered her every word. _____

   _____

   _____

7. Each worker had to take a cut in pay, according to the manager of the mill. _____

_____

_____

8. Can you help me with this account, or will I have to solve this problem myself? _____

_____

_____

9. After the severe rains, most of the plains were flooded, as a result, the farmers could not sow their crops until late spring. _____

_____

_____

10. Despite his gruff manner, he is a gentle person who tries to mind his own business and stay out of trouble. _____

_____

_____

11. The garden store in the new mall was a success, the bookstore located near it was not successful, however. _____

_____

_____

12. The magician turned to us with a smile then he disappeared. _____

_____

_____

13. Crystal loves to collect antique coins and jewellery she travels all over Canada making her purchases. _____

_____

_____

COMMA SPLICE

When you use a comma to join two sentences, you have committed a kind of run-on sentence fault called a **comma splice**. According to today's rules of punctuation, a comma is not used to join items; in fact, its function in sentences is quite the opposite—to separate items. Use the semicolon to join related sentences.

Comma Splice:	The students investigated the possibility of starting a newspaper, several volunteers wanted to organize the first meeting.
Correction:	The students investigated the possibility of starting a newspaper; several volunteers wanted to organize the first meeting.
Correction:	The students investigated the possibility of starting a newspaper, and several volunteers wanted to organize the first meeting.
Correction:	The students investigated the possibility of starting a newspaper. Several volunteers wanted to organize the first meeting.

Conjunctive Adverbs

As you will recall from Chapter 14, conjunctive adverbs are weak joiners. To strengthen their power to join parts of the sentences together, you must use a semicolon along with the conjunctive adverb. Generally speaking, conjunctive adverbs, along with a semicolon, join two independent (main) clauses together.

Conjunctive Adverbs

therefore	however
consequently	moreover
likewise	nevertheless
similarly	nonetheless
also	afterwards

Notice that a comma follows each conjunctive adverb in the examples below.

Meiki supports the candidate's platform; *however*, she worries about his inexperience.

The dog sustained a leg injury in the accident; *consequently*, he could not run properly.

The clause in your contract stipulates you cannot do freelance work for any other company; *therefore*, you cannot accept that offer.

Wadley enjoyed the sudden fame; *moreover*, he enjoyed being pestered by photographers and journalists.

The strong winds lasted for 10 hours; *afterwards*, the town's water supply was in jeopardy because of fallen debris.

Some imported china contains high levels of lead in their glazes; *likewise*, some types of pottery show dangerous amounts of toxic chemicals saturated in the clay.

Mrs. Jabi's financial advisor warned her about investing in Bumblebee's Beauty Patches; *nevertheless*, she went ahead to buy $100 000 worth of shares.

Common Errors with Conjunctive Adverbs

Incorrect:	Polly put the kettle on consequently we all had tea. (run-on fault)
Correct:	Polly put the kettle on; consequently, we all had tea.
Correct:	Polly put the kettle on, and consequently, we all had tea.
Correct:	Polly put the kettle on. Consequently, we all had tea.
Incorrect:	Tara was upset by the meeting therefore she plans to complain to the supervisor. (run-on fault)
Correct:	Tara was upset by the meeting; therefore, she plans to complain to the supervisor.
Correct:	Tara was upset by the meeting, and therefore, she plans to complain to the supervisor.
Correct:	Tara was upset by the meeting. Therefore, she plans to complain to the supervisor.

Exercise 4   Run-on Sentences, Level of Difficulty 2

Read each of the following sentences. Write **RO** after the word group if you think it is a run-on fault. Write **S** after the word group if you think it is a correct sentence. Check your answers in the Answer Key.

1. Learning more about helicopter flying was Adam's dream. _____

2. The racket kept us up all night consequently we feel a bit grumpy today. _____

3. Warner Brothers has been in the business of making Hollywood movies for over 70 years they are still producing some blockbusters. _____

4. Her garden was a small paradise with a tiny pool full of fish, lush ferns and shrubs, and flowers of many colours. _____

5. Brian had never been to the opera surprisingly, he enjoyed the performance on TV. _____

6. Montague Stately was an eccentric millionaire who decided to retire to one of the smallest islands in the St. Lawrence. _____

7. If you do your own house renovations, be sure to get all the proper permits and inspections. _____

8. They were expecting lots of customers for the holiday rush, they were stocked up on items in September. _____

9. Cuddles, her prize Doberman pinscher, was trained to guard the property, furthermore, he was expected to alert the household about any suspicious activities. _____

10. *Oliver Twist* is my favourite Dickens book, however, my sister insists *Martin Chuzzlewit* is better. _____

11. The dispatch came from Colonel Upstart, but the lieutenant refused to acknowledge it. _____

12. At one time, almost everyone's intelligence was measured by a test called an IQ, or intelligence quotient, test. _____

13. These vegetables need to be pared, then they need to be steamed for dinner service at six. _____

14. A small meteor struck Earth just outside Calgary and left a crater seven metres across. _____

15. The sculpture was placed on exhibit just outside city hall; it became an object of interest to visitors. _____

16. He shouted for assistance, then he lay still. _____

17. The shaman of the tribe came forward he wanted to assist the RCMP in their search for the lost child. _____

18. Those pesticides are toxic; please refrain from using them. _____

Exercise 5   *Fragments and Run-ons, Level of Difficulty 3*

Read each of the following sentences. If the sentence is correct as it stands, write **CORRECT** after it. If the sentence is a run-on fault, write **RO** after it. Then repair the sentence and rewrite the correct version in the space provided. If the sentence is not a sentence, but a fragment, write **FRAG** after it. Then repair the fragment and rewrite the correct version in the space provided. You may work in pairs. Be prepared to share your answers.

1. The city had become a sprawling megalopolis the citizens found themselves choking in the exhaust-filled air. _____

_____

_____

2. We are sorry to inform you that you did not win the contest your drawing however was noted by the judges to be exemplary. _____

_____

_____

3. Justin was appointed to the Order of Canada because of the work he had done with Southeast Asian immigrants since 1965. _____

_____

_____

4. Organizing a club for older women returning to formal education. _____

_____

_____

5. Her youngest, a child of four, has been selected to appear in a commercial for Canadian Tire. _____

_____

_____

6. Juanita, Esther, and Estella are sisters from Mexico who recently arrived in Canada, they are not familiar with Canadian slang. _____

_____

_____

7. The protest ended peacefully. Although some people on the roadblock had been slightly injured. _____

_____

_____

8. Most teenagers love to be independent; they enjoy the feeling of being in charge. _____

_____

_____

PRONOUN REFERENCE PROBLEMS

Sometimes errors occur in sentences because writers make incorrect or unclear pronoun references. You must pay particular attention to the **antecedent** of a pronoun in order to determine what the meaning of a sentence is. *The word the pronoun refers to in a sentence is called an antecedent.* Furthermore, you must make sure that a pronoun agrees with its antecedent; otherwise, you will make a grammatical or sentence-level error called a **pronoun reference fault**.

Vague or Ambiguous Pronoun Reference

If you do not provide a clear antecedent for your pronoun, you will have a *vague pronoun reference* problem. If your pronoun can refer to more than one antecedent, you have a pronoun reference problem called *ambiguous pronoun reference*.

Incorrect: Several large herons were fishing in the shallow lagoon; it was moving so slowly that we could not tell when it had actually moved. (vague pronoun reference. What is the antecedent for *it*?)

Correct: Several large herons were fishing in the shallow lagoon; they were moving so slowly that we could not tell when they had actually moved. (*Herons* is the antecedent of *they*.)

| Incorrect: | The dispute between the workers and the managers did not end until they invited them to a weekend retreat. (ambiguous pronoun reference) |

(The problem is ambiguity because the antecedent could be *workers* or *managers*. Who invited whom?)

| Correct: | The dispute between the workers and the managers did not end until the workers invited the managers to a weekend retreat. |

| Correct: | The dispute between the workers and the managers did not end until the managers invited the workers to a weekend retreat. |

| Incorrect: | Donald told Alfie he had won the championship. (ambiguous pronoun reference) |

(Who won the championship?)

| Correct: | Donald told Alfie, "I have won the championship." |

| Correct: | Donald told Alfie, "You have won the championship." |

| Correct: | Donald, who had won the championship, told Alfie about it. |

| Correct: | Alfie, who had won the championship, told Donald about it. |

Each of the above corrections has a different meaning. Be clear and choose your correction carefully.

Problems with the Pronoun This

One of the worst offenders when it comes to creating vague pronoun reference is the use of the word *this*. Usually, *this* has no clear antecedent in the sentence. If you want to use *this*, then use a noun right after it.

| Incorrect: | My friend Elmore loves to hang-glide in foreign countries and to fly wherever he wants to practise his sport; this has cost him quite a bit of money over the years. |

What exactly does *this* refer to? Can you tell? Is there a clear antecedent?

| Correct: | My friend Elmore loves to hang-glide in foreign countries and to fly wherever he wants to practise his sport; these activities have cost him quite a bit of money over the years. |

PRONOUN AGREEMENT

Be sure the pronoun agrees with other parts of the sentence in number and in gender.

| Incorrect: | Every woman was given their assignments at the meeting. |

| Correct: | Every woman was given her assignment at the meeting. |

The understanding is that *assignment* should reflect back to *every woman* since that is the subject. *The pronoun must agree with its antecedent in gender and number.* The subject is a singular, feminine subject; therefore, the pronoun must also be singular and feminine—*her*.

| Incorrect: | Some of the men brought his own transportation. |

| Correct: | Some of the men brought their own transportation. |

The indefinite pronoun *some* refers to a count noun—a plural—*men*. The pronoun must also be in the third person plural—*their*.

Incorrect: All of the boys wanted his own bicycle.

Correct: All of the boys wanted their own bicycles.

The indefinite pronoun *all* refers to a count noun (*boys*). Since it is in the plural, the pronoun must also be in the plural—*their*.

Incorrect: Everyone has to make up his own mind.

Correct: Everyone has to make up his or her own mind.

Also Acceptable: Everyone has to make up their own minds.

Everyone is also an indefinite pronoun. You may structure your sentence to avoid sexism as shown by the second correction—*Everyone has to make up their own minds*. It is now becoming accepted practice to use the word *their* when referring to indefinite pronoun expressions such as *everyone, everybody, every person, all,* and so forth in order to refer to people in general. The use of *their* in these cases avoids sexism in the language; in other words, using *their* with indefinite pronouns helps you avoid naming a specific gender. It is important, however, to find out if your instructor welcomes this practice. Some instructors do not allow the use of *their* with indefinite pronouns.

Exercise 6   *Pronoun Reference, Level of Difficulty 2*

Work in pairs. Find the pronoun reference problems in each of the following sentences. Then repair the error by rewriting the sentence correctly in the given space. Share your answers with others in the class, and check your answers in the Answer Key.

1. Erica told Gabrielle she was coming to lunch.

   _____

   _____

2. People could get a special pass to see the clipper ship and meet the crew; this made them very enthusiastic.

   _____

   _____

3. Everyone in the lineup must have his identification card verified.

   _____

   _____

4. When Elvis's first song was recorded in 1955, he quickly became popular.

   _____

   _____

5. Hasim told Roger about his new portfolio for art school.

   _____

   _____

6. The boy was caught speeding and driving without a licence, and this shocked his parents.

   _____

   _____

7. Every boy can have their own racquets on the court.

   _____

   _____

8. Kimi sent Tina to pick up the team uniforms after she returned from the game.

   _____

   _____

9. Every woman was given their own set of documents for the meeting.

   _____

   _____

10. Some of the girls brought her own lunch.

   _____

   _____

11. Mrs. Norman asked her if she would sing at the reception.

   _____

   _____

12. No one really knew who the missing man was, but everyone had a theory about it.

_____

_____

SHIFTS IN SENTENCES

A **shift** in a sentence is a _sudden change in tense, mood, voice, person, or number_.

Tense has to do with the times of the verbs. If you write more than one verb with more than one tense, be sure the times are in sequence. **Voice** has to do with verbs. _Active voice_ means that the subject does the action in the sentence. _Passive voice_ means that the subject receives the action of the verb.

Active Voice: I scrubbed the sink with disinfectant.

Passive Voice: The sink was scrubbed with disinfectant by me.

Try to use the active voice whenever you can in your writing. It makes your ideas more direct for the reader. It also makes plain who the agents are and what actions they are responsible for.

Person has to do with subject and point of view. You may recall the earlier discussion on point of view.

Person and Point of View

I	first person point of view (called personal point of view)
you	second person point of view (singular)
he	third person point of view
she	third person point of view
it	third person point of view
we	first person point of view (plural)
you	second person point of view (plural)
they	third person point of view (plural)

Number has to do with whether the subject is plural or singular. For example, _he, she,_ and _it_ are singular pronoun subjects, while _we_ and _they_ are plural.

Person and Number Shifts

Changes from one subject to another or _from one verb tense to another_ in the same sentence are _two common types of shifts_ that make sentences confusing to read. Look over the following examples.

SHIFTS IN PERSON

Incorrect: The spectators jumped up excitedly from their seats; we were thrilled by the power play.

Spectators is the subject. The second part of the sentence has *we* as the subject. A reader would expect to read *they* as the second subject because *they* agrees in number with *spectators*.

Correct: The spectators jumped up excitedly from their seats; they were thrilled by the power play.

Correct: We spectators jumped up excitedly from our seats; we were thrilled by the power play.

Incorrect: A worker in a large organization often feels as if they have been overlooked.

The subject of the first clause is *a worker*; the subject of the second clause is *they*.

Correct: Workers in large organizations often feel as if they have been overlooked. (non-sexist)

Incorrect: If one wants to learn about birds, you should take part in nature walks.

One is the subject of the first clause, and *you* is the subject of the second clause.

Correct: If you want to learn about birds, you should take part in nature walks.

SHIFTS IN TENSE

Be sure that the tenses you use make sense. If they are illogically sequenced, your reader will have trouble following your idea.

Incorrect: Marlon walked along the beach, and then he goes in.

The first verb *walked* is past tense; the second verb *goes* is present tense.

Correct: Marlon walked along the beach, and then he went in.

Correct: Marlon walks along the beach, and then he goes in.

Incorrect: Hannah goes to the flea market every Saturday and hunts for bargains; she loved showing off her purchases.

The verbs in the first part of the sentence, *goes* and *hunts*, are in the present tense. The verb in the second part of the compound sentence, *loved*, is in the past tense. The verbs are inconsistent in the sequence of tense.

Correct: Hannah goes to the flea market every Saturday and hunts for bargains; she loves showing off her purchases.

Exercise 7 Group Activity: Shift Errors, Level of Difficulty 3

Work in groups. Read each of the following sentences. Each contains an error in shifts: person, number, or tense. Rewrite your correction in the space provided. After you have agreed, check your answers in the Answer Key.

1. Helen is pleased with the promotion; she intended to do well in her new position as manager.

   _____

   _____

2. The epidemic spread throughout the countryside, and the doctors attempt to inoculate all residents.

   _____

   _____

3. If one wants to learn about fruit farming, you should talk to an orchardist.

   _____

   _____

4. Lola had never tried parachute jumping before; she listens carefully to the instructor's directions.

   _____

   _____

5. Several children were playing hopscotch and skipping, but we did not hear the sound of the siren.

   _____

   _____

6. The stunt crew was setting up outside the Empress Hotel, and he had some expensive technical equipment.

   _____

   _____

7. If you don't know about it, one should ask.

   _____

   _____

8. Because it was the long weekend, the trailer park is packed with vehicles.

   _____

   _____

9. Everyone should be careful about getting too much sun exposure if you do not want to increase the risk of skin cancer.

_____

_____

10. After we discussed the idea, we leave.

_____

_____

PARALLELISM PROBLEMS

Perhaps the most subtle error of all for you to spot in your own sentences is a **parallelism fault**. Faulty parallelism means that *all grammatical structures in a series are not in the same form.*

The economy was slowed because of poor production, loss of workers, and many people were getting too greedy.

Does the sentence sound incorrect to you?

The problem with the sentence is that the grammatical structures do not match in form. It contains faulty parallelism.

In the first case, you see an adjective–noun combination.

poor production

In the second case, you see a noun followed by a prepositional phrase.

loss of workers

In the third case, you see a clause.

many people were getting too greedy.

To repair the faulty parallelism, make all of the parts of the sentence the same grammatically.

The economy was slowed because of *poor production, worker loss*, and many people's *excessive greed*. (All parts are now adjective and noun combinations.)

The economy was slowed because *production was slower, workers were lost*, and *many people were getting too greedy.* (All parts are now in clause form.)

The economy was slowed because of *slow production, worker loss*, and *excessive greed.* (This version tidies up the adjective and noun combinations.)

Here are more examples of *faulty parallel* structure:

The new park is quiet, well-maintained, and has low landscaping costs.

Emile loves to dance, cook, and playing the classical guitar.

Morris can draw just as well as, if not better, than Trudy.

Why are the three sentences above not parallel in structure? Can you figure out where the faulty parallelism lies in each sentence?

Here are some examples of *correct* sentence parallelism:

       adj   noun   adj   noun   adj   noun
She is an excellent student, a loyal mother, and a helpful reader in the library.

                      verb phrase
The general manager of marketing **was planning** to visit all the plants in the Stouffville

                  verb phrase
region in the coming year, **was scheduling** meetings with new managers in October, and

verb phrase
was organizing a planning session for the month of June.

Hints to Finding Parallelism Faults

1. **Grammatical structures must match in all parts of the sentence.**
   Examine the structure in the first part of the sentence; then check to see whether the next structures are the same grammatical element.

                 gerund   gerund   gerund
   Correct: Tilling the soil, planting a variety of seeds, and weeding the garden took up most of Vaughn's long weekend.

2. **Balance comparisons.**

   Incorrect: The report showed that boys spend more money on items in the computer store than girls.

   Correct: The report showed that boys spend more money than girls do on items in the computer store.

3. **Balance the modifiers.**

   Incorrect: They requested a plumber and poet.

   Correct: They requested a plumber and a poet.

4. **Verb forms should be balanced in all parts of the sentence.**

   Incorrect: He has been writing songs, thinking about producing an album, and is happy to receive any interest in his project.

   Correct: He has been writing songs, has been thinking about producing an album, and has been happily waiting to receive any interest in his project.

5. **Balance *neither–nor, either–or, not only–but also* constructions.**

   Incorrect: She not only finished the typing but also the filing.

   Place *not only* and *but also* next to the similar grammatical structures in the parts of the sentence. Such positioning will make a smoother sentence.

   Correct: She *not only* finished the typing *but also* completed the filing.

   Correct: She finished *not only* the typing *but also* the filing.

Exercise 8   Parallelism Errors, Level of Difficulty 3

Each of the following sentences contains faulty parallelism errors. Find the errors and then rewrite the sentences to eliminate the parallelism problems. Use separate paper for your work. Be prepared to share your answers.

1. Thinking through the problem, discussing its possible solutions, and to want to change the situation contributed to the new policy.

2. My dog has, and will continue to attempt, to beg for food.

3. The student survey showed that women own more computers than men.

4. The company hired a security expert and priest.

5. She not only likes chocolate but also marshmallows.

6. The gorilla was large, hated his owners' poodles, and scared them daily.

7. The eagle had been circling for hours and waited for salmon in the stream.

8. Loulou is attractive, rich, and a penny-pincher.

9. Not only did the artist paint with oils, but also the properties of acrylics intrigued her.

10. Playing the harmonica, to do carving, and being a volunteer occupy my grandfather's time.

Exercise 9   Sentence Faults, Level of Difficulty 3

The following sentences contain one of these sentence faults:

a. fragment

b. run-on

c. shift in person/number

d. shift in verb tense

e. pronoun reference error

f. parallelism error

Work in pairs. First, read each sentence. Decide what the error is within each sentence. Then repair the error and write the corrected version of the sentence in the space provided. Check your answers in the Answer Key.

1. All of the girls wanted to get her camping gear at the same sporting goods store.

_____

_____

2. Although he knew the shed really needed an undercoat. Bobby felt too lazy to do the job properly.

_____

_____

3. Some foods rich in beta carotene.

_____

_____

4. At the registration desk, Alan rented a locker and pays for it for one term at the college.

_____

_____

5. My friend Baker is very photogenic, however, she does not like having her picture taken.

_____

_____

6. One could safeguard against accidents in the home if we just paid attention to safety details.

_____

_____

7. Sodium fluoride has been added to the water system of the city. Despite the fact that many claim this chemical is poisonous.

_____

_____

8. Walter really wanted to build a solar house, he checked the building regulations with the regional planning office.

_____

_____

9. The family bought a tandem bicycle; we particularly want to use it on vacation.

_____

_____

10. The weary visitors were so exhausted after their long flight from Taiwan that they fall asleep immediately.

_____

_____

11. Her testimony at the trial necessary to the defence.

_____

_____

12. Walking, riding, and to climb were her exercise manias.

_____

_____

Exercise 10   Sentence Faults, Level of Difficulty 3

The following sentences contain one of these sentence faults:

a. fragment

b. run-on

c. shift in person/number

d. shift in verb tense

e. pronoun reference error

f. parallelism error

First, read each sentence. Then repair the error and write the corrected version of the sentence in the space provided. Check your answers in the Answer Key.

1. It seems the whole world fearful of terrorist attacks.

_____

_____

2. Everyone should decide what is best for his own children.

_____

_____

3. Woody Allen became renowned as a popular stand-up comic, moreover, his fame earned him a job as a screenwriter.

_____

_____

4. Since that terry cloth robe was so expensive. It should look better after only three washings.

_____

_____

5. Because Lord Peakinloft managed his estate well, one was left with no debt.

_____

_____

6. The Morgan brothers had a contract to do all the plumbing in the new housing development, then their company went bankrupt.

_____

_____

7. The selector on our stereo was broken, and they couldn't fix it.

_____

_____

8. With all the self-assurance of a king. Marmaduke entered the ballroom.

_____

_____

9. The soggy tomato sandwiches did not make an appetizing lunch when we go on the picnic.

_____

_____

10. The tea tastes bitter perhaps it has been brewed too long.

_____

_____

11. The proprietor of the bed and breakfast wanting to please all of her guests.

_____

_____

12. Some people enjoy sewing because they found sewing their own clothes saved money.

_____

_____

13. Although the condo is small. There is plenty of storage space in the basement.

_____

_____

14. One ought to check with the head server before you make a complaint.

_____

_____

15. He and his brother Manny bought a cottage near Bala, and he loves going to it on weekends.

_____

_____

Exercise 11   _Group Activity: Some Final Editing Practice_

This final editing exercise is made up of three paragraphs, each containing specific grammatical or mechanical errors. Try working on each one in a group, so that you can help each other and share ideas. Be prepared to provide answers to the whole class. Check your answers in the Answer Key.

The following editing practice contains these common faults:

a. punctuation (comma, semicolon, colon) errors

b. fragments

c. run-ons

d. S–V disagreement

e. parallelism errors

f. possessive (the apostrophe) errors

g. adverb and adjective usage errors

Paragraph 1: Punctuation and the Use of the Apostrophe in Possessives

Read the paragraph. Underline all errors you spot. Correct each error.

No one knew who was to inherit Mrs. Blethershotts estate and her enormous fortune, it remained a great mystery to everyone. Because Ethyl the maid had remained in Mrs. Blethershotts service for so long all of the staff expected her to receive some small compensation for her years of loyalty. The butler Archibald felt certain he was to win something as well he had served the Blethershott Manor for over 40 years, he had not had one days absence from his duties. It was the cooks opinion that she should receive the most, she had done three things in her opinion that counted the most, served fresh nutritious food to the Mistress kept a tight budget and made herself available to the Mistress every whim. The chauffeur Kendrick did not agree that the other members of staff were worthy of receiving any more than a few dollars. Since he had arrived at Blethershott Manor he had given the Blethershotts his devoted attention not once had he complained about their unreasonable demands. In fact Kendrick had said very little, moreover, he now believed he was the most likely to inherit. Everyone's suspicion had begun to create peculiar tension in the household no one seemed able to sleep the night before the reading of the will.

Paragraph 2: Fragments, Run-ons, Comma Splices

Read the paragraph Underline all errors you spot. Correct each error.

Taking children to their first daycare can be an unnerving experience for new parents, the day of tearful and loud protests of a child can make even the most calm parent feeling flustered and guilty. Weeks in advance, many parents try to explain to their children what wonderful places daycares are. Because the parents are trying to avoid the "big scene" on the daycare steps. Some children seem to listen carefully. To understand what their parents are telling them. Some children seem to understand their parents' explanation fully, these children seem relaxed and happy about the new arrangement. Of course, once the new parents and their new daycare students arrive at the destinations, it becomes another matter entirely, teachers, students, parents, assistants, and children all seem to be talking at once. Frightened and anxious faces tell the tale. Because no one seems to want to leave and no one seems to want to stay! It is hard to imagine. That in just a few short weeks. Most children seem to love their new "schools" and welcome each day's activities.

Paragraph 3: Parallelism, and Adjective and Adverb Use

Read the paragraph. Underline all errors you spot. Correct each error.

According to *Monday Magazine*, Victoria is Canada's "city of poisons" because of the overuse of pesticides and herbicides by residential gardeners and sellers are enthusiastic to sell these chemicals. The situation has naturalists and environmentalists real upset.

Monday Magazine, April 24–30, 1997, states that "some of these compounds are tested for their cancer-causing potential, but most have been introduced without any of assessment of their effects on the immune and nervous systems" (8). To ensure that gardening chemicals are being used good, to eliminate their overuse, and controlling garden pests and diseases will take better management on the part of the industry and government. There are still few laws that are real effective and can be enforced. For example, although many residential gardeners in Victoria feel badly about the harm that garden chemical agents create, these same citizens continue to use agents such as malathion, propoxur, and captan. These chemicals act very slow on the environment, and years later, dangerous traces can be found in the soil and the drinking water supply. Beneficial insects, songbirds, garter snakes, and amphibians are also sure harmed by the abuse and we tend to overuse commonly available garden chemicals.

Chapter 16: Review Test

Part 1: Identifying Fragments and Sentences, Level of Difficulty 1

Read the following groups of words. Some are correct sentences; others are not. Write **S** after the groups of words that are correct sentences. Write **FRAG** after the groups of words that are fragments. (1 point each, 10 points)

1. Experiencing the great outdoors. _____

2. Madge photographing the new totem pole. _____

3. After his late shift was over. _____

4. Speeding causes accidents. _____

5. The Calgary Stampede was a huge success this year. _____

6. If we telephone after midnight. _____

7. Forecasts the weather accurately. _____

8. Connie tying the dried flower wreath. _____

9. When the course was offered through the Access Network. _____

10. Making mistakes is part of learning. _____

Part 2: Identifying Run-ons and Sentences, Level of Difficulty 2

Read the following groups of words. Some are correct sentences; others are not. Write **S** after the groups of words that are correct sentences. Write **RO** after the groups of words that are run-on sentence faults. (1 point each, 10 points)

1. The new telescope lens was delivered to the observatory the scientists supervised the unloading of the expensive lens. _____

2. Because he was out at third base, we lost the game. _____

3. That little sparrow has a beautiful song, however, it is not spectacular in appearance. _____

4. The racehorse stood in its stall, and it tried to watch the pedestrians in front of the stables. _____

5. The best vegetable stew is made with root vegetables, dill dumplings make a tasty addition to the meal, too. _____

6. The striking workers would not yield on any of the issues, consequently, management locked out the workers. _____

7. He got a substantial inheritance, then he quit his job and retired to Costa Rica. _____

8. The dessert squares were unusually rich and sweet; each of us could eat only a tiny piece. _____

9. The substitute teacher was exhausted at the end of the day, the Grade 7 class had worn her out. _____

10. Some illnesses are hereditary, others are caused by poor diets. _____

Part 3: Identifying Fragments and Run-on Faults, Level of Difficulty 2

Read each of the following word groups. If the word group is a correct sentence, write **S** after it. If the word group is a fragment, write **FRAG** after it. If the word group is a run-on, write **RO** after it. (1 point each, 10 points)

1. In Greek mythology, Hades was the underworld, it was ruled by Pluto and Persephone. _____

2. The council did not pass the motion to expand bus service to the campus, therefore, many students had to find alternate forms of transportation. _____

3. Colour therapy is a technique used for stress relief and relaxation purposes. _____

4. Deciding which letter to answer first. _____

5. Nintendo's Wii and Sony's Playstation seem to be world leaders in video game production, but competition from Microsoft's Xbox is pushing the gaming envelope. _____

6. Nathan decided not to apply for the job he believed he would not get it anyway. _____

7. Since Dawn has taken her training in pediatric nursing. _____

8. Debating the bill in Parliament. _____

9. Kenneth, troubled by her letter, gave Simi a call. _____

10. The commercial advertised a handy tool for peeling apples, however, I sent away for the gadget and found it did not work as demonstrated. _____

Part 4: Finding and Repairing Fragments and Run-ons, Level of Difficulty 2

Read each of the following groups of words. If the word group is a fragment, write **FRAG** after it. Then correct the fragment error, and write the correction in the space provided. If the word group is a run-on, write **RO** after it. Then correct the run-on error, and write the correction in the space provided. (1 point for each correct identification, 1 point for each correction of error, 20 points; to be marked by the instructor or the marker.)

1. Delivering furniture for a summer job. _____

    _____

    _____

2. Trudi wanting a change in scenery. _____

    _____

    _____

3. The trainer spoke to the athletes on the field, then she posted their training schedule in the locker room. _____

    _____

    _____

4. The frost in California destroyed the citrus crop, consequently, prices for oranges and grapefruits skyrocketed in Canadian supermarkets. _____

    _____

    _____

5. Rock climbing is a popular sport today, however, everyone needs some training before setting out. _____

    _____

    _____

6. Beside the old school grounds near a Garry oak a baseball glove. _____

    _____

    _____

7. The blackberries grew in dense thickets, walkers enjoyed picking the berries in early fall. _____

_____

_____

8. Although the player was interested in the trade. _____

_____

_____

9. Practising her dancing every day after school. _____

_____

_____

10. The women made rag dolls from the old clothes the children made stick toys. _____

_____

_____

Part 5: Repairing Sentence Faults, Level of Difficulty 3

The following sentences contain one of the following sentence faults: fragment, run-on, pronoun reference or agreement error, shift in person/number, or shift in verb tense. First, read each sentence. Then repair the error and write the corrected version of the sentence in the space provided. You do not need to tell what kind of error the sentence contains. (2 points each, 30 points)

1. Everybody cheered and got to his feet.

_____

_____

2. If one becomes negative in attitude, your health suffers.

_____

_____

3. Plutonium is a deadly radioactive poison, detected in some milk sources, but most consumers were unaware of this fact.

_____

_____

4. Practising snowboarding in the early spring.

   _____

   _____

5. Because the customer is angry.

   _____

   _____

6. She grooms her dog, Pokey, then she plays ball with him.

   _____

   _____

7. Manuel was a marvellous painter. Who died of AIDS.

   _____

   _____

8. All of the men brought his own ideas.

   _____

   _____

9. Kim counts all the day's cash, then she makes a deposit.

   _____

   _____

10. Jojo was spending too much money, staying out late, and sleeping in every day, this made his parents angry.

    _____

    _____

11. Buying lottery tickets is his passion, however, his wife doesn't understand it.

    _____

    _____

12. Marla told Pipi she got a raise.

_____

_____

13. Because the accounts aren't in order.

_____

_____

14. Everybody should decide for himself.

_____

_____

15. Malcolm informed Ahmed that he was the better athlete of the two.

_____

_____

CHECKOUT

1. Sentence-level errors—fragments, run-ons, shifts in person/number, shifts in verb tense, pronoun reference errors, and parallelism faults—are considered serious faults because they disrupt meaning.

2. Try to use the active voice whenever you can in your writing.

3. Keep track of the sentence-level errors you make.

4. Faulty parallelism errors are tricky and take some analysis to connect.

5. Good editing skills make you a better reader.

chapter 17

ESL Pointers

Chapter Objectives

After completing this chapter, you will be able to

- distinguish count from non-count nouns
- use the definite article *the* and indefinite articles *a* and *an* correctly
- work with expressions of quantity
- distinguish and use time-order transitions
- recognize and use expressions of comparison and contrast
- identify and employ classification and division transitions
- distinguish and apply cause/effect words: *since, because, so*, and *therefore*
- recognize what subordination is and how to apply it
- differentiate passive and active voice
- use simple, perfect, and progressive verb tenses
- work with indefinite pronouns and verb agreement
- use quotation marks in direct speech
- employ prepositions of place and time
- compose conditional sentences using the conjunction *if*
- identify and work with verbals and parallelism

INTRODUCTION

If you are a student whose first language is not English, you will find this chapter particularly helpful because it is meant especially for non-native speakers. In this chapter, you will see particular topics that will help you pay attention to features of the English language that can be troublesome. You will study and discuss these topics in order to improve your written English.

The chapter is broken into 15 parts. Each part introduces and discusses a particular topic. After each topic, you will find practice exercises to complete. Most of the time, you can check your answers in the Answer Key.

PART 1: COUNT AND NON-COUNT NOUNS

A noun names a thing, whether it is real (concrete) or imagined or felt (abstract).

Think of a **count noun** as a thing you can count or number.

Juanita has a cat with yellow-green eyes.

She paid a tax on the shoes.

Georges made a suggestion.

Can you count cats? Can you count taxes? Can you count or number suggestions? A **non-count** noun refers to a noun that cannot be counted. In the English language, think of non-count nouns as whole concepts that cannot be enumerated or divided into parts.

The weather was bad today.

Can you count weather? No. If you say "a weather," you are saying that weather is countable.

The furniture was expensive.

Can you count furniture without dividing it up? No. In this case, furniture is a collective noun. You can count pieces of furniture, but not furniture.

The warmth of the fire felt good to Roman.

Can you count warmth? No. If you say "a warmth," you are using the word *warmth* as a countable noun.

Here are more examples of non-count nouns.

Some Non-Count Nouns

courage	stress	machinery
anger	homework	equipment
knowledge	leisure	clothing
work	traffic	milk
love	progress	advice

However, some non-count nouns can become countable if they are used to designate varieties or types, or if they are used in general ways.

Work is difficult on the farm. (non-count)

He enjoys *works* of art. (countable)

Phillipa found the *stress* in her life overwhelming. (non-count collective)

Everyone endures the *stresses* and *strains* in life. (countable in general ways)

Tea can be good for your health. (non-count collective)

The store carries 16 different *teas*. (countable, referring to varieties)

Wine tastes delicious with this fish dish. (non-count collective)

This restaurant serves six German *wines* and seven French *wines*. (countable, referring to varieties or separate types of wines)

Maurice is having *difficulty* with his computer. (non-count, meaning trouble)

Several *difficulties* on the job led to his firing. (countable, indicating categories of trouble)

Exercise 1   *Count and Non-Count Nouns*

Decide if the noun is a count or non-count noun. Write **C** or **NC** in the blanks. Be prepared to share your answers.

1. news _____

2. assistance _____

3. course _____

4. building _____

5. fish _____

6. guidance _____

7. punctuation _____

8. research _____

9. trust _____

10. software _____

11. information _____

12. intelligence _____

13. luxury _____

14. curtain _____

15. truth _____

16. laundry _____

Exercise 2   *Count and Non-Count Nouns*

Decide if there is an error in count and non-count use in each of the following sentences. Correct the errors. Check your answers in the Answer Key.

1. Paulo wanted to have his freedoms when he was a little boy at school.

2. I don't think the supervisor knows about the new works we are expected to do.

3. He had to control his anger and many fears.

4. They were stopped on the freeway for 15 minutes because the traffics held them up.

5. She takes out the garbages every second day on her way out to work.

6. The farm machinery stood by the side of the road.

7. I enjoy popcorns with butter when I go to the movies.

8. Do not buy new equipment for the office until we check the price.

9. Marcella hates doing houseworks on the weekends.

10. It takes courage to do what you think is right.

PART 2: THE USE OF ARTICLES *A*, *AN*, AND *THE*

In the English language, words such as *a*, *an*, and *the* are used to point out something specific (a **definite article**) or something general in a non-specific sense (an **indefinite article**).

A man delivered these flowers for you.

The man delivered these flowers for you.

Can you tell the difference in meaning between these two sentences? In the first sentence, *a man*, not specific or known, delivered flowers. In the second sentence, the definite article *the* implies a particular, or definite, man who made the delivery.

A teacher can make a good salary.

The teacher can make a good salary.

In the third sentence, the meaning is a general one: the writer is implying that teaching is a good profession because a teacher can make a good salary. In the fourth sentence, the writer is referring to a specific, or definite, teacher. Perhaps the writer is pointing out that a particular teacher—here a definite one—has the possibility of earning a good salary for a number of reasons.

Some Useful Tips

1. Use *an* when the noun or word after it begins with a vowel or vowel sound. (In English, it is too difficult to pronounce *a* with an immediate vowel sound after it.)

an expression	an honest person	an eagle
an hour	an obstacle	an army
an iceberg	an Irish terrier	an umbrella

2. However, some words may begin with a vowel, but sound as if they begin with a consonant.

   a useful tool

   a European trip

   a Ukrainian dance

   In these examples, the *u* sounds like *you*, so the indefinite article *a* is used.

3. Use *a* or *an* when you are referring to a person being a member of a professional or political group, a particular religion, or a nation.

   Chieko is an engineer.

   Marco is a federalist.

   René is a Liberal.

   Miguella is a Catholic.

4. Use the definite article in the singular or plural to refer to a specific or particular one or group. Use the indefinite article *a* in the singular and use *some* in the plural when you wish to generalize.

   However, if you are referring to species, then non-count nouns can be countable.

   the fish (particular) *The fish* in the small pool swam around the little castle.

   a fish (general) *A fish* will recognize its feeders.

   fishes (variety of species) *Many fishes* are affected by the spawn of fish farms.

5. Some nouns do not usually take articles, for example, some sports and academic subjects.

hockey	baseball	basketball	biology	history

6. Some nouns of nationality, when used as adjectives, do not use articles. When you are using a nationality as an adjective, do not use an article. Do not make these nouns plural by adding *-s* or *-es*.

> He is Chinese. (*not* He is a Chinese; *compare with* The Chinese do not want war.)
>
> Emile is French. (*not* Emile is a French; *compare with* The French were absent from the talks.)
>
> Hakata is my student; she is Japanese. (*not* She is a Japanese; *compare with* The Japanese import wood from Canada.)

7. However, other nouns of nationality can be used with articles and can be made plural by adding *-s* or *-es*.

> He is German.
>
> He is a German.
>
> The Germans are having a national election.

Remember, certain nouns of nationality are not made plural by adding *-s* or *-es*. Here are some examples:

> British, Polish, Scottish, Danish, Spanish, Russian, English

Exercise 3   Indefinite Articles

Write *a* or *an* before each of the following nouns. Check your answers in the Answer Key.

1. _____ hockey game
2. _____ organ transplant
3. _____ field of daisies
4. _____ piece of cheese
5. _____ used car
6. _____ enraged customer
7. _____ few ounces of gold
8. _____ loud noise
9. _____ walk on the beach
10. _____ egg carton
11. _____ unusual job
12. _____ endangered species
13. _____ young child
14. _____ plate of cookies
15. _____ intelligent woman
16. _____ orange from Japan

Exercise 4   Articles

Complete each sentence using *a*, *an*, or *the*. Do not fill in a blank if you do not think an article is needed. Check your answers in the Answer Key.

1. José wants to take _____ orange from the ones in the fridge.

2. _____ dog in the hallway belongs to my friend.

3. Lucia wants to study _____ Spanish.

4. _____ Canadians love their national sport.

5. She purchased _____ eggplant for the curry.

6. My friend Gordon really enjoys the game of _____ curling.

7. The children found _____ lost cat and don't know to whom it belongs.

8. My teacher speaks _____ Danish.

9. Eduardo wants to study _____ molecular biology.

10. Because _____ professor was absent, _____ students had to work by themselves on the assignment.

11. He wants to play _____ volleyball on the university team.

12. He went to catch _____ airplane, but _____ airport was closed.

13. _____ engineer can earn extra money for original designs.

14. Her uncle is _____ priest in South America.

15. Please hand me _____ fork that is on the table next to you.

16. I love to have _____ apple in my lunch every day.

17. _____ manager of the hotel is not available to talk to the patron.

18. Have you got _____ money to pay for _____ new computer?

19. We spoke to _____ man who had saved the boy from drowning.

20. Ottawa is _____ capital city of Canada.

PART 3: EXPRESSIONS OF QUANTITY

Most count nouns form their plural by adding -s or -es.

dog	→	dogs	calendar	→	calendars
melon	→	melons	church	→	churches
fox	→	foxes	dish	→	dishes

Non-count nouns do not have a plural form.

furniture	knowledge	education	courage
work	traffic	equipment	homework
information	weather	research	warmth
leisure	progress	news	transportation
advice	music	grass	sugar
lumber	clothing	cash	wisdom

Some Useful Tips:

1. Singular count nouns can use

   the, *this* (close to you), the banana, this banana (close by)

   that (away from you), that banana (farther away)

2. Plural count nouns can use

   the, *these* (close to you), the bananas, these bananas (close by)

   those (away from you), those bananas (away from you)

Quantity Words with Count and Non-Count Nouns

Some words show quantity and go with nouns. Some quantity words that go with singular count nouns are *each*, *every*, *any*, and *one*.

each person, every boy, any dog, one banana

Some words show quantity and go with plural count nouns: *some, any, most, more, all, a lot (of), many, several, a few, a couple of, both*.

some people	any boys	most dogs	more bananas
all trees	a lot of vegetables	many shoppers	several men
a few children	a couple of cars	both women	most pastries

Some words show quantity and go with non-count nouns:

a little, some, any, much, more, all, less, a lot (of), very little, no.

Examples

a little excitement	some cash	more applause	a lot of traffic
less dirt	all information	very little justice	no soap
any food	much love	less trouble	more water

Use *few* or *fewer* with plural count nouns.

few birds	fewer tourists	few mistakes	fewer roads

Exercise 5   *Expressions of Quantity*

Complete each expression with an appropriate quantity word. Some may take several answers; choose one. Check your answers in the Answer Key.

1. _____ apples
2. _____ intelligence
3. _____ sheep
4. _____ chocolate
5. _____ plums

6. _____ work
7. _____ humans
8. _____ rain
9. _____ advertising
10. _____ workers

11. _____ wealth   13. _____ glasses

12. _____ child   14._____ magazine

Each sentence contains errors that relate to quantity words or count and non-count nouns. Find the errors. Then correct each sentence. Write your corrections above each sentence. Be prepared to share your answers.

1. Several heavy traffics were outside my apartment today.

2. A couple of student were talking about the assignment.

3. A lot of lemon were spoiled in the bin at the store.

4. Lee had a lot of troubles with his new car this week.

5. Were there many advertisings about the orientation session today?

6. Both child wanted to go out to the park to enjoy the sunny afternoon.

7. Less sandwiches were available at the cafeteria after five o'clock.

8. More girl wanted to play on the beach than boy.

9. He has a lot of energies for such a small man!

10. More educations is needed in today's world.

11. Several knowledges about diving is important for a couple of person on the trip.

12. She has decided to put fewer furnitures in her bedroom this semester.

13. Every women in the bakery knows Giorgio, who always comes to buy a couple of bun each morning.

14. A few equipment was broken when we bought them.

15. These advices does not help me get a few informations I need.

PART 4: UNDERSTANDING TIME TRANSITIONS

You use special transitional words and phrases when you want to employ a time-order mode. These transitions are used in English to help your reader follow your ideas from point to point. You will use transitions and other connectors for two main reasons: first, you want your ideas to relate in some reasonable way, and secondly, you want your ideas to "stick together," or cohere. Transitions can help give your writing coherence.

These transitions can indicate a process is just beginning:

first, to begin with, now, and in the first place

Other transitions can show that another step or stage will be introduced:

next, then, after that, later, secondly, thirdly, and later

Some transitions indicate what first happened in a sequence:

first, before, to begin with, in the first place, now

Useful Transitions in Time-Order Mode

first	later	before	to begin with
following that	next	meanwhile	afterward
until	after a while	then	when
finally	soon	secondly, thirdly	after that
now	presently	in the first place	in due time
last			

Other transitions tell what happened in a sequence after the first stage or step:

next, afterward, following that, after that, second, secondly.

Some transitions indicate time has elapsed, so if you are explaining a process that happened over time, use these:

following that, after a while, when, in due time, later, finally, last.

Exercise 7   *Transitions*

Choose transition words that could fit into each of the following short passages. Check your answers in the Answer Key.

1. Alejandro and Emile were planning a meeting. _____, they decided their agenda. _____ they had to book a room. _____ they had to inform members of the community where and when the meeting was to be held.

2. My grandmother and I always prepared pickles together. _____, we would go out to the garden and gather the freshest, ripest cucumbers and onions we could find. _____ we washed the cucumbers carefully and scrubbed them with a soft brush. _____ we set them in a cool place, and _____ we began to peel and chop the onions. _____, we would prepare the brine for the cucumbers.

3. Kiyoshi got tired of waiting for his girlfriend. _____ he called her on his cell phone. _____ he tried calling her at work. _____, he gave up and went home for the evening, annoyed that she had not turned up.

4. Bathing your dog can be quite simple. _____ assemble all of the things you will require, like towels, dog shampoo, leash, and a large plastic container. _____ fill the tub with warm water, but be careful not to fill it to the top. _____, call your dog sweetly and nicely, so he won't suspect what you have planned for him. _____ clip on his leash and lead him to the bathing area, speaking softly to him in a friendly manner.

5. _____ fill these orders and _____ pack them into these boxes.

6. Follow these procedures in an earthquake. _____ seek protection from falling objects. _____ try to shelter your body from injury by moving away from windows. _____, act quickly because earthquakes give you little time to think.

7. To play this game, _____ put your game piece on the game board in the box marked "start." _____ roll the dice. _____ count the number of squares you will move on the board according to the number on the dice. _____, move your game piece the number of squares.

8. To stir fry this delicious vegetable, _____ wash it, _____ dry it, and _____, cut it into bite-sized pieces.

PART 5: SPECIAL COMPARISON AND CONTRAST WORDS

In the English language, some words are called conjunctions because they join parts of sentences together; however, some conjunctions show differences. A coordinating conjunction, joining two equal elements together, can show a contrast between the two parts of the sentence. *But* is a coordinating conjunction that joins two main clauses; it indicates a difference between the ideas. Notice that in a compound sentence, you should use a comma in front of coordinating conjunctions.

I walked to work, *but* my husband took the car.

He wanted to speak, *but* the words would not come.

Different from is another expression that also indicates difference. It usually appears in a sentence in which two items have been named.

Bob is *different from* his brother.

A rat is *different from* a mouse.

Her work at the university is *different from* her work at home.

Words can also show similarity. Two such expressions in English are *the same as* and *similar to*. These expressions are used when you want to indicate that two things are the same. However, *the same as* means the two items are identical, whereas *similar to* implies some qualities are the same while others are not.

For Lian, a shopping trip is *similar to* a vacation. (In some ways, the two items have similarities.)

For Lian, a shopping trip is *the same as* a vacation. (Lian sees both items in exactly the same way.)

His smoking is *similar to* his drinking. (In some ways, the two items have similar qualities.)

His smoking is *the same as* his drinking. (In some sense, the two habits are exactly the same.)

Her dress is *the same as* her mother's. (They are identical items.)

Her dress is *similar to* her mother's. (In some ways, the two dresses are alike, but they are not identical.)

Exercise 8   *Writing Sentences*

Write sentences according to the instructions given below. Use separate paper. Your instructor may want to see your sentences.

Example:

Write a sentence in which you tell that your car and your brother's car have some characteristics that are the same.

Answer:

My car is similar to my brother's.

or

My car and my brother's car are similar.

1. Write a sentence in which you tell about your work and your partner's work and how they are similar.

2. Write a sentence in which you tell about your computer and Maj's computer and how they are different.

3. Write a sentence in which you tell about one meal yesterday and one meal today and how they are the same.

4. Write a sentence in which you tell about your dog and Hoshi's dog and how they share some of the same characteristics.

5. Write a sentence in which you tell about your suitcase and Max's suitcase and how they are identical.

6. Write a sentence in which you tell about your neighbourhood and your sister's neighbourhood and how they are different.

7. Write a sentence in which you tell about Tony's sweater and Guy's sweater and how they share some of the same characteristics.

8. Write a sentence in which you tell about Misu's lawnmower and your lawnmower and how they are identical.

9. Write a sentence in which you tell about your father's microwave and your microwave and how they share some of the same characteristics.

Exercise 9   *Expressions of Comparison and Contrast*

Use *but*, *different from*, *the same as*, or *similar to* in each of the following sentences. Check your answers in the Answer Key.

1. My briefcase is _____ yours because it has the same colour and lock.

2. After some years, Kim realized he was _____ his brother, so he began to appreciate their differences.

3. The instructor wanted to finish her marking, _____ she was just too tired to do it.

4. The table that Lars bought is _____ the one I bought, because it does not have the extra leaf.

5. The news story you told me is _____ the one I heard earlier, except I understood the incident happened today.

6. Her singing is _____ it was when she was my student; I think if she practises more, she will improve.

7. Miguel wanted to quit smoking, _____ he could not break the habit.

8. Turkish coffee is _____ Greek coffee.

9. My grade in the English course is _____ Joan's, _____ I did more work.

10. Her umbrella is _____ mine, even though we purchased our umbrellas at different stores.

PART 6: WORKING WITH CLASSIFICATION AND DIVISION TRANSITIONS

In the English language, transitions give your writing coherence. They make the ideas "stick together." They bridge ideas, too. Your reader is able to understand how you have arranged your points because the transitional word or phrase has a specific meaning, according to the mode. It is important to think about the meaning of transitions and how they work.

Useful Transitions in Classification Modes

one category	as well as	furthermore
the first type (of)	another group	another sort (of)
a further category	in addition to	one kind (of)
the second type (of)	one sort of	the second kind (of)

Useful Transitions in Division Modes

accordingly	besides that	another part
the first component	next	the first ingredient
the second component	another component	one component
the first part	the second part	another ingredient
the first element	the second element	

> ### Useful Transitions for Giving Examples
>
> for example   such as   for instance   specifically
>
> to illustrate   also

Study these examples showing the use of transitions:

One sort of sports car is the R-class. The Porsche Boxster, for example, has a specific design patented by Porsche International.

Three types of chemicals are dangerous and should be kept out of reach of small children. The first kind is corrosive chemicals. These can do harm on contact with a person's skin. Chemicals that unclog a drain, for instance, are extremely harmful when added to water.

The first component of good speaking is complete control over tonality of voice and modulation.

Another group of cereals that is taking a high share of the market is the microwaveable type, such as instant oats.

A third part of the system includes a sophisticated fibre-optic cable.

The first ingredient of a good cake is a fresh egg.

One element of an elementary school education is caring instruction; another element is lively "talk."

Note that in English you say

one kind of + singular noun

one part of + singular noun

one component of + singular noun.

One exception is the expression one type of + noun. The noun is seen as generic, representing a class of things, so you should consider it as a non-count noun.

One type of car runs on batteries. (generic)

One component of work is purpose. (one component + non-count noun)

One part of transportation is planning. (one component + non-count noun)

One type of animal that lives in the jungle is the sloth. (generic)

Exercise 10   Transitions

Complete each sentence with *one type of, one component of, one part of,* or *one kind of.* Check your answers in the Answer Key.

1. Rada bought herself _____ chocolate.

2. My mother-in-law will wash with only _____ soap.

3. _____ the game is tricking your opponents.

4. The customer wanted to exchange _____ software.

5. She claimed that _____ the toaster had been damaged in shipment.

6. _____ the concert will be dedicated to the early music of Mozart.

7. Sylvestine tried to purchase _____ pop at the corner store, but the store did not carry the product.

8. Misha says that _____ her housework includes mopping.

9. _____ weather sailors really hate is hail.

10. _____ the civil engineering program is calculus.

You should also note that when you use *such as*, you do not require commas. When you use *for example*, put a comma in front of the expression and after it.

Services *such as* home support are being cut from the provincial budget.

Services are being cut from the provincial budget, *for example*, home support.

Exercise 11   *Practice with Transitions*

Choose a transition from one group—classification, division, or example—to fit into each of the following. Check your answers in the Answer Key.

1. There are three basic types of crucifers. _____ of crucifer is broccoli.

2. _____ of the interview begins as you enter the interview room.

3. The government's ferry schedule consists of four categories. _____ is the holiday schedule.

4. The menu was separated into six parts. _____ contained appetizers. _____, a diner could choose from 15 appetizers, either hot or cold. _____ contained main dishes.

5. Roscoe, my dog, is _____ of terrier.

6. The equipment room contained _____ of steamer.

7. A mosquito deterrent, _____ Deet, will keep these insects away for several hours.

8. The company has decided to reorganize its information technology section. Company executives have decided to create five groups. They say that _____ will be responsible for budget and marketing directives.

9. My grandfather is an avid fly fisherman. He claims there are seven types of flies you can tie and _____ fly is capable of catching a lake trout.

10. Canadians prefer _____ of winter sport.

11. One _____ of screwdriver, _____, the Robertson, is important to have in your household tool kit.

12. Marmalade, _____ of condiment found on the breakfast table, is often served with muffins, scones, or toast.

13. As well as _____ of copier, our company can _____ offer you _____ that is far more efficient for your business needs.

14. Nels has three types of shoes in his closet: _____ is for good wear when he needs to dress up; _____ is for walking; and _____ is for casual wear around the house.

15. The technologist has designed a system with three components. _____ it is different from our design.

PART 7: CAUSE AND EFFECT: USING *SINCE, BECAUSE, SO,* AND *THEREFORE*

Since and *because* are called subordinating conjunctions. A subordinating conjunction works in a complex sentence to join dependent clauses to main clauses in order to show a relationship between the two clauses. *So* is a coordinating conjunction, usually used in compound sentences. *Therefore* is a weak conjunction called a conjunctive adverb in a sentence. Remember: in compound sentences, place a comma in front of the coordinating conjunction unless the sentence is very short.

Read the following example sentences. Pay attention to which part of the sentence can be considered the cause and which part can be considered the effect (or result). Also note that if a subordinate clause comes first in a complex sentence, put a comma after it.

> George took a taxi home because he was too tired to walk.
>
> Since it was raining, Stella took her umbrella.
>
> Abdul walked to work, so his wife could use the car.
>
> The guest arrived early at the hotel, so he could have a rest before dinner.

In English, *therefore* is a conjunctive adverb that usually appears in a compound sentence. However, it is a weak joiner that requires a semicolon (;) in front of it. Use a comma after *therefore*.

> He was absent from work; *therefore*, he lost pay.

Exercise 12   *Punctuating Sentences with Commas*

Supply commas where you think they belong in each of the following sentences. Note: some sentences may not require commas. Be prepared to share your answers.

1. Because the chef was sick the meal was delayed.

2. The young soldier sent a letter to his girlfriend so he could say goodbye.

3. He was afraid of the dogs since he had been bitten by one previously.

4. We ordered a pizza because we were hungry and in a hurry.

5. Deana loved the movie therefore she plans to buy the DVD.

6. Because our house is up for sale we must keep it very tidy.

7. Since the princess was lost she sat down and cried.

8. The shoes were too tight for Angelo therefore he returned them to the store.

9. His parents worked hard so Igor could get a good education.

10. Because the dinner was delicious we all applauded the cook.

Exercise 13   *Distinguishing Causes and Effects*

Write **CAUSE** (reason) and **EFFECT** (result) over the appropriate part of each sentence. Be prepared to share your answers.

1. Since the children are not going to school today, let's all go on a picnic.

2. The factory closed; therefore, many families were in financial turmoil.

3. Some snakes make bad pets because they do not relate to humans.

4. Several managers invented a new management strategy, so the workers felt more appreciated.

5. Since it is so sunny in the summer, we should wear sunscreen.

6. Herbert's drinking was out of control, so he lost his job.

7. Candles are easy to make because materials are easy to get anywhere.

8. Her Aunt Mazy insisted on arriving late to dinner because she thought it was dramatic.

9. Lemons and oranges were colourful in the fruit punch; therefore, Jana added more.

10. The little girl waited along the street, so she could watch the parade.

11. I wait for you after class because I have a crush on you.

PART 8: SUBORDINATION

A complex sentence usually contains two clauses. One clause is called the main clause. It can stand alone. The other clause is called a dependent or subordinate clause, which cannot stand alone. It is important for you to recognize that the clauses relate to one another in a number of ways. Sometimes the clauses show time, condition, place, or reason because of the meaning of the subordinating conjunction that begins the dependent clause.

Some Subordinating Conjunctions

after	if	when	although	since
whenever	as	unless	where	because
until	wherever	before	though	while

Exercise 14   Clauses

Identify each of the clauses in each of the following complex sentences as main or subordinate clauses. Use a comma when the dependent clause comes first in the sentence. Check your answers in the Answer Key.

1. After the students left the classroom, the teacher organized the bookshelves.

2. She has hardly spoken to me since we had our argument.

3. Tulips and daffodils are cheery spring flowers because they provide bright splashes of colour in the landscape.

4. Whenever Thomas goes out to eat, he takes his cocker spaniel along with him.

5. Shelly ordered a new washing machine before she left the store.

6. Unless you give me a raise, I will quit this job!

7. I notice happiness wherever I go.

8. Magda studies hard since she wants to be a doctor.

9. While Stephen tossed the salad, Monique set the table.

10. The report is on Lou's desk although he has not read it yet.

11. If Eda arrives late, she will miss the speaker's presentation.

12. Wherever Mim goes, her little white poodle follows.

13. Because the tablecloth is stained with tea, we will have to bleach it.

14. Jamal will partition the new hard drive after I back up my data on the portable hard drive.

15. In the late summer afternoon, Dell and his family sailed on the small lake until the sun went down.

Exercise 15   Clauses

Tell if the clauses relate by time, condition, place, or reason. Be prepared to share your answers.

1. Before you wash the car, please buy the groceries for our supper.

2. Ngozi wishes to take a break while the other students work.

3. If bears scare you, would you go into the woods?

4. Whenever we are in Ottawa, we like to visit the National Gallery.

5. The dentist worked quickly as the small child was quite anxious.

6. Several members of the theatre community stay at my house whenever they are in town for a performance.

7. The Association for Animal Rights was boycotting the pet food factory because it was in violation of several by-laws.

8. Do you enjoy eating vegetables because they are good for you?

9. The receptionist jumped up with a start when the fire alarm rang.

10. Since the roofer will not be able to complete the job this week, Yasha will hire a new roofing contractor.

11. Do you enjoy eating cotton candy whenever you go to the fall fair?

12. Although Yasuo spoke with an accent, he had very good English.

13. My brother Royce loves to go out for dinner before he goes to a movie.

14. The bird sang sweetly on the fence while its mate bathed energetically in a little pool of water between the rocks in the garden.

15. When I give you the signal, everyone should laugh hysterically.

Exercise 16   Clauses

Combine the pair of clauses to form a complex sentence, using the subordinate conjunctions suggested. Use separate paper. Check your answers in the Answer Key. Remember: if you use a dependent clause at the beginning of a sentence, use a comma after it.

1. Salim writes his own songs. He is shy about performing publicly. (although)

2. The owl sat silently watching from the highest branch of the tree. The mouse scurried through the grasses below. (while)

3. Does Yasmina visit you? Is Yasmina in town? (when)

4. Slice the mushrooms. Heat the butter. (after)

5. The choreographer spends his time rehearsing. The show starts. (until)

6. Her relatives arrived from India. Harpreet was delighted. (because)

7. Marina is having a baby in April. She is looking at baby clothing in the flyers. (since)

8. Zoe hates cooking. She won't admit it. (though)

9. The cat goes. Her kittens follow. (wherever)

10. He went to Cuba. He went to Spain. (before)

11. Do not turn off the computer. You will be away for more than one day. (unless)

12. Kira went to the marketplace. She bought eggplant for the stew. (where)

PART 9: PASSIVE AND ACTIVE VOICE

Voice is an expression used in relation to verbs. If a verb is in the active voice, it means the subject does the action. If a verb is in the passive voice, it means the subject is the recipient of the action indicated by the verb.

> At the annual meeting, Taye made a motion to increase club fees. (active)
>
> At the annual meeting, a motion was made by Taye to increase club fees. (passive)
>
> Moia loves good poetry. (active voice)
>
> Good poetry is loved by Moia. (passive voice)
>
> The company employees enjoy a spring break. (active voice)
>
> A spring break is enjoyed by the company employees. (passive voice)

The print media (newspapers and magazines) often use the passive voice when reporters write or report stories. You will see the passive voice used frequently in science and technical writing. Passive voice is used in these circumstances because the subjects of the sentences may be unknown or less important than what happened.

Useful Tips for Passive Voice

1. You cannot use the passive voice with these common verbs:

stay	walk	sleep	arrive
appear	come	cry	go
happen	die		

2. Usually the passive voice consists of a form of *to be* plus the past participle of the main verb.

3. Only transitive verbs (those that take objects) can be written in the passive voice.

4. Use the active voice whenever you can.

5. You can use the passive voice in these particular circumstances:

   - Use the passive voice when the object of the action seems to be more important than the subject.

     We instituted a new sexual harassment policy at the college. (active)

     A new sexual harassment policy was instituted at the college. (passive; the policy is more important in this case than who instituted it.)

   - Use the passive voice when the subject is unknown.
     The car was hit on the front passenger side. (It is not clear who hit the car.)

• Use the passive voice if you wish to blur agency or responsibility. Sometimes the subject or agent of an action may be protected by having a statement reported in the passive voice. It removes responsibility from the subject or agent.

Several shots were fired. (You may not wish to name who did the shooting.)

Exercise 17   Voice

Identify whether each statement is in the active or passive voice. Check your answers with the Answer Key.

1. French is spoken in many parts of Canada._____

2. The lieutenant studied for his exams._____

3. Lemon sauce will complement the fish._____

4. His wallet was stolen on Tuesday night._____

5. The guests were invited to dine on the deck of the ship._____

6. Morgan was not pleased by the arrangement._____

7. Brushing your teeth helps prevent cavities._____

8. The orchestra conductor was interpreting the passage of music in a new way._____

9. The gift was boxed and ready for shipment._____

10. Hockey sticks are made in Quebec._____

11. The doctor appeared tired after surgery._____

12. An unusual occurrence is happening in the southwest._____

13. Groober was elected to Parliament on June 24th._____

14. The prisoner was escorted from the court by a guard._____

Exercise 18   Voice

Change each of the following passive constructions into active voice. Rewrite each sentence on the lines provided. Check your answers in the Answer Key.

1. The cat was leashed to the bike rack by its owner.

_____

2. A feast was prepared by Chef Bonhomme.

_____

3. The umbrella was found by the station master.

_____

4. The novel was written by Margaret Atwood.

   _____

5. The saddle was placed on the horse by the ranch hand.

   _____

6. The murder was solved by Detective Goodley.

   _____

7. He was held responsible by the board.

   _____

8. My party was arranged by my children.

   _____

9. She was made upset by the accident.

   _____

10. I was convinced to quit smoking by my brother.

    _____

PART 10: SIMPLE, PERFECT, AND PROGRESSIVE VERB TENSES

You learned about verbs and verb tense in Chapters 11 and 12. You may wish to review those chapters before doing the following exercises.

Exercise 19 *Working with Verb Tenses*

Change each verb tense as indicated. Check your answers in the Answer Key.

1. They will not listen to my sad story. (past perfect)

   _____

2. Felicia went for an interview on Tuesday. (simple future)

   _____

3. Her neighbour's dog barks all day. (simple past)

   _____

4. Sandra played the accordion for the Community Players Band. (present perfect progressive)

_____

5. The clown does card tricks at children's parties. (simple future)

_____

6. Vicky will bandage her hand after each tennis match. (simple present)

_____

7. Lisa will not tolerate shoplifting. (past progressive)

_____

8. We collected returnable bottles for the Girl Scouts. (simple future)

_____

9. At the bus depot, the schedule was out of date (simple present)

_____

10. Each morning Joanne scans the headlines. (future progessive)

_____

11. The sheriff will note your new address. (simple present)

_____

12. The child tears her jacket in the rough brambles. (past perfect progressive)

_____

13. He spun the Wheel of Fortune on the game show. (simple present)

_____

Exercise 20   Sentences and Tenses

On a separate sheet of paper, make sentences according to the directions given below. Your instructor may want you to hand in your work. Be prepared to share your answers.

1. Use _fish_ as a noun in a sentence containing a past progressive verb.

2. Use _sail_ as a future perfect progressive verb in a sentence.

3. Use _worry_ as a noun in a sentence containing a present simple verb.

4. Use *plant* as a past progressive verb in a sentence.

5. Use *stage* as a simple past verb in a sentence.

6. Use *work* as a noun in a sentence containing a past perfect verb.

7. Use *sour* in a sentence containing a present progressive verb.

8. Use *shop* as a noun in a sentence containing a future perfect progressive verb.

9. Use *juice* as a noun in a sentence containing a simple future verb.

10. Use *fly* as a present progressive verb in a sentence.

PART 11: INDEFINITE PRONOUNS AND VERB AGREEMENT

Some words called indefinite pronouns usually take singular verbs. Remember: they are called indefinite because they do not refer to a specific person or thing.

Indefinite Pronouns

anyone	everybody	most	somebody
neither	none	one	any
someone	each	more	nothing
some	anything	everything	all
nobody	another	anybody	everyone
few	no one	either	

Indefinite pronouns such as *all*, *few*, *some*, *more*, and *most* may be either singular or plural depending on what they are referring to.

All of the paper was ruined when I spilled my coffee. (refers to a single page)

All of the men were upset by their new marching orders. (refers to men)

Most of the banana was good. (refers to a single banana)

Most of the bananas were good. (refers to a bunch of bananas)

Some of the cheese was spoiled. (refers to a single piece of cheese)

Some of the cheeses were spoiled. (refers to a variety of cheeses)

Exercise 21   Agreement and Indefinite Pronouns

Read the following sentences. Find subject–verb agreement errors having to do with indefinite pronouns. Repair the errors. Some sentences may be correct as shown. Pay attention to count and non-count nouns. Check your answers in the Answer Key.

1. A few of the people was buying extra bread on sale.

2. Some of the movie were really funny.

3. Most of the children loves to play in the water of the splash pool.

4. One of his marriages were successful.

5. None of the wine in the antique bottle taste good.

6. Both of my partners want to stay in business.

7. All of the furniture were destroyed in the fire.

8. Drago and most of his friends drinks too much on the weekends.

9. I feel sad because no one want to come to my party.

10. Most of the questions were difficult to answer on the nutrition exam.

11. All of the paint were used up for the barn.

12. Some of the evidence are unconvincing.

Exercise 22   More Subject–Verb Agreement

Read the following sentences. Find subject–verb agreement errors. Repair the errors. Some sentences may be correct as shown. Check your answers in the Answer Key.

1. The audience at the concert were throwing insults at the stage.

2. Under the counter there was piles of free samples for customers.

3. A case of carbonated juices was donated by Safeway.

4. Neither the dictator nor his henchmen were held responsible for the crimes.

5. Students or the professors votes in the coming campus election.

6. Someone on the rooftops was shooting at police.

7. Most of the photographs is memorable.

8. Nobody question his authority.

9. Do you know whether there is extra computers for student use?

10. The manager of the stores and his three assistants are developing a new marketing plan.

11. No one from these two campuses have been notified.

12. Each of the missing reports have been recovered by police.

13. Neither of the departments we contacted have a student rep.

14. The committee make its recommendations to the dean.

15. None of the conference were worthwhile.

16. The CD or the memos contains the needed information.

17. Nearly two-thirds of the town were destroyed by floods.

18. A loud flock of starlings were gathering in the cornfield.

PART 12: THE USE OF QUOTATION MARKS IN DIRECT SPEECH

Quotation marks look like this: " ". They are used to surround the words a speaker says directly. Open quotation marks show the beginning of the speaker's words like this: ". Closed quotation marks show the end of the speaker's words, like this: ".

In the English language quotation marks are essential when you are directly quoting what someone says. In other words, use quotation marks to indicate direct speech.

> Stephano said, "I will never love anyone the way I love you!"

Notice that the quotation starts with a phrase identifying who the speaker is and a verb—Stephano said. In most direct quotations you will see

- a comma used to separate the speaker identification from his or her words

- open quotation marks followed by the speaker's actual words

- a closing mark of punctuation at the end of the speaker's sentence

- closed quotation marks.

If the speaker's words are interrupted because the identifying phrase is placed in the middle of the sentence, do not use a capital letter for the second part of the speaker's words unless the beginning word requires it (a name, the pronoun I, or a specific place).

> "I will never love anyone," Stephano said, "the way I love you!"
>
> "I will never love anyone," said Stephano, "the way I love you!"

Do not use quotation marks if you are reporting speech indirectly. In these cases, what the speaker said is a fact you are reporting. You will usually introduce the indirect quotation with *that*.

> Stephano said that he will never love anyone the way he loves you.

You are reporting what Stephano said; therefore, no quotation marks are needed.

Exercise 23   *Using Quotation Marks in Direct Speech*

Where needed, add correct punctuation to each of the following quotations. Work in pairs. Try to determine the correct answers together. Be prepared to share your answers.

1. The small child whined I want another cookie!

2. Through the action of the waves the teacher explained the shoreline is ever-changing.

3. I don't want to walk by myself said Milla it is too dark outside.

4. The mechanic said he would not be able to fix my car until Thursday.

5. No one can predict the economy accurately mused Professor Plumply.

6. When I arrived, no one was in the meeting room explained Mrs. Garr.

7. Tell them to stop making that terrible racket ordered the frustrated writer.

8. Alain exclaimed all my emails are lost!

9. The chief surgeon told the patient you will have to stop smoking.

10. What does it matter asked Marie if I finish this on time or not?

Exercise 24   *Practice with Direct and Indirect Speech*

Change the form of each sentence as requested. Check your answers in the Answer Key.

1. The clerk replied, "The cost of mailing the package is $20.00." (change to indirect speech).

2. My sister-in-law said she is afraid of mice and spiders. (change to direct speech)

3. One television reporter said that he was shocked by the damage to the building. (change to direct speech)

4. "In about two months' time," Chula explained, " I will be on a train in the Sudan." (change to indirect speech)

5. "One of the things I dislike the most," the president stated, "is being misquoted by the press." (change to indirect speech)

6. The two students complained to Professor Nguyen that their marks were incorrect on the economics exam. (change to direct speech)

7. Lara remarked, "I won't work on weeknights any longer unless I get a raise." (change to indirect speech)

PART 13: PREPOSITIONS OF PLACE AND TIME

In the English language, some prepositions are commonly used to indicate time. These prepositions are *on*, *at*, and *in*.

Use *on* to indicate a particular date or day.

Use *at* to indicate the hour something is expected. It is also used with midnight, noon, or night.

Use *in* to indicate the number of minutes or hours something is expected. Use *in* to indicate a part of the day, a month, a season, or a year.

I will arrive *in* Germany *on* December 12, 2005.

Jenny will have her interview *on* Friday afternoon.

The choir is singing *at* 8 o'clock this evening.

At midnight, the church bell will ring.

Her students will meet with her *in* 10 minutes.

My grandmother loves to rest in the afternoons *in* the summer.

Exercise 25   *Prepositions of Place and Time*

Use *in*, *on*, or *at* in each of the following sentences. Check your answers in the Answer Key.

1. Kiley is expected to arrive _____ 35 minutes.

2. We think the plane will arrive _____ 5:00 a.m. today.

3. _____ six o'clock, I am going to visit an old friend in the city.

4. He must be going to his meeting _____ nine this morning.

5. The family loves to vacation _____ the winter.

6. _____ the late evening, Hyston loves to read murder mysteries.

7. My aunt's social club meets _____ noon every second Tuesday downtown.

8. Tavi said he would join us for a drink _____ 50 minutes.

9. One of the passengers will wait for a flight _____ August.

10. _____ Sunday I will bring you some parcels.

11. May I call you at home this evening _____ eight?

12. Budgie birds like a cover on their cages _____ night.

13. _____ Thursday, my uncle is having surgery on his knee.

14. _____ fall many species of birds leave Canada for warmer climates.

15. The restaurant manager called to say you have a reservation _____ Saturday, March 12th.

Adjective + Preposition Arrangements

Some common adjectives often have particular prepositions following them. You will notice these combinations frequently in speech and in writing.

Here are some common combinations:

Common Adjective + Preposition Arrangements		
Adjective + *of*	Adjective + *to*	Adjective + *with*
quality of	similar to	pleased with
aware of	accustomed to (used to)	popular with
capable of	suitable to (or for)	satisfied with
suspicious of	related to	
afraid of	opposed to	
proud of	attached to	

Exercise 26   Adjectives + Prepositions

Fill each blank with the appropriate preposition. Check your answers in the Answer Key.

1. Fernand is pleased _____ his new decorating job.

2. The priest is opposed _____ the policy on fundraising.

3. Are these green sweatshirts popular _____ younger teenagers?

4. A tiger is capable _____ eating half its weight in food every two days.

5. I think the new supervisor is suspicious _____ our plan to develop the area.

6. The mayor and city council are not aware _____ our group's proposal.

7. Some children feel closely attached _____ favourite toys.

8. Do you think the criminal is capable _____ such a violent act?

9. The house is suitable _____ a family of four.

10. I believe Saeed's argument is similar _____ his brother's.

11. My friend Joy is related _____ a famous opera singer.

12. Was the customer satisfied _____ the repair we did?

13. His mother is very proud _____ her children's accomplishments.

14. The little boy is afraid _____ dogs.

15. Vito is not yet accustomed _____ the harsh Canadian winters.

Exercise 27   Adding Modifiers

Work in pairs. Use separate paper. Add adjectives, adverbs, adjective prepositional phrases, or adverb prepositional phrases according to directions. Be prepared to share your answers.

1. Make up a sentence about a dog. Your sentence should contain two adjectives and one prepositional phrase of your own choosing.

2. Make up a sentence about a dream. Your sentence should contain three prepositional phrases of your own choosing.

3. Make up a sentence about a news story. Your sentence should have two adverbs, three adjectives, one adverb prepositional phrase, and one adjective prepositional phrase.

4. Make up a sentence about tea. Your sentence should contain one adjective prepositional phrase, two adverbs, and one adjective.

5. Make up a sentence about a child. Your sentence should contain five modifiers of your own choosing.

PART 14: CONDITIONAL SENTENCES USING THE CONJUNCTION *IF*

Although *if* is a little word, it can cause confusion because the conditions it can express can be complicated. *If* is a subordinate conjunction used when you wish to state a conditional relationship of some sort. If may be used in three conditional cases:

Case 1: To express facts or generalizations that are true in the world

If people do not drink enough water, they will die.

If the plant is not given this fertilizer, it will not flourish.

Case 2: To express predications or to make inferences

If this book is by Agatha Christie, it is probably a mystery novel.

If Rini uses her mother's recipe, the casserole will be delicious.

If the library is not open on Sunday, Josef cannot access the internet.

Case 3: To express fantastic ideas—ones that cannot come true

If I were you, I would leave him. (I cannot be another person. Notice the verb *were*.)

If he were a prizefighter, he would be dangerous. (It is not likely the subject will ever be a prizefighter. Notice that *were* is the verb.)

If cats could fly, there would be fewer birds. (Cats cannot fly.)

Exercise 28 *Identifying Conditions*

Read each sentence. Decide whether it expresses case 1, 2, or 3. Write your answer after each sentence. Check your answers in the Answer Key.

1. If the employee bought the company, he would fire all of us. _____

2. If ice melts, it leaves a puddle of water. _____

3. If the game is against the team from Oshawa, we might win. _____

4. If rainbows had pots of gold at the ends of them, most people would be rich. _____

5. If the sulphuric acid is placed in this plastic container, it will dissolve it. _____

6. If a mouse were to have a credit card, its house would be full of cheese. _____

7. If the train arrives at midnight, the passengers will be unable to take public transit in our city. _____

8. If the food contains too many additives, I will get a migraine. _____

9. If people sleep in too often, they will find it difficult to get up early. _____

10. If they offer us a good price, we will sell our condominium. _____

11. If the traffic is heavy at three o'clock, I will miss my meeting. _____

12. If she were 10 years younger, she would marry him. _____

13. If I were a witch, I'd cast a spell on you. _____

14. If you leave the butter out, it will go rancid in the warm room. _____

Exercise 29   *Constructing Sentence Patterns*

Before you complete this exercise, review the sentence patterns covered in Chapter 15. Work in pairs. Construct sentences according to the directions given below. Use separate paper. Be prepared to share your answers with others.

1. Write a compound sentence using *but* as the coordinating conjunction.

2. Write a compound–complex sentence using *who* in a relative, restrictive clause.

3. Write a simple sentence containing a compound verb.

4. Write a complex sentence using *because* as the subordinate conjunction.

5. Write a simple sentence with a compound subject.

6. Write a compound–complex sentence using *that* in a relative, restrictive clause.

7. Write a complex sentence using *which* in a relative clause.

8. Write a complex sentences using *when* as a subordinate conjunction.

9. Write a compound–complex sentence using a semicolon effectively.

PART 15: VERBALS AND PARALLELISM

About Verbals

A verbal is a word or phrase constructed from verbs but acting as other parts of speech. The following section discusses three types of verbals:

1. ***Gerunds* are verbals that act as nouns**.

   Exercising in the gym can be lacklustre.

   Exercising is a gerund, a verbal that ends in *-ing* and acts as a noun. *Exercising* is the subject of the sentence.

   Hunting for mice and dust balls keeps my cat occupied.

   Hunting is a gerund in a special phrase: Hunting for mice and dust balls. The whole gerundial phrase is the subject of the sentence.

2. ***Participles* are verbals that often end in *-ing* or *-ed*. They usually act as adjectives in sentences**.

   Walking to work, Wilma lost her new silk scarf.

   Walking to work is a participial phrase describing Wilma. It acts as an adjective.

   Playing with matches, Little Bratso set the wood shed on fire.

Playing with matches is a participial phrase modifying Little Bratso.

Worried about his money, Leroy decided to make a budget.

Worried about his money is a participial phrase describing Leroy.

3. **Infinitives are verbs that consist of to + the present simple tense of a verb (usually). Infinitives can function as nouns, adjectives, or adverbs**.

To win was Theo's goal.

To win is an infinitive. It is acting as a noun subject of the sentence.

The dog to groom is waiting for your attention.

To groom is an infinitive. It describes which dog, so it functions as an adjective.

About Parallelism

Parallelism means that all structures in the sentence are in the same grammatical form.

Washing the strawberries, chopping the fruit, and *measuring the sugar* are all part of jam making. (all gerund phrases)

Finding parallelism faults is rather difficult at times, but you can be guided by examining the verbals. All verbals must be in the same form if the sentence has parallel structure.

Exercise 30   *Verbals and Parallelism Faults*

In each of the following sentences, underline the verbals. Then identify them. Finally, be sure the verbals in the sequence are the same (parallel); if they are not, make the sentence parallel by making the verbals all the same type. Check your answers in the Answer Key.

1. Smoking, reading, and to cook were Aunt Lulu's passions.

2. Trudging up the hill, pulling his little red wagon, and reddened in the face, the little boy continued his paper route.

3. Yuni wanted to sing, to dance, and drinking on her anniversary.

4. Catching flies, to sit in the sun, and to move very little are how a frog spends its day.

5. Earning a salary as an engineer, paying off his student loans, and to have a family of his own were the young student's dreams.

6. Staring out the window, brushing her hair, and talked on the cell phone, Phillis noticed a raccoon in the garbage can in the neighbour's backyard.

7. The manager told the two workers that having long breaks, being late for work, and to be glib with the customers were the reasons they were fired.

8. The ballet teacher taught her students to be enthusiastic, free, and to be energetic.

Exercise 31 Eliminating Parallelism Faults

These sentences have parallelism problems. Find the errors and repair them. Work in pairs. Decide on corrections together.

1. Working with children is stimulating, challenging, and has its rewards.

2. Not being able to speak the language causes confusion, is frustrating, and it's sometimes embarrassing.

3. To prevent crime, attending to victims of accidents and crimes, and how to apprehend safely those suspected of crime are a police officer's responsibilities.

4. Being sound of mind and physically strong, the elderly man was able to live quite happily by himself.

5. Three of the issues the committee will have to deal with right away are camp maintenance, how to get staff for the camp, and promoting camp.

6. His doctor advised him to eat less, exercise more, and no smoking at all.

7. For many people, attending AA meetings is first embarrassing, possibly even humiliating, then helpful, and finally it is a success.

8. A high level of motivation, experience in problem solving, and you should not be concerned about your every decision are necessary if you hope to run a successful business.

9. Influential factors in any nation's economic regression are bad management of natural resources, policies regarding national debt might be unwise, and the unions' inflationary demands.

10. Although the first applicant seemed scared and showed shyness, the second was a composed person and outgoing.

chapter 18

Paragraph Readings

Chapter Objectives

After completing this chapter, you will be able to

- recognize how rhetorical modes have been used to organize ideas
- spot key words and phrases that indicate the rhetorical pattern
- make note of the vocabulary, evidence, and purpose in readings
- think critically while reading other writers' work

INTRODUCTION

This chapter provides readings for you to read and analyze. The paragraphs are organized according to the rhetorical modes you have been studying. These professional pieces are excerpts from longer selections; however, each still stands on its own as a good example of writing according to a mode of development. You will also notice a wide range of topics discussed in the readings. These readings should help you focus on modes, but at the same time, they should assist you in thinking about and discussing other more global ideas that relate to people, their interactions, and the issues in their lives and environments.

Your instructor may ask you to read the paragraphs and then work in groups to answer the questions. As you read, pay attention to how the writers have structured their ideas, what evidence they use, what vocabulary they have selected, and what purpose they may have had in writing the pieces. Also observe your own reactions to the ideas the writers present.

TIME-ORDER, OR PROCESS, MODE

Reading 1: Poutine

Jennifer Ogle

A beloved staple of Quebec cuisine, poutine is served at fast-food restaurants and fine dining establishments alike. Popular variations replace the gravy with Bolognese sauce or add sausages, and Montreal's famous Au Pied de Cochon serves its poutine with foie gras! There are many stories about the origin of poutine, but the consensus is that it originated in rural Quebec in the 1950s. Ultra-fresh cheese curds are the key ingredient in authentic poutine. They must be fresh enough to become soft (but not melt) once nestled in amongst the hot fries and gravy. A great indication of their freshness is how they squeak between your teeth when you chew them. The very popular fry-making method produces excellent, crisp fries with a creamy interior. It is a little extra work because it requires "blanching" the potatoes in oil at a low temperature to cook them, then frying them again at high temperature to brown them, but it is worth the effort if you are going to indulge anyway.

The Canadian Cookbook: History, Folklore & Recipes with a Twist *by Jennifer Ogle, Lone Pine Publishing, 2006, page 98.*

1. Why is Ogle's article an example of time-order development?

2. What are some of the transitions she uses?

3. What is "poutine"?

4. Why do you think Ogle describes poutine as a "beloved staple"?

5. How do you know the cheese curds are fresh in the poutine you order at a restaurant?

6. We can refer to poutine as a regional food. Can you name other foods that might be considered regional?

7. Food is an important cultural component. Today we see many foods and ingredients from different cultures cross into a form of cooking called "fusion." Can you think of fusion foods that come from different cultures in Canada?

8. In a paragraph composition of 150–200 words, discuss how particular foods and culture relate to daily life in Canada. Use the third-person point of view only.

Reading 2: Miss Bessie
Margaret Atwood

Miss Bessie was the best English teacher in the school. Possibly she was one of the best in the city: our parents said we were lucky to have her. She drove us briskly through the curriculum as if herding sheep, heading us off from false detours and perilous cliff edges, nipping at our heels when we slowed down in the wrong places, making us linger in the right ones so we could assimilate the material of importance. She described our task of learning as a race, a sort of obstacle course: there was a lot of ground still to be covered before the final exams, she said, and it had to be covered rapidly. This ground was strewn with hurdles and rough parts, and other difficulties. The days were speeding by, and we still had *Tess of the d'Urbervilles* looming up ahead of us like—we felt—a big steep hill of mud. It was true that once we got to the top of it, Miss Bessie—who'd been up there many times before—might show us a view; but meanwhile there would be a lot of slipperiness. We'd tangled with Thomas Hardy in the form of *The Mayor of Casterbridge* the year before: it was going to be heavy slogging. Therefore we needed to polish off "My Last Duchess" before week's end so we could catch our breath over the weekend and then get a good run at *Tess*.

Excerpt from "My Last Duchess," p. 56 from Moral Disorder *by Margaret Atwood © 2006. Published by McClelland & Stewart. Used with the permission of the publisher.*

1. What is Atwood discussing in the paragraph?

2. How would parents know that their children were "lucky to have" Miss Bessie as a teacher?

3. What metaphors does Atwood use to describe the process going on in English literature class?

4. How do the metaphors work in the piece?

5. Why do you think "Miss Bessie was the best English teacher in the school"?

6. How do you think the writer feels about Miss Bessie? How do you know?

7. In a comparison and contrast paragraph of 150–200 words, discuss how Atwood views the world of the teacher and the world of the student. Use the third-person point of view only.

Reading 3: Optical Microscope and Electron Microscope
Dr. R. C. Brooks

Invented in 1591, the optical microscope uses light and lenses to magnify objects. By 1870 scientists realized that the nature of light would limit magnification to only 2000 times. In 1932, the first electron microscope was invented. It replaced light with streams of electrons and used magnets instead of lenses. Albert Prebus and James Hillier built Canada's first electron microscope at the University of Toronto in 1939. Today, electron microscopes can magnify an object by over 500 million times.

"Optical Microscope and Electron Microscope," Dr. R. C. Brooks, Curator Physical Sciences and Space, Canada Science and Technology Museum, What Does It Do?, 2003, **www.science-tech.nmstc.ca/ english/collection/lab_equipment.cfm**.

1. Is there a topic sentence or a main idea in this piece of writing?

2. Are transitions used that show a chronological relationship? Which ones are used?

3. What problem may have motivated scientists to invent the electron microscope?

4. What are some differences between optical and electron microscopes?

5. Can you explain how lenses work in an optical microscope?

6. Do you think electron microscope images would be rendered black and white or colour?

7. Can an electron microscope enable you to see the movements of living cells?

8. For what purpose would it be useful to magnify an object 500 million times?

Reading 4: More about Good than Evil
T. F. Rigelhof

Sonny Rollins, the tenor saxophone colossus who was recently awarded the Polar Music Award by the Royal Swedish Academy as "one of the most powerful and personal voices in jazz for more than fifty years," likes to tell the people who ask him what he thinks about when he plays that "you can't think and play at the same time." What Rollins, one of the most dedicated craftsmen on the scene, means is that he practises and practises until he internalizes all the elements he needs and then lets the music play him and explicate "in the moment" whatever it dares to do. The result is music that is tightly focussed and casually brilliant, inexorably logical yet unpredictable, remarkably intelligent yet deeply felt.

"More about Good than Evil" by T. F. Rigelhof in Books in Canada: The Canadian Review of Books *March 2007. Volume 36, No 2, p. 4.*

1. What is the main idea of the paragraph from Rigelhof's piece?

2. What is a "colossus" and why does Rigelhof use it to describe Rollins?

3. Explain Rollins' statement that, "you can't think and play at the same time."

4. What comment is the passage presenting about the process of making music or art?

5. In what ways does Rollins' creative process differ from yours?

6. After doing some research on the internet and in a paragraph of about 150–200 words, describe the artistic process of a writer, visual artist, musician, or performing artist. Use the third-person point of view only.

Reading 5: Mackenzie House, Historic Buildings of Toronto
Sandra Alexandra

Mackenzie House is located at 82 Bond St. and was the home of William Lyon Mackenzie from 1859 until 1861, the year he died. Mackenzie came to York in 1820 from Scotland and was the driving force behind the reform movement in Upper Canada. He gave reformers a voice through his newspapers, the *Colonial Advocate* and the *Constitution*. Mackenzie won the first mayoralty race in the newly formed city in 1834. In 1837 he led the largely unsuccessful rebellion which culminated in a brief clash at Toronto, after which Mackenzie fled to the United States. In 1849 he returned to Toronto after an amnesty was proclaimed for those who had participated in the rebellion. This building, built in 1857, would have been part of a terrace (several adjoining buildings of the same design). Today it is a museum, restored to the period.

"Mackenzie House, Historic Buildings of Toronto," Sandra Alexandra, History of Toronto and County of York, Ontario, Canada, **www3.sympatico.ca/stillh2o/history/buildings3.html***, Stillwater Productions, 2001, 2002, p. 3.*

1. What shows that chronological order is used as a method of organizing ideas in this piece?

2. Is there a topic sentence in the paragraph?

3. How long did William Lyon Mackenzie live in Mackenzie House?

4. What is meant by the expression "restored to the period"?

5. What is meant by the architectural term "terrace"?

6. In a paragraph of 150–200 words, explain how a Canadian rebel leader could find sanctuary in the United States today.

COMPARISON AND CONTRAST MODE

Reading 6: The Devil in Ms. Griffiths
R. M. Vaughan

Indeed, a closer look at the paintings reveals an almost fanatical attention to the gradation of skin tone, to all the smudges and streaks underneath even the healthiest glow. Griffiths' new paintings are also markedly softer than her previous works. Hair sits atop heads like glowing haloes, in diaphanous counterpoint to the finely etched faces it encircles. Clothing is rendered as a series of watery folds, more like damp seaweed than constructed garments. And her backgrounds, formerly detailed vistas packed with biographical, character-defining details, have dissolved into soupy visions of innocuous trees and empty, monochromatic fields—the kind you see before you in a dream.

"The Devil in Ms. Griffiths," R. M. Vaughan, Canadian Art, *Spring 2002, Volume 19, Number 1, p. 40.*

1. Has Vaughan used both comparison and contrast in this piece?

2. Can you find differences and similarities that are highlighted by Vaughan?

3. Has Vaughan used block form or point-by-point organization?

4. What do you think Vaughan means by "details have dissolved into soupy visions"?

5. In a paragraph of 150–200 words, discuss how Vaughan's article may influence the way Griffiths paints.

Reading 7: The Liontamer
David Elliott

Questions of moral weight and identity politics apply even to her mechanics of painting. When she talks about the development of her craft, she acknowledges a career-long struggle between two very different ways of rendering. On the one hand there is the detailed busywork of earnestly copying what you see and the pleasure of patient, meditative labour. This is realism, but it also has links to the decorative arts and to folk tradition, which connect it, in her mind, to women's work. Think van Eyck, the Pre-Raphaelites, Klimt, but think also weaving and embroidery. Then there is the grand style of European oil painting, in which the world is translated through the virtuosic shorthand of the artist's brush. Dramatic naturalism, full of bravado, it is the more exalted approach. Or at least it used to be. It also carries heavy-duty white, male connotations. Think Rubens, Degas, de Kooning. This is the kind of painting that Wagschal was both honouring and challenging in her *Cyclops* self-portrait.

"The Liontamer," by David Elliott, Canadian Art, *Fall 2001, Volume 18, Number 3, p. 92.*

1. How can you tell David Elliott's piece is an example of comparison and contrast development?

2. Can you find similarities and differences pointed out by Elliott?

3. What does Elliott mean by the expression "questions of moral weight"?

4. What is identity politics?

5. In a paragraph of 150–200 words, discuss what you would expect feminists' paintings to look like. Use the third-person point of view only.

Reading 8: Winter Tick on Different Host Species
F. A. Leighton

Mooring and Samuel (1998a, b, c) studied the response of moose, elk, and bison to Winter Tick and concluded that the high susceptibility of moose to high levels of parasitism and severe disease compared to the much lower susceptibility of the other ungulate species studied could be explained, in large measure, by the grooming behaviour of moose compared to that of other species. Winter Ticks infest their ungulate hosts in September and October, but moose do not respond to the presence of the larvae or nymphs with intensive grooming. It is only when adult ticks begin to feed, in February and March, that moose groom intensively and in proportion to the number of ticks on their skin. Thus, moose go into winter carrying most of the Winter Ticks that infested them in the fall, and may have vast numbers of adult ticks on their skin, beginning to feed, before they start to respond to them in any protective way, by grooming. In contrast, white-tailed and mule/black-tailed deer, bison, and elk groom more intensively in fall and early winter. This early grooming effectively removes a substantial proportion of the Winter Tick larvae and nymphs before they can become adults. Thus, these species seldom have large numbers of adult Winter Ticks on their skin and, therefore, seldom suffer significant disease.

"Winter Tick on Different Host Species," Grooming Behaviour and Winter Ticks, Winter Tick in Moose and Other Ungulates, *F.A. Leighton, Reviewer: W. M. Samuel (August 2000),* **http://wildlife.usask.ca/ bookhtml/Winter%20Tick/wintertick3.htm**.

1. What ideas are compared and contrasted in Leighton's piece?

2. Which sentence is the topic sentence?

3. What does the term "ungulate hosts" mean?

4. What is meant by "lower susceptibility"?

5. Can you think of a reason why winter ticks infest their hosts in September and October but begin feeding in February and March?

6. In a paragraph of 150–200 words, suggest a theory to explain why the grooming behaviour of some ungulates is different from that of others.

Reading 9: Canadian Experience
Austin Clarke

The sun is brighter now. He can smile in this sun and think of home. He is getting warmer, too. A shaft of dust plays within the arrow of September light that comes through the window. It lands at his feet. The light and the particles of dust on the bright leather of his shoes attract his attention for a moment only. He smiles in that moment. And in that moment, his past life fills his heart and shakes his body like a spasm, like a cold blast of air. His attention then strays to the things around him, his possessions, prized so fondly before, and which now seem to be mere encumbrances: the valise he brought from Barbados and carried through so many changes of address in Toronto, heavier always in winter when he changed rooms, when he carried it late at night on his shoulder, although each time that he moved, he had accumulated no more possessions; the two Christmas cards that the actress had mailed to him, even though she was living in the same house, placed open like two tents and which he keeps on the top of a wooden kitchen cupboard, used now as his dressing table. "TO GEORGE, AT XMAS" is written in ballpoint, in red, on each, in capital letters; and an unframed photograph taken, in Barbados, and fading now, showing him with his father and mother and two younger brothers and three sisters: eight healthy, well-fed Barbadians, squinting because the sun is in their eyes, standing like proprietors in front of a well-preserved plantation house made of coral stone, covered in vines so thick that their spongy greenness strangles the windows and the doors. The name of this house in Barbados is Edgehill House. His present residence has no name. It is on a street named Major. It is a rooming house, similar in size, in build, and in dirt to the other houses on the street.

Excerpt from "Canadian Experience" in Choosing His Coffin: The Best Stories of Austin Clarke *by Austin Clarke, Thomas Allen Publishers, 2003, p. 35. Reprinted with permission of the publisher.*

1. What do you think the sharpest contrast is in the passage?

2. What does Clarke mean when he says, "his possessions, prized so fondly before, and which now seem to be mere encumbrances"?

3. Who do you think the character is, and how do you think the character feels about his new experiences in Canada?

4. Why does Clarke mention the sun in the passage?

5. Clarke uses several similes in the passage to help describe what things are like. He says, "his past life fills his heart and shakes his body like a spasm," "like a cold blast of air," "placed open like two tents," and "standing like proprietors." In a few sentences, explain what the similes mean to you.

6. What distinctions does Clarke make between the two residences?

7. In a paragraph of 150–200 words, compare or contrast the physical surroundings and the man's feelings.

CAUSE AND EFFECT MODE

Reading 10: Give Girls a Chance
Cheryl Embrett

Homemaker's believes that every girl child in every country around the world has the right to an education. Lack of basic education is at the root of poverty, sickness, and conflict. Last year the World Bank identified education of girls as the key to effective development, saying countries that promote women's rights and increase their access to schooling have lower poverty rates, faster economic growth, and less corruption than countries that do not. But in developing countries today almost 900 million adults are illiterate, two-thirds of them women and girls. There are 42 million fewer girls in primary schools than boys, and gender disparities exist at all levels of education. Meanwhile, in Canada, Aboriginal girls are 16 percent less likely to complete high school and 20 percent less likely to complete university than non-Native girls.

"Give Girls a Chance," Cheryl Embrett, Homemaker's, *May 2002, p. 77.*

1. Why is Cheryl Embrett's piece an example of cause and effect development?

2. What are some of the transitions the writer uses?

3. What evidence does the writer supply?

4. Do you find the author's argument compelling? Why or why not?

5. What is the topic sentence?

6. What issue is the author raising?

7. In a paragraph of 150–200 words, discuss whether Canadians should be concerned about the issue.

Reading 11: The Fall of an Arrow
Murray Peden

Like some nightmarish reversal of the standard Horatio Alger story, a reversal in which the climax saw multiplying misfortunes cascading upon the hero, the demise of the CF-105 Arrow produced a series of scenes that taxed credulity, even amongst the government's staunchest supporters. Having just completed the spending of over 340 million dollars of the Canadian taxpayers' money for the purpose of designing and building an interceptor aircraft to have a performance unsurpassed anywhere in the world—and having been spectacularly successful in producing an aircraft carrying those prestigious credentials—here was the Prime Minister cancelling the six-year long program at the very moment it was about to reach fruition, seemingly not fully realizing what would shortly ensue. The February 20th cancellation announcement caused the discharge that very afternoon of approximately 14 000 skilled employees at the A.V. Roe Canada Limited's plants in Malton, and the abrupt cessation of work for an estimated 15 000 other skilled tradesmen employed by the 2500 subcontractors and suppliers linked with A.V. Roe on this great project. Many of those subcontractors and suppliers, firms that had expanded to handle Avro Aircraft Ltd.'s growing requirements, were soon petitioned into bankruptcy.

Excerpt from The Fall of an Arrow *by Murray Peden, © 2001, pp. 10–11. Reprinted by permission of the Dundurn Group.*

1. What is the writer describing in the paragraph?

2. Who is Horatio Alger, and why does Peden make this reference?

3. How much money had Canadian taxpayers spent in developing the Arrow?

4. What direct impact did the cancellation of the Arrow project have?

5. What is the author's tone (attitude to the subject) in the piece?

6. What government project has been cancelled in recent times that you believe to have been of great benefit? Why was the project cancelled? What, in your opinion, will be the impact?

7. In a paragraph of 150–200 words, discuss the impact of a municipal decision that affected your neighbourhood. Use the third-person point of view only.

Reading 12: A Bad Bunch
Andrea Davis

Was it just a blur or have grocery stores turned into war zones? First a dreaded E. coli outbreak sent spinach lovers into their bathrooms. Then it was botulism in carrot juice and salmonella in tomatoes and cantaloupe. What's causing these recent attacks? Uneven food-handling practices in other countries and more fruit and vegetable consumption? (As people eat produce, the odds of outbreaks go up.) Plus, global authorities are getting better at tracking the outbreaks. Since it doesn't look like we'll ever be out of the woods, soak all fruit and veggies before you eat them, even if they're prewashed and prepackaged. Wash your hands when prepping other foods to avoid cross-contamination. And forgo illicit snacking in the veggie aisle. There are up to 13 million cases of food-borne illness hitting Canada annually, so help halt another outbreak before it starts.

"A Bad Bunch" by Andrea Davis from Chatelaine, *February 2007, p. 51. Reprinted with permission of the author.*

1. Why does Davis liken grocery stores to war zones?

2. In what other foods has botulism been found?

3. The water contamination in Walkerton, Ontario, was due to E. coli. How did this get into the water system?

4. Why is regulating food contamination so difficult?

5. What three causes does Davis provide for the increase in food poisoning?

6. What does Davis mean when she says, "Wash your hands when prepping other foods to avoid cross-contamination"?

7. In a paragraph of 150–200 words, write about the effects that safe food-handling practices have in the workplace. Use the third-person point of view only.

Reading 13: Global Warming in the Canadian Arctic: Canada at Risk
WWF-Canada

Canada's Arctic is warming faster than anywhere else on the planet. Certain regions have already experienced temperature increases of as much as 3 to 4°C in the past 50 years. Nearly one million square kilometres of sea ice have already disappeared, posing serious implications for seals, polar bears, and entire Arctic communities. Climate conditions that are suitable for existing forests will be moving north so far and so fast that trees will not be able to keep up. Unable to migrate and colonize fast enough, important commercial tree species will be left stranded where they are now, even when climate conditions are no longer suitable for them. Under such hostile conditions, these trees are likely to reduce in productivity and be more vulnerable to disease, pest damage, and fire.

"The Effects of Global Warming: Canada at Risk" from the WWF-Canada Website. Retrieved from **http://www.wwf.ca/AboutWWF/WhatWeDo/ConservationPrograms/GlobalWarming/effects.asp** *February 20, 2007. © WWF-Canada Used with permission.*

1. What is the immediate impact of global warming on wildlife in Canada's Arctic according to the Canadian branch of the World Wildlife Federation?

2. What does the article predict for tree growth?

3. How much sea ice has already vanished?

4. How might industry be impacted by the changes in the Canadian Arctic?

5. Why do you think such slight temperature increases have such a broad climate influence?

6. In a paragraph of 150–200 words, discuss the plight of the polar bear due to global warming. Use the third-person point of view only. If you research the topic, be sure to indicate quotations and sources in your final draft.

DEFINITION MODE

Reading 14: Letter to the Editor
Kevin Neish

How do you define "terrorism"? In the 1960s, I marched and protested to support a person the U.S. government then defined as a dangerous subversive who supported terrorism, and now Martin Luther King, Jr. has a national holiday in his name. In the 1970s, I took part in civil disobedience in the name of a man [sic] the U.S. and Canadian governments considered a dangerous subversive and now Rigoberta Menchu has a Nobel Peace Prize. Had the state back then had the power of this new "anti-terrorism" bill, I would have been jailed for my support of many people they then defined as terrorists, but who are now heroes. This bill will do nothing to address the true causes of "terrorism," Third World inequality and injustice, but it will be used to attack and hamper Canadian activists in their quest to create a just and terror-free world.

Letter to the Editor, Kevin Neish, Times-Colonist, *October 25, 2001, p. A11.*

1. What is the writer saying about the definition of "terrorist"?

2. What is the writer's diction like?

3. What point of view does the writer express?

4. What does the writer use as evidence?

5. Do you agree with the writer? Why or why not?

6. What do you think the author's purpose is in writing a letter to the editor?

Reading 15: Dracula without Kitsch

John Arkelian

Vampires have been with us for as long as we have been telling stories. Just as they mesmerize their victims, vampires transfix their audiences, holding us spellbound by an irresistible power. Their power is their ability to inspire what Coleridge called "desire with loathing strangely mix'd." We may envy the vampire's earthly immortality, not to mention his potent sexuality and seductive charm, but we recognize and abhor the essential emptiness of his existence. To survive, the vampire must steal the blood, and hence the life, of others. The new Canadian musical *Dracula*, written by Richard Ouzounian with music by Marek Norman and now playing at the Stratford Festival, brings fresh blood to an oft-told tale.

"Dracula without Kitsch," John Arkelian, The Canadian Forum, *July 1999, p. 26.*

1. How is John Arkelian's piece an example of definition development?

2. What ideas are supplied by the author?

3. Do you find the author's definition complete—why or why not?

4. Who was Coleridge?

5. What does Arkelian mean by the expression "earthly immortality"?

6. In a paragraph of 150–200 words, explain the relationship between monsters and society's fascination with them.

Reading 16: What Is a Megathrust Earthquake?

Ralph G. Currie

A megathrust earthquake is a very large earthquake that occurs in a subduction zone, a region where one of the earth's tectonic plates is thrust under another. The Cascadia subduction zone is located off the west coast of North America. From mid Vancouver Island to northern California the Juan de Fuca Plate is subducting beneath the North American Plate. The two plates are continually moving towards one another, yet become "stuck" where they are in contact. Eventually the build-up of strain exceeds the friction between the two plates and a huge megathrust earthquake occurs.

"What Is a Megathrust Earthquake?," Ralph G. Currie, Head, Pacific Geoscience Centre, All About Earthquakes, 2003, Geological Survey of Canada, Frequently Asked Questions, **www.pgc.nrcan.gc.ca/ seismo/equinfo/q-a.hem#mega-what**.

1. Is there a topic sentence in Currie's piece of writing?

2. To what general class of things does a megathrust earthquake belong?

3. What is the main distinguishing feature of a megathrust earthquake?

4. What is meant by "subducting beneath the North American Plate"?

5. How long is the Cascadia subduction zone?

6. Why do tectonic plates become "stuck"?

7. Can you suggest how a megathrust earthquake could be predicted?

8. In a paragraph of 150–200 words, tell what people ought to do during an earthquake. Use the third-person point of view only.

CLASSIFICATION AND DIVISION MODE

Reading 17: Constructing Crime: Media, Crime, and Popular Culture

Ken Dowler, Thomas Fleming, and Stephen L. Muzzatti

Crime is central to the production of news in Canadian society (Dowler, 2004a, p. 574; Fleming 1983, 2006). Although crime is considered newsworthy and often produced as informative, it is also a central component in entertainment in Canadian and North American society. It grips the collective imagination of television viewers, theatre-goers, internet browsers, and readers of true-crime books. Moreover, the boundary between crime information and crime entertainment has been increasingly blurred in recent years through the rise of reality crime shows. Crime as entertainment has cemented a place in popular culture, reflected in all the above-mentioned media formats and beyond. Canadian viewers are now exposed to American reality television shows including *American Justice*, *Cold Case Files*, *COPS*, *Court TV*, and *Dallas SWAT*, while "cop" shows focus on the investigation and arrest of suspects for a variety of offences. *The First 48* tracks cases through the investigative process, showing the arrest and interrogation of suspects. *Court TV* presents sensational trials that typically focus on murder, serial murder, or sexual assault. *The Nancy Grace Show* selectively targets specific kidnappings, sex crimes, or murders, with a particular focus on retribution and punishment. Canada boasts its own equivalent of *COPS*, the less sensational *To Serve and Protect*, which follows everyday police patrols in various Canadian cities. Ideas about crime emerge not only from news sources and reality television shows but also from dramatic movies and television shows that adopt crime as their subject. The massive popularity of crime shows has spawned some of the most enduringly popular television series of the 1990s and beyond, including *Law & Order*, *DaVinci's Inquest*, and *CSI*. The enormous appeal of crime as entertainment is also reflected in the many spinoffs of these series, all of which are currently running alongside the original series and their re-runs.

"Constructing Crime: Media, Crime, and Popular Culture" by Ken Dowler, Thomas Fleming, and Stephen L. Muzzatti in Canadian Journal of Criminology and Criminal Justice, *October 2006, Volume 48, Issue 6, p. 837, published by University of Toronto Press, Inc. Reprinted by permission of Canadian Criminal Justice Association.*

1. According to the researchers, why is crime "central to the production of news in Canadian society"?

2. What do you think the writers mean when they say the "boundary between crime information and crime entertainment has been increasingly blurred"?

3. How can crime be entertainment?

4. What criminal events have recently become entertainment in the mass media?

5. Crime series on television have become more and more popular. Which show is the most popular? Why do you think it is so "successful"?

6. In a paragraph of 150–200 words, discuss three types of crime drama currently on television. Use the third-person point of view only.

Reading 18: Participation, Participants, and Providers
Gordon Selman, Mark Selman, Michael Cooke, and Paul Dampier

Research into non-participation has found that it is possible to divide barriers into three categories: situational, dispositional, and institutional. The situational barriers are the circumstances of the potential learner and include such describable items as disposable income, means of transportation, and availability of child-minding services. The dispositional barriers likewise belong to the learner, but in this case are a function of the individual's personality. Psychological factors such as fear of returning to the evaluative attention of a teacher, the feeling of intellectual inadequacy after being away from schooling for a long time, or a general disinterest in learning once a good job has been secured are three examples of dispositional barriers. The last category of barrier, institutional barriers, are those put up by the institutional sponsor of the learning activity. These barriers are not seen as being intentionally erected by the institution to discourage participation; rather they reflect the operating practices of the particular institution which have adverse consequences. Thus the decisions taken by the institution in offering an adult education course, such as scheduling, class location, prerequisites, instructor selection, and so on, will for some potential participants become reasons for their not participating. Of the three barriers to participation, then, it is evident that "ownership" of the situational and dispositional barriers resides with the individual, while the institutional barriers reside with the provider. Thus any attempts to lower these barriers to the point where participation is enabled requires understanding and communication between the non-participant and the provider.

"Participation, Participants, and Providers," Gordon Selman, Mark Selman, Michael Cooke, and Paul Dampier, The Foundations of Adult Education in Canada, *Second Edition, 1998, pp. 138–139.*

1. Why is Selman, Selman, Cooke, and Dampier's piece an example of classification and division development?

2. What are some of the transitions the writers use?

3. What evidence is supplied by the authors?

4. Do you find the authors' argument compelling? Why or why not?

5. Why do you think they wrote this paragraph?

6. In a paragraph of 150–200 words, discuss what makes up an adult learner. Use the third-person point of view only.

Reading 19: Formulating Research Questions or Hypotheses
Barbara Kozier et al.

Once nurse researchers have identified a research problem and are knowledgeable of the literature, they formulate a research question. The question may be stated in one of three ways: a statement, a question, or a hypothesis. If researchers are going to describe something, they may make a statement, such as, "The purpose of this study is to identify gender differences in the nursing care of patients admitted to rehabilitation units." They could also ask a question, such as, "What are the communication styles of nurses that indicate client satisfaction with nursing care?" If conducting an experiment, researchers must have a hypothesis as to what the outcome will be so that hypothesis-testing statistics may be applied. For example, "Family members of palliative care patients attending support groups will demonstrate more positive-coping strategies than those who do not" is a testable hypothesis. In whichever way a research question is stated, it must be clearly expressed.

"Nursing Research in Canada, The Research Process, Formulate the Research Question or Hypothesis," by Barbara Kozier et al., from Fundamentals of Nursing; The Nature Of Nursing Practice In Canada; *Chapter 3; Prentice Hall, New Jersey, 2000, p. 37.*

1. What two conditions must be met before the nurse researcher formulates a research question? Why?

2. What is a "research question"?

3. What is the difference between a question and a hypothesis?

4. Why is it so important that the research question be "clearly expressed"?

5. In what courses at college or university have you completed research papers?

6. In a paragraph of 150–200 words, discuss the component parts of an effective research question. Use the third-person point of view only.

Reading 20: Engineering Rice Plants with Trehalose-Producing Genes Improves Tolerance to Drought, Salt, and Low Temperature
Ray Wu and Ajay Garg

Rice is a major source of food for more than 2.7 billion people on a daily basis. Rice is planted on about one-tenth of the earth's arable land and is the single largest source of food energy to half of humanity. Of the 130 million hectares of land where rice is grown, about 30 percent contain levels of salt too high to allow normal rice yield. Another 20 percent of this land is periodically subject to drought conditions that routinely affect food production. About 10 percent of the locations where rice is grown occasionally experience temperatures that are too low for healthy plant development. It is difficult to improve rice tolerance against these abiotic stresses because they involve not a single gene but a network of genes. Fortunately, recent developments in transgenic approaches offer new opportunities to elucidate the functions of many useful candidate genes from different organisms and to improve the resilience and yield of rice plants. Moreover, developing salt-tolerant transgenic rice plants can introduce new areas of land that currently contain salt too high to grow rice. It is expected that genetically engineered, improved rice varieties will help combat world hunger and poverty.

"Engineering Rice Plants with Trehalose-Producing Genes Improves Tolerance to Drought, Salt, and Low Temperature," Ray Wu and Ajay Garg, AgNet, Information Systems for Biotechnology, March 4, 2003, **www.c-ciarn.uoguelph.ca/whats_in_the_news.html**.

1. Can you see a cluster of points that supports an idea?

2. What does the term "abiotic stress" mean?

3. Why is it difficult to improve rice tolerance?

4. Will genetic engineering increase rice production? How?

5. Do the authors of this piece support genetic modification of rice plants? Why or why not?

6. From what "different organisms" might "useful candidate genes" be obtained?

7. What is meant by the expression "elucidate the functions"?

8. In a paragraph of 150–200 words, discuss the importance of food research. Use the third-person point of view.

Reading 21: Urban Oil Spills as a Non-Point Pollution Source in the Golden Horseshoe of Southern Ontario
James Li and Peter McAteer

Being the economic engine of Canada and the home of 5 million people, the environmental health of the Golden Horseshoe is very important. Among various pollution sources into the lake, urban oil spills as a non-point pollution source have not caught the attention of most residents. These spills can cause terrestrial impacts by poisoning animals and plants, groundwater contamination by infiltration, and surface water pollution by algal bloom and fish kills and destruction of freshwater invertebrates and vertebrates. In order to investigate the significance of this pollution source, 10 years of spill records in the Golden Horseshoe have been compiled. On the average, about 1050 L per day of oil escaped to the land, water and air environment in this region. About one-third of these spills eventually entered Lake Ontario. Among various types of spilled oil, gasoline, diesel fuel, aviation fuel, and furnace oil accounted for the highest reported volume. The former Metropolitan Toronto led the frequency and volume of spills, while Hamilton-Wentworth followed closely. Spills frequently occur on roads, at service stations and at electrical transformers, while the highest spill event volumes occur at bulk plants/terminals/depots and at refineries. The predominant causes of spills are related to leaks from containers, pipes and hoses, and cooling systems. However, the principal reasons for oil spills are human error and equipment failure. The transportation, public and petroleum sectors are responsible for 60% of the reported spill cases, while the petroleum sector alone accounts for nearly 50% of the reported spill volume. Given the significant volume of spilled oil, it is important that all levels of government and private industries increase their effort to promote pollution prevention such as preventive maintenance, improved employee training and/or retraining, and proper vigilant supervision. Additionally, control devices such as oil-water interceptors should be sized properly and implemented at strategic locations across the Golden Horseshoe.

"Urban Oil Spills as a Non-Point Pollution Source in the Golden Horseshoe of Southern Ontario," James Li and Peter McAteer, Department of Civil Engineering, Ryerson Polytechnic University, Toronto, Ontario M5B 2K3, Water Quality Research Journal of Canada, *Volume 35, Issue 3, pp. 313–340 (2000). Theme issue: Stormwater Pollution,* **www.cciw.ca/wqrjc/35–3/35–3–331.htm**.

1. How are ideas clustered in this piece of writing?

2. How can you tell that division was used as an organizing device in this paragraph?

3. How are transitions used to help the flow of writing in this paragraph?

4. What do you think is meant by the expression "non-point pollution source"?

5. What are some examples of animals scientists class as invertebrates?

6. Do small pollution incidents contribute significantly to environmental degradation? Is this idea supported in the paragraph?

7. In a paragraph of 150–200 words, discuss three types of oil spills. Use the third-person point of view only.

chapter 19

Longer Readings

Chapter Objectives

After completing this chapter, you will be able to

- recognize rhetorical modes in longer readings
- be more aware of writers' specialized vocabulary
- read and think critically while reading
- respond analytically to focussed questions requiring interpretation

INTRODUCTION

The following readings contain several paragraphs and are written about a variety of subjects. They have been grouped under one of four themes: each reading is assigned to one of five rhetorical patterns.

Your instructor will assign several of these readings. Read each assigned reading carefully. After you read each selection, answer the questions that follow it. Your instructor may ask you to complete these. Be prepared to discuss your ideas with others in the class.

Along with what each writer is saying, try to pay attention to how each writes. Here are some tips for reading longer selections:

1. Read the entire article in order to get the gist of it. (The gist is the general idea.)

2. Read the article again, paying attention to the specific content. Write down the main ideas as you come across them.

3. Pay attention to words that you do not understand. Look up these words in a dictionary, or ask someone else what they mean.

4. Look at the way the author has arranged his or her ideas. Do you see one rhetorical pattern that seems to influence the piece in general?

5. Pay attention to the writer's argument. Can you list the arguments the writer is making?

FAMILY AND RELATIONSHIPS

Reading 1: Bad Boys

Mordecai Richler

Finding the "right" partner seems to preoccupy people of all cultures. In this selection, Richler takes a humorous look at these encounters from the days of his youth by classifying date types. He chooses the rhetorical pattern of classification and division to drive his points home. Richler, born and raised in Montreal and author of 10 novels, several collections of essays, and screenplays, is best known for the biting satire and social commentary in his writing. Richler was awarded many prizes for his writing, including the Giller Prize in 1997 for *Barney's Version*. Prior to his death on July 3, 2002, he was made a Companion of the Order of Canada.

When we were horny teenagers, me and my bunch dreaded the coming of Saturday nights. Our anxieties, such as they were, struck as we left high school on Friday afternoons, loping home to begin to work the phones. Would we manage to get a date for the following night or would we be humiliated yet again? We were sixteen years old at the time, grade 11 students in Montreal, and the ungrateful girls we had invested in selflessly for years—treating them to double features at the Rialto, followed by toasted tomato and mayo sandwiches, washed down with Cokes or milkshakes at Ben Ash's, never mind the cost—had suddenly turned against us. Upwardly mobile in their nifty sweaters, tight skirts, nylons, and high heels, reeking of some cheap perfume shoplifted at Woolworth's, they now preferred the company of older guys, later to prosper as dentists or accountants, who were already at McGill. This being the case we often had to put up with being men without women, as Mr. Hemingway had it, on Saturday nights, settling for going out together to shoot pool at the Park Billiards. However, there were Saturday nights when we did make out, repairing to neck on a bench in Outremont Park after the movie.

Be that as it may, I'm glad dating is no longer a problem for me and my bunch, because we would now all be classified as either the Show-Off, Know-It-All, Cheater, Sex Guzzler, Mr. Ego, Bug-Eyed Boy, or Boozer, dismissed as Losers to Watch Out For. I am indebted for this information to a fascinating book which recently came my way, RED *FLAGS! How to Know When You're Dating a LOSER*, published by Plume, the down-market imprint of Penguin Books. It is the seminal work of two eminent shrinks, doctors Gary S. Aumiller and Daniel A. Goldfarb. Aumiller is an "internationally known" lecturer and Goldfarb serves as webmaster to several psychology self-help sites on the internet. Both authors have put in time as the prez of the Society of Police and Criminal Psychology and helped some 4000 patients solve problems and make better decisions before combining to warn women about the 25 Losers to Watch Out For and How to Dump Them and Move On.

Consider, for instance, the Show-Off. In an idiom refreshingly free of academic prose, the authors warn, "If the man you are dating does more strutting than a rooster on Viagra in a brand-new hen house," this guy's a turkey. Cook his goose. The Show-Off, according to the prescient authors, can easily be recognized. He is a braggart, and a sharp dresser, who flexes his muscles a lot, and looks at himself frequently in the mirror, and, um, "other reflective substances" but is very insecure underneath his plumage. Reminds me of Hershel Greenbaum. Show him the Red Flag, girls.

"The Game for the Know-It-All is Jeopardy! Beat Him to the Buzzer," say Aumiller and Goldfarb. Signals to watch out for: his eyes dart, he namedrops, puts his friends down, and insists on ordering dinner for you. Yes, but like Arnie Debrofsky of blessed memory, he also showers a lot, and reads lots of non-fiction, which don't strike me as such bad things. But the doctors also adjudge him a Loser and highly recommend a clean break, goodbye: "Then go home and turn on the Discovery Channel and learn about the mating rituals of the giant Galapagos turtles. You too can know it all."

The Sex-Guzzler, as you might have expected, is very bad news. "The Way to Your Heart is Not Through Your Pants." Happily such villains can be easily spotted. They tend to wear gold jewellery, neck chains, bracelets, touch you very quickly on the first date, and talk about life being an adventure and about the need to take risks. Watch out, girls. If the sex is great, you could end up a Guzzler yourself.

With equal ease the doctors dispose of Mr. Ego ("If He Thinks He's God's Gift, Exchange Him!"); the Cheater, who tends to look at your breasts or legs and to invade personal space; the Bug-Eyed Boy, yet another eye-darter, who looks at body parts, not faces, when he is talking to you or other women (gosh, I used to know guys like that); and the Boozer, no eye-darter he, but he does tend to be restless, and at times has a rumpled look. Worse news. He has more than two drinks on the first date. Aumiller and Goldfarb recommend boozers to rely on the three Ms: meetings with Alcoholics Anonymous, meditation, and masturbation, "because he should not have a woman around."

RED FLAGS! takes no prisoners. It provides women with further good advice against Neglecters, Pleasers, Possessors, Abusers, and Loners, taking in just about all of my cherished male friends. Girls, beware of these two shrinks. Dump Them. Cook Their Goose. Lest you end up old maids.

"Bad Boys" by Mordecai Richler, Saturday Night *(March 2000), Volume 115, Issue 2. Reprinted with permission.*

1. Richler uses a lot of slang in his article. Can you spot some? Can you explain what some of the terms mean?

2. What, according to Richler, was a typical date when he was a teenager?

3. What does Richler mean by "upwardly mobile" (underlined in your text)?

4. What classifications does the article mention for the person called "a date"?

5. What are some of the characteristics of each type of date?

6. What is the tone of Richler's article? (The tone has to do with the author's attitude to his or her topic or reader.) Why do you think Richler wrote the article?

7. What is the difference, in your opinion, between dating in Richler's time (during the 1950s) and dating today?

8. Do you agree with the classifications of a date mentioned in the article? Why or why not?

9. In a short classification/division essay of about 500 words, describe the date stereotypes currently seen on television. Use the third-person point of view only.

Reading 2: A Personal Journey through Genetics and Civil Rights

David Suzuki

Famous for his work in popularizing science through his long-running television program, *The Nature of Things*, David Suzuki, also a renowned geneticist, author, professor of genetics at the University of British Columbia, and passionate environmentalist, provides a perspective on his life story and how it helped to shape him as a scientist and as a person. Suzuki uses a time-order, or process mode, to express his views. He also asks his readers to consider what responsibility science has to society.

The most powerful force shaping society today is science applied by industry, medicine, and the military. New scientific ideas and techniques pervade every aspect of our lives, changing the way we do things and how we perceive the world, thus altering our aspirations and notions of who we are, why we are here, and where we are going. Yet, with rare exceptions, scientists are virtually invisible in the popular media and in debates and reports on economic, social, and even environmental issues. As a geneticist and a journalist, I am constantly reflecting on the nature of the relationship between science and society. Here I recount the path that I have followed as a means to convey my experiences around, and opinions on, this complex relationship.

My grandparents emigrated to Canada early in this century, driven from their homeland by terrible poverty. Both of my parents were born in Vancouver, British Columbia, as was I in 1936. Insulated from widespread racism and the ravages of the Great Depression by my parents and childish innocence, my earliest memories are of a happy childhood. On 7 December 1941, when Japan attacked Pearl Harbor, my life was changed forever. The racism that had festered in British Columbia ever since Japanese and Chinese began coming to the province in the late 1800s could now be vented openly under the guise of self-defence and patriotism. My family and I felt completely Canadian because we had never been to Japan, and at home English was our spoken language. In the months following Pearl Harbor, the Canadian government moved to control the feared treachery of its Japanese population by invoking the *War Measures Act* against all people of Japanese descent.

The *War Measures Act* was a heinous piece of legislation that failed to recognize that while it is easy to guarantee civil rights and freedoms when times are good, those guarantees only matter when times are difficult. Twenty-two thousand Japanese, most Canadian citizens by birth, were rounded up and sent to internment camps in abandoned mining settlements deep in the Rocky Mountains. My father was separated from our family and shipped to a different camp for one year before being reunited with us. We were impoverished by the loss of our savings, our home, and almost all of our possessions (each person was allowed to take 70 pounds of luggage to the camps). When the war drew to a close, we were expelled from British Columbia and my family ended up working as farmhands in southern Ontario. As a child I learned that hard work and a good education were the only means to extricate myself from this poverty. Pearl Harbor, incarceration, and expulsion from British Columbia shaped my psychic demons—a knee-jerk aversion to any perceived discrimination or bigotry—and I developed a compulsive need to excel at whatever I did to prove my worth as a human being.

I did well in high school and received a scholarship to Amherst College, where I majored in biology. In embryology and genetics courses, I was enthralled by the exquisite beauty and elegance of development and heredity. After graduating in 1958, I enrolled in the doctoral program in zoology at the University of Chicago. The launch of Sputnik by the Soviet Union electrified the world and stimulated a frantic rush to bolster science, mathematics, and engineering in North America. It was a golden period of enthusiasm and expansion in all of the natural sciences, including genetics. As a graduate student during this exuberant time, I acquired the belief that science could eliminate superstition and ignorance by providing us with an understanding of the underlying mechanisms of all the cosmic forces impinging on our lives. In genetics, I believed that through a better understanding of mutation, recombination, and gene activity, we would eventually be able to manage, and possibly even eliminate, the hereditary problems that afflict humankind.

In the early 1960s there were numerous job opportunities in the United States as universities expanded their science departments. Nevertheless, I chose to return to Canada. Even though Canada had incarcerated my family during the war and expelled us from British Columbia, it was still my home and I wanted to contribute and work to make it a nation that could live up to its boast of being a place where all of its citizens were treated equally. I returned in 1962 as an assistant professor in the Department of Genetics at the University of Alberta in Edmonton.

As the most junior member of the department, I was assigned to teach genetics to students majoring in agriculture. They constantly pushed me to explain the agricultural implications of genetics with questions about the green revolution, about ways to improve milk output or weight gain by gene engineering, and about the possibility of the perpetuation and amplification of highly productive animals by cloning. As a snobby scientist who revelled in basic research, I had not paid attention to the practical consequences of genetics research and was now forced by students to read more widely on this topic, whereupon I discovered a vast and interesting literature.

In 1963 I moved to the University of British Columbia. Most students in my classes hoped to go to medical school, so they would quiz me about medical genetics, human heredity, and the possibility of genetically altering people. I gave a talk about genetic engineering to students at a campus dorm in which I discussed the techniques of DNA transfer by transformation and transduction, the possibility of cloning, and the implications for people. At the end of my talk a student demanded to know why, if such terrible possibilities come from new ideas and techniques, was I still doing research in genetics. I glibly answered that I was doing basic research into mechanisms of cell division and chromosome behaviour in fruit flies, not applied work. The student rejected my answer. Knowledge, he pointed out, was like a huge pool of information. Like water added to a lake, any scientific result becomes diffused throughout the pool of information. So when someone comes up with a practical application, there is no way to identify the specific studies that made it possible. Ideas are built on the collective base of accumulated knowledge, thereby blurring any distinction between practical and basic science. The student had a point, and I was spurred to read more about applied genetics.

To my shock, I discovered that eugenics, the attempt to apply hereditary principles to improve the human genetic condition, was not some weird aberration, but had been created and supported by leading geneticists. Eugenics was considered a legitimate scientific discipline. Eugenicists made pronouncements about the supposed hereditary nature of tuberculosis, syphilis, indolence, sloth, drunkenness, criminality, and deceit. Indeed, Edward East, a distinguished Harvard professor and president of the Genetics Society of America, once wrote: "In reality, the negro is inferior to the white. This is not hypothesis or supposition; it is a crude statement of actual fact."

As geneticists discovered principles governing heredity and showed that most were universal, there was an understandable sense of excitement. Geneticists believed that they had their hands on the levers of life and were on the verge of elucidating principles that could be applied to eliminate hereditary disease and abnormalities while increasing the level of intelligence and ability. Extrapolating readily from studies on inheritance of physical traits like flower colour in plants or wing shape in flies, geneticists jumped to conclusions about the inheritance of intelligence and behaviour, often confusing their beliefs and values with scientifically meaningful categories. By invoking the word "inferior"—like the words "better" or "worse"—East, too, was treating a value judgment as if it was not something that could be measured scientifically.

To my horror, I found that Josef Mengele, the infamous "angel of death" at Auschwitz, was a human geneticist who held peer-reviewed research grants to carry out studies on twins at the death camp. Race purification, an element of Nazi policy, was in part justified by the climate of optimism surrounding genetics as a means to improve the human condition. By the end of the war, when the horrors of the Holocaust were revealed, the accepted wisdom was that human behaviour and intelligence were primarily an expression of environmental factors. Even though I had received an outstanding liberal arts education and a thorough training in genetics, I had not been taught this aspect of the history of my discipline.

To add to my discomfort, I began to understand that genetics had been the underlying rationale that had justified the incarceration of Japanese-Canadians. Parliamentary transcripts indicate that a British Columbian member of Parliament, A. W. Neill, stated in 1937: "To cross an individual of the white race with an individual of a yellow race, is to produce in nine cases out of ten a mongrel wastrel with the worst qualities of both races." While not quite a Mendelian ratio, it was, nevertheless, an apparently quantified claim. In February 1941, Neill told the Prime Minister: "We in British Columbia are firmly convinced that once a Jap, always a Jap." Implicit in Neill's statement was a belief in the hereditary nature of perceived racial traits, such as perfidy and deceit. Thus, bigotry was cloaked by the legitimizing claims of scientists. At the very least, this lesson from recent history can warn us about the hazards of extending the boundaries of scientific claims beyond immediate experiments.

This grotesque intersection of two great passions in my life—genetics and civil rights—was an agonizing confrontation with the intersection of science and society. I concluded that, above all, scientists are fallible human beings with all of the foibles, idiosyncrasies, talents, and shortcomings of any other group. Our perspective is shaped by professional self-interest, training, and ambition, and it is easy to become so enthralled with our work that, without reflection, we make grand claims about the potential of our discoveries and ideas. Moreover, in the flush of research and its exciting results, it is easy to forget that science progresses by conjecture and supposition, and that hypotheses will be evidentially modified, corroborated, or discarded. The ideas about gene and chromosome structure and regulation that excited me when I graduated in 1961 seem laughably far from what we believe today, and most of today's cutting-edge notions will be just as far off the mark 20 or 30 years from now. So what is the hurry to apply our notions so quickly? Often we make discoveries simply because our knowledge base is so tiny that we are bound to learn new things. This means that our ignorance is so great that we have virtually no capacity for prescription, that is, little capacity to recommend ways to correct problems that we encounter.

Scientists need to learn more about the social ramifications of their activity as revealed by history. We need to understand more intimately the nature of scientific knowledge, its strengths, weaknesses, limits, and how it differs from other ways of knowing. Above all, we must encourage public discourse about the interface between science and society and support those among our students and colleagues who enter this arena.

From "A Personal Journey through Genetics and Civil Rights," by David Suzuki, Science, *281: 1796–1797 (18 September 1998). © 1998 AAAS. Reprinted with permission from AAAS.*

1. What does Suzuki mean when he says "scientists are virtually invisible in the popular media"?

2. What is the *War Measures Act*? Why does Suzuki mention it? How did it affect him personally?

3. What was the "launch of Sputnik" Suzuki mentions, and why do you think he believes the event was such a turning point for science?

4. What does Suzuki say about how he first perceived the role of science when he was a graduate student?

5. What is the metaphor for knowledge used in the article? (A metaphor is an implied comparison between two things or ideas so that one illuminates the imagined common qualities of the other.)

6. What is "eugenics"? Why was Suzuki upset when he discovered this area of study?

7. Does the article contain an important irony? (Irony is a development that is opposite to, or a mockery of, an expected result.)

8. In your opinion, what is Suzuki's purpose in writing this article? Was he successful?

9. Re-read Suzuki's final paragraph. In a short process essay of about 500 words, discuss ways everyday people can begin to do what Suzuki suggests. Use the third-person point of view only.

ENVIRONMENT AND THE OUTDOORS

Reading 3: Betrayal of Trust

ONCE AGAIN, CANADIANS ARE ASKING, "HOW COULD THIS HAPPEN?"

Sharon Butala

Due to the serious events in Walkerton, Ontario, and North Battleford, Saskatchewan, Canadians have taken a sober look at the safety of their public drinking water. Sharon Butala, a writer and thinker concerned about the environment of the Canadian prairies, was born and raised in rural Saskatchewan. She worries about the conditions of rural life, particularly for women. Her essay describes how the difficulties she experienced in finding safe drinking water on her first ranch connected with her beliefs that the government must act responsibly in regard to the safety of its citizens. She employs a cause and effect mode to outline her views on that relationship.

I was raised in rural and small-town Saskatchewan. We children used to raft every spring on sloughs swollen by meltwater, falling in and splashing one another, and swam—our parents poised to grab us, so swift was the current—in the Saskatchewan River. I remember narrow, hilly, sandy roads lined with a thick deciduous forest that we used to take instead of highways for sheer pleasure in the beauty. We didn't have indoor plumbing until the early 1950s when we moved to Saskatoon. Like us, most small-town or rural people had pumps in the kitchen and outdoor biffies. We bathed once a week in tin tubs of water—melted snow in winter—heated on the cookstove. Yet we were more likely to suffer from gas poisoning from our coal-fired furnaces, or from a fall downstairs, than from illnesses caused by drinking or bathing in the water.

In the mid-'70s, when I moved from Saskatoon to the Butala ranch near the Montana and Alberta borders, I soon developed a problem with diarrhea. I didn't notice it had become chronic until one day I realized I had a half-dozen bottles of anti-diarrhea medication sitting on windowsills and shelves in every room of the old ranch house. I went to the doctor, who, despite testing, was unable to find a cause. But through happenstance, I discovered the origin of my ailment. It was the ranch water, which, in this semi-arid region of southwestern Saskatchewan, came from a well, the blessed presence of which decided where the Butalas would put their house and ranch buildings, in fact, whether they could live there at all.

My husband, Peter, and his family had always used that water. Their bodies had adapted to it, but mine, accustomed to better quality urban water, couldn't handle it. Testing showed the well water was so hard it was barely fit for human consumption. I weighed only 98 lb. at the time and the accompanying pain, fatigue and dehydration could conceivably have killed me, if my husband hadn't immediately begun bringing me water from elsewhere.

Then, in the late 1970s, we built our new house only 20 m from the small Frenchman River, which supplied our household, our cattle and horses, and our local flood irrigation system. I was warned against using this water for cooking or drinking. A number of families, nevertheless, drank it as it was, without any attempt to filter or purify it. We, however, put nearly $10,000 into a seepage filtration well beside the river, plus various other paraphernalia to provide us with safe, clean water. No government helped us to pay for this, although if help had been available we would have accepted it. When it came to water, like most rural families, we were pretty much on our own.

When I was born, Saskatchewan had been a province for only 35 years. I think we all had a sense of "roughing it" in a raw, new place, and that in the years to come everything would improve. Well, yes and no. In a country the United Nations has declared for several years running to be the best in the world to live in, how can we not feel it a betrayal that the water running from taps in homes, not just in North Battleford, Sask., but all over Canada, is no longer safe to drink. Worse, the agencies established to provide clean, safe water apparently can't be relied on to do the job properly. And as residents of Walkerton, Ont., and North Battleford would probably say, they can't be trusted either to warn us when equipment breaks down, or when floods or other non-usual sources of pollution render the water supply questionable. Premier Lorne Calvert has announced an independent judicial inquiry into the failure of the North Battleford system, so we're also being treated to the sight of officials scrambling to distance themselves from blame for the presence of Cryptosporidium, the parasite that caused illnesses in the city's water supply. In the year 2001, in the darkest part of the night, North Battleford residents must have been wondering what happened. Why, when we are so advanced compared to 50 years ago, could the things we trusted in most completely fail us, so that suddenly we feel no safer than the much-pitied poor of developing countries?

I think that one answer lies in the reluctance of governments to provide money for projects that lack glamour. All over Canada, infrastructure for cleaning and purifying water is archaic in design and/or decaying, and the repair or replacement of such equipment hasn't paid off in political capital, and thus, has been neglected. Also, we are suffering from the effects of governments buying into the odd idea that less government is better, and from the odious notion of user pay, an erosion of the most basic democratic principle of equality of opportunity for rich and poor, rural and urban alike.

The result, as the residents of Walkerton and North Battleford know all too well, has been that governments began to pare services and to charge individuals for others that had been free. In Saskatchewan, for example, rural folk didn't pay the provincial laboratory to test our water until about five years ago. And such testing has never been, and isn't now, mandatory. Now people are asking, if governments refuse to be responsible for the provision of safe water, just what are our governments for? Are they there only to satisfy the demands of the corporate fat cats while the vast majority, the so-called ordinary people, must fend for themselves?

Each province sets it own water quality guidelines for Cryptosporidium—and these can vary widely. But our whole idea of what constitutes a safe and adequate water supply has to be rethought. With a huge increase in human populations, and in animals held in giant feedlots and barns, all producing vast amounts of waste, water pollution is more likely to occur. And we continue to drain wetlands and mow down forests, our natural filtration systems, as if we didn't know that doing so lessens our precious water supply and destroys its quality.

Today, just about everything has become a commodity, from trips into space to human embryos. In such a milieu, having to buy our drinking water, an idea that 50 years ago would have horrified people, has become normal. In all this uproar about water contamination in North Battleford, and in the rapid backpedalling of officials, we seem to have lost sight of the basic, unadulterated fact that water is not merely nice to have, or pretty when in lakes or rivers: water is life itself.

Sadly, the great beauty that was once Saskatchewan is disappearing at a frightening pace. The trees that lined our country roads have been cut down; the fields of wildflowers plowed under; the sloughs drained and filled to make room for farms or urban sprawl. The wild, dangerous Saskatchewan River of my childhood is dammed, its once pristine waters no longer safe. Along with its purity, something else equally vital has been destroyed: the trust of people, far from the centres of power, in the ideal we were all raised with—that in a democracy, the government is not them, but that it is us.

"Betrayal of Trust," by Sharon Butala, S, from Maclean's, *Volume 114, Issue 21 (21 May 2001), p. 28. © Sharon Butala. With permission of the author.*

1. Butala's article begins with several terms that are specific to the Canadian prairies. In the first paragraph, you will see "sloughs," "meltwater," and "biffies." What do these terms mean?

2. What implications are to be derived from Butala's statement, "When it came to water, like most rural families, we were pretty much on our own"?

3. What contrast does Butala use in her article?

4. What are Butala's views on why the safety of our drinking water has declined?

5. How is the title, "Betrayal of Trust," appropriate in your opinion?

6. What environmental damage has contributed to the state of unsafe drinking according to Butala?

7. What does the concept of trust mean in regard to democracy?

8. Do you agree with Butala's position? What do you think should be done to rectify the problem of adequate and safe drinking water?

9. In an essay of about 500 words, discuss the relationship between stewardship and citizenship. Use the third-person point of view.

Reading 4: The Worst Kind of Ice-Breaker

I FELT TOTALLY INCAPABLE OF THOUGHT, POSSESSED BY THE PUREST FORM OF PANIC. THE INSTINCT TO SAVE IS SOLID AND CAN OBLITERATE COMMON SENSE.

Judy Plaxton

Personal and almost tragic experiences can cause us to appreciate more fully who we are and what other people in our lives mean to us. In the next selection, Judy Plaxton remembers an accident on the ice that almost claimed the life of her husband and her dog. She recalls the feeling of helplessness she experienced in trying to rescue them from the freezing waters. Plaxton relates her story in a time-order, or process mode, so that the events feel more immediate to the reader. She considers how fragile life really is.

There was a time when my sleep was disturbed by anxious dreams. I would see deep, dark water surrounded by sharp ice and feel its numbing cold. To dispel these images, I would replace them with others. Fields of grass, running brooks and shimmering sunlight would help me return to sleep.

The desire to live in a country setting drew my husband and me out of the city. After retirement, we bought a small farm. We settled in effortlessly. Frogs croaking from our pond and murmuring breezes replaced the intrusive drone of city air-conditioners. Summer flies were the only pests. Colourful autumn became winter. The breeze became a fierce wind that howled around the house. The snow sparkled with sunlight and scrunched underfoot. We were delighted with it all.

But one quiet winter afternoon, we experienced a dark side to <u>our pastoral</u> Eden. I had returned from a short trip to town to find that my spouse had been searching the sideroads; his words "I've lost the dog" were distinctly ominous, conjuring pictures of speeding cars or dog-nappers.

Our Labrador Retriever is very playful and friendly but after our move from the city had demonstrated a distinct desire to stay close to us. On this day, with my spouse busy in the barn, she slipped away. She may have seen his concentration on his work as an absence of fun, but also as a chance to investigate a wider world.

We dressed warmly and began the search. Soon we heard a distant barking and headed in the direction of the sound. As we got closer, the barking had a howling, desperate sound. We found her in the middle of a neighbouring pond, only her soaking wet, seal-like head visible; surrounded by ice, unable to climb out.

Seeing her in that state launched us immediately into a rapid no-time-to-think mode. This proved to be our undoing. There was a small boat near the edge of the pond. We quickly turned it upright, untied it and pushed it towards the edge of the ice. My husband climbed in and began to scoot his way towards the open water, intending to reach out and pull the dog into the boat. When he tried to haul her out, the boat tipped over under his leaning weight, and he was in the water!

My heart immediately went into overload. I slid and shuffled my way rapidly to the edge of the ice, hearing it creak beneath me, and grabbed his hands. I noticed that they were bleeding from holding onto the edge of the ice. We held on hard to each other, the phrase "for dear life" acutely meaningful. He laboured to try and get his breathing under control, then tried to heave himself out of the water but, weighted with soaking-wet winter clothing, was unable to do so.

I continued to feel totally incapable of thought, possessed by the purest form of panic. I called for help but we were alone in our struggle on this beautiful winter afternoon. Some-how we managed a rhythmic effort as, with each attempt to launch himself out, my spouse broke some more ice and I nimbly stepped back out of the way, still managing to grimly hold on. He was afraid of pulling me in and I was afraid to let go. Finally, with one huge exertion, the inevitable happened and I crashed through the ice into the water. This mishap proved to be helpful. By breaking a larger amount of ice with that force, we were closer to shore. Moments later, he could touch bottom for the first time and by continuing to smash the ice with our hands, we were finally able to clamber up onto the bank, dog included.

There followed a numbing race through fields of snow to our house. Towels, blankets and hot tea eventually restored our circulation and calmed us. I had difficulty sleeping that night because of the recurring vision of my husband neck-deep in icy water, gasping for breath. We talked about the experience a great deal afterward, imagining terrible conclu-sions that might have been. If we had not found the dog within the time frame that we did, she would have slipped under the water and we would never have known what had happened to her. We wondered how long she would have been able to stay afloat. If my shopping trip had kept me longer in town, and if my husband had found and attempted to rescue the dog by himself, he also would have struggled alone. This was a thought too horrible to pursue. We were amazed, too, that I had been able to hold onto him as I am approximately half his weight. Simple buoyancy was probably one reason, and grim determination fuelled by masses of adrenaline another.

Our children, upset by our story, chided us for our lack of logic. Our son's vehement "You do not risk your life for the dog!" expressed their alarm. Attempted pet rescues with terrible results, sadly, do occur, but the instinct to save is solidly there and can obliterate common sense.

Like any other near-fatal accident, it has been a powerful learning experience. We now have at our pond a long rope with a wooden handle, which could be thrown to someone struggling in the water. We also placed at the site an extension ladder to use to reach out across an icy surface.

We continue to find immense pleasure in the beauty of our surroundings, our home, but perhaps with a little less romanticism and a dollop more of caution. I no longer have bad dreams, but when I hear our dog whimper in her sleep, I wonder if she is chasing a rabbit or dreaming that she is drowning.

"The worst kind of ice-breaker" by Judy Plaxton, The Globe and Mail, *7 March 2003, p. A16. Reprinted with permission.*

1. What rhetorical mode does Plaxton use?

2. What does "pastoral Eden" (underlined in your text) mean? How is the expression fitting?

3. What is the contrast Plaxton describes between urban and rural life?

4. How does Plaxton make use of description?

5. What do you think Plaxton means when she says "the instinct to save is solidly there and can obliterate common sense"?

6. Why are such incidents as Plaxton describes "powerful learning experiences"?

7. Why do you think Plaxton wrote the article?

8. Have you ever had a trying experience similar to Plaxton's? In a few sentences, can you describe it?

9. In an essay of about 500 words, describe how someone that you know or have read about rescued someone else. Do Plaxton's words, "The instinct to save is solidly there and can obliterate common sense," ring true for the incident? What do rescues tell us about human nature?

Reading 5: Sonar Surveillance Despite Whale Injuries
Peter Carter

Concerned environmentalists point out that orca whale populations in the Pacific Northwest are on the decline. Some specialists argue that decreases in fish populations, exposure to toxins like PCBs in the water, and the increase of surface and underwater boat traffic are all contributing factors in the dropping numbers of orca whales off the coast of Vancouver Island and the state of Washington. Peter Carter is a physician and environmental activist living on the Gulf Islands of British Columbia. His claim is that testing by American naval experts is also adding to the harm of coastal water orcas, and he utilizes a cause and effect rhetorical pattern to establish that link.

For the last several years the US Navy has been moving ahead with plans to deploy Low Frequency Active Sonar, or LFA—a new extended-range submarine-detection system that will introduce into the world's oceans noise billions of times more intense than that known to disturb large whales. Now the National Marine Fisheries Service has proposed issuing a permit that would allow the navy to proceed with LFA deployment and, in the process, to harass, injure, or even kill marine mammals while flooding the ocean with intense noise.

Undeniable evidence that high-power "active" sonar systems can and do kill marine animals emerged in March 2000, when beach strandings of four different species of whales and dolphins in the Bahamas coincided with a Navy battle group's use of extremely loud active sonar there. Despite efforts to save the whales, seven of them died; a National Marine Fisheries Service and US Navy investigation established with virtual certainty a connection between the strandings and the sonar—and that active sonar system put out mid-frequency sound, which generally does not travel as far as LFA.

Although active sonar has been suspected in previous strandings, analysis of the heads of several dead whales enabled scientists to confirm, for the first time, the dangerous role of active sonar to a level of certainty that even the Navy could not ignore. All but one of the whales suffered hemorrhages in and around the ear, almost certainly the result of acoustic trauma. And in February 2001, a marine scientist observed that at least one of the whale species that was stranded in the Bahamas had virtually disappeared from the area, raising questions about impacts well beyond the initial strandings and deaths.

According to the Navy, LFA functions much like a floodlight, scanning the ocean at vast distances with intense sound. Each transmitter in the system's long array can generate 215 decibels of sound, a level millions of times more intense than is considered safe for human divers. Worse yet, not far from the array of transmitters the signals begin to combine, and the result as the signals travel is sound as forceful as if as much as 240 decibels had been transmitted at the source. (To understand just how powerful these sounds are, keep in mind that the decibel scale used for measuring noise is like the Richter scale used for measuring earthquakes—both use small differences to express increasing orders of magnitude.) Thanks to the combined power of all these sound waves, LFA can illuminate hundreds of thousands of square miles of ocean at one time. In 1991, scientists produced a loud, low-frequency signal off the coast of Heard Island in the southern Indian Ocean, and found that it was still detectable off the West Coast of the United States. That signal was effectively 100 times less powerful than LFA's.

For years the Navy had been testing the LFA system in complete secrecy and in violation of environmental laws. In 1995, Natural Resources Defence Council (NRDC) brought the sonar tests to light and demanded that the Navy comply with federal and state statutes and disclose how the sonar would affect marine mammals, sea turtles and other ocean species. As a result, the Pentagon agreed to conduct a full-scale study of environmental impacts before putting the LFA system into use across an estimated 80% of the world's oceans.

In late January 2001, the Navy released its Environmental Impact Statement, which according to law should be a "rigorous and objective evaluation" of environmental risks. Yet the US Navy's study fails to answer the most basic questions about its controversial system: How will LFA affect the long-term health and behaviour of whales, dolphins and hundreds of other species? Taking place as it does over an enormous geographic area, what effect might it have on marine populations?

According to the US Navy's study, scientists briefly exposed a 32-year-old US Navy diver to LFA sonar at a level of 160 decibels—a fraction of the intensity at which the LFA system is designed to operate. After 12 minutes, the diver experienced severe symptoms, including dizziness and drowsiness. After being hospitalized, he relapsed, suffering memory dysfunction and seizure. Two years later he was being treated with anti-depressant and anti-seizure medications.

Whales use their exquisitely sensitive hearing to follow migratory routes, locate one another over great distances, find food and care for their young. Noise that undermines their ability to hear can threaten their ability to function and survive. As one scientist succinctly put it: "A deaf whale is a dead whale." But what concerns marine scientists even more than short-term effects on individual animals is the potential long-term impact that the Navy's LFA system might have on the behaviour and viability of entire populations of marine mammals.

Sound has been shown to divert bowhead and gray whales and other whales from their migration paths, to cause sperm and humpback whales to cease vocalizing, and to induce a range of other effects, from distressed behaviour to panic. A mass stranding of beaked whales off the west coast of Greece in 1996 has been associated with an LFA-type system being tested by NATO. And last year's whale deaths in the Bahamas add further evidence of the risks of intense active sonar. Leading marine experts say the Navy's limited assessment cannot tell us how long-term exposure to LFA sonar will affect the breeding, feeding, and migration of whales and other marine species. It is exactly such long-term effects on vital activities, say the experts, that pose the greatest risk of pushing endangered species over the brink into extinction.

The National Marine Fisheries Service announced its proposal to permit LFA even as its own investigations into the Bahamas strandings continue. In the wake of the recent dramatic confirmation of the dangers of active sonar, NRDC is calling on the Fisheries Service to withdraw its proposed permit and deny the Navy's application to deploy LFA.

"Sonar Surveillance Despite Whale Injuries" by Peter Carter, Island Tides, Volume 14, Issue 16 (15–28 August 2002), p. 2.

1. How does LFA work?

2. How does LFA disrupt whales' hearing?

3. What is "acoustic trauma" (underlined in your text)?

4. Why would this article be seen to have a cause and effect arrangement of ideas?

5. What examples does Carter use to prove his point?

6. Why do you think Carter wrote this article?

7. According to Carter, why is hearing so critical to whales?

8. What is your opinion of military testing? Should it be kept secret? Why or why not?

9. In an essay of about 500 words, relate how scientific testing can be damaging to an animal species. Use some specific facts by doing a bit of research on the internet. Cite your sources. Use the third-person point of view only.

Reading 6: Whose Trail Is It Anyway?
Tom Cruickshank

The clash between those who wish to be stewards of the land and those who wish to develop it is an issue frequently raised in the media and newspapers. In the next selection, Tom Cruickshank provides a pointed example of such a conflict in a beautiful and popular region of Quebec. One group wishes to keep the area peaceful and natural for walking, horseback riding, and hiking, while another group wants to use the trail for recreational vehicles and sport. Cruickshank divides the issue by classifying the users of the trail system, and this classification and division rhetorical pattern works effectively to outline the problems entailed by the conflict.

Things came to a head in St-Lazare last summer. Accusations flew and fingers were pointed as two factions argued over who has access to the much-beloved trail system in this growing bedroom community just west of Montreal. On one side was the horsy set, for whom St-Lazare has been a refuge for generations. On the other were enthusiasts of a different kind: dirt bikers and ATV owners. At issue was the extent to which motorized vehicles should be allowed to use town pathways.

And what great pathways they are. The trail system, hundreds of kilometres long, winds through pine woods and open meadows surrounding this town of 13,000, linking various neighbourhoods to each other and to the great outdoors. For years, horseback riders had them to themselves, but as St-Lazare evolved from hobby farm community to commuter town, the riders were soon joined by legions of newcomers. At first the new users—joggers, birdwatchers, hikers, cyclists and cross-country skiers—seemed to co-exist without incident. It wasn't until the arrival of motor-enthusiasts that things turned ugly.

Last spring, equestrians were aghast at the number of ATVs on local paths, particularly a four-kilometre stretch through a corner of a pine forest, which provided a much-needed link in the regional network of ATV trails. Not only did the presence of motorized vehicles shatter the peace, they argued to town council, but it also posed a safety hazard because, as every rider knows, <u>a horse can easily spook</u> when confronted with unexpected noise. As the summer progressed, tensions mounted, reaching a boiling point at not one, but two council meetings, where the police were called to keep the peace. Meanwhile, a local ATV club did nothing to defuse the situation when it purchased an ad in a French-language newspaper and <u>decried the equestrians as a bunch of Anglo elitists</u> bent on preserving the trails as their exclusive domain. Sensing a clash of cultures, the *National Post* picked up the story and ran it on its front page.

The battle for the bridle path in St-Lazare is a microcosm of an issue dogging trail development across Canada. Although enthusiasts of all stripes agree that trails are a wonderful asset to country living, there is no consensus over who should be allowed to use them. Invariably, the lines are drawn when the issue of motorized vehicles arises and the argument goes much further than spooked horses. It's a classic showdown between those who equate the outdoor experience with peace and quiet and those who favour the roar of an engine with the call of the wild. It seems the twain shall never meet: Safety is often voiced as the main objection to motor bikes, ATVs and snowmobiles, but at the root of it all is a general disdain for anything noisy in what is supposed to be an unspoiled setting. For its part, the motorized crowd—snowmobilers especially—is far more numerous and apt to be better organized. In fact, they support and maintain more trails than all the other users combined.

The debate has even affected the Trans Canada Trail, the 18,000 kilometre cross-country route currently under development. Acknowledging the importance of snowmobilers to its long-term viability, it has no problem with motorized use in winter, but ATVs are so far banned in light of potential conflicts with other summertime users. Meanwhile in other locales, the most common solution has been separate trails for separate functions. The debate in St Lazare was resolved this way, with a new four-kilometre link through the woods reserved for ATV use. Meanwhile, motorized vehicles have been banned from other local paths. However, there is still the nagging question of policing. Volunteers from ATV and equestrian clubs alike are patrolling for violators, but all it will take is one stray vehicle and one startled horse and you can bet the battle will heat up all over again.

"Whose Trail Is It Anyway?" by Tom Cruickshank, Harrowsmith Country Life, *Volume 27, Issue 170, (June 2003), p. 34. Reprinted with permission from the May–June 2003 edition of* Harrowsmith Country Life Magazine.

1. What is an ATV?

2. Cruickshank uses the expression "a horse can easily spook" (underlined in your text). What does this expression mean?

3. What does Cruickshank mean when he says, "decried the equestrians as a bunch of Anglo elitists" (underlined in your text)?

4. What is the issue that Cruickshank outlines in his article?

5. How might the issue have been seen as a "clash of cultures," as Cruickshank says?

6. Why is Cruickshank's article a good example of classification and division?

7. Who is right in the debate in your opinion? Why?

8. How should trails be developed in your view?

9. In an essay of about 500 words, analyze an issue in your local neighbourhood or city. How are the issues divided? What are the types of concerns? What kinds of measures to solve the problem have been suggested? Who is served by the various solutions? Use the third-person point of view only.

BUSINESS AND MARKETING

Reading 7: The Trouble with "How's it going, ladies?"

DON CHERRY'S OPENING LINE IN THE MOLSON BUBBA COMMERCIAL MARS AN OTHERWISE HILARIOUS AD.

Richard Rotman

In the next reading, Richard Rotman examines language use and advertising. He points out how viewers are strongly influenced by the sometimes sexist language used in commercials. Viewers can be persuaded or dissuaded because icons such as Don Cherry are employed as key figures in the advertiser's message. Rotman chooses a comparison and contrast mode to convey his distinctions on the subject.

In beer advertising, sexism often rears its ugly head, but a recent lesson that my 12-year-old daughter taught me showed how ingrained it is in the daily imagination. Not just ingrained but part of the negative messages with which sports-minded young girls like her are bombarded every day.

It happened watching one of our favourite TV spots: Don Cherry, the hockey sage of "Coach's Corner" fame, meets up with beer-loving sports fans featured in a series of Bensimon·Byrne spots. The cast later dresses in Cherry's trademark <u>vertiginous</u> sport jackets and buys the new Molson Canadian Bubba beer keg emblazoned with the outspoken coach's image.

In the spot, he walks into the apartment with the beer-guzzling guys and derisively says: "Hey, how's it going, ladies?" Any male who has ever been on a sports team has heard that one before. When the game or the play is going badly, the coach will employ reverse psychology by goading the players with the terms "girls" or "ladies." To a young man, this is the ultimate emasculating insult.

But my bright, engaging daughter viewed that and said, "Why does he call them 'ladies'?" On her soccer teams (one of which I coach), the coach never uses that term. Her female basketball coach never calls the girls "boys" or something like that. In fact, her coaches probably call the girls "guys" more often than not.

She asked me to explain and I was at a loss; she had me cold. I fumbled through stuttering attempts to rationalize a male in-group term. Truthfully, there was no reasonable explanation that would hold water with my daughter. The whole thing was so lame—lame because Cherry, the Coach of All Coaches, used the term exactly as it is tossed off in countless locker rooms all across North America. "How's it going, ladies?" expresses to young men that they are beneath contempt and are therefore described as girls, the most provocative derogatory term possible.

But looking at it another way, Molson has made a monumental mistake, hidden in a small line of dialogue. Starting the action with a well-known sports figure, who is a kind of perverse role model, contemptuously referring to young men as "ladies" is a breach of corporate responsibility. With its cavalcade of bouncing busty bimbos, beer advertising is the last time-honoured refuge of sexist values. The prototypical young men in the Molson spot, the future husbands and fathers of the world (if that seems imaginable), take their social cues from these ads. Sadly, the consumption of beer is presented as the key to good times (of course in moderation, as the brewers would respond) and winning over the opposite sex. Even more sinister is the placement of the women in this series of spots: When the beer is poured and the party starts, the most buxom woman is positioned next to the main character, as if he's won the prize. In this spot, coach Cherry is standing next to the vavoomy woman at the happy conclusion.

I am mad at myself for enjoying this clever series of spots, for they have shown my sports-enthusiast daughter that being described as a girl is what boys fear most. They have given her a window into the <u>misogynistic</u> world of men's sports, which is a different universe than the one women experience. In men's sports, to be inadequate is to be a girl. That message is particularly traumatic when many studies report that girls' self-image declines following the onset of maturity.

Brewers and other companies entwined in promoting sports should be more careful. This is a time of female empowerment, and a small phrase such as "How's it going, ladies?" creates a larger ripple effect. Are there not other derogatory terms that coach Cherry could have said to this gaggle of geeky losers? How about "Hello, little boys" or "Hi, turkeys." Or simply, "Well, who do we have here?" All of which would adequately convey the coach's scorn for this crew of Molson-loving jellyfishes.

It's always remarkable what does seep through in ads, given how many people vet them, from agencies to focus groups and clients. One would give much to be a fly on the wall to hear the debate about the spot. Was there some young woman at the client or the agency, perhaps a sports participant herself, who heard "How's it going, ladies?" and remained silent, not daring to protest the insult in what surely must be a macho-charged, Hockey Night in Canada atmosphere?

Moreover, this is not to try to censor an ad that fits into network standards, was mostly in good taste and downright hilarious. (Kudos to Don Cherry for letting himself be parodied.) Instead, it's to advocate that advertisers, especially those influencing young males, rise above the milieu in which they work.

Pandering to all the usual prejudices in beer advertising is more passé than one can imagine. What's worse, it's bad public relations to continue to spread those tired old macho attitudes to the easily influenced. Surely the creative minds that produced the funny idea of the boys with the Bubba garbed like Don Cherry can come up with something less insidious than "How's it going, ladies?"

"The trouble with 'How's it going, ladies?'" by Richard Rotman, Marketing Magazine, *Volume 108, Issue 20 (26 May 2003), p. 8. Reprinted with permission.*

1. What is sexism?

2. In your opinion, why did Rotman write the article?

3. Who is Don Cherry?

4. What does "in beer advertising, sexism often rears its ugly head" mean?

5. Can you give examples of sexism in beer advertising?

6. What do "vertiginous" and "misogynistic" mean (underlined in your text)?

7. Who should advertising serve? Do advertisers also have a social responsibility? Why or why not?

8. Have you seen some ads on television lately that you consider sexist? What were they? Why do you consider them sexist?

9. In an essay of about 500 words, compare or contrast a beer ad from the 1980s with a current beer ad. What distinctions do you see? What similarities? In what ways do these differences comment on accepted social values of the time? Are these values actual or constructed by advertisers? Use the third-person point of view only.

Reading 8: Reinventing Our Food for Fun and Profit
Pam Freir

The food industry is a multi-billion dollar enterprise that is constantly looking for ways to re-package its food products. In her article, Pam Freir takes an amusing look at ways in which products are "reinvented" to appear to be new to the consumer. She uses many examples to prove her point that companies and advertisers will use any means possible to sell something, and her use of the comparison and contrast mode keeps the reader in tune with her thinking.

If what we eat is any indication of who we are, we've got a lot of explaining to do. Two recent stories, one from Paris, the other from the U.S., tell us all we need to know.

On the uncomfortably-close-to-home front, the *Wall Street Journal* reports that H.J. Heinz Co. has "transformed one of the planet's most <u>mundane</u> food products . . . into a star." (Note that familiar weasel, *food product*, which means, of course, it's not actually food at all). Anyway, the reinvented "star" on the <u>ersatz</u> food horizon is ketchup. And its new claim to fame is its colour. Green.

People are eating it up.

But that's not all. There's been a packaging breakthrough too. Green ketchup comes in a user-friendly, easy-squeeze container cunningly contoured to fit a child's hands. And children love it. With every happy squirt and splat they are unleashing a flood of ketchup on a scale never seen before.

Green, of course, looks especially good on the corporate bottom line. Which explains the current <u>euphoria</u> at ketchup headquarters. Heinz has created a marketing phenomenon: Increased sales are no longer a reflection of increased consumption. People aren't necessarily eating more ketchup. They're just emptying the containers faster.

"As long as they're putting it on their plates, we're happy," says spokesman Michael Mullen.

Waste not, profit not. That's the dictum.

The Heinz success story has got others scrambling for a toehold in this kiddie-food play land. Quaker Oats has children digging through their oatmeal in search of edible jewels, gold coins and treasure chests. Parkay has just unveiled two new margarines—in shocking pink and electric blue. These too are packed for squeezability and fun.

"They're good for drawing pictures," we are told. Whether anyone actually eats the stuff is of no particular interest. It's selling.

Things are different in Paris. John Henley wrote this in a report to the *Guardian Weekly*:

> "For lunch yesterday my son had cream of spinach soup, gigot d'agneau accompanied by petits pois and puree of new potatoes, and a slice of tarte tatin topped off with a dollop of creme fraiche."
>
> "All that was missing was a glass or two of Burgundy and a nice fat cigar."

Henley is quick to concede the appropriateness of this seeming lapse. His son, Nathan, is nine months old.

The menu is a typical one at the day-care his son attends. And although it employs a full-time chef, it is not, as Henley points out, "a posh crèche stuffed full of toffee-nosed little Pierre-Henris." This is your standard, urban neighbourhood day-care and the kids are just regular kids.

The French, you see, like their children to get "an early start on the important things in life," Henley explains. When Nathan was barely three months old his pediatrician suggested introducing a little Roquefort cheese into his diet. "Taste development is essential," she advised. So even if Nathan turns up his little nose at the offering, his world is richer for the encounter.

So what'll it be? Green ketchup on a Velveeta slice? Or creme fraiche on a tarte tatin? And another question: Who cares? Does it matter? If that oft-quoted gastronome, Brillat-Savarin, is to be believed, it does: "The destiny of nations depends on what and how they eat."

It's an unsettling thought. Personally, I'm reluctant to throw in my lot with a culture defined by green ketchup and electric blue margarine. I'm uneasy with a generation that plays with its food, profits from the leftovers, and has forgotten that apples grow on trees. Besides, I have a hunch that a nation preoccupied with diving for treasure in its breakfast cereal could wind up choking on its own party favours.

No, I'm betting on Nathan. Not just because of the food that's set in front of him but because of the values that food embodies. Nathan will grow up knowing the difference between a Happy Meal and a joyous one. He will approach his food with a keen palate, an open mind and what M.F.K. Fisher calls "inquisitive gusto." And chances are he will approach his life and the larger world with the same curiosity, acceptance and enthusiasm.

I think Nathan's going to turn out O.K. He may never acquire a taste for Roquefort cheese but he'll at least recognize it as food, not play dough.

"Reinventing Our Food for Fun and Profit" by Pam Freir, Times Colonist, *14 November 2001, p. D1.*

1. What do "mundane," "ersatz," and "euphoria" mean (underlined in your text)?

2. What do you think Freir means when she says, "a posh crèche stuffed full of toffee-nosed little Pierre-Henris" (underlined in your text)?

3. What do you think "weasel" means? (Freir says: "that familiar weasel, food product.")

4. Can you name other "weasel words" advertisers like to use in descriptions of their products?

5. What does Freir mean when she says, "green, of course, looks good on the corporate bottom line"? What does it mean when a company is "in the red" or "in the black"?

6. What is the tone of Freir's article? Why do you think that?

7. How can some products be a "packaging breakthrough" as Freir suggests? Can you name other "packaging breakthroughs"?

8. In your opinion, why do advertisers aim their ads at children?

9. In an essay of about 500 words, compare or contrast how food preferences can be called "lifestyle differences." Use the third-person point of view.

Reading 9: Old Levi Would Not Be Proud
Arthur Black

Three-time winner of the Stephen Leacock Memorial Medal for Humour Award, Arthur Black is a well-known Canadian writer and broadcaster. From 1983 to 2002, he hosted *Basic Black* on CBC radio. He's the author of 10 books. In "Old Levi Would Not Be Proud," Black investigates the rather "rags to riches" history of jeans.

I knew it. I could have predicted this would happen from the moment they came out with Stay Prest. You remember that? Levi's Stay Prest? Wash-and-wear jeans. You could climb into 'em as soon as they came out of the dryer?

What a joke. Levi's always *were* wash-and-wear. Only a terminal nerd would consider ironing them. That's the whole point of jeans. Jeans are for people like you and me—and Gilda Radner, who once bragged that she based all her fashion choices on what didn't itch.

Back in the 1960s, the brain trust at Levi Strauss understood that their role in life was to put out a cheap pair of denim pants that would practically stop bullets. Perfect product. And then they tried to finesse. They bought out Stay Prest wash-and-wear—and eventually bell-bottoms and hiphuggers and pastels and flare legs and stonewashed and tapers.

This is not what [a] horny-handed Bavarian merchant by the name of Levi Strauss had in mind back in 1853, when he emigrated to San Francisco.

Strauss was a merchant, an odd jobber who got his hands on a bargain heap of tough, heavy-weight brown canvas. He noticed that the hardrock miners generally wore crummy torn and patched trousers. They need better pants, he thought to himself, and he started cutting up his canvas into trouser patterns—double-seaming the legs, even putting rivets in the stress corners for extra strength. Strauss didn't know it, but he had created the trouser equivalent of the Volkswagen Beetle. His pants were cheap, tough, and terribly common. Just like his newly adopted country.

Strauss gave the pants his first name, and Levi's were off and running.

And run they did. For more than a century, jeans meant Levi's and Levi's meant jeans. During the Second World War, you couldn't even buy them on the open U.S. market. Levi's were strictly reserved for American defence workers. But in the mid-1950s, two things happened to the Levi Strauss image. One was named James Dean, and the other was called Marlon Brando. Their movies—*Rebel without a Cause* for Dean and

The Wild One for Brando—featured the stars wearing Levi's. The sales went through the roof.

The company could have run with that. It could have kept on turning out merely the best-value pants on the market. But that's not how it works in big business—if it was, we'd still have a six-team NHL.

Nope. By the 1970s, Levi's had become chic. Boutiques all over the world were selling jeans at unbelievable prices. Faded jeans. Patched jeans. Ripped jeans. Even jeans with no knees. In 1973, the president of Levi Strauss admitted that he "found it a little strange to rise from workclothes to fashion, but we're not fighting it."

They should have fought it. Instead, Levi Strauss tried to go high market—opening the door to all manner of foppy foreign designers' mutations. Suddenly, the market was awash in glitzy brands like Gap, Tommy Hilfiger, Big Star, Guess—even Diesel and Gasoline and Kik Girl, for crying out loud.

And somewhere in that swirl, Levi's—like its anagram, Elvis—lost its way.

Really lost its way. In 1998, the one-time giant of the garment trade lost a cool billion dollars. Not long after, Levi Strauss announced the closing of half its 22 North American plants.

The buzz on the street? The Levi's people lost it. Tried to be highsteppers, forgetting that they couldn't dance. Their pants just aren't cool any more.

But this is refreshing, because I fell in love with Levi's before they were cool. Back in the 1960s, when only hoods and louts wore them—oh, yeah, and a rumpled, chain-smoking guy by the name of Gzowski, who back in the late 1960s quit as editor of *Maclean's* magazine, announcing that he would never again take a job where he couldn't wear jeans to work.

And he didn't. Got a job at CBC Radio instead, as host of *This Country in the Morning*.

And so I find myself on the high inseam of the millennium: pursuing a work philosophy by Gzowski, wearing a wardrobe by Levi Strauss.

Except that Gzowski is no longer with us. And these Levi's I'm wearing cost more than I paid for my first car.

Plus, they're . . . kinda tight.

"Old Levi Would Not Be Proud" from Black Gold: Nuggets from a Lifetime of Laughs, *by Arthur Black, 2006, Harbour Publishing Co.*

1. Who was Levi Strauss and what is he famous for?

2. What two movie stars does Black suggest were responsible for the popularity of jeans?

3. What is the author's tone?

4. What does "high market" mean (underlined in your text)?

5. How does a product become a blockbuster?

6. How do marketers work today to get product placement and gain market share?

7. John Berger, a famous British art critic said, "Fashion is making the old seem ridiculous." In an essay of about 500 words, discuss how Berger's view is different from Black's. Which viewpoint sells more products? Use the third-person point of view only.

Reading 10: Put Your Money Where Your Mouth Is

SOCIALLY AND ENVIRONMENTALLY RESPONSIBLE INVESTING COMES OF AGE

Wendy Priesnitz

Wendy Priesnitz, once leader of the Green Party, is a social activist, author, and award-winning journalist. She is editor of *Life Magazine*, which advocates adopting a green lifestyle, and *Life Learning Magazine*, which promotes learning in life. Founder of the Canadian Alliance of Home Schooling, she continues to contribute to the home schooling movement.

Investing money to gain profit in relation to the public good is not a new notion; however, within the past decade, many North American investors have linked their financial lives with their moral beliefs. This practice, called ethical investing or socially responsible investing, is the subject of Wendy Priesnitz's article. She discusses the categories and principles of socially responsible investing.

Seemingly one of the last bastions of fiscal conservatism, the investment industry has been greening itself up over the past decade or so. Shareholders have realized that by voting with their dollars, they have the potential to leverage markets in favour of the planet and of those less fortunate who live on it—and to make some money for themselves at the same time.

And that, in turn, is slowly but steadily leading the business community and governments toward becoming part of the solution rather than part of the problem. With the responsible investment sector watching over their shoulders and primed to pounce at missteps, they are finding that rhetoric and greenwashing advertisements are no longer enough.

Socially Responsible Investing

Shareholder advocacy is one aspect of socially responsible investing (SRI). SRI is defined as the integration of investment with social responsibility and environmental sustainability. It includes all the financial decision-making processes that are a part of a prudent investment management approach, but it also includes the selection and management of investments based on issues of sustainability or social responsibility.

That selection and management is accomplished through screening or the application of social and environmental guidelines or "screens" to the investment process. It can be done directly by investing in particular stocks or other investments selected according to specific screens, or through socially responsible mutual funds employing pre-established screens.

Negative screens can include such issues as companies operating with sweatshop or child labour, or that manufacture alcohol, tobacco, or pornography, or that are heavy polluters. Companies falling into these categories are excluded from portfolios containing these screens. Examples of positive screens include seeking out companies with good employee relations, strong records of community involvement and exemplary environmental impact policies and procedures.

Besides shareholder advocacy and screening, a third aspect of SRI is community investing, whereby investors place their money in businesses or investments reflecting a vision of an alternative kind of economy. Community investors generally place money in community loan funds providing capital to local entrepreneurs, cooperative or community-oriented enterprises such as worker or consumer co-ops, regional development bonds, not-for-profit enterprises or community loan funds. Community investment funds provide capital that cannot be offered by banks and other for-profit financial institutions. In addition, by bringing mentoring or government-funded resources to the process, community investment helps to provide training, networking, and other technical support.

Social investing can be done by individuals or institutions such as foundations, religious organizations, trusts, investment pools, and pension plans. And all these types of socially responsible investors have been ramping up their corporate engagement activity in recent years, as a way of holding companies accountable for their social and environmental behaviour on the international stage.

According to the Shareholder Association for Research and Education (SHARE), Canadian investors have filed close to 30 shareholder proposals on a wide range of socially responsible and sustainability-related issues in 2006, including the rights of local communities in development projects, biodiversity, and climate change.

There is even an award for excellence in this sector. The Capital Markets Award for Sustainable Investment & Banking is a category of the GLOBE Awards for Environmental Excellence, presented at the GLOBE environmental conference held in Vancouver. The Capital Markets Award is based on "an explicit recognition that financial markets are increasingly integrating environment factors into investment and banking decisions, and are placing more capital into sustainable technologies and ventures," states the Globe Foundation, sponsors of the awards and organizers of the conference. This year's winner was Jantzi Research Inc., an independent investment research firm that has been evaluating and monitoring the environmental, social, and governance performance of securities for a number of years.

Shareholder Activism

A good example of shareholder activism is resolutions filed this spring by two groups of Canadian investors: the Ethical Funds Company, a Vancouver-based socially responsible mutual funds company, and the Missionary Oblates of Mary Immaculate. The resolutions demand that Alcan create an improved policy of stakeholder engagement. They cite community opposition to the company's Utkal project in India, a large new bauxite development. Some local groups in India have opposed the project for a number of years and public protests have been marked by police violence. As part of its recently announced Share Power campaign, Amnesty Canada urged its members who hold shares in Alcan to support the resolutions and to write to mutual fund companies holding Alcan shares asking them to support the proposals.

Although the Alcan annual meeting hadn't been held at press time, at another such meeting, the American energy giant Dominion Resources had just been given a strong message by its shareholders who had been seeking greater analysis and disclosure from the company about the financial impacts posed by global climate change, including foreseeable greenhouse gas emission limits on U.S. power plants.

Twenty-two-and-a-half percent of the company's shareholders, who collectively own about $5.85 billion worth of shares, supported a resolution requesting that the company undertake a comprehensive review on how it is responding to growing regulatory, competitive, and public pressure to reduce greenhouse gas emissions. Shareholders requested that the climate risk report be completed by September 1, 2006 and be reviewed by a board committee of independent directors.

The 22.5% support is nearly three times higher than the 8.3% voting support a similar resolution received at Dominion's 2005 annual meeting. The measure was backed by many of the company's largest shareholders, including public pension funds in California.

"Shareholders have sent a loud and clear message that they expect Dominion to be far more active to reduce greenhouse gas emissions and a plan for a future in which carbon constraints change the way electric companies do business," says Shelley Alpern, director of social research and advocacy at Trillium Asset Management, which filed the resolution along with the New York City Employees Retirement System.

The UN Principles for Responsible Investment
As institutional investors, we have a duty to act in the best long-term interests of our beneficiaries. In this fiduciary role, we believe that environmental, social, and corporate governance (ESG) issues can affect the performance of investment portfolios (to varying degrees across companies, sectors, regions, asset classes, and through time). We also recognize that applying these principles may better align investors with broader objectives of society. Therefore, where consistent with out fiduciary responsibilities, we commit to the following.

1. We will incorporate ESG issues into investment analysis and decision-making processes.

2. We will be active owners and incorporate ESG issues into our ownership policies and practices.

3. We will seek appropriate disclosure on ESG issues by the entities in which we invest.

4. We will promote acceptance and implementation of the principles within the investment industry.

5. We will work together to enhance our effectiveness in implementing the principles.

6. We will each report on our activities and progress toward implanting the principles.

"Put Your Money Where Your Conscience Is" by Wendy Priesnitz, Natural Life, *July/August 2006.*

1. According to Priesnitz what is "socially responsible investing"?

2. The author says that guidelines or screens can be applied to a company's investment history. What are some of the negative screens that can be applied?

3. What is "community investing"?

4. According to the writer, what can shareholders do to make companies more socially responsible, in other words, involve "shareholder activism"?

5. Review the "UN Principles for Responsible Investment" found at the end of the article. What principles do you believe to be most important? Are there other principles you would like to see added to the list?

CULTURE AND COMMUNICATIONS

Reading 11: Employee Privacy at Risk, Research Warns

KEYSTROKE MONITORING, CLOSED-CIRCUIT TELEVISION SYSTEMS, GPS—A CONFERENCE EXPLORES HOW TECHNOLOGY IMPLEMENTED FOR ONE PURPOSE CAN BE USED FOR ANOTHER. PLUS: THE FUTURE OF RFID

Laura Eggertson has worked as a journalist for the Canadian Press, the *Globe and Mail*, and *The Toronto Star*. In 1995–1996, she was awarded a Nieman Fellowship in Journalism at Harvard University. She currently works as a freelance writer for a variety of magazines and specializes in health, science, business, and politics. In "Employee Privacy at Risk," Eggertson examines how definitions of privacy policies in Canada are often misapplied in the workplace.

Researchers at a symposium hosted by Canada's privacy commissioner today called on legislators and employers to strengthen employee privacy guarantees and to anticipate the implications of emerging technologies that threaten privacy rights.

Employers already have access to technologies that range from key-stroke monitoring to closed-circuit television systems, access control systems (magnetic key cards), global position systems, radio frequency identifiers, telephone and e-mail monitoring and drug and genetic testing, conference speakers pointed out. Even if employers initially install the technologies for different purposes, they have surveillance capabilities that can be detrimental to employee privacy, said Avner Levin, coordinator of the law area at Ryerson University's business faculty.

In a recent case in Highlands East, Ont., hidden video cameras installed for security surveillance caught volunteer firefighters drinking beer. The fire station's commander was fired.

"The issue here is the <u>function creep</u> of these technologies as they are introduced for one purpose and used for another," said Levin.

Levin and three other colleagues at Ryerson surveyed companies representing three per cent of the Canadian workforce, asking employers about their workplace privacy policies.

Fully two-thirds of the representatives at companies the Ryerson researchers contacted would not co-operate with their survey, including CIBC and Wal-Mart, Levin said. Managers responsible for privacy at the 15 firms that did co-operate were often unaware of legislation that governed employee privacy, he said.

In Quebec, privacy legislation requires employers to protect the dignity of their employees. Privacy legislation in Alberta and B.C. stipulates that employers must be governed by a "reasonable" standard of conduct in collecting information about their employees.

In the companies that the Ryerson researchers spoke to, "there was absolutely no awareness that this was the state of affairs," Levin said. Most thought they had no restrictions on the information they could gather, and none of those surveyed provided privacy policies for their employees.

In all other provinces, including Ontario, there is no legislation specifically governing employee privacy in the workplace, Levin said. He called on the province to amend its

Employee Standards Act to put in place at least "minimal" guarantees, as West Virginia has done, that there will be no surveillance in place in restrooms, shower stalls or other personal spaces.

Employers should also consider the reasons they are collecting employee information, Levin said.

"It means thinking very seriously about what your role is as a corporate citizen in this post-911 world. You know if you create databases governments may want to have access to them," he said.

In a democracy, said Levin, "It's not always a good thing to create a database simply because you have some new technology that can create a database about your employees."

Richard Rosenberg, president of the BC Freedom of Information and Privacy Association, also cited the potential for genetic testing to violate employee privacy and, potentially, cost jobs.

"That's of great concern," Rosenberg said, citing a lack of legislation or public policy debate about the impact of that kind of employer surveillance.

Individuals have the right to seek genetic testing for health reasons, but "that doesn't automatically mean that information should become available for management to make decisions on," said Rosenberg, also a professor emeritus in computer science at the University of British Columbia.

Currently, most companies don't have policies governing genetic testing, he said, and nor are employees or their union representatives requesting it.

Rosenberg is also worried about the increasing use of RFID technology to track people, not just animals. As of 2004, 40 million Americans were already carrying an RFID tag, or implantable computer chip, Rosenberg said.

One Cincinnati corporation called CityWatch.com, a surveillance company, has already implanted VeriChip tags in some of its employees. The chips permit the employees to access secure data centres.

Both Levin and Rosenberg urged employees to ask their employers for their policies concerning collection of employee information, and where one doesn't exist, to draft one.

Such a request would encourage employers to think through the process and ensuing policies could "leave the employees in a better state," said Levin.

"Employee Privacy at Risk," by Laura Eggertson, retrieved from **http://www.itbusiness.ca/it/client/en/ComputerCanada/News.asp?id=42416**. Reprinted by permission of the author, Laura Eggertson, a freelance journalist, Ottawa, Ontario

1. What in general is this article about?

2. Why is Canada's privacy commissioner interested in strengthening employee privacy guarantees?

3. Avner Levin refers to the issue as "function creep" (underlined in your text). What is it?

4. How should employees' right to privacy be protected in the modern workplace?

5. What is RFID technology?

6. According to the article, why is collecting information and creating a database not always a good thing in the workplace? What is your opinion on worker privacy issues as they relate to the workplace?

7. In an essay of about 500 words, define employee privacy and the rights to privacy. Then discuss how your definition might conflict with current business practices. Use the third-person point of view only.

Reading 12: The Simplification of Culture

Neil Bissoondath

Neil Bissoondath was born in Trinidad and came to Canada where he was educated at York University. He is a well-known writer and television host. The following selection is an excerpt from Chapter 5 of Bissoondath's controversial book, *Selling Illusions: The Cult of Multiculturalism in Canada*, which criticized the Canadian government's policy on multiculturalism. In the excerpt, Bissoondath examines language and culture, and argues that acquiring a new language does not necessarily mean letting go of one's culture and its traditions. The rhetorical mode he uses is comparison and contrast because he distinguishes his experiences and beliefs about language from those of his grandparents.

> In Canada, I don't think we've really explored how the <u>immigration experience</u> changes people when they move from one country to another. It's easier just to comment on different foods and folkloric dances than to really understand what people go through when they emigrate. . . . In Canada, there has been a tendency to trivialize.
> —*Nino Ricci, quoted in Profiles, February 1994 (underlining added)*

It is at times strange to me that for my great-grandparents English was a second language. They were Brahmins, members of the learned caste, but poor. In Trinidad they led <u>tenuous</u> lives working the land, going about their daily tasks—cutting sugar-cane stalks, tending rice paddies—mostly in Hindi. That I find this strange says much about the change that the years have brought. Both the lives they led and the language they spoke have now grown impossibly remote, their faces, even their names, long drifted, for my generation at least, into an irretrievable anonymity.

Change, made inevitable by time and space and Bible-toting missionaries from another British colony called Canada, marked itself on their children. In the schools that <u>bartered</u> education for religious conversion (the bargain always kept, my paternal grandfather and one of his brothers remaining loyal to the old faith, while two other brothers embraced the new), a greater facility in English was acquired. In an agrarian society, this could not have been easy—but forever after, my grandfather ritually read his daily newspaper, lips soundlessly forming the words.

For both my grandfathers, the new language offered escape from the <u>enervating</u> labours of the field. My paternal grandfather found success in commerce, while my mother's father, less practical, more of a dreamer, engaged what little literary life the island had to offer by becoming a newspaper reporter who wrote short stories in his spare time.

Success, though, exacted a price. For my father's parents (my mother's father died before I was born), Hindi eventually became little more than a language of religion and secrets, spoken only in prayer and for privacy between themselves. In both families, English, the language of success, was the language of communication with the children, the result being that my parents spoke no Hindi save a word here and there, mostly terms of endearment or disparagement infrequently uttered.

Within three generations, then, the language of my great-grandparents had all but disappeared, and along with it had gone a way of life: dependence on the land and religious belief. We felt no sense of loss, no <u>tincture</u> of regret, no romantic attachment to a language that no longer served the purposes of our circumstance. And those of my parents' generation who still clung to the distant past—the few women who wore only saris, the few men who went to India in search of wives—came to be viewed as eccentric and foolish.

My own world was very different from the one in which my parents had grown up. While, for them, going abroad to study remained a grand and lengthy journey—farewells at the docks, the slow progression of the ship towards the horizon—for my generation it was one more step in a normal progression. Like my contemporaries', my mode of travel was jet-powered, the trip a few short hours. My only language was English, my popular cultural influences in an island independent only ten years less British or Indian than American: not Ravi Shankar or Laurence Olivier but the Temptations and Clint Eastwood. Through schooling, I acquired French, Spanish and the cultural influences they entailed, including an enduring love of the poetry of the Spanish poet Federigo García Lorca.

When, at the age of eighteen, I left Trinidad for Canada, the journey that had begun in India a century before—and here I mean not just the physical journey—was simply proceeding to its next logical step. Members of my family now live not only here but in England and the United States as well. After twenty years, this country now claims all of my loyalty, intellectual and emotional.

India and many things Indian have been left behind. Trinidad and many things Trinidadian have been left behind. Much else, though, has been assumed along the way. In a way, then, time and circumstance have succeeded where the Canadian missionaries failed—not in terms of religion but in terms of culture. It is a change that can be viewed as a loss to be mourned but there is, too, a less nostalgic way of looking at it.

In his novel *A Bend in the River*, V. S. Naipaul writes: "The world is what it is; men who are nothing, who allow themselves to become nothing, have no place in it." Making a place for ourselves is what my families have long been good at: it is one of the effects of the fear of becoming nothing. Both families are now replete with doctors and lawyers, teachers and writers. All this has come, in great part, through a refusal to brood over the loss of one language and its cultural baggage and a willingness to fully embrace another. English, then, is not for us a borrowed language but an acquired one, as fully part of my families today as Hindi was a hundred ago: the distinction is vital.

The languages I speak are central to me. My attachment to them is strong and passionate. They have made me what I am; have provided me with a way of looking at the world, of exploring and understanding it. Perhaps most important of all, they have given me the means of expressing what I see. For in being a writer, in engaging through my imagination the varied elements of familial experience, I am linked to my maternal grandfather and to all of the faceless, nameless people who came before.

1. What do "tenuous," "bartered," "enervating," and "tincture" mean (underlined in your text)?

2. What tone has the writer chosen? Why do you think so?

3. What do you think is meant by "the immigration experience" (underlined in your text)?

4. What is irony? Are there some examples of irony in Bissoondath's article? What are they?

5. What comments do you suppose Bissoondath is making about language and cultural ties?

6. What contrasts does Bissoondath mention?

7. In your opinion, what does Bissoondath mean when he says, "Making a place for ourselves is what my families have long been good at: it is one of the effects of the fear of becoming nothing"?

8. What is "multiculturalism"? A policy promoted by provincial and federal governments in Canada? Can multiculturalism exist if people are not willing to give up some cultural ties of their own?

9. In an essay of about 500 words, compare or contrast Bissoondath's view with this passage from "Best of Both Worlds," *Canada and the World Backgrounder*, 2006: "The argument is that dual citizenship helps immigrants integrate into their new societies more smoothly. There are some statistics to back up this theory. Countries that allow dual citizenship find that more immigrants naturalize and become citizens of their new home than countries that insist on renunciation. This leads to more immigrants getting involved in the political process and forming deeper ties with their adopted nation."

Reading 13: Crows of the World

Candace Savage, raised on the Canadian prairies, still makes her home there. She is a graduate of the University of Alberta and is the author of 19 books of non-fiction, many of them on wildlife, particularly birds of Western Canada. In "Crows of the World," Savage reviews how crows and ravens have been defined by group and behaviour.

There are about forty-five species of crow in the world (a couple more by some estimations, a couple fewer by others, depending on whether local varieties are split into separate entities or lumped together). Although they are known by a variety of common names, including ravens, jackdaws, and rooks, all are members of the genus *Corvus*, or crow; and all are variations on a theme, with their glossy black (or sometimes black-and-white) plumage, their raucous voices, and their seemingly endless capacity to fly out of the frame of our expectations and surprise us. They are medium-sized or largish birds—the smallest, the European jackdaw, *Corvus monedula*, is about the size of a large cockatiel—with sturdy bills, strong feet, and venturing minds that are formed for exploration and discovery. The burliest member of the crow tribe, the common raven, *Corvus corax*, is as big and brassy as a macaw and just as impressive, with its liquid calls, rustling cape of feathers, and keen alertness. (One of the most widespread birds in the world, the common raven is found throughout the northern hemisphere, from Europe and North Africa east through Asia and across the northern reaches of the New World.)

In between these extremes in size lie the other members of the global crow congregation, including a dozen species found exclusively in Europe and Asia—among them the gregarious rook, *Corvus frugilegus*, a familiar bird of farmland across both continents, pied hooded crow, *Corvis cornix*, and its all-black cousin, the carrion crow, *Corvus corone.* Another eight or nine species are native to Africa, and five or six are found only in Australia: the Australian raven, *Corvus coronoides*, for example, with its mournful, fading wail, and the only-slightly-smaller little crow, *Corvus bennetti*, which is famous for its exuberant aerial displays. Yet another dozen-plus species are unique to islands in the South Pacific and the West Indies, from New Caledonia and New Guinea to Jamaica.

Strangely, there are no crows at all in South or Central America, where *los observadores de pájaros* have to be content with a profusion of brightly colored jays and magpies, the crows' closest relatives. (Crows, magpies, and jays belong to different genera, or kinship groupings, within the larger family connection of the tribe *Corvini*.) North America is blessed with four species all its own: the sociable northwestern crow; *Corvus caurinus*, of the west coast; the glossy fish crow, *Corvus ossifragus*, of the eastern seaboard, with its distinctive nasal caw; the heavyset Chihuahuan raven, *Corvus cryptoleucus* of northern Mexico and the southwestern United States; and the lively American crow, *Corvus brachyrhynchos*, which is seen and heard almost everywhere else. Rounding out the clangorous chorus, in North America as elsewhere in the Northern Hemisphere, is the common raven, which drifts over gloomy forests and bleak tundra from sea to sea to sea, uttering its sonorous commentary.

Crows and ravens make a statement just by being themselves. Everything about them says, "It's me. I'm here. This is my world, my place in the world, and don't you forget it." They are the opposite of shyness, the antithesis of camouflage, the very embodiment of self-promotion. And although their showy behavior is primarily intended to attract the attention of others of their kind, their "advertising package" is also ideally pitched to attract the human ear and eye. Unlike the little dickey-birds that set us scrambling for binoculars and frantically twiddling knobs, crows are big and bold, making them easy to observe and identify. As a rule, individual species of *Corvus* are not difficult to tell apart, if you spend a few minutes learning their particular field marks. The common raven, for example, can be distinguished from all the other crows that share its range by its large size; its big schnoz, or heavy bill; its slotted wing tips; and its diamond-shaped, rather than fan-shaped, tail.

Even the crows' harsh voices are—if not exactly music to our ears—surprisingly companionable. Technically speaking, crows are songbirds, though you wouldn't know it from what comes out of their mouths. Not for them a soaring aria that would put the Three Tenors to shame. Instead, crow vocalizations are earthy; studded with what sound to us like consonants and vowels, as if their caws and "quorks" were pronouncements in some unintelligible tongue. And this attunement between humans and crows, this resonance, is both striking and unexpected. Why the connection between bird and mammal? For whatever reason, crows stir our senses, and, over the centuries, their harsh calls have echoed loudly through our dreams and myths. When the legendary Crow or Raven speaks, even the gods listen.

"Crows of the World" excerpted from Crows: Encounters with the Wise Guys of the Avian World *by Candace Savage, published 2005 by Greystone Books, a Division of Douglas & McIntyre Ltd. Reprinted by permission of the publisher.*

1. What characteristics do birds in the *Corvas* family share?

2. Although crows can be found in almost all countries of the world, there are two continents in which they are absent. What are the two continents?

3. What four species are found in North America?

4. How are crows and ravens different in appearance?

5. Do you know of any legends connected to the crow? Describe one.

6. Have you ever watched a crow or a raven? What did you observe? Did you discover any surprises?

7. Write an essay of about 500 words on an animal and modern myths about the animal. Use a classification and division mode. Use the third-person point of view.

Reading 14: Intellectual Property: A Different Kind of Inuit Ownership
Denise Rideout

Businesses' and corporations' copyrights protect their company logos; the use of one without the appropriate permission and payment can cost someone a lot of money in legal fees. In the next reading, Denise Rideout explores how an Inuit cultural symbol has been co-opted as a marketing tool by business and government. Using the rhetorical pattern of definition, Rideout investigates the characteristics of a cultural icon.

The inuksuk, a symbol of Inuit culture that appears on the Nunavut flag and directs hunters on the tundra, is somewhat of a marketing device in southern Canada. Its image is popping up on T-shirts and key chains, found on company logos, and is even used to sell brands of beer.

And Inuit groups across the country don't like the way non-Inuit businesses are exploiting the inuksuk to make a profit.

"The inuksuk is a big item when it comes to it being misappropriated by other individuals, non-Inuit or non-Aboriginals, for business purposes," said John Cheechoo, a director at Inuit Tapiriit Kanatami (ITK) who has been looking into ways to protect Inuit cultural symbols.

"It's a problem and it's been there for a while," Cheechoo said in an interview in Ottawa.

The major Inuit organizations in Canada sent representatives to Ottawa last week to brainstorm ways to prevent Qallunaat businesses and companies from using Inuit symbols to promote and sell their products.

The Inuit groups want the law to protect what is known as their "intellectual property rights." Current federal legislation designed to protect intellectual property covers art, trademarks, and technologies—but only if they are new or original. This makes it difficult to protect old designs, such as the traditional inuksuk symbol.

Along with ITK, Pauktuutit, Nunavut Tunngavik Inc., the Inuvialuit Regional Corp., the Labrador Inuit Association and the Avataq Cultural Institute attended the discussions with officials from the federal department of foreign affairs who specialize in intellectual property laws. Since this was a gathering of policy advisors, and not a meeting of politicians, the discussions weren't open to the public.

Robert McDougall of the department of foreign affairs said the aim of the National Roundtable on Intellectual Property and Traditional Knowledge was to get the perspective of Inuit and First Nations groups.

It turned out they had much to say. Inuit organizations worry their cultural icons are being exploited. Sometimes that misuse is happening in their own communities.

In Labrador, for instance, some Qallunaat are making and selling soapstone carvings—an artform usually mastered by Inuit carvers.

"We were always concerned with the Japanese making plastic carvings. Now it seems we've got a fight on the other front. We're now competing with non-Inuit soapstone carvers, especially in Labrador," said Gary Baikie, a representative of the Labrador Inuit Association.

Baikie recounted how these soapstone carvings are being mistaken for genuine Inuit pieces. "A buddy of mine went into an art gallery and bought a carving and he was all happy about how he'd gotten this Inuk carving. I looked at the bottom of it and the name wasn't even an Inuk one."

Another sore spot for Labrador Inuit is when Qallunaat get access to traditional knowledge and then make money off it, Baikie said.

"The one thing that we noticed is that when we [published] our 'Footprints Are Everywhere,' which is the basis of our land claim, it contained a lot of traditional knowledge talking about the best hunting areas and best fishing areas. All of sudden, after that was published, we see lodges popping up in the best hunting and fishing spots," he said.

"So we became aware of how sensitive this information is."

Since then, the LIA has adopted guidelines outlining how outside researchers can conduct studies in Labrador and what they can do with the information gathered.

Incidents like this prompt Inuit organizations to take a look at how they can protect their intellectual property and traditional knowledge. Five years ago, Pauktuutit, the national Inuit women's association, laid the groundwork. Pauktuutit made it its mission to protect the design of the traditional women's parka, the amauti.

Veronica Dewar, Pauktuutit's president, said Inuit women didn't want to see fashion designers appropriate the design of the amauti.

"We've already lost our kayak design many years ago and we don't want to go that route with the amauti," Dewar said. "Inuit own that. But how do we protect it?"

In May 2001, Pauktuutit brought a group of Inuit seamstresses and intellectual property rights experts to Rankin Inlet for a workshop on current laws and regulations.

Indigenous women from Panama also attended, telling the Inuit seamstresses that their government has laws to protect their traditional clothing designs from exploitation.

Pauktuutit has invited the Panamanian women to another such workshop in Ottawa this fall. "We are really pushing this issue now," Dewar said.

"We may not adopt their legislation, but we want some ideas on how to go about it."

Rideout, D. (2003, May 30). Intellectual property: A different kind of Inuit ownership. Nunatsiaq News. *Retrieved May 30, 2003, from* **http://www.nunatsiaq.com/archives/030530/news/nunavut/ 30530_04.html**. *Reprinted with permission of Nunatsiaq News, Nunavut.*

1. Who are the Inuit?

2. What is the "inuksuk" and, according to Rideout, why is it so important to the Inuit?

3. What is Rideout's argument? Summarize it in a few sentences.

4. What is a "cultural icon" (underlined in your text)? Can you think of other examples of "cultural icons" besides the inuksuk?

5. How have some groups organized to protect traditional knowledge and cultural objects?

6. In your opinion, how can groups protect their traditions from exploitation?

7. In what ways are governments responsible for the protection of groups against exploitation by business interests? Do you agree they should be responsible? Why or why not?

8. In your opinion, are cultural symbols a form of intellectual property? Why or why not?

9. In an essay of about 500 words, define "cultural icon." Use specific examples to support your definition. Use the third-person point of view only.

answer key

Chapter 1: Preparing and Planning to Write

EXERCISE 7   *Creating Outlines from Paragraphs*

PARAGRAPH 1

Exercise 7 Paragraph 1 page 12

Topic sentence: Cell phone use should be banned from the public domain.

Major point 1: First of all, most cell phone users who make calls in unrestricted places do not respect the privacy of others around them.

Support (Explanation or example): They make the mistaken assumption that they can talk as loudly or aggressively as suits their mood. In fact, many are downright obnoxious as they yell over the noise of the mall to get their words across.

Major point 2: Another reason for the suggested ban is that cell phone users are often discourteous.

Support (Explanation or example): Many cell phone users employ profane language or say offensive things in their conversations. Some claim that to do so is their right because they are making a private call, which they are paying for, and even exclaim that if someone else is listening in on their conversation, then the other person is at fault for eavesdropping.

Major point 3: Finally, cell phone use is actually an incursion into once quiet and relaxing public places.

Support (Explanation or example): It's not unusual to hear walkers or joggers shouting over their headsets as they make their way along trails through public parks. Park benches are now often occupied by people who are talking on their cell phones as they work on their laptops.

Wrap-up sentence: Cell phone use should be prohibited from public spaces because it is removing the rights of people to enjoy open places in relative peace in favour of the individual who co-opts the space for his or her own private purpose.

PARAGRAPH 2

Topic Sentence: Consumers can "food-shop" wisely.

Major point 1: think and plan

Support (explanation or example): weekly menu

Support (explanation or example): store "specials"

Support (explanation or example): grocery list

Major point 2: convenience foods

Support (explanation or example): costly items

Support (explanation or example): ingredients

Support (explanation or example): additives

Major point 3: nutritional value

Support (explanation or example): complex carbohydrates

Support (explanation or example): available choices

Support (explanation or example): food preparation

Support (explanation or example): fresh produce

Wrap-up sentence: With some planning and attention, consumers can do some careful shopping in the grocery store, while saving money and avoiding unnecessary trips to the store.

Chapter 2: Analyzing Paragraph Development

EXERCISE 2   *Identifying Rhetorical Modes in Paragraphs*

1. Definition
2. Comparison/contrast
3. Comparison/contrast
4. Definition
5. Cause/effect
6. Classification/division

Chapter 3: Analyzing Detail Organization

EXERCISE 1   *Locating the Topic Sentence*

1. Main idea? Who was F.H. Varley? No topic sentence: it is implied.
2. Main idea? The establishment of the UN. No topic sentence: it is implied.

3. Main idea? The problematic history of tree cutting in Canada or technical difficulties in the pioneer days of lumbering in Canada. No topic sentence: it is implied.
4. Topic Sentence: Rowing is a sport that is gaining in popularity.

Chapter 11: Nouns, Pronouns, and Verbs

Self-Test: Part 1   Nouns, Pronouns, and Verbs
1. Dr. Alonzo, understanding, clients
2. representative, office, moment
3. protest, workers, petition
4. doctor, pills, depression

Self-Test: Part 2   Nouns as Subjects or Objects of Verbs
1. Eunsook (S) Pierre (S)
2. machine (S)
3. Malcolm (S) Bob (O)
4. crows (S)
5. group (S) fries (O) sandwiches (O) coffee (O)

Self-Test: Part 3   Verbs
1. had been waiting
2. will be singing
3. Have worked
4. is
5. started

Self-Test: Part 4   Verb Tenses
1. P	6. P
2. F	7. P
3. PT	8. PT
4. P	9. PT
5. PT	10. PT

Self-Test: Part 5   Verb Forms
1. eaten	5. done
2. sworn	6. brought
3. saw; did see; was seeing	7. choosing
	8. worked
4. began; had begun; did begin; were beginning	9. written
	10. drive

Self-Test: Part 6   Identifying Nouns, Pronouns, and Verbs
1. pronoun	6. pronoun
2. noun	7. noun
3. verb	8. verb
4. verb	9. noun
5. verb	10. pronoun

Self-Test: Part 7   Identifying Action and Non-Action Verbs
1. decided (A), received (A)
2. are (NA)
3. stopped (A)
4. thought (A) became (NA)
5. is (NA) will win (A)

Self-Test Part 8   Identifying Verb Tense
1. has examined (present perfect) will be expecting (future progressive)
2. are packing (present progressive), put (simple present), pack (simple present), expect (simple present), will be (simple future)
3. is (simple present), don't consume (present; helper or auxiliary verb is emphatic), said (simple past)
4. are moving (present progressive), cause (simple present), become (simple present)
5. should have been wearing (past perfect progressive with conditional modal); had done (past perfect); would have been (past perfect with conditional modal)

EXERCISE 1   Classifying
1. dogs
2. cooking *or* kitchen utensils
3. cars *or* vehicles
4. furniture
5. animals

EXERCISE 2   Nouns
foot	examination	paint	skip
wagon	planet	community	person
rum	hate	law	television
apricot	love	tent	kitchen
joke	harbour	hero	ghetto
sauce	end	hours	

EXERCISE 3   Concrete and Abstract Nouns
1. passengers (C) bus (C) rain (C)
2. Ronnie (C) models (C) collection (C or A)

3. artist (C or A) paper (C) scissors (C) glue (C) pencil (C)
4. children (C) games (C or A) boss (C or A)
5. ship (C) coat (C) paint (C)
6. prince (C) guests (C) party (A)
7. hotel (C) gunshots (A) fire (A) silence (A)
8. carpenter (C) nails (C) trim (C) window (C)
9. eggs (C) pavement (C)
10. program (A)
11. company (C or A) order (C) van (C)
12. skunk (C) bushes (C) path (C) shed (C)
13. wasp (C) woman (C) warning (A)
14. Paul (C) truck (C) farm (C)
15. fight (A) bar (C) rule (A) hockey (C)

EXERCISE 5   Subject Nouns

1. Marie
2. dog
3. boxer
4. Terry
5. Sylvia
6. workers
7. Wally
8. dancers
9. wolf
10. car
11. team, captain
12. train, snowplough

EXERCISE 6   Subject Nouns

1. actor
2. Margaret
3. paper
4. dog
5. Tom
6. Yogurt
7. soup
8. lawn
9. cookies
10. lamp
11. Philip
12. children

EXERCISE 7   Subject Nouns and Object Nouns

1. Rodd (S) plywood (O)
2. students (S) rules (O)
3. man (S) money (O)
4. puppy (S) rag (O)
5. Mrs. Pobsby (S) rug (O)
6. chef (S) salad (O)
7. boy (S) ankle (O)
8. cousin (S) pizza (O)
9. Ozzie (S) rocks (O) stones (O)
10. Madame Lem (S) disaster (O)

EXERCISE 8   Subject Nouns and Object Nouns

1. child (S) picture (O), home, subdivision
2. coffee (S) (no object), restaurant
3. crow (S) garbage (O), bins
4. girl (S) novel (O), stream, oak

5. supervisor (S) party (O), staff
6. family (S) picnic (O), weekend, Fairview Hill Park
7. Francis (S) parrot (O), salesman
8. Charlie (S) time (O), project
9. gentleman (S) sandwich (O) beer (O)
10. Harvey (S) sauce (O), supper

EXERCISE 10   Pronouns

1. it
2. he and she, him and her, they or them
3. it or she or he or him or her
4. he or she or him or her
5. it or they or them
6. it
7. he or him
8. they or them
9. He or She; it
10. They; her
11. They; them
12. She; him or her
13. He; it, they; him
14. He; it
15. They; her or him

EXERCISE 11   Subject and Object Nouns and Pronouns

1. (We) (S) cream (O), icing
2. Rhonda (S) poem (O), childhood
3. mayor (S) gallery (O), Calgary
4. (he) (S) reports (O), meeting, home
5. (I) (S) parade (O), hours
6. Books (S) papers (S) (no object), nothing
7. (we) (S) voices (O), night, backyard
8. John (S) (I) (S) charge (O), hearing
9. (She) (S) (it) (O)
10. Al (S) meat (O), counter; (it)
11. (You) (S) cold (O) chills (O), weather
12. (I) (S) Joe (O) (her) (O), tennis
13. (We) (S) program (O); audience (S) (it) O
14. dogs (S) cat (S) squirrel (O), tree
15. (He) (S) window (O), office; door (O), evening

EXERCISE 13   Action Verbs

1. rang
2. caught, carried
3. (no action verb)
4. swims
5. seeded, tamped
6. cooked, went
7. drove
8. traded, bought
9. understood, winked
10. wrote

EXERCISE 14   *Action and Non-Action Verbs*

1. lay, panted ACT
2. is NO ACT
3. had NO ACT, discovered ACT, was NO ACT
4. smells NO ACT, sounds NO ACT
5. were NO ACT, entered ACT
6. said ACT is NO ACT
7. interviewed ACT
8. are NO ACT
9. purchased ACT
10. will be NO ACT
11. was NO ACT, crawled ACT
12. is NO ACT

EXERCISE 16   *Identifying Verb Tense*

1. <u>has been wanting</u> present perfect progressive
2. <u>had left</u> past perfect
3. <u>have been standing</u> present perfect progressive
4. <u>had loved</u> past perfect
5. <u>is running</u> present progressive; <u>expects</u> simple present
6. <u>knew</u> simple past; <u>was drinking</u> past progressive
7. <u>had been sold</u> past perfect; <u>selected</u> simple past
8. <u>can be</u> simple present; <u>will ask</u> simple future
9. <u>were fighting</u> past progressive
10. <u>will have written</u> future perfect; <u>arrive</u> simple present
11. <u>have gone</u> present perfect
12. <u>suspected</u> simple past; <u>was sitting</u> past progressive

EXERCISE 18   *Adding Verb Forms*

1. written
2. forgiven
3. taken
4. broken
5. thrown, replaced
6. known, passed
7. saw, failed
8. given, swam
9. ridden
10. began, lit
11. spoken
12. became
13. chosen
14. written
15. given

COMBINED REVIEW EXERCISE 19

Here are some suggested answers. Your answers will differ; however, examine the samples for help in checking your own sentences.

1. Skye is providing assistance to the lost passenger from the tour bus.

Skye is the subject noun. *Is providing* is a verb in the present progressive. *Assistance* is the object noun.

2. The attendant and the patient will have flown to Ottawa by the time the hospital contacts them.

The attendant and the patient are two subject nouns. *Will have flown* is in the future perfect tense and uses the past participle of *fly.*

3. The young offender had been stealing cars, threatening his parents, and selling drugs; finally he was caught and charged with possession of an illegal weapon.

Had been stealing, (had been) *threatening*, and (had been) *selling* are all verbs in the past perfect progressive tense.

4. The clown and the juggler had spun the plates and the fishbowls on short poles when the circus tent began to collapse.

The clown and the juggler is a compound noun; *the plates and the fishbowls* is a compound object; *had spun* is past perfect tense.

5. The bank had frozen his accounts, and the court had frozen his assets.

Had frozen is in the past tense; *frozen* is the past participle of *freeze*. The *bank* and *court* are the subjects; *accounts* and *assets* are the objects.

Chapter 12: Subjects and Verbs

Self-Test: Part 1   Subject and Verb Identification

1. Sasha (S) Lowell (S) booked (V)
2. druggist (S) filled (V), left (V)
3. Lucinda (S) comes (V)
4. flies (S) were (V) buzzing (V)
5. Several of the customers (S) were (V)
6. child (S) seemed (V); we (S) took (V)
7. economy (S) is (V); companies (S) view (V)
8. we (S) spotted (V)
9. ice cream (S) is (V); people (S) choose (V)

Self-Test: Part 2   Subject–Verb Agreement

1. wants
2. were
3. is
4. pours
5. perform
6. is
7. are
8. make
9. Is
10. Have

Self-Test: Part 3   Identification of Subjects

1. Dawn (S) niece (S)
2. One (S)
3. case (S)
4. manager (S)
5. Marcus (S) Leo (S)
6. hoot (S)
7. instructor (S)
8. one (S)

Self-Test: Part 4   Subject–Verb Identification

1. controllers (S) direct (V) that (S) are heading (V)
2. Rafella (S) lawyer (S) left (V) who (S) had clustered (V)
3. places (S) were (V) lovers (S) could meet (V)
4. Tons (S) tons (S) are found (V) most (S) comes (V) that (S) has fallen (V)
5. Marci MacDonald (S) says (V) pollution (S) is blamed (V)

Self-Test: Part 5   Subject–Verb Agreement

1. was
2. are
3. Has
4. is
5. (correct)
6. goes
7. were
8. (correct)
9. was
10. owns
11. was
12. checks
13. have
14. are
15. harmonizes

EXERCISE 1   Subjects and Verbs

1. children (S) are (V)
2. We (S) whispered (V)
3. daughter (S) is (V)
4. Maxwell (S) worked (V)
5. I (S) phoned (V)
6. She (S) is (V)
7. You (S) should (not) make (V) you (S) will receive (V)
8. friend (S) was (V)
9. They (S) drank (V)
10. Margaret (S) lives (V)

EXERCISE 3   Verb Phrases

1. is working
2. has been driving, has enjoyed
3. has won
4. must write, will lose
5. should go, will be staging
6. are deciding
7. was picking, (was) chewing
8. can leave, will have

9. has had, met
10. may have been writing, must visit

EXERCISE 4   Verbs, Verb Phrases, and Subjects

1. Being a general (S) means one (S) must review dismiss
2. hikers (S) guide (S) were prepared
3. networks (S) should have been broadcasting making
4. approach (S) leaves history (S) is
5. mother (S) worries gives I (S) follow
6. environmentalists (S) have called ecosystems (S) have established
7. biologist (S) assistants (S) might have been coerced
8. article (S) suggests eating lightly on a hot day (S) may prevent
9. Adriana (S) mentor (S) had entered they (S) understood
10. Norman Spector (S) says (No) price (S) is (no) effort (S) should be spared few (S) are we (S) 've (have) met

EXERCISE 5   Prepositional Phrases

1. Across the valley
2. along the river; near some rocks
3. of bears; at the park gate
4. for the flock; of snow geese
5. in a foreign language
6. on the stage; of the show
7. against the odds
8. Near the swamp; beside a clump; of weeds
9. through the crowd; of protesters
10. behind the counter

EXERCISE 7   More about Prepositional Phrases

1. from a dealer (where) in Edmonton (where)
2. in the woods (where)
3. of snakeskin (what)
4. against the strong winter wind (how)
5. After the game (when)
6. from Jamaica (where) until Sunday (when)
7. on the floor (where)
8. of magpies (what) in the trees (where)
9. of flowers (what)
10. under the bridge (where)

EXERCISE 8   Verbs, Verb Phrases, Subjects, and Prepositional Phrases

1. (At the party) I (S) met (from Yellowknife) who (S) talked (about white water rafting)
2. One (S) (of the horses) escaped (from the corral ran (onto the highway)
3. driver (S) (of the commercial truck) fell (at the wheel)
4. raise (S) (of $300) was (to him)
5. bunch (S) (of flowers) arrived (for you) (by special delivery)
6. winners (S) (of the race) stayed (at the racetrack) (for a photograph) (in the winners' circle)
7. marks (S) (for his mechanics exams) were he (S) hired (for extra help)
8. (After the storm) game (S) continued fans (S) sat (on soggy benches)
9. ducks (S) loons (S) were feeding (near the shore)
10. master (S) (of ceremonies) tripped (on his way) (to the podium)

EXERCISE 9   Subject–Verb Agreement and Detail Phrases

1. are (on the desk)
2. is (to the doors) (on the wall)
3. drives (from Flin Flon)
4. is (of men) (in pay)
5. have (of the students)
6. are (in the fridge)
7. was (Up the hill) (over the bridge)
8. prepares (In the mornings) (for her family)
9. irritates (of cigarettes)
10. go (of those items)

EXERCISE 11   Verbs and Commands

1. You (S) stack (V)
2. you (S) offer (V)
3. You (S) distribute (V)
4. you (S) remove (V)
5. you (S) arrange (V)
6. You (S) stop (V)

EXERCISE 12   One and Each

1. goes
2. was
3. gives
4. is
5. needs
6. has

EXERCISE 14   Subject–Verb Agreement

1. is
2. were
3. is
4. goes
5. makes, demands
6. are
7. have
8. have, need
9. were
10. is

Chapter 13: Modifiers

Self-Test: Part 1   Finding Adjectives

1. ashamed, greedy
2. impatient, convenience
3. fresh, lemon
4. historic, wonderful, beautiful
5. excited, light-fingered, bustling
6. young, imposing, dinosaur
7. thick, blueberry
8. shaggy, stone
9. strong
10. (no adjectives)

Self-Test: Part 2   Finding Adverbs

1. quietly
2. Today, usually
3. desperately, quite, dangerously
4. intensely, now
5. certainly, unexpectedly, tomorrow
6. excitedly, not
7. extremely, just, however
8. (no adverbs)
9. tightly, then
10. commonly, rather well

Self-Test: Part 3   Finding Prepositional Phrases

1. (Despite the weather) (in the rain)
2. (about the exam) (on Monday) (with anyone)
3. (at the farmers' market) (on Blunt Street)
4. (in the lunchroom)
5. (for a beer) (at the hotel)
6. (in a short time)
7. (of students) (on the platform)

Self-Test: Part 4   Identifying Adjective and Adverb Prepositional Phrases

1. (from Brazil) ADJ (to immigration officials) ADV
2. (of pumpkins) ADJ (of sunflowers) ADJ (of the hall) ADJ
3. (of the planks) ADJ (from the deck) ADV

4. (through the mall) ADV (about their plans) ADV
5. (in her arms) ADV

Self-Test: Part 5   Using Comparisons

1. better	6. most
2. most	7. more
3. worst	8. better
4. better	9. More
5. least	10. better

Self-Test: Part 6   Your Own Sentences

Please show your work to your instructor.

Self-Test: Part 7   Usage

1. really
2. badly
3. well
4. well
5. bad

EXERCISE 3   *Adjectives That Compare*

1. bad, worse *or* good, better
2. best
3. worst *or* worse
4. better *or* worse
5. worst
6. most
7. most
8. more *or* less
9. most
10. more *or* less
11. more *or* less
12. most *or* least
13. more *or* less
14. more *or* less
15. better *or* worse

EXERCISE 5   *Adverbs*

1. Often, really, freely
2. lazily, just
3. seldom, too
4. sadly, slowly, weakly
5. very, usually, happily
6. never, quite
7. usually, there, almost
8. often, somewhat
9. always, very, generously
10. scarcely, strangely
11. perfectly, fluently
12. unhappily, just, too
13. furiously, then
14. beautifully, almost, never
15. somewhat, so, loudly

EXERCISE 6   *Adverbs*

1. really, carefully, yesterday
2. neatly, outside
3. noisily, over, there
4. clumsily
5. most
6. Here, recently
7. Seldom, intentionally
8. ferociously
9. Yesterday, quietly, happily
10. rarely, anywhere
11. Bravely, back
12. early, later
13. shyly
14. Immediately
15. Slowly, quietly
16. less
17. Today, brightly
18. too
19. more
20. extremely
21. Honestly, not, rarely
22. more, always
23. down, calmly, clearly
24. softly
25. Tomorrow, quite
26. loudly, angrily
27. so, blankly
28. completely, strongly
29. casually, immediately
30. hardly, extremely, well

EXERCISE 9   *Prepositional Phrases*

1. (Between you and me) (in honour) (of their parents' wedding anniversary)
2. (of flames and melted rock)
3. (of embroidery) (in many cultures) (of the world)
4. (in a bog) (near Copetown, Ontario)
5. (In case) (of an emergency) (beside the patient)
6. (in the waters) (around Vancouver Island)
7. (for children) (of their homes and parents) (behind them)

8. (Inside the tunnel) (from beneath them)
9. (for their great beauty) (despite their irritating voices)
10. (of clay) (in the centre) (of her wheel) (with her foot)
11. (Along the edges) (of the field) (of a red-brown mineral)
12. (of jewels) (without a trace)
13. (Across the open meadows) (through the thickets and forests) (to safety)
14. (in my notebook) (on Wednesday)
15. (Below the surface) (of the water) (of tiny blue fish)
16. (in the scene) (except Vicki) (with the nature hike)
17. (of wine) (for me)
18. (in a tangle) (of old fishing lines) (below the wharf)
19. (into my business) (about me)

EXERCISE 10   Adjective or Adverb Prepositional Phrases

1. (On Sunday afternoon) ADV (on the grounds) ADV (for a reunion) ADV
2. (of the dogs) ADJ (in the playground) ADV (on tricycles) ADJ
3. (in the city) ADJ (for better wages) ADV
4. (in the sun hat) ADJ (for the finest carnations) ADJ
5. (Inside the house) ADV (around the kitchen) ADV (for their dinner) ADV
6. (of salmon) ADJ (from the chemical spill) ADV (of garden fertilizer) ADJ
7. (at the large, decorated table) ADV (about the celebration) ADV (of her eightieth birthday) ADJ
8. (from the American ship) ADJ (on Government Street) ADJ
9. (from that region) ADJ (of the globe) ADJ (of their new Canadian home) ADJ
10. (during the Gulf War) ADV (by various countries) ADV
11. (on the upper deck) ADV (of the large ferry) ADJ
12. (with this heavy couch) ADV (to the other side) ADV (of the room) ADJ
13. (by the other man's threats) ADV (within a few minutes) ADV
14. (in the little blue sneakers) ADJ (of chocolate ice cream) ADJ
15. (of biscuits) ADJ (from Britain) ADV
16. (On an evening) ADV (during the winter) ADV (in the fourth quadrant) ADV (of the galaxy) ADJ

17. (On Laugh Night) ADV (on Tuesday) ADV (at the downtown bar) ADV (to a silent audience) ADV
18. (of campers) ADJ (along the beach) ADV (at low tide) ADV
19. (of blackbirds) ADJ (in the treetops) ADV
20. (of crunchies) ADJ (with a large saucer) ADV (of milk) ADJ
21. (of books) ADJ (up the stairs) ADV (down the hall) ADV (into my room) ADV (on the shelf) ADV (over my bed) ADJ
22. (of roses) ADJ (inside the basket) ADV (of chocolates) ADJ
23. (Despite my protests) ADV (on the trip) ADV

EXERCISE 13   Adjective and Adverb Usage

1. really *or* badly
2. really
3. badly—good *or* real
4. badly
5. really bad
6. well *or* badly
7. bad *or* real *or* good
8. bad—really *or* badly
9. really
10. real
11. really
12. well
13. really—badly *or* well
14. good *or* real—badly
15. bad—real *or* good
16. well *or* badly
17. well *or* badly
18. well *or* badly
19. real

Chapter 14: Punctuation and Capitalization

Self-Test: Part 1   Comma Use

1. beaver, eagle, bulldog,
2. finished,
3. soil, lumps, seedlings, labels, wagons, site,
4. 10, 1871,
5. (correct)
6. bang, I understand,
7. (correct)

8. day, yard,
9. 12, 1988, 16,
10. course, sarcastic, stupid,

Self-Test: Part 2 Semicolon Use

1. hutch;
2. tourist;
3. (correct)
4. broken;
5. hospital;
6. green;
7. myself;
8. (correct)
9. electronics;
10. treasure;
11. night;
12. classics;
13. pulpit;
14. (correct)

Self-Test: Part 3 Colon Use

1. parts:
2. secret:
3. gifts:
4. ridiculous:
5. (correct)
6. material:
7. orders:

Self-Test: Part 4 Commas, Colons, and Semicolons

1. students; level, schedules,
2. (correct)
3. payment, rent, limit;
4. communication; is, functions,
5. He, hand, platform; however,
6. Page, Atwood, Canada; States, Britain,
7. circle;
8. secret:

Self-Test: Part 5 Capitalization

1. Monday Uncle Robert Four Roads Motel
2. Toronto
3. Royal Canadian Mounted Police Port Renfrew
4. We Swiss French
5. Credit Union Saturdays Fridays
6. Mrs. Walsh Department Mines Resources
7. Safeway Coke Lansdowne Junior High School

EXERCISE 1 Using Commas

1. town, Dylan, Cohen,
2. baby, wash, calls, dinner,
3. (correct)
4. (correct)
5. Alberta, Columbia, Saskatchewan,
6. (correct)
7. Barbara, California, Portland,

8. cakes, cookies, juice,
9. sugar, butter,
10. dough, batter, buns, breads, baked, sorted,
11. pink, red, orange, blue,
12. breakfast, egg, toast, jam,
13. Baden Baden, Germany, 22, 6,
14. Winnipeg, Manitoba, Edmonton, Alberta, Current,
15. Rice, wheat, lentils,

EXERCISE 3 Using Commas

1. glue, nails, bits,
2. anxiety, marks,
3. Sydney, Australia, Tuesday, 23,
4. (correct)
5. Squirrels, chipmunks, rats,
6. ham, bacon,
7. beads, blocks, drawing, painting, whispering, listening,
8. psychology, philosophy,
9. (correct)
10. jalapeño, vinegar,
11. Hamilton, Ontario,
12. roll, blues,
13. sugar, milk,
14. Mo, Alice, Amanda,
15. Saturday, 1,
16. Vancouver, Oshawa,
17. Apples, quinces,
18. interesting, informative,
19. stairs, bedroom, doors,
20. wage, conditions,
21. Poodles, terriers, spaniels,
22. refrigerator, steps, fence,
23. Valencia, Mandarin,
24. 11,
25. résumés, interviews, techniques,

EXERCISE 5 Complex Sentences

1. (Since he fought with his sister), <u>little Edward was sent to his room</u>
2. (While Jens was baking the bread), <u>we prepared the salad</u>.
3. <u>You can clean the windows</u> (after you have your lunch)
4. <u>Some of the animals of the forest were frightened</u> (because the wind was so strong) (no comma)

5. (Unless I win the chess game), <u>I will be disappointed</u>

6. <u>She waited at the campus</u> (until her boyfriend picked her up) (no comma)

7. (As Mario opened the library book), <u>a $20 bill fell to the floor.</u>

8. (Since my uncle is a nervous fellow), <u>the doctor has advised him to avoid driving in rush hour traffic</u>

9. <u>The dog couldn't decide</u> (if she wanted to bury the bone or not) (no comma)

10. (While her parents were on vacation), <u>the teenager threw a wild party at the house</u>

11. <u>The supervisor will call you</u> (if there is any work) (no comma)

12. (As Rodney turned to get the box of cereal from the store shelf), <u>a mouse scampered ... bins</u>

13. (Because the snowstorm blew down some heavy trees and took out hydro lines), <u>power was lost in most of the city</u>

14. <u>Max was elected president of the club</u> (because he is a tremendous organizer) (no comma)

EXERCISE 6   Group Activity: The Semicolon

1. dogs;
2. OK
3. up;
4. OK
5. OK
6. project;
7. lot,
8. (no semicolon)
9. (no semicolon)
10. OK
11. OK
12. church,
13. OK
14. OK
15. state,

EXERCISE 7   Colon Use

1. (no colon)
2. (no colon)
3. OK
4. OK
5. (no colon)
6. OK
7. (no colon)
8. (no colon)
9. worsening:
10. OK

EXERCISE 10   Using Apostrophes

1. Zoe's she's
2. children's
3. men's
4. golfer's
5. cat's
6. Anna's
7. ship's passengers'
8. They'll
9. hospital's he'd Dad's
10. We're you're sheep's

EXERCISE 11   Capitalization

1. Has Uncle Fred Doctor Robinson
2. Did I Uncle Seth
3. The Mr. Eng
4. Early Superintendent Davis
5. Inspector Gladeau Chief Beckley

EXERCISE 12   Capitalization

1. *A Whale Killing* Farley Mowat Canadian
2. Many Indo–Canadian India
3. My I Christmas Halifax
4. Last Tuesday March April
5. Did Gwen English Italian Spanish
6. Mark *Twelve Days Better Body*
7. A Dr. Johnson Red Deer
8. New Year's Day Canadian
9. The French Moncton
10. Chef Schneider German

Chapter 15: Patterns of Sentences

Self-Test: Part 1   Identifying Patterns of Sentences

1. complex
2. compound
3. simple
4. compound
5. simple
6. complex
7. complex
8. compound
9. simple
10. compound
11. complex
12. simple
13. simple
14. complex
15. compound

Self-Test: Part 2   Identifying Clauses

1. (While you were at the store) <u>the office supervisor called you</u>

2. (Although the wind was strong) <u>no property was damaged</u>

3. <u>Please ask Adara</u> (if she is coming with us)
4. <u>Ronald played the violin</u> (until he was 12 years old)
5. <u>Tell me</u> (when Christopher can meet at the conference)
6. <u>We're having a celebration</u> (after our last exam is over)
7. (Since she left) <u>I've been lonely</u>
8. <u>The fishers caught some whitefish</u> (when they went out yesterday)
9. (As the child walked) <u>he whistled</u>
10. (When we were away last weekend) <u>the power was off at our house</u>

EXERCISE 4   Simple and Compound Sentences

1. S	8. S
2. S	9. C
3. S	10. C
4. C	11. S
5. C	12. S
6. S	13. C
7. C	

EXERCISE 5   Two Types of Clauses

1. Because we had a party last night (D), we're exhausted today (M).
2. A salesperson will help you (M) if you ring the bell (D).
3. When Mrs. Singh was in Europe (D), she visited Rome (M).
4. The kids were watching television (M) as we were playing cards (D).
5. Although Maxine is a qualified welder (D), she can't find work (M).
6. Before you go to bed (D), let the cat out (M).
7. After his family telephoned (D), Acton was depressed (M).
8. Since Aileen won't be able to be in class tomorrow (D), I'll collect the assignment for her (M).
9. If I tell you about it (D), will you keep it a secret (M)?
10. Because her son had the measles (D), Dotti missed a week of classes (M).
11. When he went for the interview (D), he lost his glasses (M).
12. He twisted his ankle (M) while he was water skiing (D).
13. If the baby cries (D), pick her up (M).

14. I wanted to go to Montreal (M), although I couldn't afford the trip (D).
15. The game was exciting (M) because the two teams were very competitive (D).
16. After the new manager was appointed (D), the employees became suspicious (M).

EXERCISE 6   Clauses and Complex Sentences

1. CONDITION	8. CONDITION
2. TIME	9. TIME
3. CONDITION	10. TIME
4. TIME	11. TIME
5. CONDITION	12. TIME
6. CONDITION	13. CONDITION
7. TIME	

EXERCISE 9   Simple, Compound, and Complex Sentences

1. SIMPLE	11. SIMPLE
2. COMPLEX	12. COMPOUND
3. COMPLEX	13. SIMPLE
4. SIMPLE	14. COMPOUND
5. COMPOUND	15. COMPOUND
6. COMPLEX	16. COMPLEX
7. COMPLEX	17. COMPLEX
8. SIMPLE	18. COMPOUND
9. COMPOUND	19. SIMPLE
10. SIMPLE	20. SIMPLE

EXERCISE 13   Review of Simple, Compound, and Complex Sentences

1. C, but	9. C, but
2. CX, appliance	10. CX, college
3. S	11. S, efforts
4. C, but	12. CX
5. S	13. C
6. C, and	14. CX, field
7. CX	15. CX, condo
8. S	

Chapter 16: Sentence-Level Errors

Self-Test: Part 1   Identifying Fragments and Sentences

1. FRAG	4. S
2. FRAG	5. S
3. FRAG	6. FRAG

7. FRAG	9. FRAG
8. FRAG	10. S

Self-Test: Part 2   Identifying Run-ons and Sentences

1. RO	6. RO
2. S	7. RO
3. RO	8. S
4. S	9. RO
5. S	10. RO

Self-Test: Part 3   Identifying Fragments and Run-on Faults

1. RO	6. RO
2. RO	7. FRAG
3. S	8. FRAG
4. FRAG	9. S
5. S	10. RO

Self-Test: Part 4   Finding and Repairing Fragments and Run-ons

Please show your work to the instructor.

Self-Test: Part 5   Repairing Sentence Faults

Please show your work to the instructor.

EXERCISE 1   *Fragments*

1. FRAG	11. FRAG
2. FRAG	12. S
3. S	13. S
4. FRAG	14. FRAG
5. S	15. FRAG
6. FRAG	16. S
7. FRAG	17. S
8. S	18. FRAG
9. S	19. FRAG
10. S	20. S

EXERCISE 3   *Run-on Sentences*

1. The young couple was arguing about the rent money; however, they seemed to settle their differences.
2. Two of the bank managers were fired from their positions; the government inspectors had found serious errors in their accounting systems.—*or*—Two of the bank managers were fired from their positions because the government inspectors had found serious errors in their accounting systems.
3. Daisy loves to play baseball in the spring; her husband, Arnold, likewise loves the game.

—*or*—Daisy loves to play baseball in the spring, and her husband, Arnold, likewise loves the game.
4. The teacher wanted to encourage discussion about Chaucer; many students, on the other hand, were more interested in Shakespeare.—*or*—The teacher wanted to encourage discussion about Chaucer. Many students, on the other hand, were more interested in Shakespeare.
5. I found the shoes very uncomfortable; however, I could not return them because the store had gone out of business.—*or*—I found the shoes very uncomfortable. However, I could not return them because the store had gone out of business.
6. On election night, the crowd gathered around the favoured candidate; they cheered her every word.—*or*—On election night, the crowd gathered around the favoured candidate. They cheered her every word.
7. CORRECT
8. CORRECT
9. After the severe rains, most of the plains were flooded; as a result, the farmers could not sow their crops until late spring.—*or*—After the severe rains, most of the plains were flooded. As a result, the farmers could not sow their crops until late spring.
10. CORRECT
11. The garden store in the new mall was a success; the bookstore located near it was not successful, however.—*or*—The garden store in the new mall was a success. The bookstore located near it was not successful, however.
12. The magician turned to us with a smile; then he disappeared.—*or*—The magician turned to us with a smile, and then he disappeared.—*or*—The magician turned to us with a smile. Then he disappeared.
13. Crystal loves to collect antique coins and jewellery; she travels all over Canada making her purchases.—*or*—Crystal loves to collect antique coins and jewellery. She travels all over Canada making her purchases.—*or*—Crystal loves to collect antique coins and jewellery, and she travels all over Canada making her purchases.

EXERCISE 4   Run-on Sentences

1. S	10. RO
2. RO	11. S
3. RO	12. S
4. S	13. RO
5. RO	14. S
6. S	15. S
7. S	16. RO
8. RO	17. RO
9. RO	18. S

EXERCISE 6   Pronoun Reference

1. Erica told Gabrielle, "I am coming to lunch."
    Gabrielle told Erica, "I am coming to lunch."
    Gabrielle was coming to lunch, and she told Erica about it.
    Erica was coming to lunch, and she told Gabrielle about it.
2. People could get a special pass to see the clipper ship and meet the crew; this possibility made them very enthusiastic.
3. Everyone in the lineup must have their identification cards verified (non-sexist).
    Everyone in the lineup must have his/her identification card verified.
4. When Elvis recorded his first song in 1955, he quickly became popular.
5. Roger bought a new portfolio for art school, and he told Hasim all about it.
    Hasim bought a new portfolio, and he told Roger all about it.
    Hasim told Roger, "You should see my new portfolio for art school."
    Roger told Hasim, "You should see my new portfolio for art school."
6. The boy was caught speeding and driving without a licence, and this behaviour shocked his parents.
7. Every boy can have his own racquet on the court.
8. Kimi sent Tina to pick up the team uniforms after Tina returned from the game.
    Kimi sent Tina to pick up the team uniforms after Melissa returned from the game.
9. Every woman was given her own set of documents for the meeting.
10. Some of the girls brought their own lunches.
11. Mrs. Norman asked Bernice (or another name) if she would sing at the reception.
12. No one really knew who the missing man was, but everyone had a theory about who he was.
    No one really knew who the missing man was, but everyone had a theory about what had happened to him.

EXERCISE 7   Group Activity: Shift Errors

1. Helen is pleased with the promotion; she intends to do well in her new position as manager.
2. The epidemic spread throughout the countryside, and the doctors attempted to inoculate all residents.
3. If you want to learn about fruit farming, you should talk to an orchardist.
    If one wants to learn about fruit farming, one should talk to an orchardist.
4. Lola had never tried parachute jumping before; she listened carefully to the instructor's directions.
5. Several children were playing hopscotch and skipping, but they did not hear the sound of the siren.
6. The stunt crew was setting up outside the Empress Hotel, and they had some expensive technical equipment.
7. If you don't know about it, you should ask.
    If one doesn't know about it, one should ask.
8. Because it was the long weekend, the trailer park was packed with vehicles.
9. Everyone should be careful about getting too much sun exposure if they do not want to increase the risk of skin cancer. *or* . . . if he or she does not want to increase the risk . . .
10. After we discussed the idea, we left.
    After we discuss the idea, we leave.

EXERCISE 9   Sentence Faults

1. All of the girls wanted to get their camping gear at the same sporting goods store.
2. Although he knew the shed really needed an undercoat, Bobby felt too lazy to do the job properly.
3. Some foods are rich in beta carotene.
    Some foods rich in beta carotene are said to be very healthful in our diets.

4. At the registration desk, Alan rented a locker and paid for it for one term at the college.

5. My friend Baker is very photogenic; however, she does not like having her picture taken.

   My friend Baker is very photogenic. However, she does not like having her picture taken.

6. We could safeguard against accidents in the home if we just paid attention to safety details.

   One could safeguard against accidents in the home if one just paid attention to safety details.

7. Sodium fluoride has been added to the water system of the city, despite the fact that many claim this chemical is poisonous.

8. Walter really wanted to build a solar house; he checked the building regulations with the regional planning office.

   Walter really wanted to build a solar house, so he checked the building regulations with the regional planning office.

   Walter really wanted to build a solar house. He checked the building regulations with the regional planning office.

9. The family bought a tandem bicycle; they particularly wanted to use it on vacation.

10. The weary visitors were so exhausted after their long flight from Taiwan that they fell asleep immediately.

11. Her testimony at the trial is necessary to the defence.

    Her testimony at the trial was necessary to the defence.

12. Walking, riding, and climbing were her exercise manias. *or* To walk, to ride, and to climb . . .

EXERCISE 10   *Sentence Faults*

1. It seems the whole world is fearful of terrorist attacks.

   It seems the whole world was fearful of terrorist attacks.

   It seems the whole world, fearful of terrorist attacks, is heightening security measures.

2. Everyone should decide what is best for their own children.

   Everyone should decide what is best for his or her own children.

3. Woody Allen became renowned as a popular stand-up comic; moreover, his fame earned him a job as a screenwriter.

   Woody Allen became renowned as a popular stand-up comic. Moreover, his fame earned him a job as a screenwriter.

4. Since that terry cloth robe was so expensive, it should look better after only three washings.

5. Because Lord Peakinloft managed his estate well, he was left with no debt.

   Because Lord Peakinloft managed his estate well, his heirs were left with no debt.

   Because Lord Peakinloft managed his estate well, his estate was left with no debt.

6. The Morgan brothers had a contract to do all the plumbing in the new housing development; then their company went bankrupt.

   The Morgan brothers had a contract to do all the plumbing in the new housing development, and then their company went bankrupt.

   The Morgan brothers had a contract to do all the plumbing in the new housing development. Then their company went bankrupt.

7. The selector on our stereo was broken, and the technician couldn't fix it.

8. With all the self-assurance of a king, Marmaduke entered the ballroom.

9. The soggy tomato sandwiches did not make an appetizing lunch when we went on the picnic.

10. The tea tastes bitter; perhaps it has been brewed too long.

11. The proprietor of the bed and breakfast wants to please all of her guests.

12. Some people enjoy sewing because they find sewing their own clothes saves money.

13. Although the condo is small, there is plenty of storage space in the basement.

14. You ought to check with the head server before you make a complaint.

    One ought to check with the head server before one makes a complaint.

15. He and his brother Manny bought a cottage near Bala, and they love going to it on weekends.

Paragraph 1: Punctuation and the Use of the Apostrophe in Possessives

No one knew who was to inherit Mrs. Blethershotts' estate and her enormous fortune; it remained a great mystery to everyone. Because Ethyl the maid had remained in Mrs. Blethershotts' service for so long, all of the staff expected her to receive some small compensation for her years of loyalty. The butler Archibald felt certain he was to win something as well; he had served the Blethershott Manor for over 40 years, and he had not had one day's absence from his duties. It was the cook's opinion that she should receive the most. She had done three things, in her opinion, which counted the most: served fresh nutritious food to the Mistress, kept a tight budget, and made herself available to the Mistress' every whim. The chauffeur Kendrick did not agree that the other members of staff were worthy of receiving any more than a few dollars. Since he had arrived at Blethershott Manor, he had given the Blethershotts his devoted attention. Not once had he complained about their unreasonable demands. In fact, Kendrick had said very little; moreover, he now believed he was the most likely to inherit. Everyone's suspicion had begun to create peculiar tension in the household; no one seemed able to sleep the night before the reading of the will.

Paragraph 2: Fragments, Run-ons, Comma Splices

Taking children to their first day of daycare can be an unnerving experience for new parents. The tearful and loud protests of a child can make even the most calm parent _feel_ flustered and guilty. Weeks in advance, many parents try to explain to their children what wonderful places daycares are _because_ the parents are trying to avoid the "big scene" on the daycare steps. Some children seem to listen carefully and to understand what their parents are telling them. Some children seem to understand their parents' explanation fully; these children seem relaxed and happy about the new arrangement. Of course, once the new parents and their new daycare students arrive at the destination, it becomes another matter entirely. Teachers, students, parents, assistants, and children all seem to be talking at once. Frightened and anxious faces tell the tale because no one seems to want to leave, and no one seems to want to stay! It is hard to imagine that in just a few short weeks, most children seem to love their new "schools" and welcome each day's activities.

Paragraph 3: Parallelism and Adjective and Adverb Use

According to *Monday Magazine*, Victoria is Canada's "city of poisons" because of the overuse of pesticides and herbicides by residential gardeners. Sellers are enthusiastic to sell these chemicals. The situation has naturalists and environmentalists _really_ upset. *Monday Magazine*, April 24–30, 1997, states that "some of these compounds are tested for their cancer-causing potential, but most have been introduced without any assessment of their effects on the immune and nervous systems" (8). To ensure that gardening chemicals are being used <u>well</u>, to eliminate their overuse, and <u>to control</u> garden pests and diseases will take better management on the part of the industry and government. There are still few laws that are <u>really</u> effective and enforceable. For example, although many residential gardeners in Victoria feel <u>bad</u> about the harm that garden chemical agents create, these same citizens continue to use agents such as malathion, propoxur, and captan. These chemicals act very <u>slowly</u> on the environment, and years later, dangerous traces can be found in the soil and the drinking water supply. Beneficial insects, songbirds, garter snakes, and amphibians are also <u>surely</u> harmed by the abuse and overuse of commonly available garden chemicals.

Chapter 17 ESL Pointers

EXERCISE 2   *Count and Non-Count Nouns*

1. freedom
2. work
3. correct
4. traffic
5. garbage
6. correct
7. popcorn
8. correct
9. housework
10. correct

EXERCISE 3   *Indefinite Articles*

1. a
2. an
3. a
4. a
5. a
6. an
7. a
8. a
9. a
10. an
11. an
12. an
13. a
14. a
15. an
16. an

EXERCISE 4   *Articles*

1. an
2. The
3. no article
4. no article
5. an
6. no article
7. a
8. no article
9. no article
10. the, the
11. no article
12. an, the
13. An
14. a
15. the
16. an
17. The
18. the, a *or* the
19. the
20. the

EXERCISE 5   *Expressions of Quantity*

1. some, any, most, more, all, a lot of, many, several, a few, a couple of, both
2. some, much, more, less, a lot of, very little, no
3. each, every, any, one, some, most, more, all, a lot of, many, several, a few, a couple of, both
4. some, most, more, all, a lot of, no
5. some, any, most, more, all, a lot of, many, several, a few, a couple of, both, few, fewer
6. a little, some, any, much, more, all, less, a lot of, very little, no
7. some, any, more, all, few, fewer, a lot of, no, many, several, a few, a couple of, both
8. any, some, most, more, all, a lot of, a little, much, less, very little, no
9. any, some, most, more, a lot of, a little, much, all, less, very little, no
10. some, any, most, more, all, a lot of, many, several, a few, a couple of, both, no
11. some, any, most, more, all, a lot of, a little, much, no
12. each, every, any, one, no
13. some, any, most, more, all, a lot of, many, several, a few, a couple of, both, no
14. each, every, any, one, no

EXERCISE 7   *Transitions*

1. Blank 1 (First, To begin with, In the first place)
   Blank 2 (Next, After that, Later, Secondly, Afterward, Soon, After a while, In due time, Then, Meanwhile, Following that)
   Blank 3 (Finally, Lastly)
2. Blank 1 (First, To begin with, In the first place)
   Blank 2 (Next, After that, Later, Secondly, Afterward, Soon, After a while, In due time, Then, Meanwhile, Following that)
   Blank 3 (Then, After that, Later, Meanwhile, Afterward, Finally, Soon, Following that, After a while, Thirdly, In due time, Next)

Blank 4 (next, after that, later, fourthly, afterward, soon, after a while, in due time, then, meanwhile, following that)

Blank 5 (Next, After that, Later, Fifthly, Afterward, Soon, After a while, In due time, Then, Meanwhile, Following that, Last, Finally)

3. Blank 1 (First, To begin with, In the first place)

Blank 2 (Next, After that, Later, Secondly, Afterward, Soon, After a while, In due time, Then, Meanwhile, Following that)

Blank 3 (Next, After that, Later, Thirdly, Afterward, Soon, After a while, In due time, Then, Meanwhile, Following that, Last, Finally)

4. Blank 1 (First, To begin with, In the first place)

Blanks 2 and 3 (Next, After that, Later, Secondly, Thirdly, Afterward, Soon, After a while, In due time, Then, Meanwhile, Following that)

Blank 4 (Next, After that, Later, Fourthly, Afterward, Soon, After a while, In due time, Then, Meanwhile, Following that, Last, Finally)

5. Blank 1 (First, To begin with, In the first place)

Blank 2 (next, after that, later, secondly, afterward, soon, after a while, in due time, then, meanwhile, following that, last, finally)

6. Blank 1 (First, To begin with, In the first place)

Blank 2 (Next, After that, Later, Secondly, Afterward, Soon, After a while, In due time, Then, Meanwhile, Following that)

Blank 3 (Next, After that, Later, Thirdly, Afterward, Soon, After a while, In due time, Then, Meanwhile, Following that, Last, Finally)

7. Blank 1 (first, to begin with, in the first place)

Blanks 2 and 3 (Next, After that, Later, Secondly, Thirdly, Afterward, Soon, After a while, In due time, Then, Meanwhile, Following that)

Blank 4 (Next, After that, Later, Fourthly, Afterward, Soon, After a while, In due time, Then, Meanwhile, Following that, Last, Finally)

8. Blank 1 (first, to begin with, in the first place)

Blank 2 (next, after that, later, secondly, afterward, soon, after a while, in due time, then, meanwhile, following that)

Blank 3 (next, after that, later, thirdly, afterward, soon, after a while, in due time, then, meanwhile, following that, last, finally)

EXERCISE 9   *Expressions of Comparison and Contrast*

1. similar to
2. different from
3. but
4. different from
5. similar to
6. the same as
7. but
8. different from or similar to
9. similar to, but
10. similar to

EXERCISE 10   *Transitions*

Other answers may also be suitable. Please check with your instructor.

1. one kind of / one type of
2. one kind of / one type of
3. One part of
4. one kind of / one type of
5. one part of / one component of
6. One part of
7. one kind of / one type of
8. one part of /one component of
9. One kind of / One type of
10. One part of / One component of

EXERCISE 11   *Practice with Transitions*

Other answers may also be suitable. Please check with your instructor.

1. One sort of / One kind of
2. The first part / The second part / etc.
3. One kind of / The first type
4. Blank 1—The first part / The second part
   Blank 2—To illustrate / Accordingly / Specifically
   Blank 3—Another part / The second part
5. one kind / one type / one sort
6. one kind / another type / the last type
7. for example,
8. one group / one / the third group
9. one sort of / the fourth type of
10. one category / one kind

11. Blank 1—category / sort / etc.
    Blank 2—for example
12. the sixth type / another kind
13. Blank 1 (one kind / the third type)
    Blank 2— also
    Blank 3—the second kind / another type
14. Blank 1—the first kind
    Blank 2—a second sort
    Blank 3—the third type
15. Furthermore/Accordingly/Besides that / Specifically

EXERCISE 14   Clauses

1.	D/M	9.	D/M
2.	M/D	10.	M/D
3.	M/D	11.	D/M
4.	D/M	12.	D/M
5.	M/D	13.	D/M
6.	D/M	14.	M/D
7.	M/D	15.	M/D
8.	M/D		

EXERCISE 16   Clauses

If you have another answer you think is correct, please check with your instructor.

1. Although he is shy about performing publicly, Salim writes his own songs.
2. The owl sat silently watching from the highest branch of the tree while the mouse scurried through the grasses below. *or* While the mouse scurried through the grasses below, the owl sat silently watching from the highest branch of the tree.
3. Does Yasmina visit you when she is in town?
4. After slicing the mushrooms, heat the butter. *or* After you slice the mushrooms, heat . . .
5. The choreographer spends his time rehearsing until the show starts.
6. Harpreet was delighted because her relatives arrived from India.
7. Since Marina is having a baby in April, she is looking at baby clothing in the flyers.
8. Though she won't admit it, Zoe hates cooking. *or* Zoe hates cooking though she won't admit it.
9. Wherever the cat goes, her kittens follow.
10. Before he went to Cuba, he went to Spain. *or* He went to Cuba before he went to Spain.
11. Do not turn off the computer unless you will be away for more than one day. *or* Unless you will be away for more than one day, do not turn off the computer
12. Kira went to the marketplace where she bought eggplant for the stew.

EXERCISE 17   Voice

1.	passive	8.	active
2.	active	9.	passive
3.	active	10.	passive
4.	passive	11.	active
5.	passive	12.	active
6.	passive	13.	passive
7.	active	14.	passive

EXERCISE 18   Voice

1. Its owner leashed the cat to the bike rack.
2. Chef Bonhomme prepared a feast.
3. The station master found the umbrella.
4. Margaret Atwood wrote the novel.
5. The ranch hand placed the saddle on the horse.
6. Detective Goodley solved the murder.
7. The board held him responsible.
8. My children arranged my party.
9. The accident upset her.
10. My brother convinced me to quit smoking.

EXERCISE 19   Working with Verb Tenses

1. had not listened
2. will go
3. barked all day
4. has been playing
5. will do
6. bandages
7. was not tolerating
8. will collect
9. is
10. will be scanning
11. notes
12. had been tearing
13. spins

EXERCISE 21   Agreement and Indefinite Pronouns

1. A few of the people were
2. Some of the movie was
3. Most of the children love
4. One of his marriages was

5. None of the wine in the antique bottle tastes
6. correct
7. All of the furniture was
8. Drago and most of his friends drink
9. no one wants
10. correct
11. All of the paint was
12. Some of the evidence is

EXERCISE 22   More Subject–Verb Agreement

1. The audience . . . was throwing
2. there were piles
3. correct
4. correct
5. Students or the professors vote
6. correct
7. Most of the photographs are
8. Nobody questions
9. there are extra computers
10. correct
11. No one . . . has been notified
12. Each of the missing reports has been
13. Neither of the departments . . . has
14. The committee makes
15. None of the conference was
16. The CD or the memos contain
17. two-thirds . . . was destroyed
18. flock . . . was gathering

EXERCISE 24   Practice with Direct and Indirect Speech

1. The clerk replied that the cost of mailing the package was $20.00.
2. My sister-in-law said, "I am afraid of mice and spiders."
3. One television reporter said, "I am shocked by the damage to the building."
4. Chula explained that, in about two months' time, she would be on a train in the Sudan.
5. The president stated that one of the things he (or she) disliked the most was being misquoted by the press.
6. The two students complained to Professor Nguyen, "Our marks are incorrect on the economics exam."
7. Lara remarked that she would not work on weeknights any longer unless she got a raise.

EXERCISE 25   Prepositions of Place and Time

1. in
2. at
3. At
4. at
5. in
6. In
7. at
8. in
9. in
10. On
11. at
12. at
13. On
14. In
15. on

EXERCISE 26   Adjectives + Prepositions

1. pleased with
2. opposed to
3. popular with
4. capable of
5. suspicious of
6. aware of
7. attached to
8. capable of
9. suitable to *or* for
10. similar to
11. related to
12. satisfied with
13. proud of
14. afraid of
15. accustomed to

EXERCISE 28   Identifying Conditions

1. case 3
2. case 1
3. case 2
4. case 3
5. case 1
6. case 3
7. case 1
8. case 2
9. case 2
10. case 2
11. case 2
12. case 3
13. case 3
14. case 1

EXERCISE 30   Verbals and Parallelism Faults

1. Smoking, reading, and cooking were Aunt Lulu's passions.
   To smoke, read, and cook were Aunt Lulu's passions.
   To smoke, to read, and to cook were Aunt Lulu's passions.
2. Trudging up the hill, pulling his little red wagon, and reddening in the face, the little boy continued his paper route.
3. Yuni wanted to sing, to dance, and to drink on her anniversary.

Yuni wanted singing, dancing, and drinking on her anniversary.

Yuni wanted to sing, dance, and drink on her anniversary.

4. Catching flies, sitting in the sun, and moving very little are how a frog spends its day.

To catch flies, to sit in the sun, and to move very little are how a frog spends its day.

To catch flies, sit in the sun, and move very little are how a frog spends its day.

5. Earning a salary as an engineer, paying off his student loans, and having a family of his own were the young student's dreams.

To earn a salary as an engineer, (to) pay off his student loans, and (to) have a family of his own were the young student's dreams.

6. Staring out the window, brushing her hair, and talking on the cell phone, Phillis noticed a raccoon in the garbage can in the neighbour's backyard.

7. The manager told the two workers that having long breaks, being late for work, and being glib with the customers were the reasons they were fired.

8. The ballet teacher taught her students to be enthusiastic, free, and energetic.

The ballet teacher taught her students to be enthusiastic, to be free, and to be energetic.

index

N

names
    brand names, 216
    buildings, 215
    geographical names, 215
    holiday names, 214
    individual's names, 213
    institutions, 215
    organizations, 215
    place names, 201
    places in addresses, 215
    product names, 216
    of relatives, 213
    seasons, 214
nation, member of, 284
nationalities, 214, 285
natural sciences, 64
Neish, Kevin, 322
neither-nor, 268
non-action verbs, 133, 134–137, 154, 191
non-count nouns, 281–283, 286–287
non-essential element, 204
non-essential information, 204–205
non-restrictive clause, 204
non-restrictive clauses, 234
non-restrictive element, 204
not only-but also, 268
nouns
    abstract nouns, 124–126
    classification of nouns, 124–126
    common noun, 124
    concrete nouns, 124–126
    count nouns, 281–283, 286–287
    described, 124
    gerunds, 310
    infinitives, 311
    non-count nouns, 281–283,
      286–287
    as objects, 126, 128–129
    plurals, 286–288
    proper noun, 124
    review of, 132–133
    review test, 145–148
    self-test, 121–123
    as subjects, 126–130
number, 264
number shifts, 264

O

object
    compound object, 129
    nouns, 126, 128–129
    objects of the preposition, 157
    pronoun, form of, 130
object nouns, 126, 128–129
objects of the preposition, 157
Ogle, Jennifer, 313–314
"Old Levi Would Not Be Proud" (Black), 349–350
on, 306
one, 164–165
"Optical Microscope and Electron Microscope"
    (Brooks), 315
or, 162
organization of ideas
    box charts, 9
    categorizing, 57
    clustering, 7–8
    contrast and comparison, 45–46
    grouping, 57
    mapping out ideas, 7–8
    spokes and wheels, 9
    time-order development, 42–43
organizations, 215
outdoors and the environment readings, 335–338
outlining
    organization of ideas, 9–14
    sketch outline, 110
overgeneralization, 65, 84
oversimplification, 65

P

paragraph compositions
    see also paragraphs
    cause and effect paragraph, 69–70
    classification paragraph, 62
    comparison paragraph, 54–55
    conclusion, 35
    contrast paragraph, 55
    definition paragraph, 78
    described, 1, 2–4
    division paragraphs, 62–63
    final draft, 44
    final drafts, 44
    ideas supporting the point, 2